Grasses of the Trans-Pecos and Adjacent Areas

A. MICHAEL POWELL

Illustrator: Patricia R. Manning

University of Texas Press
Austin

txp

Illustrations from Hitchcock-Chase Collection of Grass Drawings
and drawings by Patricia R. Manning

Copyright © 1994 by the University of Texas Press
All rights reserved
Printed in the United States of America
First edition, 1994

Requests for permission to reproduce material from this work should be sent to
Permissions, University of Texas Press, Box 7819, Austin, TX 78713-7819.

∞ The paper used in this publication meets the minimum requirements of
American National Standard for Information Sciences—Permanence of Paper for
Printed Library Materials, ANSI Z39, 48–1984.

LIBRARY OF CONGRESS CATALOGING-IN-PUBLICATION DATA

Powell, A. Michael.
    Grasses of the Trans-Pecos and Adjacent Areas / A. Michael Powell ; illustrator,
Patricia R. Manning. — 1st ed.
        p.   cm.
    Includes bibliographical references (p.   ) and index.
    ISBN 0-292-76553-3.—ISBN 0-292-76556-8 (pbk.)
    1. Grasses—Trans-Pecos (Tex. and N.M.)—Identification.
I. Manning, Patricia R., date.   II Title.
QK495.G74P76   1994
584'.9'097649—dc20   93-47656

*In memory of Cora Lee and Ervin Ridout,
early ranchers in Presidio County, Texas.*

Contents

Preface

Expansive grasslands, particularly those of mountain basins and plateaus, are a prominent feature of Trans-Pecos Texas. Grasses are found throughout the region from mountain tops to the Chihuahuan Desert, where desert grasslands are recognized. The diversity of grasses in the Trans-Pecos is high, with about 268 species in 83 genera being recognized for the region. Among the Texas species of grasses, 53 species occur only in this mountain and desert region of the state.

Most of Trans-Pecos Texas is under private ownership. Traditionally the region has been known as ranching country, from the time of the first Anglo settlers in the Big Bend area in the early 1880's to the present. Ranching activities spread quickly after 1883 when the Texas and Pacific Railroad was completed through the heart of the range country. While surviving numerous long droughts and severe winters, and increasingly difficult economic times, many of the fiercely independent ranchers and ranch families have persisted in the Trans-Pecos.

Much of the information about grasses presented here would not have been possible without the past cooperation of landowners and access to the many natural habitats in which these grasses occur. This book salutes the ranchers who have conserved native rangelands.

The present work is designed for use by the non-scientist and the scientist alike in identifying and reading about grasses of the Trans-Pecos region. The manual includes illustrations and photographs to help in identifications, along with the more technical keys and descriptions. Distributional information is presented for each grass species and specific locality data are given for most species. The locality data for most species previously have not been available in published form. The extensive collection of grasses housed in the Sul Ross State University (SRSU) herbarium, some of them dating back to the 1930's, was the source of most locality data. The major grass collections in the SRSU herbarium are those of B. H. Warnock. Forage value for livestock, flowering times, and other information are presented for each species.

The Grasses of Texas by F. W. Gould was a major source of information for the present compilation. Gould's work, the *Manual of the Grasses of the United States* by A. S. Hitchcock, the *Manual of the Vascular Plants of Texas* by D. S. Correll and M. C. Johnston, Johnston's up-date of the *Manual* (1990), the *Checklist of the Vascular Plants of Texas* by Hatch et al. (1990), and the forthcoming *Chihuahuan Desert Flora* by J. Henrickson and M. C. Johnston should be consulted for more comprehensive taxonomic information about the Trans-Pecos grasses. Discussion of Trans-Pecos grasslands and grasses and numerous color photographs of these entities are to be found in three wildflower books by B. H. Warnock (1970; 1974; 1977). The text of the present work follows the format of *Trees and Shrubs of Trans-Pecos Texas* by A. M. Powell. Some keys and descriptions are adapted from Gould's *Grasses of Texas*. The keys to tribes and to some genera were adapted from Clayton and Renvoize (1986). Most of the abbreviations of geographic names follow those in the *Manual* by Correll and Johnston. Postal Service abbreviations are used for the states, and directions (N, E, S, W) are in caps. The derivation of genus names, as well as much other information about grasses, was taken from Hitchcock's *Manual.* The common names were selected from the sources cited above, except that when there was a choice, the common names used by Gould usually were followed herein. Complete synonymy is not included, but the selected synonyms listed should be useful in recognizing changes in the scientific names. Forage value and related information is available in Stubbendieck et al. (1992), Gould (1978), and in other sources.

Metric system measurements are employed in keys and descriptions. The millimeter units commonly used in scientific works are more accurate in smaller scale, and rulers in metric units are readily available. English measurements are used for elevations and distances because these units are more easily followed by a majority of southwesterners, who are accustomed to seeing feet and miles on road signs and maps.

The taxonomic treatments of certain groups of grasses are controversial among agrostologists. Most notably the treatment of the tribe Triticeae (e.g., *Agropyron, Hordeum,* and *Elymus*) will hardly be recognizable to those who are familiar with the classic disposition of this taxon, for example, in the grass books by Hitchcock and Gould. In preparing the manuscript of Trans-Pecos grasses, I have attempted to utilize the available recent taxonomic studies accomplished by various works in the field of agrostology. Some of these new treatments will stand the test of time, and some will not, as additional systematic work is completed.

It is intended that this work may be useful to the many visitors, managers, and students who are interested in the vegetation of the large and botanically diverse national parks in the area, Guadalupe Mountains National Park (northern Culberson County) and Big Bend National Park (southern Brewster County). Many species of grasses also are found on the grounds of the Fort

Davis National Historic Site (Jeff Davis County) and along the shores and canyons of Amistad National Recreation Area (Val Verde County). In addition, perhaps this treatment will be appreciated by those who visit and study in the many state parks, wildlife management areas, and other natural areas located in or near the region. State parks found in or near the Trans-Pecos are: Franklin Mountains and Hueco Tanks (El Paso County), Fort Leaton (Presidio County), Balmorhea (Reeves County), Davis Mountains/Indian Lodge (Jeff Davis County), Monahans Sandhills (Ward County), Seminole Canyon and Devils River (Val Verde County), and Fort Lancaster (Crockett County). Big Bend Ranch State Natural Area (Presidio County), until recently a large private ranch and now managed by the Texas Parks and Wildlife Department, exhibits extensive desert grassland. State Wildlife Management Areas in the Trans-Pecos include: Sierra Diablo (Hudspeth County), Ocotillo Unit of La Paloma (Presidio County), and Elephant Mountain and Black Gap (Brewster County). Several Nature Conservancy preserves are located in the Trans-Pecos, including sites at or near: The gypsum dunes (northeastern Hudspeth County), Brushy Canyon (southern Brewster County), Diamond Y Spring (Pecos County), and Independence Creek (Terrell County). This book on grasses of the Trans-Pecos also may be consulted at the Buffalo Trail Scout Ranch, the Chihuahuan Desert Research Institute Visitor Center, and Mitre Peak Girl Scout Camp (Jeff Davis County), the B. H. Warnock Environmental Education Center (Lajitas, southern Brewster County), the Judge Roy Bean Visitor Center (Langtry, Val Verde County), and along the Rio Grande Wild and Scenic Rivers area below Big Bend National Park. Visitors to public lands should remember that plant collecting is prohibited without a specific permit.

Acknowledgments

Most of the illustrations of grasses were provided through the Hitchcock-Chase Collection of Grass Drawings, Hunt Institute for Botanical Documentation, Carnegie Mellon University, Pittsburgh, PA, on indefinite loan from the Smithsonian Institution. I am grateful to James J. White, Curator of Art, for expediting the use of these fine illustrations, and for his professional courtesy in handling the bulky process. Many original drawings were made by Patricia R. Manning, who used this project to perfect her considerable skills as a botanical artist, and who provided the great service of preparing all of the illustrations for the manuscript. Permission to use the map in Figure 1 was obtained from the Big Bend Natural History Association.

Roger Corzine has been most generous in contributing expertise to this work. He volunteered to edit the entire manuscript and his careful and thorough efforts were extremely valuable in realizing a consistent final draft. As is inevitably the case, some changes were made after the editing process, and any errors in the final product are entirely those of the author.

Special appreciation is extended to Rena Gallego, who typed most of the original manuscript and who was otherwise helpful in manuscript preparation. Daisy McCutcheon also typed much of the original manuscript, processed extensive corrections, and was very helpful in editing and in other final stages of manuscript preparation. Susan McClinton typed some of the early manuscript.

I am grateful to knowledgeable agrostologists Kelly W. Allred and J. Travis Columbus for helpful discussions regarding Trans-Pecos grasses, particularly of the genera *Aristida*, *Bothriochloa*, *Lycurus*, and *Bouteloua*. Allred identified *Aristida gypsophila*, a species not known by me to occur in the Trans-Pecos, among the Sul Ross collections. He also identified other specimens of *Aristida* and in general contributed much useful information about this genus in the Trans-Pecos. Paul M. Peterson provided the identification of *Muhlenbergia crispiseta*. Photographic expertise was generously supplied by Lee Sleeper and Barbara Richerson. Jean Hardy graciously made available some of her fine photographs. I thank David H. Riskind for making the appropriate suggestion that a list of state parks found in the Trans-Pecos (in Preface) should be included in this work. Discussions with Jackie Poole revealed to me helpful distributional information about certain rare species and about a literature source. Guy Nesom facilitated the use of grass specimens. My knowledgeable colleague James F. Scudday kindly reviewed part of the manuscript. Hillary Loring provided a Spanish translation and the illustrations of *Leersia, Melica montezumae,* and *Glyceria.* Mary Barkworth discussed the identifying features and distribution of *Stipa robusta.* Richard D. Worthington generously made available his unpublished records for grass collections in the Franklin Mountains and Hueco Moutains. Always thoughtful, B. L. Turner apprised me of pertinent literature. Jim Henrickson kindly allowed use of the grasses treatment prepared (by M. C. Johnston) for the forthcoming *Chihuahuan Desert Flora.* Over the years Shirley Ridout Powell has been my field assistant. She has also been my supportive field companion, who has allowed her vacations to be our plant collecting trips.

Grasses of the Trans-Pecos and Adjacent Areas

Never have I seen such grass as grew in West Texas. . . . Endless miles of it stretched out in every direction. It stood knee-deep to a horse everywhere . . . it seemed to me that there was enough grass growing in the Big Bend country to fatten every horse and cow in the United States.

—In 1909, between Alpine and Marathon, as recalled by J. O. Langford (*Big Bend, A Homesteader's Story,* Langford and Gipson, 1952).

Introduction

T rans-Pecos Texas is the mountain and desert part of the state west of the Pecos River, bounded to the north by New Mexico and to the south by Mexico (Fig. 1). The Pecos River enters Texas from southeastern New Mexico about 50 miles to the east of Guadalupe Peak (8,751 ft), the highest peak in Texas, and trends southeast until it enters the Rio Grande in Val Verde County. The mouth of the Pecos River is at about 1,000 ft, the lowest elevation in the Trans-Pecos. In the Trans-Pecos there are about 90 peaks that are a mile or more above sea level, most of them in the Davis Mountains in the central portion of the region. In addition to Guadalupe Peak in the Guadalupe Mountains, other major peaks include Mount Livermore (8,382 ft) in the Davis Mountains, Emory Peak (7,835 ft) in the Chisos Mountains, and Chinati Peak (7,730 ft) in the Chinati Mountains.

Brewster County is the largest (exceeding the size of Connecticut) of nine counties completely within the Trans-Pecos. Val Verde County is partially in the region. The size of the Trans-Pecos region itself is roughly equal to that of the state of Maine. Several counties border the Trans-Pecos to the east, including Loving, Winkler, Ward, Crane, Upton, Crockett, and Val Verde. These bordering Texas counties, adjacent New Mexico, and adjacent Mexico are all considered to be associated with the Trans-Pecos in this floristic account of grasses. Additional descriptions of the physiography, climate, and soils of the Trans-Pecos are presented in Schmidly (1977) and Powell (1988).

There are two national parks in the Trans-Pecos region, Big Bend National Park in southern Brewster County, and Guadalupe Mountains National Park in northern Culberson County. Most of the Trans-Pecos is under private ownership in the form of relatively large ranches. Cattle ranching has been emphasized in the Trans-Pecos since early settlement days because of the abundant and nutritious grasses to be found in the extensive grasslands. Historically the Trans-Pecos has also seen considerable sheep and goat ranching. Today most sheep and goats are found on the Stockton Plateau ranges. Farming is not ex-

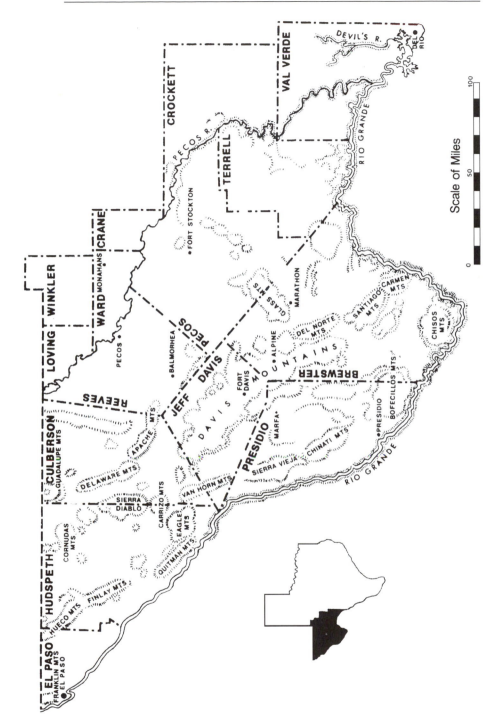

Fig. 1. The Trans-Pecos Region of Texas and adjacent counties, with major geographic features and towns (from Powell, 1988, used with permission).

Fig. 2. Chihuahuan desertscrub dominated at this site in Brewster County by creosotebush (*Larrea tridentata*), Chisos Mountains in the background.

tensive in the Trans-Pecos, with most cultivated areas today being located near El Paso, Van Horn, Pecos, Balmorhea, Presidio, and Fort Stockton.

In general the climate of the Trans-Pecos is arid, with an average annual precipitation of about 12 in. Annual average precipitation generally decreases from east to west (about 8 in for El Paso) and increases with elevation (to about 20 in), but different parts of the region are subject to wide seasonal and annual fluctuations in rainfall. At higher elevations, it is not uncommon to have over 30 in of precipitation in good years. Dry periods may last for several months or even years. Typically most rainfall occurs during the summer months (June–September), often expanded from April to October, a pattern that is also characteristic of other semidesert grassland regions in the southwestern United States (Brown, 1982).

The Trans-Pecos Mountains and Basin is one of 10 Vegetational Areas recognized for Texas (Gould et al., 1960; Correll and Johnston, 1970; Hatch et al., 1990). The Trans-Pecos Region itself is diverse biologically because it includes not only the mountains and desert habitats but also part of the Edwards Plateau Vegetational Area (Stockton Plateau), which extends eastward across the Pecos River into Pecos, Terrell, and Brewster counties. Biological diversity of the Trans-Pecos Region is increased by floristic influences (phytogeographic connections) from the Tamaulipan Province (South Texas Plains), the Edwards

Plateau, the plains country (Rolling Plains and High Plains), southern Rocky Mountains, southeastern Arizona, Sierra Madre Occidental and Sierra Madre Oriental of Mexico, and the Chihuahuan Desert of Mexico. The unique vegetative aspect of the Trans-Pecos is the Chihuahuan Desert, which characterizes essentially all of the lower elevational vegetation in the Trans-Pecos. The desertscrub (Fig. 2) vegetation dominates the lower "desert" mountains in the Trans-Pecos, and extends well up to the south slopes of major mountain systems, which are characterized by more mesic grasslands and woodlands. A more extensive discussion of general vegetation types in the Trans-Pecos can be found in Schmidly (1977) and Powell (1988).

Grasses in Perspective

Fossil Record. Reliable mega-fossil and fossil pollen evidence of Poaceae dates back to the Paleocene/Eocene boundary in geological history, more than 54 million years ago (Cronquist, 1988; Crepet and Feldman, 1991). Fossil evidence also suggests an Upper Cretaceous origin for the family (Crepet and Feldman, 1991), and that major diversification in grasses was well underway in the Miocene, more than 25 million years ago (Cronquist, 1988).

Present Day. The grass family with its estimated 7,500–10,000 species in about 600 genera is one of the largest families of flowering plants. The Poaceae (or Gramineae) ranks fifth in number of species, after Asteraceae, Orchidaceae, Fabaceae, and Rubiaceae, and third in number of genera, after Asteraceae and Orchidaceae (Gould, 1968). Grasses probably are the most widespread and abundant kind of plants on earth, and they are of the greatest use to mankind.

Importance of Grasses. The centers for development of human civilizations were in grassland regions. The major grains that today provide a staple food supply for the human race are corn (maize), wheat, rice, barley, rye, oats, sorghum, and the various millets. The first six grains listed are considered to be the most important in the development of modern human civilization (deWet, 1981; Simpson and Conner-Ogorzaly, 1986). The primary source of refined sugar in the world is the tropical cane grass sugarcane (*Saccharum officinarum*).

Native grasses have provided important forage for domestic animals throughout the history of humankind. It is estimated that nearly one-fourth of the global land surface was essentially grassland during the time of early human civilization. Original grasslands in the western United States were expansive, including about 700 million acres (Gould, 1968) and supporting tremendous numbers of bison and pronghorn. The livestock industry began after 1830 when settlers in the Mississippi Valley interacted with stockmen working north from Texas (Stoddard and Smith, 1955). Huge numbers of cattle and sheep were grazed on open ranges until 1885. Afterwards the livestock industry took on a new character influenced by continual western migration and settle-

Fig. 3. Trans-Pecos rangeland dominated by grama grasses, Presidio County, with Spanish dagger (*Yucca treculeana*) and Texas sacahuiste (*Nolina texana*) in the foreground (photo by Jean Hardy).

Fig. 4. Buffalograss (*Buchlöe dactyloides*) lawn on the Sul Ross State University campus, Alpine, Texas.

Fig. 5. Giant reed (*Arundo donax*), common along the Rio Grande, often used as an ornamental in yards of the Trans-Pecos; the compact elliptic-lanceolate inflorescence helps to distinguish this species from the other "river cane," common reed (*Phragmites australis*).

Fig. 6. Pampasgrass (*Cortaderia selloana*), commonly used as an ornamental in yards of the Trans-Pecos.

ment, fencing of rangeland, and cultivation of the fertile plains grasslands in the central United States. The range livestock industry quickly shifted westward into the arid region of the southwest, including the Trans-Pecos (Fig. 3), and into the mountains, valleys, and grasslands of the northwest.

The western rangelands are noted for supporting a large number of good forage grasses. Among the best known forage grass species in the Trans-Pecos are buffalograss (*Buchlöe dactyloides*), blue grama (*Bouteloua gracilis*), sideoats grama (*B. curtipendula*), and many other gramas, little bluestem (*Schizachyrium scoparium*), and silver bluestem (*Bothriochloa laguroides* subsp. *torreyana*). The famous tall grasses big bluestem (*Andropogon gerardii*), switchgrass (*Panicum virgatum*), and indiangrass (*Sorghastrum nutans*) also occur sporadically in the Trans-Pecos, but they are prominent components of the tall grass prairies of the Great Plains region.

In recent years there has been increasing concern about the preservation of wildlife habitat. Grasses contribute significantly to ecosystems that provide cover and food for wildlife and especially to those animals such as bison and pronghorn that depend upon a prairie environment. There are many small mammals, birds, and other animals that are associated with grassland habitats. Migratory game birds such as ducks and geese and many mammals utilize certain grasses in wetland habitats. Wetland habitats in the Trans-Pecos are of minimal size and number compared to some other parts of the country.

Perennial grass cover not only helps build fertile topsoil through the decomposition of roots, rhizomes, stolons, and leaf and culm litter, but prevents the loss of topsoil through erosion. Effective range management practices involve techniques that are designed to maintain perennial grass cover. Grassland degradation in the arid and semiarid southwest has followed the loss of topsoil from temporarily denuded rangelands.

The American way of life is associated with lawns, parks, sports playing fields, golf courses, and many other areas where mowed turfgrasses provide aesthetic or practical value. Turfgrasses are various sod-forming species that spread by rhizomes and/or stolons to form turf. Familiar turfgrasses in southern areas are bermudagrass (*Cynodon dactylon*) and St. augustinegrass (*Stenotaphrum secundatum*). Buffalograss is a native turfgrass species that is gaining in popularity in arid regions of the southwest because of its ability to maintain vigor with minimal watering (Fig. 4).

Many of the larger, more showy grass species are used as landscape plants. These include various introduced bamboos, primarily in the southeastern United States. The giant reed (*Arundo donax*) and pampasgrass (*Cortaderia selloana*) are widely used as ornamentals in the Trans-Pecos (Figs. 5, 6).

Grasslands

Because the major subject of this work is grasses of the Trans-Pecos, it is appropriate to discuss in greater detail the grassland vegetative communities of the region. Grassland communities of the Trans-Pecos are best understood in the context of other grasslands in North America. Grasslands cover more area of North America than any other vegetative type. A grassland is an herbaceous community dominated by grasses (and perhaps other graminoids, sedges, and rushes), but with other herbaceous plants (forbs) also present and perhaps even dominating in certain seasons. In classical grasslands trees are not present over wide expanses, but may be present along watercourses through the grasslands and perhaps at other localized sites. The dominant grasses in grasslands may be annuals or perennials, or both, and the perennials may be cespitose (tufted, bunchgrass) or sod-forming (turfgrasses) grasses with rhizomes or stolons.

Other terms often either associated or confused with grassland are prairie, steppe, and savanna. Prairie is perhaps best applied to a type of grassland that is dominated by tall to medium-sized sod-forming grasses, with near 100% ground cover. The term steppe has been applied to grasslands dominated by short bunchgrasses, perhaps mixed with shrubs, and with less than 100% ground cover. Grassland is often used as a general term that is applicable to prairie, steppe, and intermediates (Barbour et al., 1987). A savanna is a grassland with scattered and regularly distributed trees, and is usually thought of as an ecotone (ecological transition) between grassland and woodland (or forest) usually accompanied by a gradual increase in precipitation.

The most extensive grassland area in North America is located in the central interior region extending from Mexico and central Texas through the midwest and into Canada. This great grassland region, a 600 mi wide area often called the plains grassland, is not homogeneous in its composition of grass species. The size, growth form, and species composition changes from east to west and north to south in connection with decreases in precipitation. In general the northeastern portion of the plains grassland is referred to as the tall grass prai-

Fig. 7. Plains grassland in Presidio County, with mixed grasses on foothills and in basins between the mountains (photo by Jean Hardy).

rie, where the stems of some species are over 6 ft high. Western and southern portions are called the mixed-grass prairie (or mid-grass prairie), where component grass species may reach 3 ft high. The southwestern area of the plains grassland, in a progressively drier climate, is dominated by cespitose grasses usually less than 2 ft tall. In many areas of the southwest, in Arizona, New Mexico, and Texas (including the Trans-Pecos region), and in northern Mexico, the plains grassland gives way at lower elevations to desert grassland. Reportedly all these grasslands were once open landscapes dominated by nearly continuous grass cover, but they have been extensively altered by agricultural and other human activities, including suppression of natural fires, and perhaps by climatic change.

Plains Grassland. In Trans-Pecos Texas both plains grassland and desert grassland communities are prominent. In 1931, Cottle described the Trans-Pecos as containing " . . . the largest remaining area of native grassland in the United States." The plains grassland elements extend into the mountain areas on mid-elevation slopes, plateaus, and in the basins formed from accumulated erosional outwash materials between the mountains (Fig. 7). Desert grassland is most prominent on mesas, plateaus, and on alluvial fans or bajadas at the bases of desert mountains, or on the lower slopes of some larger mountains (e.g., the Chisos Mountains) whose slopes extend into the desert (Fig. 8). The

Fig. 8. Desert grassland, western foothills of the Chisos Mountains in Brewster County; even canopy grasses and the low shrub mariola (*Parthenium incanum*) dominate slopes in center of photo.

upward elevational contact of plains grassland is juniper-oak-pinyon woodland at about 5,200 ft (Fig. 9), and the lower elevation contact is with desert grassland at about 4,300 ft (Fig. 10). The plains grassland in the Trans-Pecos is composed of mixed-grass or short-grass communities. The principal grass species are *Bouteloua gracilis* (blue grama), *B. curtipendula* (sideoats grama), *B. hirsuta,* (hairy grama), *B. eriopoda* (black grama), and other gramas, *Bothriochloa barbinodis* (cane bluestem), *B. laguroides* (silver bluestem), *Schizachyrium scoparium* (little bluestem), *Eragrostis intermedia* (plains lovegrass), *Panicum obtusum* (vine mesquite), *Lycurus phleoides* (wolftail), *Hilaria mutica* (tobosa), *Muhlenbergia arenicola* (sandy muhly), *Aristida* spp. (threeawns), *Sporobolus airoides* (alkali sacaton), *Scleropogon brevifolius* (burrograss), *Buchlöe dactyloides* (buffalograss), *Tridens* spp. (tridens), and other species. The altered plains grasslands of today in the Trans-Pecos reportedly show increases in junipers in some areas (Fig. 9), larger shrubs (Fig. 11) and leaf succulents (Fig. 12) in other areas, e.g., *Mimosa biuncifera* (catclaw mimosa), *Atriplex canescens* (fourwing saltbush), *Ziziphus obtusifolia* (lotebush), *Koeberlinia spinosa* (allthorn), *Condalia ericoides* (javelina bush), *Yucca* spp. (yucca), *Nolina texana* (Texas sacahuiste); and also in some regions small shrubs about 2 ft high, e.g., *Gutierrezia sarothrae* (snakeweed), that are equaled or exceeded by the size of the surrounding grasses. Thus a modified plains grassland may show

Fig. 9. Plains grassland and upward elevational contact with juniper-oak-pinyon woodland, Brewster County; note numerous young plants of the rose-fruited juniper (*Juniperus coahuilensis*) occurring at the grassland margin (photo by Shirley Powell).

Fig. 10. Sierra Vieja Rim in northwestern Presidio County, illustrating physiographic contact between plains grassland above and desert grassland at lower elevations below the rim.

Fig. 11. Modified plains grassland in Presidio County, showing an increase in large shrubs, at this site mostly honey mesquite (*Prosopis glandulosa*). Photo by Shirley Powell.

Fig. 12. Altered plains grassland in Presidio County, at this site showing an increase in Texas sacahuiste (*Nolina texana*). Photo by Jean Hardy.

Fig. 13. Modified plains grassland in Brewster County, showing a low canopy of plants that includes grasses and the low shrub snakeweed (*Gutierrezia sarothrae*).

the effects of change through the large and visible shrubs (Fig. 11) or may show an evenly statured low canopy of plants (Figs. 8, 13) that includes low shrubs and grasses (Brown, 1982).

Desert Grassland. The desert grassland in the Trans-Pecos is more correctly labeled semidesert grassland (Brown, 1982), because the grassland community considered interacts with but is not actually part of classic Chihuahuan Desert vegetation. The desert grassland communities have also been referred to as desert savanna, mesquite grassland, desertscrub grassland, grassland transition (Muller, 1947), and *pastizal* (in Mexico) by various authors (Brown, 1982). Herein the term desert grassland is used, following Barbour et al. (1987) and Humphrey (1958). By any name the desert grassland in Trans-Pecos Texas is historically (Wondzell, 1984) or at least potentially (Brown, 1982) a perennial grass- and shrub-dominated community largely surrounding Chihuahuan Desert habitat (Fig. 14). Desert grassland is positioned between desertscrub (or shrub desert, Gehlbach, 1981) at lower elevations (3,500–4,000 ft) and usually plains grassland above (4,000–4,500 ft). In the southwestern United States and Mexico the desert grassland community is essentially a Chihuahuan semidesert grassland (Brown, 1982). According to Henrickson and Johnston (1986) the grasslands of the Chihuahuan Desert Region occur within the Chihuahuan

Fig. 14. Desert grassland west of the Chisos Mountains, Brewster County, where chino grama (*Bouteloua ramosa*) is co-dominant with creosotebush (*Larrea tridentata*), lechuguilla (*Agave lechuguilla*), and ocotillo (*Fouquieria splendens*).

Desert scrub as extensive stands of grama grasslands that continue outside the desert region, and as local stands of tobosa grasslands and sacaton grasslands. In Trans-Pecos Texas the contact of desert grassland and Chihuahuan desert-scrub is complex, being rather smooth at some sites along mountain slopes, and at many other localities in broken topography existing as a mosaic of vegetation types appearing in irregular habitats that support them. Average annual precipitation in the desert grassland is estimated to be about 8–14 in.

Some of the prominent grasses found in desert grassland in the Trans-Pecos include *Bouteloua ramosa* (chino grama), black grama, *B. barbata* (sixweeks grama), *Muhlenbergia porteri* (bush muhly), *Aristida* spp. (threeawns), *Digitaria californica* (California cottontop), *Dasyochloa pulchella* (fluffgrass), *Erioneuron pilosum* (hairy tridens), tobosa, alkali sacaton, and other species. Tobosa occurs in heavy soils of basins (enclosed drainages) in the desert grassland and in the plains grassland, where in some areas (Fig. 15) vast "tobosa flats" (or bolsons) are formed (Shreve, 1942). Alkali sacaton along with *Atriplex* and other shrubs (Fig. 16) dominates the localized saline or alkaline habitats (some of them sacaton grasslands), usually in lower elevational sites (Shreve, 1939, 1942; Muller, 1947). Shrub components of the desert grasslands may share or assume dominance. Prominent species include *Prosopis glandulosa* (honey

Fig. 15. Tobosa (*Hilaria mutica*) grassland or "tobosa flat" in Jeff Davis County, the western Sierra Vieja in the background.

Fig. 16. Sacaton (*Sporobolus airoides*) grassland in gypseous and saline soils near the margin of an ephemeral salt lake in Culberson County; surrounding shrubs (not recognizable) include honey mesquite (*Prosopis glandulosa*), salt cedar (*Tamarix* sp.), and fourwing saltbush (*Atriplex canescens*).

Fig. 17. Chihuahuan Desert elements increasing in plains grassland, at this site in Brewster County mostly tarbush (*Flourensia cernua*) and creosotebush (*Larrea tridentata*), the Glass Mountains in the background.

mesquite), lotebush, *Ephedra trifurca* (Mormon tea), *Acacia greggii* (catclaw acacia), *Acacia neovernicosa* (viscid acacia), *Rhus microphylla* (desert sumac), *Berberis trifoliolata* (agarito), *Fouquieria splendens* (ocotillo), *Opuntia* spp. (prickly pear), *Dasylirion leiophyllum* (sotol), *Nolina* spp. (sacahuiste), *Agave lechuguilla* (lechuguilla), and *Yucca treculeana* (Spanish dagger). The desert grassland often shares species with the Chihuahuan desertscrub and the plains grassland (Shreve, 1942).

Chihuahuan Desert elements have for many years been increasing in the desert grassland and in the plains grassland (Fig. 17). Wondzell (1984) and Shreve (1942) describe the desert grassland as ecotonal between the desert and the plains grassland. Desert shrubs have always been a part of the desert grassland (Shreve, 1942; Nelson, 1987; Brown, 1982), but small trees such as *Juglans microcarpa* (Mexican walnut), *Sapindus saponaria* (western soapberry), *Chilopsis linearis* (desert willow), honey mesquite, and others were more or less restricted to drainages. Honey mesquite has also spread through the desert proper and the plains grasslands (Johnston, 1963; Humphrey, 1958; Gehlbach, 1981; Grover and Musick, 1990).

Historical Trans-Pecos Grasslands. Most ecologists who have studied desert grasslands in the southwestern United States have concluded that a significant part of this grassland has disappeared during the past 112 years (Brown, 1982;

Barbour et al., 1987; Bahre, 1991). Questions that have been asked regarding the historical perspective of desert grasslands include: What were the grasslands like before Anglo settlement of the area? How have the grasslands changed, if at all? What factors are responsible for change? And, can change in the grasslands be reversed by management practices?

Recent paleoecological investigations (Van Devender, 1986; Van Devender and Spaulding, 1979) suggest that much of the Trans-Pecos area was a mesic woodland until about 8,000 years ago, when drying conditions and summer monsoons allowed maximum development of grasslands and expansion of the Chihuahuan Desert in the region. Historical records that give reliable accounts of Trans-Pecos grasslands are minimal, but considerable information has been drawn together from survey records, journals, photographs, and various other early records from travelers through the region to provide a good idea of what the landscape was like before Anglo settlement and widespread ranching activities (Humphrey, 1958). All of the early accounts (Bartlett, 1854, in Humphrey, 1958; Parry, 1857; Echols, 1860; Hall, 1990) suggest that the Trans-Pecos grasslands were extensive and that the grass vegetation was interspersed with shrubs (Bray, 1901; Humphrey, 1958; Cottle, 1931; Wondzell, 1984). Waist-high grass was reported along Terlingua Creek (Echols, 1860) and in Tornillo Flats (Gehlbach, 1981) where eroded desert exists today. In fact, Langford noted (in Langford and Gipson, 1952) extensive grass cover in the Big Bend area near the turn of the century during the time of heavy livestock ranching activity in the region. In 1885 Terlingua Creek was described as a running stream lined with cottonwood trees and full of beaver (Wauer, 1973; Wuerthner, 1989). Honey mesquite was not nearly as widespread as today, evidently existing as scattered shrubs in the grassland and occurring in small stands in isolated areas, including along some watercourses (Johnston, 1963; Humphrey, 1958). There is no mention of the dense viscid acacia or catclaw mimosa stands that dominate some grassland areas in the Trans-Pecos today. Interestingly, one account in the early 1850's of the Pecos River at Horsehead Crossing (30 mi NE of Fort Stockton) noted that there were no trees or shrubs along its banks (Humphrey, 1958). Today at Horsehead Crossing the Pecos River is choked with salt cedar (*Tamarix*), mesquite, and other woody plants. The presettlement grassland vegetation in the Trans-Pecos was essentially the same as in other sections of the southwestern United States, where desert grasslands consisted of abundant grasses with scattered shrubs (Humphrey, 1953, 1958; Buffington and Herbel, 1965; Hastings and Turner, 1965; York and Dick-Peddie, 1969; Stein and Ludwig, 1979; Brown, 1982; Wondzell, 1984; Bahre, 1991).

Early Ranching Activity. Extensive ranching in the Trans-Pecos began in the early 1880's when the first Anglo Americans settled in the Big Bend region (Gregg, 1933; Casey, 1972). Thereafter much of the land in the region was bought, leased, or claimed for grazing livestock. From various historical accounts it is known that there was some localized grazing of domestic livestock, mostly cattle, in the region before the 1880's (Gregg, 1933; Humphrey, 1958; Hastings and Turner, 1965; Corning, 1967; Weddle, 1990; Parsons, 1990). In the Big Bend area of Trans-Pecos Texas, the most notable and reportedly the first early Anglo rancher was Milton Faver, who moved into southern Presidio County in 1857 (Gregg, 1933; Corning, 1967) and subsequently built a sizable herd of cattle (10,000–20,000 head), along with up to 5,000 sheep and 2,000 goats. Certainly considerable localized grazing activity occurred in areas of New Mexico and Arizona before the 1880's (Bahre, 1991). Humphrey (1958) and Bahre (1991) give an account of the grazing history in the southwestern United States where it is noted that livestock raising in the region dates back to about 1500. In the mid-1500's livestock (horses, cows, sheep) were brought into the southwest from Mexico. Some of these animals strayed or were lost and gave rise to herds that grazed the region. The numbers of cattle, horses, and sheep increased steadily after 1598, although for a long time Indian hostility tended to force concentration of the herds near the towns of El Paso, Santa Fe, Taos, and Tucson (Humphrey, 1958). The relatively concentrated grazing near towns and later near fortress-ranches and villages must have had some effect on rangeland. Livestock numbers on southwestern rangelands peaked in the late 1880's soon after completion of the Texas and Pacific Railroad (in 1883) through the region (Cottle, 1931; Corning, 1967; Bahre, 1991; Hastings and Turner, 1965; Grover and Musick, 1990), but it was not long until drought and severe winters (about 1885 to 1895) drastically reduced the herds. By 1905 most of the cattle companies operating in 1885 were out of business. Range conservation and management was born subsequent to the "appalling" losses of cattle from drought and starvation, the lowered rangeland productivity, and "the associated evils of soil erosion, water loss, and encroachment by noxious weeds" (Gould, 1951).

In the Trans-Pecos area Indians were still a problem for travelers and inhabitants in 1860 and beyond the time of Anglo settlement in the region (Echols, 1860; Gregg, 1933; Corning, 1967; Weddle, 1990). By 1885 relatively large herds of livestock were being raised in the Trans-Pecos (Gregg, 1933; Parsons, 1990). One such example occurred in the lower Big Bend country, where a cattle herd on the G-4 Ranch was increased from 6,000 head to 30,000 head in about six years from 1885 (Wauer, 1973). Drought years forced reduction of the herd by 1895, but the initial success of the ranching operation served to attract other cattlemen to the Big Bend Country in subsequent years (Wauer, 1973).

Changes in Trans-Pecos Grasslands. By all accounts it is evident that desert grasslands in the southwestern United States have changed since Anglo settlement, and it is well documented that the grasslands have been reduced through increase (or invasion) of scrubby woody plants (Cottle, 1931; Parker and Martin, 1952; Buffington and Herbel, 1965; Brown, 1982; Grover and Musick,

Fig. 18. The dominant presence of shrubs, at this site in Presidio County mostly honey mesquite (*Prosopis glandulosa*), overlapping with remaining grassland (foreground and background).

1990). In the Trans-Pecos both desert grassland and plains grassland have seen an increase of Chihuahuan Desert scrub species since the mid-1880's (Bray, 1901). Prominent invaders of desert grassland include *Larrea tridentata* (creosotebush), *Flourensia cernua* (tarbush), viscid acacia, *Opuntia* spp., and honey mesquite. Plains grassland has been invaded by catclaw mimosa, *Opuntia* spp. (*O. imbricata*, cane cholla, and prickly pears), sacahuiste, snakeweed, and other species. Today the range of former grasslands is suggested by the dominant presence of shrubs overlapping with remaining grassland (Fig. 18). In effect this amounts to a generally northward expansion of the Chihuahuan Desert at the expense of adjacent vegetative associations. Some of the most striking evidence for these changes involves before and after photographs (Parker and Martin, 1952; Hastings and Turner, 1965; McBryde, 1958; Nelson, 1981; Nelson, 1987; Bahre, 1991). No perceptible shrub increase was revealed, however, in some of the 1899 photographs examined by Nelson (1987), and the early photographs (mostly 1916–1920) by Smithers (1976) in the central Trans-Pecos reveal a moderate shrub increase in areas away from settlements and other sites of heavy human activity.

The underlying causes responsible for changes in desert grasslands have been studied by a number of workers. Most investigators have hypothesized that the drastic increase in shrubs was brought about by the overgrazing of grasslands by livestock, and much evidence has been cited in support of this concept (Humphrey, 1958; York and Dick-Peddie, 1969; Grover and Musick, 1990; Gillis, 1991). Additional factors that possibly are responsible for significant vegetative changes in desert grasslands have been reviewed by Humphrey (1953; 1958), Wondzell (1984), Branscomb (1958), Grover and Musick (1990), Holechek (1991), Bahre (1991), and others. The factors most often considered, in addition to heavy grazing, are changes in climate, suppression of grassland fires, fuelwood cutting, short and long drought periods, plant competition (e.g., snakeweed or mesquite naturally controlled by competition from grasses), effects of rodents, and erosion of topsoil in denuded areas. It has been demonstrated that all of these factors probably have been and are contributing to reduction in desert grassland and increase in shrubs (Humphrey, 1958; Wondzell, 1984; Grover and Musick, 1990), although in different parts of the southwest where the particular studies were carried out, different conclusions were sometimes reached about the primary reasons(s) for desertification (Branscomb, 1958; Brown, 1950; Gardner, 1950; Grover and Musick, 1990; Hastings and Turner, 1965; Herbel et al., 1972; Humphrey, 1958; McPherson and Wright, 1990; Nelson, 1987; Stein and Ludwig, 1979; York and Dick-Peddie, 1969; Bahre, 1991).

Not all evidence points to overgrazing as a primary cause of the shrub explosions seen in southwestern grasslands. In some areas climatic change might have been the primary cause of desertification (Buffington and Herbel, 1965). Turner (1990) has demonstrated that desert communities are highly responsive to changes in particular contemporary climatic regimes. In southern New Mexico it was revealed that shrubs continued to spread at an even rate inside and outside cattle enclosures (Gardner, 1950), although work by York and Dick-Peddie (1969) would suggest that a single factor such as previous grazing of the protected enclosure area is enough to set in motion the events that promote shrub increase. Even the rate of desertification in desert grasslands may be proportional to the intensity of grazing (Branscomb, 1958; Holechek, 1991).

One can infer from the Echols (1860) journey that the Trans-Pecos climate in 1860 was much the same as it is today. In his camel expedition through the southeastern Trans-Pecos from the Pecos River to Fort Davis, Marfa, Presidio, the Lajitas region, and across to Fort Stockton during the summer months, Echols reported in his journal very dry conditions with little or no grass in some areas early in the trip, and good grass in certain areas after evidence of thundershowers later in the journey. This seems like a contemporary summer in the Trans-Pecos, and one might suspect that the climate is changing slowly if at all. Recent predictions about global warming (Kerr, 1990) and increasing aridity, however, suggest an accelerated pace of desertification in semiarid grasslands of the southwest, an area where there is already a transition between the arid desert and semiarid grasslands. Schlesinger et al. (1990) reason that long-term grazing of semiarid grasslands gives rise to an increase in heterogeneity of soil resources, including water and nitrogen. Heterogeneity of soil resources is likely to encourage an increase in desert shrubs which contributes to desertification. It is apparent that the present climate only marginally supports the desert grasslands, and that even small changes in climate could result in major changes in vegetation (Wondzell, 1984).

Natural fires in Trans-Pecos grasslands today are suppressed by human activity. Over the past 100 years the rangeland has been divided into smaller ranches and in some areas even real estate developments. People for different reasons do not want their vegetation burned, particularly if a fire removes available forage or threatens buildings, fences, telephone or electric-line poles, recreational areas, or wildlife habitat. From a historical perspective, fire suppression also has resulted from livestock grazing where grasses have been reduced or eliminated, thus facilitating the increase of woody species. The subsequent decreases in open and extensive stands of grass that fuel fires may have the effect of reducing or even eliminating the incidence of fire in some areas (Humphrey, 1958). Modern studies in fire ecology have revealed a number of beneficial effects of fires, and prescribed burning (Bock and Bock, 1992) is a range management technique very much in evidence today (Barbour et al., 1987). Not only is effective fire thought to control the increase in shrubs (Fig. 19), but burning characteristically promotes an increase in the nutrition of range grasses (Hanselka, 1989).

Erosion of topsoil suitable to support grasses (Fig. 20) perhaps is one of the most important factors leading to desertification in the southwest and in the Trans-Pecos (York and Dick-Peddie, 1969; Brown, 1982; Schlesinger et al., 1990). Once soil-binding perennial grasses have been removed from desert or plains grasslands (Herbel et al., 1972), then encroachment of opportunistic desert shrubs is not far behind. Even under carefully managed grazing regimes the loss of topsoil sometimes is unavoidable. Heavy grazing during a good summer wet season may lead to the diminution of grass cover in subsequent and unpredictable drought periods. Moderate to extensive soil erosion may follow (Fig. 21). Any process that leads to increasing heterogeneity of soil resources in space and time (Schlesinger et al., 1990) may contribute to vegetative degradation, particularly in desert grassland transition between Chihuahuan desertscrub and plains grassland.

An analysis of the current literature makes it clear that the perceived deterioration of grasslands in the southwestern United States is a complex phenomenon (Anderson, 1982; Holechek, 1991). The reasons for change at one site may not be the same at another, especially in the topographically heterogeneous desert grassland. There is little that can be done about long-term climate changes or short-term weather. In the arid Trans-Pecos region good seasonal precipitation in some years followed by periodic, moderate to severe droughts in other years is a factor that is likely to remain characteristic for some time.

Fig. 19. A rangeland fire in 1989 at this site in Brewster County removed abundant juniper and other shrubs, and promoted the growth of predominant grasses in 1990 (this photo taken in 1992).

Fig. 20. The erosion of topsoil at this site in Culberson County presented conditions unsuitable to support grasses such as those remaining, along with various desert shrubs, in the background.

Fig. 21. Gully erosion leads to the destruction of grasslands in the Trans-Pecos and in the arid southwest.

Herds of livestock grazing the Trans-Pecos ranges today are nowhere near the numbers reported for the early days. There were at least 60,000 head of cattle in Presidio County by the end of 1885, and flocks of sheep and goats all over the county (Gregg, 1933). In 1886 about 60,000 head of cattle were rounded up in the Big Bend area, and at this time the regional cattle herds had not reached their maximum (Wuerthner, 1989). Livestock numbers (Wauer, 1973) later removed from the Big Bend National Park in 1944 and 1945 (19,000–25,000 cattle, 15,000–18,000 goats, 6,000–8,000 sheep, about 1,000 horses) show the extent of early grazing pressure in the lower Big Bend.

Effective range management information and techniques are available to the ranchers of today, and these have been utilized throughout the Trans-Pecos. Holechek (1991) recently has emphasized the importance of moderate stocking rates (removal of about 30% of perennial grass forage annually) on Chihuahuan Desert rangelands. Among the desirable management techniques, grazing itself probably represents essential management of grassland systems that evolved along with grazing animals such as the bison (Stebbins, 1981; Hill, 1991; Holechek, 1991). Ranching remains a major industry in the vast region which still supports extensive plains grassland on the mountain slopes, basins, and plateaus. After normal summer rains these grasslands present spectacular green landscapes. Also, the desert grassland in the Trans-Pecos is much altered by an increase in Chihuahuan desertscrub, but it survives as a recognizable vegetative entity in the region. Studies of permanent transects located in desert grassland in Big Bend National Park (Wondzell, 1984) have demonstrated that even heavily grazed desert grassland vegetation can recover, especially on certain soil types. Soil degradation and erosion, after denudation of perennial grass cover, are probably the most critical factors in promoting desertification in the transition desert grassland in Trans-Pecos Texas, where climatic conditions particularly at the lower and drier sites are already marginal for the support of grasses.

Morphology of Grasses

Grasses are flowering plants with small and inconspicuous flowers. These specialized monocotyledonous plants of the family Poaceae (Gramineae) often are included along with the family Cyperaceae in the order Cyperales (Cronquist, 1988). Plants of both families in our region are characterized by clumped habit, slender leaves, and small flowers. The Poaceae are distinguished by stems terete or flattened, leaves two-ranked, leaf sheaths mostly open, a two-nerved bract (palea) subtending the flower, fruit usually a caryopsis, and embryo lateral to the endosperm. The Cyperaceae are recognized by stems triangular at least immediately below the inflorescence, leaves three-ranked, leaf sheath mostly closed, bract subtending the flower with an odd number of nerves, fruit usually an achene, and embryo embedded in the endosperm (Gould and Shaw, 1983).

Grass plants vary in size from 2–3 cm to more than 30 m tall (the larger bamboos). In the Trans-Pecos region the tallest grass is the riparian giant reed (*Arundo donax*), with culms 2–6 m tall. Most grass species in the region are less than 1 m high, although some members of the tribe Andropogoneae may reach 2–3 m in height.

A typical grass plant (Fig. 22) consists of roots, culms (stems), leaves, and a contracted or open inflorescence of small flowers. Prominent morphological features of the grass plant include: (1) A *fibrous* root system. (2) Jointed stems, known as *culms*, composed of often enlarged *nodes* and elongated *internodes*. (3) Leaves borne in *two ranks*, one at each node; the leaf consists of a basal *sheath* and a distal *blade*; a ciliate membrane or fringe of hairs known as a *ligule* is found at the inside (adaxial) junction of sheath and blade. (4) The most common *inflorescence* type in grasses is the *panicle*; florets are borne in *spikelets*; a spikelet (Fig. 23), composed of one to numerous florets, is treated as the basic unit of the grass inflorescence; spikelets typically are subtended below by two empty bracts called *glumes*; *flowers*, typically consisting of a pistil, three stamens, and two lodicules, are enclosed by two bracts, a *lemma* (lower)

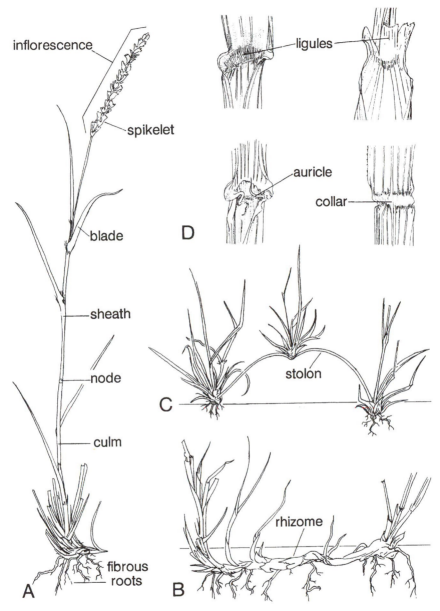

Fig. 22. Important features of the grass plant. (A) Habit (*Hilaria mutica*), showing roots, culm (stem) with nodes, leaves (sheath and blade), and inflorescence (with spikelets). (B) Rhizome (*Hilaria mutica*). (C) Stolon (*Hilaria swallenii*). (D) Auricle (*Elymus canadensis*) on adaxial surface in some grasses; collar (*Elymus canadensis*) at abaxial junction of blade and sheath; ligule, a ciliate example (*Eragrostis cilianensis*), and a membranous ligule (*Sorghastrum nutans*).

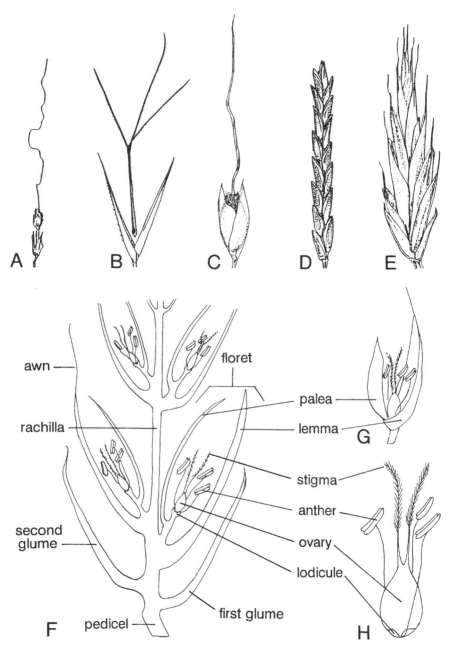

Fig. 23. Spikelets and spikelet, floret, and flower structure. (A) Spikelet with one floret (*Muhlenbergia crispiseta*). (B) Spikelet with one floret, lemma 3-awned (*Aristida ternipes* var. *hamulosa*). (C) Spikelet with one floret, indurated lemma (*Piptochaetium fimbriatum*). (D) Spikelet with 16 florets (*Eragrostis lehmanniana*). (E) Spikelet with about 10 florets, the lemmas awned (*Bromus lanatipes*). (F) Diagrammatic representation of a *Bromus* spikelet, showing four florets. (G) Representation of a grass floret, and (H) a grass flower.

and a *palea*. Collectively the lemma, palea, and flower are called a *floret* (Fig. 23). Additional information about each organ of the grass plant is presented below. More detailed discussion of grass morphology is presented in Hitchcock (1951), Gould (1968), and Gould and Shaw (1983).

Roots. The mature fibrous root system of grasses is made up of adventitious roots. The primary root system developed from the embryonic primary root and other seminal roots persists usually less than one month, giving way to the adventitious roots that develop from lower nodes of the culms. The usually slender adventitious roots produce branch roots. Roots do not have nodes and internodes but may resemble the underground stems (called rhizomes) of some grasses. Rhizomes do have nodes and internodes and may produce roots or reduced "scaly" leaves at the nodes. Roots or leaves are not produced on the internodes. Some grasses such as corn or maize (*Zea mays*) produce *prop roots* at the lower culm nodes.

Culms (stems). The jointed grass stems usually are smooth and cylindrical. Culm growth results from active apical meristems and from intercalary meristems at the base of nodes. The internodes are hollow, as in wheat, or solid, as in maize. Some grasses exhibit partially filled internodes. The nodes are solid. Culms are herbaceous in most grasses, but the stems of reeds and bamboos become hard or woody. Culm branches, leaves, or adventitious roots develop at the nodes. A "bunchgrass" habit results from basal stem branching. Spreading basal branches in grasses often are called "tillers," "suckers," or "stools." Branching in some grasses is along erect culms above the base.

Creeping culms are produced by some grass species. Slender *stolons*, often called "runners," extend above ground and may form new plants at the nodes (Fig. 22). Stolons are produced by black grama (*Bouteloua eriopoda*), buffalograss (*Buchlöe dactyloides*), bermudagrass (*Cynodon dactylon*), and many other Trans-Pecos grass species. *Rhizomes* are underground creeping stems that also may function in asexual reproduction through production of new plants at the nodes (Fig. 22). Many Trans-Pecos species such as ear muhly (*Muhlenbergia arenacea*) produce rhizomes. Some species such as bermudagrass produce either stolons or rhizomes depending upon whether the "runner" axis is above the ground or below.

Leaves. The basal leaf *sheath* is attached immediately below the culm node and tightly envelops the culm internode (Fig. 22). Leaves are borne in two ranks, one at each node, and alternate. Sheath margins are overlapping and free to the base in most grasses, but in some species the margins are partially or completely united to form a cylinder, as in most species of *Bromus*. The leaf *blade* (Fig. 22) may be flat, folded (conduplicate), or inrolled (involute). Involute leaf blades are thought to be an adaptation to hot, dry conditions and thus grass species with this leaf condition are common in the Trans-Pecos. *Auricles* (Fig. 22) are leaf appendages in some grasses on either margin at the base of the blade or at the apex of the sheath. The characteristic *ligule* (Fig. 22), a ciliate or membranous appendage at the adaxial junction of blade and sheath, is an important taxonomic character at the genus level in grasses. The abaxial (outside or back) junction of blade and sheath is known as the *collar* (Fig. 22). The margins of leaf blades in some grass species exhibit microscopic epidermal projections that give the saw-edge effect familiar to some people who have experienced cuts on bare hands while pulling grasses.

The prophyllum is a modified, short and thin first leaf associated with lateral shoots or branches that is formed in the axil of normal leaf sheaths. The *prophyllum*, or *prophyll*, is a 2-keeled organ with its concave dorsal side fitted against the culm axis and its margins clasping the bud or base of the new shoot.

Inflorescence. A common definition of inflorescence is the arrangement of flowers on a plant. In grasses the individual unit of the inflorescence is the spikelet, and the inflorescence type may be thought of as the arrangement of spikelets. There are three basic inflorescence types (Fig. 24), the *spike, raceme,* and *panicle*. Spikes, racemes, and *contracted panicles* are similar in appearance (Fig. 24) but may be distinguished, as explained below, through examination of spikelet attachment to the inflorescence axis.

The prevalent inflorescence type in grasses is the *panicle*. In a panicle, spikelets are borne not only on individual stalks or *pedicels*, but also on branches of the inflorescence axis. There are several modifications of a panicle. A panicle may be open, as in *Muhlenbergia porteri* and *Sporobolus airoides*, or contracted, densely flowered, and cylindrical, as in *Lycurus*.

Contracted panicles are referred to as *spicate* or *spikelike panicles* (Fig. 24). Another panicle type is seen in the tribe Chlorideae and in some genera of Paniceae and Andropogoneae, where the spikelets are arranged along primary inflorescence branches. The primary branches of the inflorescence may be distributed along the main axis, as in species of *Leptochloa* and *Bouteloua* (Fig. 24), or borne at the apex and *digitate*, as in some species of *Chloris*. Highly modified panicles are seen in *Setaria* and *Cenchrus*, where the ultimate branches are without spikelets, and develop as bristles near the spikelets (Fig. 24).

In a *raceme* the spikelets are borne on pedicels attached directly to the main inflorescence axis. Classical racemes with spikelets borne singly at the nodes as in *Pleuropogon* are rare in grasses. Slightly more common are modified *spicate racemes* (Fig. 24) such as in *Critesion* (=*Hordeum pusillum*), where both sessile and short-pedicled spikelets occur at the same node.

In a *spike* all the spikelets are *sessile* (without pedicels) on the main axis. Among Trans-Pecos grasses, species of *Hilaria* exemplify this type of inflorescence (Fig. 24).

Spikelet. The *spikelet* consists of the *rachilla*, a short axis bearing one or more florets above, and two empty bracts, the *glumes*, at the basal nodes

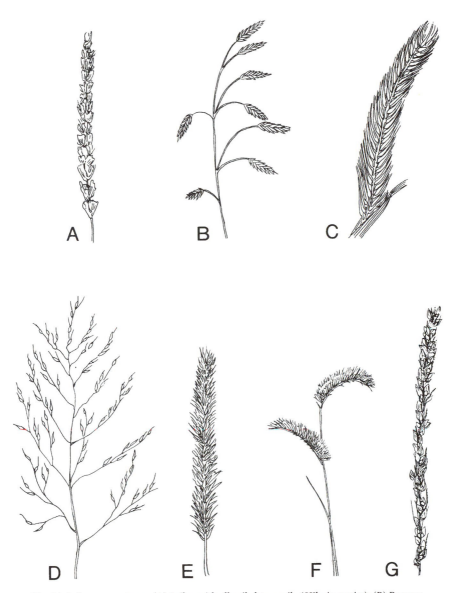

Fig. 24. Inflorescence types. (A) Spike, with all spikelets sessile (*Hilaria mutica*). (B) Raceme
(*Bromus catharticus*). (C) Spicate raceme (*Critesion* [=*Hordeum*] *pusillum*). (D) Panicle, open
(*Muhlenbergia eludens*). (E) Panicle, contracted (*Lycurus phleoides*). (F) Panicle, with primary,
spicate branches (*Bouteloua gracilis*). (G) Panicle, spicate, with spikelets subtended by bristles
(*Setaria texana*).

(Fig. 23). The glumes are alternate and closely placed. In some grasses (e.g., some Paniceae) one glume is reduced, modified, or absent. Each *floret* usually consists of two bracts, and the enclosed *flower*. The lower bract is the *lemma*, and the smaller, upper bract is the usually 2-keeled *palea*. The typical grass flower exhibits three *stamens*, a *pistil*, and two *lodicules* which are considered to be vestigial perianth parts (Fig. 23).

Perhaps most grass species produce *bisexual* or *perfect* flowers, but *unisexual* flowers also are found in grasses. *Staminate* flowers have only the three stamens and *pistillate* flowers have only a pistil. Grass flowers are *sterile* if they lack functional stamens or a functional pistil. The term *fertile* floret applies to one with a functional pistil even if stamens are absent (Fig. 25).

Some grass species are *dioecious* (Fig. 25), with separate male and female plants, including the familiar Trans-Pecos species burrograss (*Scleropogon brevifolius*) and buffalograss (*Buchlöe dactyloides*). *Monoecious* grasses, with male and female spikelets on the same plant, include the cultivated corn or maize (*Zea mays*), eastern gamagrass (*Tripsacum dactyloides*) (Fig. 25), and species of *Zizania* and *Zizaniopsis*. In the spicate racemes of tanglehead (*Heteropogon contortus*), paired lower spikelets are staminate while paired upper spikelets are staminate (pedicelled) *and* pistillate.

The most primitive grass spikelet has several florets, as seen in *Bromus, Poa*, and many other genera. It is assumed that reduction in the spikelet to one or two florets has occurred independently in several tribes (Gould and Shaw, 1983). Spikelets with single florets are seen in *Muhlenbergia, Sporobolus, Agrostis, Aristida, Stipa*, and other grasses. In Paniceae the spikelet is two-flowered, with a staminate lower floret (resembling the second glume) and perfect upper floret, usually with a hardened lemma (Fig. 25). In *Andropogon* the spikelets occur in pairs of one sessile and perfect and one pedicelled and staminate or rudimentary (Fig. 25). The Andropogoneae have paired two-flowered spikelets with the lower floret usually sterile and vestigial. In some grasses with multiflowered spikelets, the lower florets (*Blepharidachne*) or the upper florets (*Chloris* and *Melica*) may be sterile and perhaps reduced (Fig. 25).

Glumes and Lemmas. The floral bracts *glumes* and *lemmas* (and paleas) are modified leaves. Glumes and, particularly, lemmas provide important taxonomic characters. Their salient features often are emphasized in keys and descriptions.

Usually the glumes are similar in appearance, but this is not always the case. The first glume (lowest in nodal attachment) may be smaller than the second glume, and in some grasses (Paniceae) the first glume may be short or even absent. In the Andropogoneae the first glume is larger than the second, and both glumes are somewhat hardened (perhaps dark), enclosing a thin, membranous lemma. In *Hordeum* and other related grasses the glumes are awnlike. In the tribe Oryzeae glumes typically are absent.

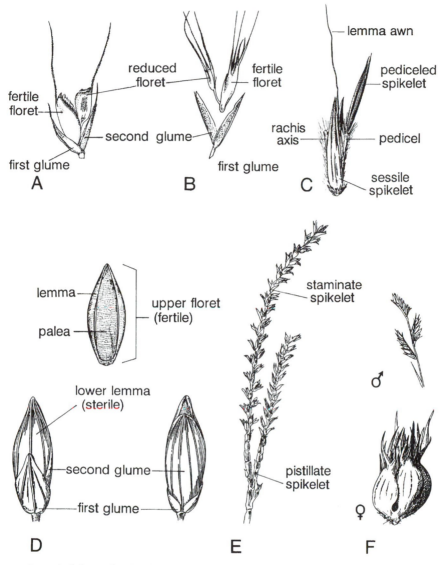

Fig. 25. Spikelets with reduced, sterile, or unisexual florets; representative genera and tribes.
(A) Spikelet of *Chloris verticillata* (Chlorideae). (B) Spikelet of *Bouteloua kayi* (Chlorideae).
(C) Spikelet of *Andropogon gerardii* (Andropogoneae). (D) Spikelet of *Panicum bulbosum* (Paniceae). (E) Spikelets of *Tripsacum dactyloides* (Andropogoneae), these unisexual (staminate and
pistillate) in same inflorescence. (F) Spikelets of *Buchlöe dactyloides* (Chlorideae), these unisexual
in separate staminate (♂) and pistillate (♀) inflorescences; pistillate inflorescence known as a
"bur," with several spikelets inside.

The lemmas of different grass genera may vary in size, shape, texture, number of nerves, awns, and surface features. In *Panicum* and related genera the fertile lemma is indurate, and noticeably harder than the glumes or the lemma of the sterile lower floret (Fig. 25). In Andropogoneae the fertile lemma is membranous. *Aristida* and *Stipa* exhibit a terete, hardened lemma, often with a sharp callus and tuft of hairs at the base. Lemma awns may vary from one to about 13 and may be weak or stout. Some long, stout, geniculate (bent) awns are hygroscopic and twist with moisture changes, supposedly facilitating contact of the grain with the soil and thus enhancing germination.

Fruit. Botanically a dry, indehiscent, one-seeded fruit with the seed coat adherent to the ovary wall is known as a *caryopsis*. In *Aristida* and *Stipa* the indurated, cylindric lemma permanently encloses the fruit. A hardened lemma, rounded on the back, confines the fruit in Paniceae. In Andropogoneae the hardened glumes permanently enclose the fruit. The term "grain" is used in reference to the fruit alone or to the fruit enclosed in persistent floral bracts.

Grasses of
Trans-Pecos Texas

The state of Texas has a rich grass flora, with approximately 40% of the species and about 60% of the genera of grasses in the United States being represented in the state (Box and Gould, 1959). In the Trans-Pecos region alone there are about 268 species in 83 genera, and 24 varieties in addition to the typical varieties. Gould (1975) lists 523 species in 122 genera for Texas. Fifty-three Texas grass species are endemic to the Trans-Pecos. During the current study one genus new to Texas, *Microchloa*, and one species new to the United States, *Muhlenbergia crispiseta*, were recorded. Of the 10 Vegetational Areas of Texas recognized by Gould et al. (1960), only the Gulf Prairies and Marshes, Pineywoods, and Post Oak Savannah are similar to the Trans-Pecos Mountains and Basins in species diversity of their grass floras.

In the Trans-Pecos region about 83% of the grass species are native, and about 17% of the species (approximately 46 species) are introduced. Approximately 72% of the Trans-Pecos grass species are perennial, and about 28% are annual. Warm-season grasses, about 84% of the Trans-Pecos species, greatly outnumber the cool-season species, about 16%.

The taxonomic arrangement of subfamilies, tribes, and most genera for the current treatment of Trans-Pecos grasses essentially follows Gould (1975). Parentheses beside each genus name indicate the number of Trans-Pecos species currently recognized for each genus. More accurate classifications for the grasses, including tribal and subfamilial arrangements, are emerging as workers continue to study the family (Soderstrom et al., 1987; Clayton and Renvoize, 1986).

Subfamilies, Tribes, and Genera Represented in Trans-Pecos Texas

(Number in parentheses is the number of species in Trans-Pecos Texas.)

SUBFAMILY I. ORYZOIDEAE

TRIBE 1. ORYZEAE

1. *Leersia* (1)

SUBFAMILY II. ARUNDINOIDEAE

TRIBE 2. ARUNDINEAE

2. *Arundo* (1)
3. *Phragmites* (1)
4. *Cortaderia* (1)

TRIBE 3. DANTHONIEAE

5. *Schismus* (1)

TRIBE 4. STIPEAE

6. *Stipa* (10)
7. *Oryzopsis* (2)
8. *Piptochaetium* (2)

SUBFAMILY III. POOIDEAE (FESTUCOIDEAE)

TRIBE 5. MELICEAE

9. *Melica* (3)
10. *Glyceria* (1)

TRIBE 6. POEAE

11. *Vulpia* (1)
12. *Festuca* (3)
13. *Lolium* (1)
14. *Poa* (8)

TRIBE 7. AVENEAE

15. *Koeleria* (1)
16. *Sphenopholis* (1)
17. *Trisetum* (1)
18. *Avena* (2)
19. *Limnodea* (1)
20. *Agrostis* (6)
21. *Polypogon* (2)
22. *Gastridium* (1)
23. *Phalaris* (2)

TRIBE 8. BROMEAE

24. *Bromus* (10)

TRIBE 9. TRITICEAE

25. *Hordeum* (1)
26. *Critesion* (3)
27. *Elymus* (4)
28. *Leymus* (1)
29. *Pascopyrum* (1)
30. *Pseudoroegneria* (1)
31. *Triticum* (2)

SUBFAMILY IV. CHLORIDOIDEAE (= ERAGROSTOIDEAE)

TRIBE 10. ERAGROSTEAE

32. *Eragrostis* (12)
33. *Tridens* (4)
34. *Triplasis* (1)
35. *Erioneuron* (3)
36. *Dasyochloa* (1)
37. *Munroa* (1)
38. *Eleusine* (1)
39. *Leptochloa* (5)
40. *Scleropogon* (1)
41. *Blepharidachne* (1)
42. *Calamovilfa* (1)
43. *Lycurus* (2)
44. *Muhlenbergia* (28)
45. *Sporobolus* (10)
46. *Blepharoneuron* (1)

TRIBE 11. CHLORIDEAE

47. *Schedonnardus* (1)
48. *Microchloa* (1)
49. *Cynodon* (1)
50. *Chloris* (6)
51. *Bouteloua* (14)
52. *Cathestecum* (1)
53. *Buchlöe* (1)
54. *Spartina* (1)
55. *Hilaria* (4)

TRIBE 12. ZOYSIEAE

56. *Tragus* (2)

TRIBE 13. AELUROPODEAE

57. *Distichlis* (1)
58. *Allolepis* (1)

TRIBE 14. PAPPOPHOREAE

59. *Pappophorum* (2)
60. *Enneapogon* (1)
61. *Cottea* (1)

TRIBE 15. ARISTIDEAE

62. *Aristida* (11)

SUBFAMILY V. PANICOIDEAE

TRIBE 16. PANICEAE

63. *Digitaria* (5)
64. *Stenotaphrum* (1)
65. *Eriochloa* (3)
66. *Panicum* (18)
67. *Paspalum* (4)
68. *Echinochloa* (4)
69. *Setaria* (11)
70. *Pennisetum* (1)
71. *Cenchrus* (4)

TRIBE 17. ANDROPOGONEAE

72. *Imperata* (1)
73. *Sorghum* (1)
74. *Sorghastrum* (1)

75. *Andropogon* (3)
76. *Bothriochloa* (5)
77. *Schizachyrium* (3)
78. *Trachypogon* (1)
79. *Elionurus* (1)
80. *Heteropogon* (1)
81. *Hemarthria* (1)
82. *Tripsacum* (1)
83. *Zea* (1)

Key to the Tribes

(adapted from Clayton and Renvoize, 1986)

1. Spikelets 2-flowered, with only the upper floret fertile (disregarding those in the few monoecious taxa, and the staminate or neuter spikelets), the lower floret staminate or empty.
   2. Glumes membranous; lemma of the sterile lower floret like the glumes in texture (spikelets with upper lemma usually convex and hard, usually shiny or wrinkled, the texture of fingernails, the margins usually clasping the flat palea of similar texture; glumes 1 or 2, the first one often reduced or absent, the second glume covering the convex back of the perfect lemma)   **16. Paniceae, p. 254.**
   2. Glumes hardened; lemma (and palea) of the fertile floret hyaline or membranous, lemma of the sterile floret like the fertile one in texture (spikelets in pairs, one sessile or nearly so and one on a pedicel, except at branch tips, which have one spikelet sessile and 2 spikelets pedicelled, rarely both spikelets short-pedicelled; pedicelled spikelet usually reduced in size or rudimentary, perhaps represented by pedicel alone, or else like the sessile spikelet)   **17. Andropogoneae, p. 312**
1. Spikelets 1- to many-flowered, the reduced florets, if any, above the perfect florets (except in *Phalaris* and *Blepharidachne*), if 2-flowered then both perfect or the upper empty.
   3. Spikelets with 1 fertile floret, with or without other staminate or empty florets.
      4. Palea 1-keeled; glumes absent; wet habitats   **1. Oryzeae, p. 43**
      4. Palea 2-keeled, or if 0–1-keeled, then glumes well-developed; various habitats.
         5. Inflorescence a panicle (except in some *Avena* of Aveneae).
            6. Ligule membranous.
               7. Lemma indurate, terete to subterete (or somewhat laterally compressed), permanently enclosing the palea and fruit, with a well-developed basal callus; awn terminal   **4. Stipeae, p. 49**

       7. Lemma not indurate, laterally compressed to terete, not permanently enclosing the palea and fruit; spikelets with or without a well-developed basal callus; awns absent or dorsal.
         8. Glumes longer than floret; awns dorsal

                                7. Aveneae, p. 77
         8. Glumes shorter than floret; awns terminal or absent.
            9. Sheath margins connate; lemmas awnless (in our species)   **5. Meliceae, p. 60**
            9. Sheath margins mostly free; lemmas awned or awnless

                                  6. Poeae, p. 65
    6. Ligule a line of hairs.
       10. Lemma awns 7–11 (or more), the apex deeply cleft or lobed   **14. Pappophoreae, p. 233**
       10. Lemma awns 0–3, the apex not cleft or lobed.
          11. Awn of the lemma 3-branched, the lateral awns perhaps minute; lemma indurate, slender, and subcylindrical, permanently enclosing the palea and fruit

                               15. Aristideae, p. 239.
          11. Awn of the lemma single, or awn absent; lemma otherwise   **10. Eragrosteae, p. 120**
  5. Inflorescence a spike or a panicle of racemose branches.
    12. Lemma 3-nerved.
      13. Spikelets (second glume) bearing stout hooked bristles
                              12. Zoysieae, p. 228
      13. Spikelets not bearing hooked bristles
                              11. Chlorideae, p. 195
    12. Lemma 5–9-nerved (obscurely 3–5-nerved in some).
      14. Spike bilateral; awn not geniculate   **9. Triticeae, p. 104**
      14. Racemose branches of panicle unilateral; awn geniculate (dorsal), reduced, or absent   **7. Aveneae, p. 77**
3. Spikelets with 2 or more fertile florets.
  15. Lemmas 1–3-nerved   **10. Eragrosteae, p. 120**
  15. Lemmas 5-or-more-nerved.
    16. Ligules membranous, sometimes with a minutely fringed margin.
      17. Inflorescence a simple or compound bilateral spike, the spikelets oriented flatwise to the rachis **9. Triticeae, p. 104**
      17. Inflorescence a panicle, or a unilateral raceme, with spikelets oriented edgewise.
        18. Upper glume longer than adjacent floret; awn dorsal and usually geniculate   **7. Aveneae, p. 77**
        18. Upper glume shorter than adjacent floret or nearly so; lemma awnless, or awn terminal and straight.

      19. Spikelets exceeding 1.5 cm (usually 2–3.5 cm) long (lemmas awned from a bifid apex, or awns absent) **8. Bromeae, p. 95**

      19. Spikelets less than 1.5 cm (usually 0.3–1.4 cm) long.

        20. Sheath margins connate; lemmas awnless **5. Meliceae, p. 60**

        20. Sheath margins mostly free; lemmas awned or awnless **6. Poeae, p. 65**

16. Ligule a line of hairs, the hairs sometimes on a membranous base (the ligule membranous in *Muhlenbergia*, *Lycurus*, and some *Leptochloa*).

    21. Spikelets disarticulating between the florets.

      22. Plants 2–6 m high, in large clumps 1 m wide or more, cane- or reedlike, with leaves evenly distributed on the stems **2. Arundineae, p. 44**

      22. Plants usually less than 1 m high.

        23. Tufted annuals; leaf blades weak and filiform; spikelets bisexual **3. Danthonieae, p. 48**

        23. Strong perennials with rhizomes or stolons; leaf blades stiff, distinctly 2-ranked, terminating in a sharp point; spikelets unisexual, male and female similar **13. Aeluropodeae, p. 229**

    21. Spikelets not disarticulating between the florets (except in *Cottea* of Pappophoreae).

      24. Glumes falling with the spikelet **10. Eragrosteae, p. 120**

      24. Glumes persistent on inflorescence.

        25. Inflorescence a panicle (lemmas with 9 or more awns) **14. Pappophoreae, p. 233**

        25. Inflorescence a panicle with racemose unbranched primary branches **11. Chlorideae, p. 195**

Descriptive Grass Flora

SUBFAMILY I. ORYZOIDEAE

Tribe 1. Oryzeae

The tribe Oryzeae includes about 12 genera and 70 species distributed characteristically in riverside, marshland, or aquatic habitats in tropical and warm temperate regions of the world (Clayton and Renvoize, 1986). Included in this tribe are rice (*Oryza sativa*), annual wildrice (*Zizania aquatica*), the rare Texas wildrice (*Zizania texana*) of the headwaters of the San Marcos River in Hays County, Texas, and southern wildrice (*Zizaniopsis miliacea*). Of these important and potentially important economic species, only annual wildrice is not reported to occur in Texas (Gould, 1975). Among other characters the tribe is characterized by the absence of glumes, which may appear only as obscure lobes at the pedicel apex.

1. LEERSIA Swartz

A genus of about 18 species of temperate and tropical regions of both hemispheres, most typical in marshy and moist woodland habitats. Five species occur in Texas. The genus is named for J. D. Leers.

1. Leersia oryzoides (L.) Swartz RICE CUTGRASS. Fig. 26. Perennial with creeping rhizomes. Culms usually 80–150 cm long, bases often decumbent or stoloniferous, the nodes retrorsely hispid. Leaves retrorsely scabrous; ligules membranous, firm, short-truncate; blades usually 7–10 mm wide, firm, midnerve and margins serrate. Inflorescence a panicle, usually 10–20 cm long, lax and drooping, often partially included in sheath, the slender lower branches bare of spikelets for basal 1–4 cm. Spikelets 1-flowered, flattened laterally, sharply keeled, awnless, 5–6 mm long, narrow, oblong, asymmetrical; glumes

Fig. 26. *Leersia oryzoides*. Panicle; stem with
leaf; spikelet.

absent; lemmas indurate, boat-shaped, 5-nerved, with marginal nerves often indistinct, tightly enclosing the palea, short-hispid or scabrous, with stiff hairs on the keels.

Limited distribution along permanent water sources. Brewster Co., 101 Ranch Hdq., in pool. 5,000 ft. Flowering Jul. Throughout much of TX (perhaps not the High Plains) in aquatic or moist habitats. Throughout most of the U.S. except NV, WY, and MT; also southern Canada.

Reported by Gould (1978) as a warm-season grass that is of little or no forage value for livestock, but its seeds provide food for ducks and other birds.

SUBFAMILY II. ARUNDINOIDEAE

Tribe 2. Arundineae

The tribe Arundineae includes about 40 genera and 300 species of worldwide distribution, but with most taxa concentrated in southern latitudes. Single representatives of three genera occur in the Trans-Pecos, but only one species, *Phragmites australis*, is considered to be native.

Fig. 27. *Arundo donax.* Dense growth of the river cane, giant reed, also locally known as carrizo, along the Rio Grande, Brewster County.

Key to the Genera of Arundineae

1. Plants cespitose, without rhizomes; leaves crowded at the base, the blades 0.5–1.5 cm wide; ornamental   **4. *Cortaderia*, p. 47**
1. Plants tall and canelike, with stout rhizomes, forming colonies; leaves evenly arranged along the culms, blades 2–6 cm wide; mostly along the Rio Grande and Pecos River, but used also sometimes as an ornamental.
    2. Panicle tightly elliptic-lanceolate in outline; rachilla glabrous; lemmas hairy; plants 2–6 m tall   **2. *Arundo*, p. 45**
    2. Panicle somewhat triangular or ovate in outline, often with longer branches reflexed; rachilla hairy; lemmas glabrous; plants 2–4 m tall
    3. *Phragmites*, p. 46

2. ARUNDO L.

A genus of approximately three Asian species. One species occurs in Texas. *Arundo* is an ancient Latin name used in reference to a reed.

1. Arundo donax L.   GIANT REED.   Figs. 6, 27.   Bamboolike perennial with thick rhizomes. Culms 3–6 m high, glabrous. Leaves glabrous, evenly spaced along the stem; sheaths rounded; ligules ciliate, ca. 1 mm long; blades to 4–7 cm wide. Inflorescence a dense, contracted panicle, 30–60 cm long, branches scabrous. Spikelets 1–4-flowered, 10–15 mm long; glumes unequal, thin, 3-or-more-nerved, acute or acuminate; lemmas 5–10 mm long, 3–5-nerved, densely pilose, acuminate and usually short-awned; paleas shorter than lemmas.

Scattered along the Rio Grande and lower Pecos River. Flowering mostly Sep–Nov. Widely propagated from rhizomes, becoming a pest, difficult to eradicate in yards. An Old World species, widespread in the southern U.S.

When in flower the giant reed is easily distinguished from the common reed by its longer, narrowly elliptic, dense panicles and usually longer stems. The common reed has usually much shorter and less dense panicles with the branches flexing laterally. Woodwind reeds are made from dried stems of the giant reed.

3. PHRAGMITES   Adans.

A genus of perhaps three species. One species occurs in Texas. The genus name *Phragmites* is taken from the Greek, *phragma*, in reference to its growth like a fence along streams.

1. Phragmites australis (Cav.) Trin. *ex*. Steud.   COMMON REED.   Fig. 28.   [*Phragmites communis* Trin.]. Canelike perennial with thick, creeping rhizomes and often stolons. Culms 2–4 m high, glabrous. Leaves glabrous, evenly spaced along the stem; sheaths rounded; ligules ciliate; blades mostly 1.5–5 cm wide. Inflorescence a dense panicle 25–40 cm long, the longer branches tending to flex laterally at maturity; disarticulation above glumes, between florets. Spikelets 10–15 mm long, usually with 4–8 florets; joints between florets with long silky hairs, the florets glabrous; first glume 3-nerved, about one-half as long as the second; second glume 3–5-nerved, 6–8 mm long; lower floret infertile, with lemma 11–14 mm long, much longer than lemmas of the other florets.

Common along the Rio Grande and lower Pecos River, colonies often side by side with the more scattered *Arundo donax*. Also scattered throughout the Trans-Pecos, including 2 mi S of Pecos in alkali soils; widely propagated from rhizomes. Flowering mostly Jul–Nov. Scattered throughout Texas, most frequently along the Gulf Coast, along streams, lakes, and other permanent water. More widely distributed in the western and northern U.S. than in the southeast. Widespread in tropical and temperate areas of both hemispheres.

The stems of common reed usually are smaller in diameter than are those of giant reed, allowing tentative identification when the plants are not in flower.

Fig. 28. *Phragmites australis.* Plant with rhizome and stem; floret (left) and spikelet (right). Photo inset, inflorescence.

4. CORTADERIA Stapf

A genus of about 24 species native to South America. One species occurs in Texas. The genus name is derived from the Argentine word, *cortadera*, meaning cutting, in reference to the cutting edges of the leaf blades.

1. Cortaderia selloana (Schult.) Ashers. & Graebn. PAMPASGRASS. Fig. 6.   Densely clumped perennial, 1 m or more wide, plants dioecious. Leaves with rounded sheaths, glabrous or with a ring of hairs at the collar; ligule a tuft of hairs, 3–5 mm long; blades firm to 1 m or more long, 3–10 mm wide, sharply toothed with stout spicules on margins and midnerve. Inflorescence a densely flowered, bright white panicle, usually several of these per plant and 25–100 cm long. Spikelets 2–3-flowered, disarticulating above the glumes; glumes thin, glabrous, 1-nerved, attenuate at apex; lemmas thin, narrow, attenuate, with long hairs on the back in pistillate spikelets, glabrous in staminate spikelets.

Grown as an ornamental in some Trans-Pecos towns. Flowering mostly Aug–Nov. More commonly used in coastal areas and south Texas, and in the southern U.S. Native to South America, especially Brazil, Argentina, and Chile.

Fig. 29. *Schismus barbatus.* Plant; spikelet
(upper right) and florets (upper left).

The large, white panicles provide a main ornamental feature of this large clump grass. Reportedly pampasgrass is good forage for cattle (Hitchcock, 1951) when planted for that purpose.

Tribe 3. Danthonieae

The only Trans-Pecos representative of this tribe (Gould, 1975), *Schismus*, is included in the tribe Arundineae by Clayton and Renvoize (1986).

5. SCHISMUS   Beauv.

Approximately five species native to Africa, Asia, and Europe, with two species adventive in the southwestern United States. One species occurs in Texas. The genus name is from the Greek, *schismos*, meaning splitting, alluding to the deeply notched lemmas.

1. Schismus barbatus (L.) Thell.   Fig. 29.   Tufted annual. Culms weak, glabrous, 7–30 cm long. Leaves with rounded sheaths; collar with long hairs on either side; ligule a short, ciliate membrane; blades glabrous or hirsute, slender, 0.5–2 mm wide. Inflorescence a dense, contracted panicle, 1–5 cm long, with spikelets on short branches. Spikelets 4.5–6.5 mm long, usually 5–7-flowered, disarticulating above the glumes; glumes subequal, acute to acuminate with prominent whitish margins, nearly equaling the entire spikelet in length; lemmas rounded, several-nerved, 2–2.5 mm long, glabrous or hairy on margins and back, apex with a deep notch, this often with a minute bristle; palea nearly as long as lemma. Caryopsis shiny, clear, obovate, 0.6–1 mm long.

Infrequent in El Paso Co., in yards of El Paso and Fabens, McKelligon Canyon, Franklin Mts. Flowering Feb–Jun. W to AZ and S CA. Adventive from Mediterranean region.

This introduced species is of limited occurrence and probably of minor forage value.

Tribe 4. Stipeae

This tribe consists of about 400 species in nine genera distributed in temperate and warm temperate regions of the world. The Stipeae are characterized by spikelets with a single terete or hardened floret, usually with a terminal awn. Three genera of Stipeae occur in Texas, according to traditional treatments (Gould, 1975), and all three genera occur in the Trans-Pecos.

Barkworth (1993) revised the Stipeae for the United States and Canada, and five genera were recognized among the Trans-Pecos species of the tribe. The more traditional, and probably unnatural, treatment of Stipeae is maintained at the present time for practical reasons only. The nomenclature presented by Barkworth (1993), however, is included below in discussion under species of Stipeae.

Key to the Genera of Stipeae

1. Lemma awn not twisted, straight or curved, readily deciduous; body of lemma dorsally compressed, broad, ovate, with a blunt callus at base
   7. *Oryzopsis*, p. 56
1. Lemma awn twisted and bent, persistent or later deciduous; body of lemma not compressed, terete and slender to obovoid, the callus short and blunt to pointed.
   2. Palea grooved between the two keels; body of the lemma cylindrical to gibbous-ovoid; the callus blunt; lemma margins inrolled along median line, not meeting at the apex and exposing tip of palea; awn 1–2 cm long
      8. *Piptochaetium*, p. 58
   2. Palea not grooved, not keeled; body of the lemma slender, terete, fusiform; the callus pointed and bearded; lemma margins flat, overlapping or not, but usually meeting at the apex and covering tip of palea; awn 1.5–15 cm or more long **6. *Stipa*, p. 50**

6. STIPA   L.   NEEDLEGRASS.

Clumped perennials. Culms stiffly erect or spreading, 30–150 cm long. Leaves long and narrow; ligules membranous; blades mostly involute. Inflorescence a panicle, narrow or contracted, often drooping. Spikelets 1-flowered; disarticulating above the glumes; glumes longer than body of the lemma, thin, several-nerved, acute, acuminate, or aristate; lemmas usually terete and slender, hard or firm, tightly enveloping the palea, flower, and caryopsis at maturity; lemma awn commonly bent (geniculate) and twisted below, pubescent or scabrous, usually persistent; palea membranous; base of lemma (and rachilla) developing a callus, usually sharp-pointed and densely pubescent; caryopsis usually fusiform.

A genus of temperate and subtropical regions, and about 300 species. In the United States about 35 species occur mostly in the western states (Gould, 1975). All 10 of the Texas species occur in the Trans-Pecos. The genus name is from the Greek, *stupe*, in reference to the feathery awns of the type species, *S. pennata* L. Comprehensive taxonomic studies involving the tribe Stipeae (Barkworth and Everett, 1987; Barkworth, 1990) have resulted in the rearrangement of species groups and genera (Barkworth, 1993). Native *Stipa* does not occur in North America according to the interpretation by Barkworth (1993).

Key to the Species

1. Awns plumose (hairs mostly 0.6–2.5 mm long) on terminal portion
                                                        1. S. neomexicana.
1. Awns not plumose on terminal portion.
    2. Lemmas 2–3 mm long   **10. S. tenuissima.**
    2. Lemmas 5 mm or more long (including callus).
        3. Lemma apex with a smooth, whitish neck ca. 1 mm long, the neck just below a ring of stiff hairs (0.5–1 mm long) formed around awn base   **4. S. leucotricha.**
        3. Lemma apex without a smooth, whitish neck below a ring of hairs around awn base.
            4. Awns densely plumose below (between apex of lemma and bend of awn)   **3. S. curvifolia.**
            4. Awns scabrous, nearly glabrous, or with rather short appressed hairs.
                5. Awns 10–15 cm long   **2. S. comata.**
                5. Awns less than 7.5 cm long.
                    6. Awns 3.5–7 cm long; panicles open or contracted.
                        7. Panicles open but narrow (not dense), the branches and pedicles slender, some spreading; ligules (1.5–)2–6 mm long   **5. S. eminens.**

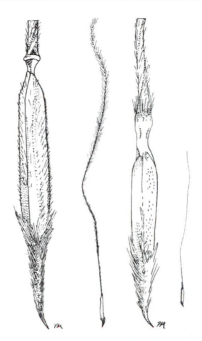

Fig. 30. *Stipa neomexicana* (left) and *S. leuco-tricha* (right). Lemmas with base of awn (enlarged) and whole florets with awns. Both same scale.

    7. Panicles contracted, usually dense, the branches and pedicles short and erect; ligules less long   **7. *S. arida.***
  6. Awns 1–3.5 cm long (to 3.8 cm long in *S. robusta*); panicles contracted, usually dense.
    8. Lemma apex with membranous lobes 0.6–1.5 mm long at sides of awn base   **6. *S. lobata.***
    8. Lemma apex without lobes.
        9. Leaf blades 5–8 mm wide; culms stout 3–6 mm across at the base   **8. *S. robusta.***
        9. Leaf blades 3(–4) mm wide; culms slender 1.5–2.5 mm across at the base   **9. *S. nelsonii.***

    1. Stipa neomexicana (Thurb.) Scribn. NEW MEXICO FEATHER-GRASS. Fig. 30. Widespread and only locally common on open rocky slopes. El Paso Co., Franklin Mts.; Hueco Pass. Hudspeth Co., 10 mi E Hueco. Culberson Co., Sierra Blanca; Sierra Diablo, Victorio Canyon; Guadalupe Mts., mid to lower slopes. Presidio Co., SW San Estaban Lake. Jeff Davis Co., Davis Mts. State Park. Brewster Co., Chisos Mts., upper Cattail Canyon; Glass Mts.,

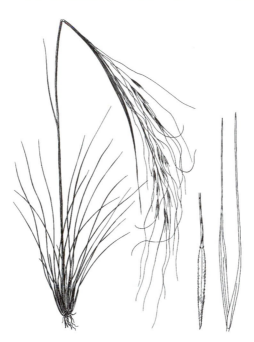

Fig. 31. *Stipa comata*. Plant; lemma with base
of awn, and glumes.

near Altuda Point; 19–25 mi E Marathon. Pecos Co., 15–30 mi S Fort Stockton; Sierra Madera; 4 mi W Longfellow. 2,800–6,500 ft. Flowering Apr–Jun. E to Crockett Co., the Edwards Plateau, and the plains country. W to AZ, CO, UT. N Mex.

Stipa neomexicana is closely related to *S. comata*, from which it differs conspicuously by plumose awns and shorter ligules. Both of these species have only fair to good forage value for livestock, and relatively poor value for wildlife. In addition the sharp-pointed callus of the long awns may cause injury to eyes, tongue, and ears, particularly of sheep. In Barkworth (1993) this species is recognized as *Hesperostipa neomexicana* (Thurb.) Barkworth.

2. Stipa comata Trin. & Rupr.   NEEDLE-AND-THREAD.   Fig. 31.   Frequent on the plains and grasslands, reportedly infrequent in the Trans-Pecos mountains (Gould, 1975). Flowering May–Jun. NE in the TX Panhandle. Widespread N to Canada, and W to the coast. Treated as *Hesperostipa comata* (Trin. & Rupr.) Barkworth by Barkworth (1993).

3. Stipa curvifolia Swallen   GUADALUPE NEEDLEGRASS.   Fig. 32. Steep, north-facing, open, rocky limestone slopes and cliffs. Hudspeth Co.,

Fig. 32. *Stipa curvifolia, S. eminens, S. lobata* (with enlargement of
lemma apex, right), *S. nelsonii*, and *S. tenuissima* (left to right).
Lemmas and whole florets with awns. All same scale.

Guadalupe Mts., 120 ft E of streambed and SW of Cutoff Peak, 0.8 mi SW of
the summit of Cutoff Peak. Culberson Co., Guadalupe Mts., W escarpment;
Coyote Peak; Patterson Hills. 3,600–6,400 ft. Flowering Apr–Jun. Adjacent
Eddy Co., NM (originally collected, Rocky Arroyo, Guadalupe Mts.) and Doña
Ana Co., NM (specific localities, Hatch and Bearden, 1983).

Stipa curvifolia, recently studied by Hatch and Bearden (1983), is highly
restricted in distribution, and closely related to the more widely ranging *S.
occidentalis* Thurb. (western needlegrass). Barkworth (1993) regarded *S. curvifolia* as *Achnatherum curvifolium* (Swallen) Barkworth.

4. Stipa leucotricha Trin. & Rupr.   TEXAS NEEDLEGRASS.   Fig. 30.
Hills, slopes, and mesas, including mostly open sites. Brewster Co., roadside in
N Alpine. Pecos Co., ca. 20 mi W Sanderson; 4 mi N Fort Stockton; 3 mi W
Pecos River bridge. Val Verde Co., near Comstock; near Juno. 1,000–4,700 ft.
Flowering mostly Apr–Jun. Throughout most of TX. Also OK. NE Mex.

Texas needlegrass is also known as Texas wintergrass. Good to fair forage is
afforded by Texas needlegrass in the early spring, although the awns may cause

some problems later in the season. Barkworth (1993) treated *S. leucotricha* as *Nassella leucotricha* (Trin. & Rupr.) Pohl.

5. Stipa eminens Cav. SOUTHWESTERN NEEDLEGRASS. Fig. 32. Mountains, canyons, rocky slopes, and mesas. El Paso Co., Franklin Mts., McKelligon Canyon. Hudspeth Co., Sierra Diablo, Victorio Canyon and elsewhere; Eagle Mts. Culberson Co., Guadalupe Mts.; 2 mi S Kent. Presidio Co., Sierra Vieja; Capote Mt.; Chinati Mts.; Elephant Mt.; N rim, W rim of Solitario; 2 mi S Shafter. Jeff Davis Co., Sawtooth Mt., H. O. Canyon; near Reeves Co. line; Davis Mts. State Park. Reeves Co. Brewster Co., 5 mi SW Marathon; Iron Mt.; Glass Mts., Altuda Point; Mt. Ord; Doubtful Canyon; Paisano Campground; Cathedral Mt.; Goat Mt.; Cienega Mt.; 20 mi NE Alpine; Steamboat Mesa, 02 Ranch; Packsaddle Mt.; Elephant Mt.; Nine Point Mesa; Chisos Mts.; Dead Horse Mts., Heath Canyon. Pecos Co., mesas and canyons near Fort Stockton. 3,100–7,500 ft. Flowering Jun–Oct (to Nov). W to AZ. Central Mex.

This is probably the most widespread needlegrass species in the Trans-Pecos. Although fairly common in some areas, southwestern needlegrass probably is of limited forage value. Barkworth (1993) included *S. eminens* in another genus as *Achnatherum eminens* (Cav.) Barkworth.

6. Stipa lobata Swallen LITTLEAWN NEEDLEGRASS. Fig. 32. Rocky slopes and canyons, mostly above 5,000 ft. El Paso Co., Franklin Mts. Hudspeth Co., Sierra Diablo, Victorio Canyon and at Bat Cave. Culberson Co., Guadalupe Mts. Brewster Co., Glass Mts.; Mt. Ord; Goat Mt.; Chisos Mts., Chinese Wall, Cattail Canyon; Dead Horse Mts., Heath Canyon. 4,400–8,000 ft. Flowering May–Aug (to Sep). Also NM.

Littleawn needlegrass probably is of limited forage value, although it is often locally common. *Stipa lobata* is regarded as *Achnatherum lobatum* (Swallen) Barkworth by Barkworth (1993).

7. Stipa arida M. E. Jones MORMON NEEDLEGRASS. Fig. 33. Reported for the Trans-Pecos (Gould, 1975) on open rocky slopes. Flowering summer. W to AZ, Funeral Mts. of CA and UT, CO.

The author has not observed this species to occur in the Trans-Pecos, and no specimens are available at Sul Ross. Barkworth (1993) listed *S. arida* as *Achnatherum aridum* (M. E. Jones) Barkworth.

8. Stipa robusta (Vasey) Scribn. SLEEPYGRASS. Fig. 34. Reported for the Trans-Pecos (Gould, 1975) on slopes and mountain valleys. To be expected in the Guadalupe Mts., if actually extant in the Trans-Pecos. Flowering Jun-Sep. N to NM, CO, W to AZ. N Mex.

According to Barkworth (1993), *Stipa robusta* is best distinguished from robust *S. lobata* by a line of pubescence on the back of the collar on upper leaves. The collar of *S. lobata* is glabrous. *Stipa robusta* has not been docu-

Fig. 33. *Stipa arida*. Plant; glumes and floret.   Fig. 34. *Stipa robusta*. Plant; glumes and floret.

mented for Texas. Barkworth (1993) treated *S. robusta* as *Achnatherum robustum* (Vasey) Barkworth. Sleepygrass is named after a narcoticlike effect it has on horses, cattle, and sheep. Horses have been known to doze for seven days after grazing on sleepygrass, but the more usual effect, which is seldom fatal, is sleepiness for a few hours, more or less. Tests in New Mexico reportedly demonstrated that when cattle were fed sleepygrass they "ate it with gusto," but that they would not eat it again after they had once experienced its effects. The cattle would "freeze" in one position and remain motionless for up to 45 minutes. Reportedly some ranchers have tried with success to feed their herds sleepygrass hay under controlled conditions, before moving them on the range, so that the cattle would later avoid the grass instead of getting "spaced out" and losing weight. The narcotic substance has been identified as diacetone alcohol. Gould (1975) reports that the narcotic effect of sleepygrass varies from region to region, and with the stage of growth. Sheep are not as strongly affected by sleepygrass as are cattle. White et al. (1992) suggested that the narcotic effects of *S. robusta* and other grasses may be due in part to alkaloids produced by endophytic fungi living in the grass plants. These authors further suggested that the endophytic fungi in certain grasses may have a negative impact on the livestock industry, because once animals have experienced the extreme narcotic effects, they tend to avoid the grasses and suffer reduced weight gain.

9. Stipa nelsonii Scribn.   COLUMBIA NEEDLEGRASS.   Fig. 32.   [*Stipa columbiana* Macoun]. Burgess and Northington (1981) reported two collections from Culberson Co., Guadalupe Mts., vicinity of Bush Mt., although they note that the two collections may represent aberrant *S. lobata*. Worthington (pers. comm.) has tentatively identified this taxon to occur in the Franklin Mts. (El Paso Co.). Flowering late spring and perhaps summer. The name *S. nelsonii* follows Barkworth and Maze (1979), who proposed that the name *S. columbiana* be rejected. Barkworth (1993) recognized *S. nelsonii* as *Achnatherum nelsonii* (Scribn.) Barkworth. Gould (1975) reports this taxon for the mountains of the Trans-Pecos. N to cen. Canada, W to CA.

10. Stipa tenuissima Trin.   FINESTEM NEEDLEGRASS.   Fig. 32.   Locally abundant in alluvial valleys and on rocky slopes, commonly under oaks. Culberson Co., South McKittrick Canyon. Presidio Co., top of Chinati Peak; Elephant Mt. Jeff Davis Co., Madera Canyon; near McDonald Observatory; Bloys Encampment; Limpia Canyon; Davis Mts. State Park; Rockpile; E of Girl Scout Camp. Pecos Co., 30 mi E Fort Stockton. Brewster Co., Bird Mt.; Mt. Ord; Goat Mt.; Twin Peaks; Elephant Mt.; Cathedral Mt.; Cienega Mt.; 7–8 mi W Alpine; Chisos Mts. (3,300)4,400–8,000 ft. Flowering Jun–Sep or later into fall. Also NM. Cen. Mex. Also Argentina.

Finestem needlegrass is one of the most widespread stipas of the Trans-Pecos, particularly in Jeff Davis and Brewster counties, commonly growing in dense stands under oaks, junipers, and pines in alluvial basins. The species is easily distinguished by its short lemmas, only 2–3 mm long. According to Barkworth (1993) *S. tenuissima* belongs in *Nassella* as *N. tenuissima* (Hitchc.) Barkworth.

7. ORYZOPSIS   Michx.   RICEGRASS.

Cespitose perennials. Culms slender. Leaves with membranous ligules; blades narrow, flat or involute. Inflorescence a narrow or open panicle. Spikelets 1-flowered; disarticulation above the glumes; glumes (in our species) hyaline or papery, subequal, acuminate or attenuate; lemmas subterete, dorsally compressed, indurate, callus blunt; awns deciduous, 3–10 mm long, straight or twisted and bent; palea enclosed by lemma. Caryopsis enclosed by lemma.

A genus of about 35 species of cool and temperate regions of both hemispheres. Two species occur in Texas. The genus name was inspired by the resemblance of its species to rice (*oryza*, rice, and *opsis*, appearance). The genus name of true rice is *Oryza*. The dorsally compressed floret of *Oryzopsis* is the main character distinguishing the genus from the closely related *Stipa*.

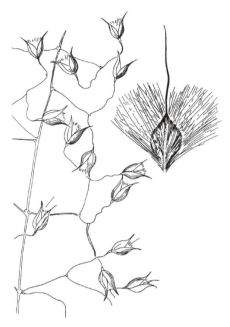

Fig. 35. *Oryzopsis hymenoides.* Part of panicle;
floret.

Key to the Species

1. Lemmas densely pubescent with hairs 2–4 mm long; spikelets 5–8 mm long; pedicels kinked or curved, usually 7–30 mm long **1. *O. hymenoides.***
1. Lemmas glabrous (rarely short-pubescent); spikelets 2.5–4 mm long; pedicels straight, very short to ca. 4 mm long   **2. *O. micrantha.***

1. Oryzopsis hymenoides (Roem. & Schult.) Ricker, in Piper   INDIAN RICEGRASS.   Fig. 35.   Usually in gypsum or quartz sand. Hudspeth Co., valley W of eastern ridge of Hueco Mts.; 9 mi E of Hueco Inn; 12.5 mi E Dell City. 3,500–4,700 ft. Flowering May–Jul. Also High Plains in TX. NM and most of western states, W to CA and WA, N to ND.

This species is locally common in the white gypsum dunes west of the Guadalupe Mountains, and also at White Sands, New Mexico. Reportedly the grains were used for food by the Indians. Indian ricegrass is highly palatable to livestock, but usually not abundant enough to be important forage. Barkworth (1993) included *Oryzopsis hymenoides* in *Achnatherum* as *A. hymenoides* (Roem. & Schult.) Barkworth.

2. Oryzopsis micrantha (Trin. & Rupr.) Thurb. LITTLESEED RICE-GRASS. Fig. 36. Forested areas. Culberson Co., Guadalupe Mts., top of South McKittrick Canyon. 8,000 ft. Flowering May–Jul, extending into Sep. Also High Plains in TX. NM W to AZ and NV, N to ND and MT.

Littleseed ricegrass is palatable and evidently restricted in the Trans-Pecos to the top of the Guadalupe Mountains. According to Barkworth (1993) little-seed ricegrass is not closely related to Indian ricegrass and instead belongs in a separate genus as *Piptatherum micranthum* (Trin. & Rupr.) Barkworth.

8. PIPTOCHAETIUM   Presl

Tufted perennials. Culms 40–100 cm long, glabrous or hairy at nodes, slen-der, erect to declining. Leaves mostly basal, glabrous; ligules membranous, 0.5–3 mm long; blades 5–35 cm long, ca. 1–3 mm wide, flat or involute, flexuous. Inflorescence an open or loosely contracted panicle, 6–15(–20) cm long, few-flowered; panicle branches slender, the lowermost 2–10 cm long, spikelets absent on proximal one-half; disarticulation above the glumes. Spike-lets 1-flowered, plump; glumes 5–11 mm long, subequal, thin, acuminate or short-awned, faintly 3–9-nerved, with hyaline margins at apex; lemmas 3.8–8.5 mm long, ca. 1.5 mm wide, oblong, firm, tightly enclosing palea and cary-opsis, unequal at apex, at maturity dark brown with reddish hairs, tufted at base; lemma awn stout, 1.2–3 cm long, weakly twice-geniculate, the lower por-tion twisted and scabrous; palea sulcate, as long as lemma. Caryopsis usually fusiform.

A genus of mostly South American species, about 30 in all, with three spe-cies in North America. The genus name is from Greek *piptein*, to fall, and *chaite*, bristle, in reference to deciduous awns of the type species. The grooved palea of *Piptochaetium* distinguishes the genus from *Stipa* (Clayton and Ren-voize, 1986). Both Trans-Pecos species of *Piptochaetium* were retained in this genus by Barkworth (1993).

Key to the Species

1. Leaf blades involute, ca. 1 mm wide; glumes usually 5–6 mm long, faintly 3–7-nerved; lemmas 3.8–5 mm long, faintly 3-nerved; lemma awn 1.2–1.8 cm long   **1. *P. fimbriatum.***
1. Leaf blades flat or somewhat involute, 1–3 mm wide; glumes 9–11 mm long, 5–9-nerved; lemmas 7–8.5 mm long; lemma awn 2–3 cm long
                                                                  2. *P. pringlei.*

1. Piptochaetium fimbriatum (H.B.K.) Hitchc. PINYON RICEGRASS. Fig. 37. Mountains and canyons, mostly in protected areas and under pines and oaks. Culberson Co., Sierra Diablo, Victorio Canyon; Guadalupe Mts.,

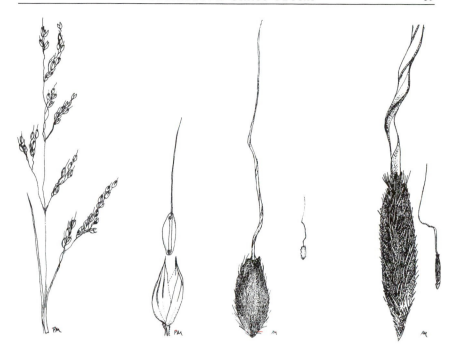

Fig. 36. *Oryzopsis micrantha*. Panicle; spikelet.

Fig. 37. *Piptochaetium fimbriatum* (left) and *P. pringlei* (right). Lemmas with awn or awn base, and florets. Both same scale.

South McKittrick Canyon; top of Guadalupes. Presidio Co., Chinati Mts., big canyon above Fred Shely ranch house. Jeff Davis Co., Sawtooth Mt.; Madera Canyon; Davis Mts. State Park; Mt. Locke; Rockpile; slopes of Mt. Livermore; Haystack Mt. Brewster Co., Iron Mt.; Mt. Ord; Cathedral Mt.; Cienega Mt.; Elephant Mt.; Chisos Mts. Usually 4,700–8,000 ft, rarely 3,100–4,100 ft. Flowering Jun–Oct. NM, AZ, CO. Also Mex.

Pinyon ricegrass is highly palatable but usually not sufficiently abundant to be important forage.

2. Piptochaetium pringlei (Scribn.) Parodi   PRINGLE NEEDLEGRASS. Fig. 37.   [*Stipa pringlei* (Beal) Scribn.]. Infrequent on slopes and canyons, open or under trees. Culberson Co., top of South McKittrick Canyon; Bowl. Jeff Davis Co., upper slopes Mt. Livermore; Madera Canyon; upper Limpia Canyon. 6,800–8,000 ft. Flowering summer. W to AZ. N Mex.

Pringle needlegrass probably is good forage where it is locally abundant. Gould recognized this species as a *Stipa*, although most agrostologists now include the taxon with *Piptochaetium* (Barkworth and Everett, 1987; Barkworth, 1993).

SUBFAMILY III. POOIDEAE (FESTUCOIDEAE)

Tribe 5. Meliceae

The eight genera and approximately 130 species of Meliceae occur in temperate regions of the world. Important tribal characters include the connate sheath margins and the peculiar lodicules that are usually connate, fleshy, and truncate. There are two genera of Meliceae in Texas, and both are represented in the Trans-Pecos.

Key to the Genera of Meliceae

1. Glumes papery; 3–5-nerved   9. *Melica*, p. 60
1. Glumes not papery, 1-nerved   10. *Glyceria*, p. 63

9. MELICA   L.

Clumped perennials, some rhizomatous, usually 40–100 cm tall in our species, with cormlike culm bases in some species mostly outside the Trans-Pecos. Leaves with closed sheaths, the margins fused to near the top; ligules membranous, continuous with sheath margins. Inflorescence a panicle, usually simple and contracted, more open in some taxa. Spikelets with 2 (rarely 1)–several perfect florets and 2–3 reduced, neuter florets above; reduced florets with successively smaller empty lemmas, these together termed "the rudiment"; disarticulation below the glumes in our species (except *M. bulbosa*); broad, thin, 3–5-nerved, with clear or paperlike margins and apices; lemmas more firm than glumes, usually 7-nerved, awnless in our species, with clear upper margins; palea usually three-fourths as long as lemma. Caryopsis smooth, wrinkled, shiny.

A genus of about 80 species in temperate regions of both hemispheres, except in Australia, with some species extending to the subtropics in North America. Approximately 20 species occur in the United States. Five species occur in Texas. In addition to the three species treated below, Gould (1975) indicated that *M. bulbosa* Porter & Coulter has been reported from the Trans-Pecos but not recently documented from this region, and Hatch et al. (1990) listed *M. bulbosa* for the region. I have not verified *M. bulbosa* to occur in the Trans-Pecos. *Melica bulbosa* (oniongrass) can be identified by basal culms usually bulbous, disarticulation above the glumes, and purple-tinged lemmas. The spikelets with broad, thin, shiny glumes are an identifiable feature of the genus. The origin of the genus name, *Melica*, is from an Italian word for a type of sorghum, probably (*mel*, honey) from the sweet juice.

Fig. 38. *Melica porteri*. Plant; and spikelet.

Key to the Species

1. Perfect florets usually 4–5; rudiment (reduced upper florets) narrowing above, not club-shaped or obconic   **1. *M. porteri.***
1. Perfect florets usually 1–3; rudiment club-shaped or obconic, rarely narrowing above.
    2. Back of the lemma usually with prominent twisted hairs; spikelets with 1 perfect floret   **2. *M. montezumae.***
    2. Back of the lemma scabrous; spikelets with 2–3 perfect florets
                                  3. *M. nitens.*

1. Melica porteri Scribn. PORTER MELIC. Fig. 38. Infrequent in mountains and canyons. Culberson Co., Guadalupe Mts. Jeff Davis Co., Limpia Canyon, 10 mi above Fort Davis; Mt. Livermore, Madera Canyon and elsewhere in shaded moist pockets near the top. 4,700–8,000 ft. Flowering Apr–Oct. W to AZ and CO.

Porter melic is probably palatable to cattle and wildlife, but not abundant enough to provide good forage.

Fig. 39. *Melica montezumae.* Plant;
and spikelet.

Fig. 40. *Melica nitens.* Partial plant; floret.

2. Melica montezumae Piper   MONTEZUMA MELIC.   Fig. 39.   Infrequent to locally common, usually N slopes and canyons, juniper-oak woodland. Brewster Co., Chisos Mts., Pulliam Bluff, Maple Canyon; Panther Canyon; Packsaddle Mt.; 19 mi E Marathon; Housetop Mt., ca. 28 mi E Marathon. Pecos Co., N end Glass Mts.; 20–35 mi S Fort Stockton; Sierra Madera 24 mi S Fort Stockton. Terrell Co., 10 mi S Sheffield. Crockett Co., Lancaster Hill just E of the Pecos. Sutton Co., 1 mi W Sonora. Val Verde Co., 2 mi S Juno. 2,000–5,200 ft. Flowering Mar–May (rarely Jun). TX. N Mex.

Montezuma melic probably is excellent forage for grazing animals where it is abundant. Immature florets may lack identifiable features of this species, including the clavate rudiment, broad glumes and lemmas, and twisted hairs on the back of the lemmas, although the single perfect floret is a reliable character in the Trans-Pecos. Some specimens from Sierra Madera (Pecos Co.) appear to have glabrous lemmas. A first chromosome number report ($2n = 18$) and range extensions (included above) for *Melica montezumae* were recorded by Read and Simpson (1992).

3. Melica nitens (Scribn.) Nutt. ex Piper   THREEFLOWER MELIC.   Fig. 40.   Infrequent in mountains and canyons, igneous or limestone soils, mostly moist and cool sites. Culberson Co., South McKittrick Canyon. Jeff Davis Co., Limpia Canyon near Wild Rose Pass; Mt. Livermore. Pecos Co., Sierra Madera. Val Verde Co., 3 mi N Comstock; 10 mi S Juno. 1,600–8,000 ft. Flowering Apr–Jun. E and NE to Edwards Plateau, Cross Timbers, and plains country. N to VA, PA, WI, and KS.

Melica nitens is related to *M. mutica* Walt., which reportedly does not occur in the Trans-Pecos (Gould, 1975). The common name threeflower melic is not appropriate for Trans-Pecos and other Texas (Gould, 1975) populations of *M. nitens*, which characteristically exhibit only two fertile flowers per spikelet. The Trans-Pecos distribution of *M. nitens* appears to overlap with *M. porteri* on Mt. Livermore, and with *M. montezumae* in the Sierra Madera (Pecos Co.). Like other Texas melic grasses, this species is notably palatable to most grazing animals.

10. GLYCERIA   R. Br.

A genus of approximately 40 species preferring moist to aquatic habitats in temperate regions of both hemispheres. Three species are reported for Texas (Gould, 1975). *Glyceria* is from the Greek, *glukeros*, meaning sweet, after the sweet grains of the type species.

Fig. 41. *Glyceria striata*. Plant; spikelet and
floret (above).

1. Glyceria striata (Lam.) Hitchc. FOWL MANNAGRASS. Fig. 41.
Perennial, often with slender rhizomes. Culms 35–85 cm long, glabrous.
Leaves glabrous; sheaths rounded, uppermost with margins fused nearly to
top; ligules membranous, 1.5–3.5 mm long; blades 2–7 mm wide, flat or involute. Inflorescence an open to loosely contracted panicle 10–20 cm long, the
lowermost branches 4–9 cm long, flexuous, glabrous or scabrous, bare of spikelets on lower one-half to one-third. Spikelets usually 4 mm or less long, 3–
6-flowered, or more commonly, 5–6-flowered; disarticulating above glumes,
between florets; glumes with membranous margins, the first ca. 1 mm long,
the second slightly longer; lemmas ca. 2 mm long, obovate, prominently 7-
nerved, apex rounded, hyaline, ciliolate-lacerate; palea broad, as long as the
lemma except for hyaline apex. Caryopsis black, ca. 0.8 mm long.

Along permanent streams and at spring margins. Culberson Co., Smith
Canyon; Smith Springs; South McKittrick Canyon. 5,300–6,500 ft. Flowering
Apr–Sep. E to Edwards Plateau and SE TX. Widely distributed throughout the
U.S.; British Columbia to Newfoundland.

Fowl mannagrass is palatable to livestock, like other species of the genus,
but too localized to be of much forage value.

Tribe 6. Poeae

The tribe Poeae as treated by Clayton and Renvoize (1986) consists of about 1,200 species in 49 genera, distributed in temperate and cold regions of the world. *Poa* and *Festuca* are the largest genera of the tribe. Gould (1975) recognized 10 genera of Poeae for Texas, including *Bromus*, which herein is relegated to a separate tribe Bromeae. Four genera of Poeae occur in the Trans-Pecos. *Dactylis glomerata* L. (orchard grass), an adventive weed from Europe and Asia and introduced to the United States as a forage grass, occurs in Texas on the High Plains and eventually may be found in the Trans-Pecos.

Key to the Genera of Poeae

1. Inflorescence a bilateral spike, the spikelets oriented edgeways; first glume absent (except on the terminal spikelet); plants annual   **13. *Lolium*, p. 69**
1. Inflorescence a panicle, infrequently a raceme, but then the spikelets oriented flatways; first glume present; plants perennial or annual.
    2. Plants perennial.
        3. Lemmas rounded on the back, at least near the base
            12. *Festuca*, p. 67
        3. Lemmas keeled throughout   **14. *Poa*, p. 70**
    2. Plants annual.
        4. Lemmas awned   **11. *Vulpia*, p. 65**
        4. Lemmas awnless   **14. *Poa*. p. 70**

11. VULPIA   K.S. Gmel.   SIXWEEKSGRASS.

A genus of about 32 species widely distributed in temperate and subtropical regions of the northern hemisphere. *Vulpia* has been introduced to the southern hemisphere, perhaps with some endemic species in South America. In Texas there are four species, all short-lived annuals flowering in the spring. *Vulpia* was regarded as a section of *Festuca* (Hitchcock, 1935; 1951), while Gould (1975) followed other authors including Fernald (1950) and Lonard and Gould (1974) in according *Vulpia* generic status.

1. Vulpia octoflora (Walt.) Rydb.   COMMON SIXWEEKSGRASS.   Fig. 42.   [*Festuca pusilla* Buckl.; *F. octoflora* subsp. *hirtella* Piper]. Annual, short-lived. Culms 10–45 cm long, slender, weak, erect or decumbent, often geniculate at dark nodes. Leaves glabrous or short-pubescent; ligules membranous, 0.5–1 mm long; blades to 10 cm long, 0.5–1 mm wide. Inflorescence a panicle usually, or spicate raceme, 1–17 cm long, branches short, appressed. Spikelets

Fig. 42. *Vulpia octoflora*. Plant; spikelet.

glabrous to short-pubescent, 7–11 mm long excluding awns, florets 6–17, uppermost reduced; first glume 2.5–4.5 mm long, second glume 3–6.6 mm long; lemma of lowermost floret 3–6.4 mm long; awn 0.3–6 mm long. Caryopsis cylindrical, elongate, 1.7–3.2 mm long, brown at maturity.

Infrequent to rare, usually in disturbed habitats. El Paso Co., Franklin Mts., McKelligon Canyon, Fusselman Canyon, E slopes; Hueco Tanks. Hudspeth Co., 22 mi E El Paso, Hueco Mts.; 15 mi E Indian Hot Springs; W slopes of Guadalupe Mts. Culberson Co., Eagle Mts., Panther Peak; Sierra Diablo; Pine Spring service station. Presidio Co., 32 mi S Marfa, bed of Alamito Creek; near old San Estaban Lake; Cibolo Creek at Shafter. Jeff Davis Co., Haystack Mt., N slope. Brewster Co., Calamity Creek, 20 mi S Alpine; Cienega Mt.; Elephant Mt., N slope; Big Hill, ca. 6 mi S Alpine. Pecos Co., 1 mi S Sheffield. Terrell Co., 31 mi S Sheffield. Val Verde Co., Mile Canyon, Langtry; mouth of Pecos River. 1,200–6,500 ft. Flowering Mar–Jun. Throughout TX, except deep southern part. Western U.S. to British Columbia. Northern Mex., Coahuila to Baja CA.

According to Gould (1975) the Trans-Pecos entity is *V. octoflora* (Walt.) Rydb. var. **hirtella** (Piper) Henr., and this variety grades into *V. octoflora* var.

octoflora as seen particularly in characters of the lemma. Common sixweeks-grass is small, ephemeral, and consequently of little forage value except perhaps where it might be abundant in early spring.

12. FESTUCA   L.   FESCUE.

Tufted perennials, some rhizomatous. Culms usually slender, wiry, erect or decumbent. Leaves with flat or (in our species) involute blades. Inflorescence a contracted or open panicle. Spikelets with 2–several florets. Disarticulation above glumes and between florets; glumes slender, 1–3-nerved, acute or acuminate; lemmas rounded on back, usually 5–7-nerved, acute (in our species), awned or awnless. Caryopses usually ovoid or ellipsoid, free from palea.

This genus of perhaps 450 cool-season species is widely distributed in temperate and cool regions of the world, including mountains in the tropics. Many of the species are important forage grasses in Europe and in the western United States. The seven fescue species of Texas (Gould, 1975) are not usually abundant enough to rank as important forage grasses, although one introduced species, *F. arundinacea* Schreb. (tall fescue), is cultivated in fields. Tall fescue is listed to occur in the Trans-Pecos (Hatch et al., 1990), and Worthington (pers. comm.) reported it from the Franklin Mountains in El Paso County. The generic name, *Festuca*, is derived from an old Latin name for a weedy grass.

Key to the Species

1. Ligules 3–4 mm long; spikelets awnless, with 2–3 florets, perhaps more
   1. *F. ligulata.*
1. Ligules 0.1–1.5 mm long; spikelets awned or awnless, with (3–)4–8 florets.
   2. Plants densely tufted, culms mostly erect; lower sheaths grayish or brownish, not shredding in age; blades usually glaucous **2. *F. arizonica.***
   2. Plants not densely tufted, culms usually decumbent at base; lower sheaths purplish, usually shredding into fine fibers with age; blades not glaucous **3. *F. rubra.***

1. Festuca ligulata Swallen   GUADALUPE FESCUE.   Fig. 43.   Rare on higher mountain slopes or in canyons, endemic. Culberson Co., Guadalupe Mts., McKittrick Canyon (*H. H. Nixon N-5*, tentatively identified as *F. ligulata*); upper McKittrick Canyon. Brewster Co., Chisos Mts., trail to Boot Spring (*B. H. Warnock 21424*). 4,700–6,500 ft. Flowering Jun–Sep. Reported by Jackie Poole (pers. comm., 1986), Guadalupe Mts., North and South McKittrick canyons, and around Pratt Lodge; Chisos Mts., Boot Spring area, and more recently reported from Boot Canyon Trail up to the Colima Trail. Coahuila, Mex.

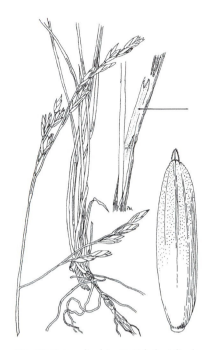
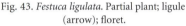

Fig. 43. *Festuca ligulata*. Partial plant; ligule   Fig. 44. *Festuca arizonica*. Panicle; floret
(arrow); floret.   and spikelet.

Guadalupe fescue is one of the truly rare species in the Trans-Pecos, occurring in both the Guadalupe and Chisos mountains, but apparently not in the Davis Mountains. Reportedly this perennial may produce rhizomes.

2. Festuca arizonica Vasey   ARIZONA FESCUE.   Fig. 44.   Locally common at higher elevations. Culberson Co., McKittrick Canyon; South McKittrick Canyon, near the top; Bowl. Jeff Davis Co., Tobe's Gap; higher slopes of Mt. Livermore, W ridge, near the top. 4,700–8,250 ft. Flowering Jun–Sep. Also NM, AZ, CO, NV.

Arizona fescue is relatively abundant in protected areas and on some open slopes near the top (7,200–8,250 ft.) of Mt. Livermore in Jeff Davis County, and apparently it is also reasonably common on top of the Guadalupe Mountains. This fescue is not accessible to livestock, but probably provides some forage and cover for wildlife.

3. Festuca rubra L.   RED FESCUE.   Fig. 45.   Reported (Gould, 1975) to be infrequent in moist, shaded places, highest slopes of the Davis Mts. No collections of red fescue were identified among the Davis Mts. collections of

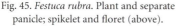

Fig. 45. *Festuca rubra*. Plant and separate
panicle; spikelet and floret (above).

Fig. 46. (A) *Lolium perenne*; inflorescence.
(B) Awned form of *L. perenne*; plant; spikelet
and floret (above).

Festuca. Northern U.S., E to GA, W to AZ, CA. Mountains of Mex. Also widespread in the cooler regions of the world, mostly Northern Hemisphere.

13. LOLIUM   L.   RYEGRASS.

A genus of about eight species native to the temperate regions of Eurasia,
but introduced and cultivated over much of the world with temperate climate.
Two species are reported for Texas (Gould, 1975). Some species, including *L.
perenne*, are among the most important forage grasses in Europe. The genus
name, *Lolium*, is an old Latin name for darnel (darnel, *L. temulentum* L., is a
toxic species).

1. Lolium perenne L.   RYEGRASS.   Fig. 46.   Annual or short-lived perennial. Culms glabrous, 22–65 cm long, fleshy when green. Leaves glabrous,
dark green; sheaths with membranous, hyaline upper margins, these often
forming auricles; ligules membranous; blades 2–10 mm wide, flat or folded,
thin when dry. Inflorescence a spike, these 10–25 cm long. Spikelets usually
5–12-flowered, borne singly at nodes, oriented with edge toward rachis;

glumes usually 5–10 mm long, 3–7-nerved, first glume absent except on terminal spikelet; lemmas obscurely 5-nerved, about same length as glumes, their awns, if present, to 8 mm long, from just below a notched apex, or absent and apex blunt and membranous; paleas nearly as long as lemmas.

Introduced from Europe, usually in disturbed areas. El Paso Co., scenic drive above El Paso, waste water from water tank. Culberson Co., Sierra Diablo. Presidio Co., old Army Air Base ca. 10 mi E Marfa. Brewster Co., Sul Ross campus; near train depot, Alpine; Chisos Mts., Laguna Trail. Pecos Co., Comanche Springs. Val Verde Co., near Devils River bridge. 1,200–5,000 ft. Flowering Mar–Jun. Throughout TX except the deep south plains. Widespread in the U.S., especially in northern states.

Collections from El Paso, Presidio, and Brewster counties exhibit awns and were referable to *L. multiflorum* Lam. (Fig. 46) in Hitchcock (1951), but are now considered to represent a form of *L. perenne* (Gould, 1975). *Lolium perenne* was brought into the United States for use as a pasture grass, where it is now a commonly escaped weed that is good forage for livestock, but poor grazing for wildlife (Gould, 1978). White et al. (1992) have identified *L. perenne* as one of the several species that might be infected with potentially toxic endophytic fungi. Numerous commercial strains have been developed for use in seeding lawns and pastures, an appropriate historical trend after *L. perenne*, also known as English ryegrass, was the first pasture grass to be cultivated in Europe. Another ryegrass species, *L. temulentum* L. (darnel), eventually might be found in the Trans-Pecos. Darnel is noted for its toxicity. The deadly poison is an alkaloid, temulin, which is produced by a fungus that infects the fruit of the ryegrass. The reputation of darnel as a toxic weed of cultivated fields dates back to earliest history, with infected grains having been discovered in an Egyptian tomb dated about 2000 B.C. (Gould, 1978).

14. POA   L.   BLUEGRASS.

Perennials or annuals, many species with rhizomes. Culms low to tall. Leaves with flat or folded blades; ligules membranous. Inflorescence usually a panicle, open or contracted, rarely a raceme. Spikelets smallish, florets 2–7, awnless; disarticulation above the glumes and between florets; glumes somewhat broad, 1–3-nerved; lemmas usually thin, broad, 5-nerved, the nerves often puberulent, rounded or keeled on the back, in some species the base with long, kinky hair, margins membranous, apices acute or obtuse; paleas glabrous, scabrous, or ciliate.

A relatively large genus with about 500 species in temperate regions of the world, extending through the tropics in high mountains. Most bluegrass species are palatable and nutritious, and they are often important forage grasses in many regions of the world, including the western United States. Some species are cultivated in pastures and lawns, most notably *Poa pratensis* (Kentucky bluegrass), perhaps the most important of these grasses in the United States. About 15 species of *Poa* occur in Texas, with probably eight species in the Trans-Pecos. Gould (1975) pointed out that *P. interior* Rydb. (inland bluegrass) has been reported but not documented by him to occur in the Trans-Pecos. Hatch et al. (1990) reported both *P. interior* and *P. compressa* L. to occur in the Trans-Pecos. The taxonomy of Trans-Pecos bluegrasses, including those in the Guadalupe Mountains (Burgess and Northington, 1981), is in need of careful study. The genus name is from the Greek word, *poa*, for grass.

Key to the Species

1. Plants annual; lemma nerves pubescent (to nearly glabrous in *P. annua*).
    2. Panicle somewhat open, at least the lower branches spreading; leaf sheaths glabrous   **1. *P. annua.***
    2. Panicle contracted, the branches erect and close to main axis; sheaths usually scabrous   **2. *P. bigelovii.***
1. Plants perennial; lemma nerves pubescent or glabrous.
    3. Spikelets typically with cottony or woolly hairs webbed at the base of lemmas, or on the rachilla below the lemmas.
        4. Plants with rhizomes, these slender but well developed.
            5. Panicles open, at least the lower branches spreading and usually ascending, usually bare of spikelets on the lower one-half or more; plants with perfect flowers   **3. *P. pratensis.***
            5. Panicles dense, the branches contracted at the main axis, the branches with spikelets at or near the base; plants dioecious   **4. *P. arachnifera.***
        4. Plants without rhizomes.
            6. Panicles spreading, usually exceeding 15 cm long; culms to 1 m or more long; leaf sheaths retrorsely scabrous; lemmas 4.5–5 mm long   **5. *P. occidentalis.***
            6. Panicles nodding, usually less than 15 cm long; culms usually less than 40 cm long; leaf sheaths glabrous or faintly scabrous; lemmas ca. 3 mm long   **6. *P. reflexa.***
    3. Spikelets without cottony or woolly hairs at base of lemmas or elsewhere.
        7. Lemma nerves glabrous; spikelets with perfect flowers; leaf blades filiform, 1–2 mm wide, usually involute   **7. *P. strictiramea.***
        7. Lemma nerves pubescent or glabrous; spikelets unisexual, the pistillate flowers perhaps with non-functional anthers; leaf blades flat or filiform, 1–4 mm wide, often involute   **8. *P. fendleriana.***

1. Poa annua L. ANNUAL BLUEGRASS. Fig. 47. Usually in and around lawns and golf courses, associated with ample moisture. El Paso Co., Hueco Mts. (Worthington, pers. comm); Brewster Co., Sul Ross State Univer-

Fig. 47. *Poa annua*. Plant; spikelet.   Fig. 48. *Poa bigelovii*. Plant; floret and spikelet.

sity campus, beneath dripping faucets and on watered lawns. Presidio Co., 32 mi S Marfa, Ridout Ranch in stock tank overflow, this collection tentatively identified as *P. annua*. 3,500–4,500 ft. Flowering Feb–Nov. Throughout TX, mostly in lawns and in waste areas. Introduced from Europe, now a weed throughout much of North America.

Annual bluegrass is usually the first grass to flower in the fall and winter (Gould, 1975). This cool-season grass persists in early spring but tends to disappear with warm weather. The species is probably more common in Trans-Pecos lawns than the few collections for the area would suggest, but it is of no significance as a forage grass.

2. Poa bigelovii Vasey & Scribn. BIGELOW BLUEGRASS. Fig. 48. Mountains and canyons at low to medium elevations. El Paso Co., E slopes Franklin Mts.; Hueco Tanks. Hudspeth Co., 1.5 mi E Indian Hot Springs; W slopes Eagle Mts.; lower W slopes Guadalupe Mts. Culberson Co., N slopes, Beach Mts.; Panther Peak, Eagle Mts.; lower slopes Guadalupe Mts. Presidio Co., E slopes Capote Mt.; Fresno Creek, 5 mi above its mouth; Contrabando Mt.; Cibolo Creek at Shafter; 6 mi below Redford; lower slopes Chinati Peak; W side Solitario uplift. Jeff Davis Co., near top of Mt. Livermore; Limpia Can-

Fig. 49. *Poa pratensis*. Plant; floret and spikelet.

yon 13 mi NE Fort Davis; 10 mi N Fort Davis; Haystack Mt. Brewster Co., 18 mi S and 16 mi E Marathon; Sierra Madera; Green Valley, Little McKinney Mt.; Chalk Draw, Schuler Ranch; Cienega Mt.; Calamity Creek; Spring Well, 101 Ranch; N slopes Elephant Mt.; NW slopes Wildhorse Mt.; Heath Canyon, Black Gap Refuge; Chilicotal Mt.; Chisos Mts., E slopes of Pulliam Peak; Dog Canyon and Dog Canyon Flats. Pecos Co., Sierra Madera. Terrell Co., 31 mi S Sheffield. Val Verde Co., Mile Canyon, Langtry; Pecos River crossing on Pandale Road; mouth of Pecos River. 2,000–8,000 ft. Flowering Jan–May or Jun (Aug on Mt. Livermore) in TX. E to Crockett Co. and N in plains country. OK, CO, UT, S CA. N Mex.

Bigelow bluegrass is one of the most widespread bluegrass species in the Trans-Pecos. Possibly it is of some localized winter forage value.

3. Poa pratensis L. KENTUCKY BLUEGRASS. Fig. 49. Mostly disturbed sites as a weed, valleys in the central mountain region. Jeff Davis Co., Limpia Canyon at Wild Rose Pass. Alpine, various sites, probably escaped from cultivation. Pecos Co., 30 mi E Fort Stockton. 3,000–5,500 ft. Flowering Apr–May (Jul). In TX reported from Pineywoods, Cross Timbers, and High Plains regions; native to Old World and possibly northern North America.

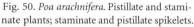
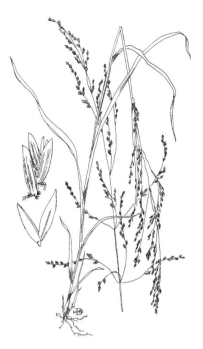

Fig. 50. *Poa arachnifera.* Pistillate and staminate plants; staminate and pistillate spikelets.

Fig. 51. *Poa occidentalis.* Plant; glumes
and florets.

Various strains of Kentucky bluegrass have been artificially selected for use
as pasture and lawn grasses, and many of these have been widely introduced
in all but the warmest parts of the United States. Throughout its range,
but particularly in cooler northern regions, the species is of excellent forage
value for cattle and wildlife, but it is not abundant in the Trans-Pecos unless
cultivated.

4. Poa arachnifera Torr.   TEXAS BLUEGRASS.   Fig. 50.   Rare in the
Trans-Pecos, in the Sul Ross Herbarium known by one collection, B. C. Tharp,
2 Apr 1929, from halfway between Alpine and Marathon. Throughout most of
Texas except perhaps the South Texas Plains and High Plains. E from KS and
OK to NC and FL; also ID.

Where abundant this species is reported to be good forage for livestock and
wildlife. In mountain valleys of the Trans-Pecos, Texas bluegrass might be a
good choice as an introduced cool-season perennial in disturbed areas.

5. Poa occidentalis Vasey   NEWMEXICAN BLUEGRASS.   Fig. 51.   Reported by Burgess and Northington (1981), a single collection, Culberson Co.,

Fig. 52. *Poa reflexa*. Plant; spikelet and floret
(above).

Fig. 53. *Poa strictiramea*. Plant; floret.

Guadalupe Mts., forested slope E of the earth dam in the Bowl, 7,700 ft. Flow-ering August (Jul–Sep). Distributed from S NM to SW CO and E cen. AZ. Soreng and Hatch (1983).

6. Poa reflexa Vasey and Scribn. NODDING BLUEGRASS. Fig. 52. Reported from the tentative identification of plants collected in Culberson Co., Guadalupe Mts., N slope of Bush Mt., by Burgess and Northington (1981), who also recommended that the poas of the Guadalupe Mts. are in need of further collection and study. Distributed throughout most of the western states (Hitchcock, 1951), except for the west coast; NM and AZ, N to MT; also British Columbia.

7. Poa strictiramea Hitchc. CHISOS BLUEGRASS. Fig. 53. [*Poa in-voluta* Hitchc.]. Higher slopes and canyons. Brewster Co., Chisos Mts., Big Bend National Park, most commonly observed on the trail to Boot Spring in Boot Canyon, and on trails to the South Rim, Emory Peak, Laguna Meadow, upper Pine Spring Canyon, and upper Cattail Canyon. 5,000–7,500 ft. Flow-ering May–Sep. NE Mex.

Fig. 54. *Poa fendleriana.* Plant; glumes and
florets; ligule (above).

The flowering times of the Chisos bluegrass correspond almost to those of
warm-season grasses. This species, possibly related to *P. napensis* Beetle (Soreng, 1991), is rather common in the higher Chisos Mountains. Until recently
(Soreng, 1991), *P. strictiramea* in Texas was regarded as *P. involuta* and endemic
to the Chisos Mountains. The species can be recognized vegetatively by its
slender, usually involute leaves.

   8. Poa fendleriana (Steud.) Vasey   MUTTON BLUEGRASS.   Fig. 54.
Mountain slopes and canyons. El Paso Co., W and E slopes, Franklin Mts.
Hudspeth Co., Eagle Mts. Culberson Co., Eagle Mts., Panther Peak; Guadalupe
Mts., The Bowl. Presidio Co., Chinati Peak, near top and lower slopes; E slopes
Capote Mt.; 6 mi NW San Estaban Lake. Jeff Davis Co., Davis Mts., Mt. Liv-
ermore and upper canyons on its flanks; Haystack Mt., at top; Timber Mt.
Brewster Co., Mt. Ord, upper slopes and canyons; Ranger Peak; Cathedral Mt.;
Cienega Mt.; Elephant Mt.; Nine Point Mesa. 4,000–8,000 ft. Flowering Apr–
Jun (Sep). NM, AZ, and CA, N into Canada.
   Mutton bluegrass is the most common bluegrass species in the central
mountains of the Trans-Pecos, where it likely provides useful forage for mostly

wildlife. This incompletely dioecious species usually has slender, involute leaves.

Tribe 7. Aveneae

The tribe Aveneae comprises 1,000 or more species in about 57 genera, these distributed throughout the world in temperate and cold regions. Important tribal characters include long, usually scarious glumes, geniculate dorsal awns (these two traits not always occurring together), and a soft or liquid endosperm that does not solidify even in older herbarium specimens (Clayton and Renvoize, 1986). *Koeleria* is atypical in its shorter glumes and awnless lemmas. Gould (1975) recognized 14 genera of Aveneae for Texas, with nine of these genera also occurring in the Trans-Pecos.

Key to the Genera of Aveneae

1. Spikelets with 2 or more fertile florets.
    2. Plants annual; ovary hairy   18. *Avena*, p. 81
    2. Plants perennial; ovary glabrous.
        3. Spikelets falling entire at maturity   16. *Sphenopholis*, p. 78
        3. Spikelets breaking apart at maturity.
            4. Lemma dorsally awned (the awns usually 5–8 mm long)
                        17. *Trisetum*, p. 80
            4. Lemma awnless, or awned from a bifid apex (awns to 2 mm long)
                        15. *Koeleria*, p. 78
1. Spikelets with 1 fertile floret.
    5. Fertile floret with 1 or 2 staminate or sterile (and rudimentary) florets below (disarticulation in clusters of 1 fertile and ca. 6 sterile spikelets)
                23. *Phalaris*, p. 94
    5. Fertile floret solitary (without staminate, sterile, or rudimentary florets below).
        6. Spikelets disarticulating above the glumes.
            7. Plants perennial   20. *Agrostis*, p. 84
            7. Plants annual.
                8. Panicle spikelike.
                    9. Glumes swollen below   22. *Gastridium*, p. 93
                    9. Glumes not swollen below   20. *Agrostis*, p. 84
                8. Panicle open or contracted   20. *Agrostis*, p. 84
        6. Spikelets disarticulating below the glumes, falling entire.

10. Spikelets falling with a basal stipe (the pedicel); lemma 5-nerved
21. *Polypogon*, **p. 90**
10. Spikelets falling without a basal stipe; lemma 3-nerved
19. *Limnodea*, **p. 83**

15. KOELERIA   Pers.   JUNEGRASS.

A genus of about 35 species widely distributed in temperate regions of both hemispheres. Two species occur in Texas. The genus was named after G. L. Koeler.

1. Koeleria macrantha (Ledeb.) Schult. JUNEGRASS. Fig. 55. [*Koeleria cristata* (L.) Pers.; *K. gracilis* Pers.; *K. nitida* Nutt.]. Perennial, tufted. Culms to 65 cm long, minutely pubescent near nodes and inflorescence. Leaves mostly basal. Sheaths usually rounded, perhaps keeled, pubescent; ligules membranous 0.5–2 mm long; blades 1–4 mm wide, flat, folded, or involute, glabrous to pubescent. Inflorescence a contracted panicle, 5–14 cm long, the branches puberulent, short, erect, and densely flowered. Spikelets 4–5 mm long; glumes slightly unequal, scabrous on midnerve, minutely scabrous on back, the second glume obovate, nearly equaling the lowermost lemma; lemmas shiny, smooth or minutely scabrous on the back; scabrous on midnerve, apex acute or minutely apiculate; paleas hyaline, translucent and shiny, as long as lemmas.

Mountains and canyons, often on protected slopes in partial shade. El Paso Co., Franklin Mts. Culberson Co., Pine Spring to Bowl; McKittrick Canyon. Jeff Davis Co., Mt. Livermore; Limpia Canyon; Madera Canyon; Wild Rose Pass; Timber Mt.; Mt. Locke. Brewster Co., Sul Ross Hill; Ranger Canyon; 16 mi S Alpine; Cienega Mt.; Goat Mt.; Cathedral Mt.; Elephant Mt.; Glass Mts.; Iron Mt.; Altuda Point; Mt. Ord; Chisos Mts., upper elev. 4,000–8,200 ft. Flowering May–Sep. In TX also Edwards Plateau and plains country. Throughout much of United States except southeastern states. Widespread in both hemispheres. Coahuila, Mex.

Junegrass is of high forage quality for livestock and wildlife. *Koeleria pyramidata* (Lam.) Beauv. has been used by many workers (e.g., Gould, 1975; Correll and Johnston, 1970) as the name for the American species of *Koeleria* treated here. Arnow (1994), however, has concluded that *K. pyramidata* is restricted to Europe, and that *K. macrantha*, which occurs in both hemispheres, is the correct name for our species.

16. SPHENOPHOLIS   Scribn.   WEDGESCALE.

A genus of five North American species with three of these in Texas (Gould, 1975). All are palatable grasses, although usually they are not abundant. The

Fig. 55. *Koeleria macrantha.* Plant; glumes and floret.

Fig. 56. *Sphenopholis obtusata.* Plant; glumes and floret.

genus name is from Greek *sphen*, wedge, and *pholis*, horny scale, in reference to the shape and texture of the second glume.

1. Sphenopholis obtusata (Michx.) Scribn. PRAIRIE WEDGESCALE. Fig. 56. Annual or perennial, tufted. Culms 40–75 cm long. Leaves glabrous, scabrous, or with spreading hairs; sheaths rounded on back; ligules membranous, 1.5–3 mm long; blades flat, 2–8 mm wide, 5–14 cm long. Inflorescence a panicle 5–25 cm long, contracted and densely flowered but perhaps open along the length. Spikelets usually 2.0–4.5 mm long, 2–3-flowered; glumes with nerves glabrous or scabrous, first glume acute 1–4 mm long, 0.1–0.3 mm wide, second glume 1.2–4.2 mm long, 0.5–1 mm wide, prominently obovate (wedge-shaped), apex rounded or acute; lemmas acute to obtuse, 1.4–4.3 mm long, glabrous or minutely scabrous.

Usually near springs, streams, and other permanent water sources, often in mountain canyons. El Paso Co., Franklin Mts.; Rio Grande, 3–4 mi above El Paso. Culberson Co., trail to Smith Spring; Smith Canyon Spring; Guadalupe Mts., McKittrick Canyon. Jeff Davis Co., mid–Little Aguja Canyon; Musquiz bog 18 mi N Alpine; 10 mi N Fort Davis. Brewster Co., Kokernot Ranch, Leoncita Spring; 16–20 mi S Alpine; Elephant Mesa; Chisos Mts., Boot Spring Canyon, below Windows. 3,900–6,900 ft. Flowering Apr–May, rarely Sep. Throughout TX except South Plains and south coastal area. Throughout much of the United States, Canada, Mex. south to Puebla, Mex. Caribbean Islands.

According to Gould (1975) the Trans-Pecos variety is *Sphenopholis obtusata* var. **obtusata**. Another variety of this species, *S. obtusata* (Michx.) Scribn. var. *major* (Torr.) Erdman, occurs in Texas east of the Trans-Pecos and elsewhere in North America, and eventually may be found in the Trans-Pecos. Reportedly prairie wedgescale is good forage, but in the Trans-Pecos it is found only near water sources and thus is not abundant enough to be of much value to livestock. Gould (1975) described prairie wedgescale as an annual in Texas, while many of the specimens in the Sul Ross Herbarium are labeled as perennials. This species is also known by the common name prairie wedgegrass (Hitchcock, 1951).

17. TRISETUM   Pers.   TRISETUM.

A temperate- (except Africa) and cold-region genus of about 70 species. One species occurs in Texas. Some species provide valuable forage. The genus name is derived from Latin *tri*, three, and *setum*, bristle, in reference to the one awn and two teeth of the lemma.

1. Trisetum interruptum Buckl.   PRAIRIE TRISETUM.   Fig. 57.   Annual, tufted. Culms 10–48 cm long, weak, erect or spreading-geniculate, glabrous or pubescent particularly just below the nodes. Leaves with rounded sheaths, these pubescent to densely so; ligules membranous, 1.5–2 mm long; blades nearly glabrous to densely pubescent, flat and thin, usually 1–4 mm wide, 2–14 cm long. Inflorescence a contracted panicle, 2–15 cm long, 5–14 mm wide. Spikelets 2–3-flowered, 4–6 mm long excluding awns, upper floret often reduced and sterile; disarticulation between florets and below glumes; glumes glabrous or scabrous, obovate, subequal in length but second broader, about as long as lemmas, first glume 3-nerved, second glume 3–5-nerved; lemmas glabrous, the body 3.5–5 mm long, rounded and minutely rugose on back, obscurely nerved, apexes with an awn arising between two setaceous teeth, these 1.5–2 mm long, the awns usually 5–8 mm long, twisted and usually twice-geniculate; paleas hyaline, about two-thirds as long as lemmas.

Various habitats and soil types including sand and gypsum, usually disturbed conditions. El Paso Co., Franklin Mts., lower E slopes; Hueco Mts. Culberson Co., below Guadalupe Mts., 2 mi S of state line, gyp hills. Pecos Co.,

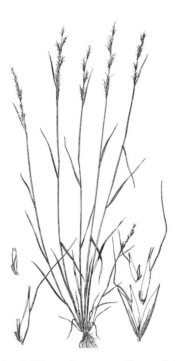

Fig. 57. *Trisetum interruptum.* Plant; spikelet
(right) with fertile florets and reduced upper
floret; fertile and reduced floret (left).

20 mi NE Fort Stockton; between Fort Stockton and Sheffield; N end of Glass
Mts., 20–40 mi S Fort Stockton. Terrell Co., just S Sanderson; 4.2 mi W Sanderson. Val Verde Co., 7 mi W Langtry; Mile Canyon; near Pumpville turnoff.
1,300–5,400 ft. Flowering Mar–May. Ward, Ector, and Crockett counties, occasional throughout TX, except in extreme south and east. NM, AZ, CO.

Prairie Trisetum is palatable but probably not often abundant enough to be
valuable forage.

18. AVENA L. OATS.

Annuals. Culms thick, succulent, glabrous, 35–110 cm long. Leaves with
sheaths glabrous or hispid; ligules membranous, 2–4 mm long, continuous
with sheath margins; blades flat, 5–11 mm wide, usually glabrous, rarely hispid. Inflorescence a loose panicle or raceme, slender curved or bent pedicels

supporting large spikelets. Spikelets 2–4-flowered, when more than 2, upper ones usually reduced and sterile; disarticulation between the florets; glumes 1.5–2.5 mm long, broad, glabrous, usually acuminate, 7–9-nerved. The nerves not extending to hyaline margins and apex; lemmas indurate, rounded on back, the lower one longest, 1.5–2 cm, with dorsal awn straight, curved, or geniculate, 2–4 cm long, or awn absent; paleas thin, shorter than the lemmas, nerves ciliate.

Native to temperate regions of Europe and the Middle East. This is a genus of about 25 species, probably six or seven of them widely cultivated in the world. One or two species occur in Texas, depending upon taxonomic interpretations (Gould, 1975). *Avena* is the old Latin name for oats.

Key to the Species

1. Awn of lemma straight or gently curved, or absent; spikelets usually 2-flowered; lemmas glabrous   **1. *A. sativa.***
1. Awn of lemma geniculate; spikelets usually 3–4-flowered; lemmas with prominent, stiff hairs, these whitish to reddish-brown   **2. *A. fatua.***

1. Avena sativa L.   COMMON OAT.   Fig. 58.   [*Avena fatua* L. var. *sativa* (L.) Hausskn.]. An occasional cool-season weed in disturbed areas, usually along roads. El Paso Co., 2 mi W El Paso, lower slopes Franklin Mts.; Hueco Mts. Culberson Co., Guadalupe Mts., Upper Pine Springs. Jeff Davis Co., Davis Mts., Madera Springs. Brewster Co., Alpine, S city limits; 20 mi NE Alpine; Chisos Mts., Laguna Meadow. Pecos Co., 20 mi NE Fort Stockton. Terrell Co., 7 mi E Longfellow; 30 mi NE Sanderson; 20 mi E Dryden. 2,000–5,500 ft. Flowering Apr–May, often into Jun–Jul, rarely Sep. Throughout TX as cool-season weed in disturbed areas. Introduced from Europe as a crop plant, common in the United States except the southeast, a cultivated plant and escaped weed.

The common oat is seeing new popularity in human nutrition, and oat bran muffins have received attention as a natural and healthy way to help reduce ingested cholesterol before it reaches the bloodstream. Oats are not widely cultivated in the Trans-Pecos, but are rather common weeds at roadside, possibly because oats are frequently transported in this region for horse feed. Gould (1975) recognized both the common oat and wild oat as varieties of one species, *A. fatua* L.

2. Avena fatua L.   WILD OAT.   Fig. 58.   [*Avena fatua* L. var. *fatua*]. Seemingly rare in the Trans-Pecos, usually in disturbed areas at roadside. Pecos Co., 3 mi W Pecos River bridge, I 10. 2,500 ft. Flowering in May. Generally in

Fig. 58. (A) *Avena sativa*; floret. (B) *A. fatua*;
plant; spikelet and floret.

northern half of TX. A European grass throughout most of the United States, especially coastal CA, but not found in the southeast (Gould, 1975).

This cool-season species usually germinates in the early winter, exhibits vegetative growth in the spring, and flowers in Mar–May. It is highly palatable until the awns of mature spikelets cause problems.

19. LIMNODEA　L. H. Dewey

A monotypic genus of the central southeastern United States, perhaps spreading westward in Texas. The genus name is derived from *Limnas*, a genus of grasses.

1. Limnodea arkansana (Nutt.) L. H. Dewey　OSARKGRASS.　Fig. 59. Annual, in small clumps. Culms weak, thin, 20–58 cm long. Leaves with sheaths rounded on back, often hispid; ligules membranous, 1–2 mm long, lacerate; blades flat, glabrous or pubescent, 2–8 mm wide, 3–11 cm long. Inflorescence a contracted panicle, 5–18 cm long. The short branches with flo-

Fig. 59. *Limnodea arkansana.* Plant; floret
(with awn) and glumes.

rets to the base or nearly so. Spikelets 1-flowered, 3.4–4 mm long, excluding
awn; disarticulation below glumes; glumes firm, equal, as long as spikelet,
obscurely 3–5-nerved, rounded and hispid to scabrous, sometimes glabrate,
acute; lemmas nearly as long as glumes, thinner, glabrous, with a twisted and
geniculate awn, 8–11 mm long, arising just below the apex, the apex acute or
minutely bifid; paleas hyaline, shorter than lemmas, nerved at base only.

Infrequent in disturbed habitats, southeastern periphery of the Trans-Pecos;
perhaps ultimately to be found west of the Pecos River. Val Verde Co., E bank
at Pecos River bridge, Hwy 90; 3 mi N Comstock. Crockett Co., 23 mi W
Ozona. 1,600–2,400 ft. Flowering Apr–May. Throughout TX except the High
Plains and western Trans-Pecos. OK and AR to FL. NE Mex.

20. AGROSTIS   L.   BENTGRASS.

Annuals and perennials, some with rhizomes or stolons. Culms erect or
decumbent. Leaves with membranous ligules; blades flat or involute. Inflores-

cence a panicle, open or contracted. Spikelets one-flowered, small; disarticulation above glumes, except in *A. semiverticillata*; glumes thin, lanceolate, acuminate to acute, nearly equal in length, the first glume usually 1-nerved, the second glume 1–3-nerved; lemmas thin, 3–5-nerved, apex acute or blunt, awnless in most of our species, or awned from the back; paleas present or absent.

A genus of about 220 species, occurring mainly in temperate regions of the world and on mountains in tropical areas. Most of the species are good forage, either in native habitats or under cultivation. Certain species are used for lawns, sports turf, and golf greens. The term agrostology (the study of grasses) is from the same Greek root as the genus, *agrostis*, a type of grass, from *agros*, a field. The Trans-Pecos species of *Agrostis* require further study, and the treatment herein is to be regarded as preliminary, mostly following that of Gould (1975).

Key to the Species

1. Spikelets 3–4 mm long; lemmas with awns 3–6 mm long   **1. *A. avenacea.***
1. Spikelets 1.5–2.5(–3.5) mm long; lemmas awnless.
   2. Glumes less than 2 mm long or barely 2 mm.
      3. Panicles dense with branches in close verticils, these densely flowered nearly to the base; stolons present   **2. *A. semiverticillata.***
      3. Panicles diffuse, open at maturity, the branches usually spreading, with spikelets mostly toward the apical portions; stolons absent
                                                                3. *A. hyemalis.*
   2. Glumes more than 2 mm long.
      4. Paleas 1 mm or more long; plants perennial with rhizomes or stolons
                                                                5. *A. stolonifera.*
      4. Paleas absent, or a mere scale 0.5 mm or less long; plants perennials without rhizomes.
         5. Panicle open, at least some branches spreading, spikelets absent on lower portion   **4. *A. scabra.***
         5. Panicle contracted, tightly or loosely, the branches short, appressed, or slightly spreading, spikelets borne nearly to bases
                                                                6. *A. exarata.*

1. Agrostis avenacea J. F. Gmel.   PACIFIC BENTGRASS.   Fig. 60.   According to Correll and Johnston (1970) known in Texas only from a collection in Culberson Co., May 1902 at Kent, a waif found by Tracy and Earle (Gould, 1975) near the railroad, probably not a normal member of the Trans-Pecos

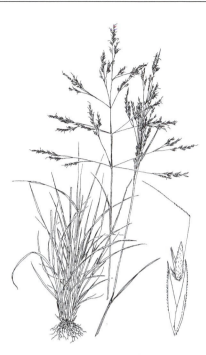

Fig. 60. *Agrostis avenacea*. Plant; glumes
and floret.

flora. Introduced in central CA, and in OH (Hitchcock, 1951) from the South
Pacific.

Pacific bentgrass is a tufted perennial.

2. Agrostis semiverticillata (Forsk.) C. Chr.   WATER BENTGRASS.
Fig. 61.   Moist habitats along streams, in canyons, near springs, and ponds.
El Paso Co., Franklin Mts. Culberson Co., Guadalupe Mts., McKittrick Can-
yon; 12 mi SW of Texline. Presidio Co., Sierra Vieja, Vieja Pass; lower Pinto
Creek, 4 mi N Ruidosa. Reeves Co., Balmorhea. Jeff Davis Co., Madera Springs
S of Toyahvale. Brewster Co., Alpine, Kokernot Spring; 9 and 20 mi S Alpine;
Nine Point Mesa; N Rosillos Mts., Buttrill Spring; Chisos Mts., Lower Oak
Canyon, Alamo Spring; Paint Gap Hills; Fresno Creek, S side Chisos Mts. Ter-
rell Co., Independence Creek; Pecos River. Val Verde Co., Devils River. 1,500–
6,500 ft. Flowering Apr–Nov. E in TX to South Texas and Blackland Prairie.
NM and CO W to WA. Introduced from the Old World.

Water bentgrass, a stoloniferous perennial, is one of the most common spe-

Fig. 61. *Agrostis semiverticillata.* Panicle; glumes and floret. Photo, panicles.

cies of *Agrostis* in the Trans-Pecos, along with *A. hyemalis.* Water bentgrass is easily recognized by its densely flowered panicles.

3. Agrostis hyemalis (Walt.) B.S.P.   WINTER BENTGRASS.   Fig. 62. Protected habitats in mountains and canyons, usually near permanent water. El Paso Co., Hueco Tanks, above rockwall dam. Jeff Davis Co., Davis Mts., upper Limpia Canyon; 1 mi N Wild Rose Pass; N slopes Timber Mt.; mouth of Madera Canyon; near second pool, Mitre Peak Girl Scout Camp; Musquiz Canyon. Brewster Co., Iron Mt.; Chisos Mts., Pine Canyon; Cattail Canyon. 3,500–6,000 ft. Flowering May–Sep. Throughout most of TX. OK, KS, IA, E to the Atlantic Coast. Chihuahua and Coahuila, Mex.

Winter bentgrass, a relatively common tufted perennial in the Trans-Pecos, is recognizable by its diffuse panicle with long, slender branches, branching most distally.

4. Agrostis scabra Willd.   ROUGH BENTGRASS.   Fig. 63.   Protected areas in high canyons and on high slopes. El Paso Co., Hueco Mts. Jeff Davis Co., Davis Mts., upper Limpia Canyon; upper Madera Canyon of Mt. Liver-

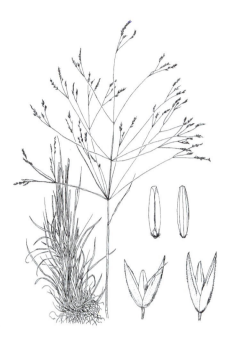

Fig. 62. *Agrostis hyemalis.* Plant; spikelets (left
one with a lemma awn) and florets (above).

more; shaded areas near top of Mt. Livermore. 6,500–8,000 ft. Flowering
Aug–Sep. Reported to occur in NE TX (Correll and Johnston, 1970).
Throughout most of the United States except the southeast, also Canada,
Alaska.

Agrostis scabra appears to be a tufted perennial closely related to *A. hyemalis.*
The collections referenced here as *A. scabra* have the habit of *A. hyemalis* but
differ by having longer spikelets 2.2–2.5 mm long, and they occur at higher
elevations on Mt. Livermore.

5. Agrostis stolonifera L.   REDTOP BENTGRASS.   Fig. 64.   Protected
mountains and canyons, usually near perennial water. Jeff Davis Co., Musquiz
Swamp, 18 mi N Alpine; Girl Scout Camp, ca. 11 mi N Alpine. Brewster Co.,
Chisos Mts., Boot Springs. 4,600–7,500 ft. Flowering Jul–Aug. Reported for N
and E TX and plains country. Widespread in temperate North America. Introduced from Eurasia.

The recognition of *A. stolonifera* for Trans-Pecos Texas follows the treatment in Correll and Johnston (1970). Correll and Johnston include *A. gigantea*

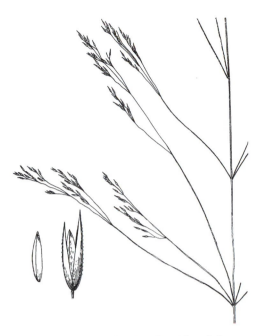

Fig. 63. *Agrostis scabra.* Partial panicle; spikelet
(right) and floret (left).

Roth (redtop) as a synonym of *A. stolonifera*, while Gould (1975) treated *A. gigantea* as a distinct species and reported the taxon to have been introduced in the Trans-Pecos, but probably is not now persisting in this region. Gould also treated *A. palustris* Huds. (creeping bentgrass) as a variety of *A. stolonifera* that occurs only in Texas in the upper Gulf Coast region. Stubbendieck et al. (1992) map *A. stolonifera* in the Trans-Pecos. *Agrostis stolonifera* incorrectly has often been called *A. alba* L. Redtop bentgrass is a highly palatable rhizomatous perennial but not abundant enough in the Trans-Pecos to serve as an important forage grass.

6. Agrostis exarata Trin.   SPIKE BENTGRASS.   Fig. 65.   Near perennial water, limestone habitats. Culberson Co., foothills of the Guadalupe Mts., Choisya Springs. Jeff Davis Co., near Boy Scout Ranch. 5,000–5,800 ft. Flowering Sep–Oct. Throughout most of the western United States, E to NE and ND.

The collection from Choisya Springs is cited tentatively as *A. exarata* because the specimens exhibit the narrow panicle described for the species by

Fig. 64. *Agrostis stolonifera.* Partial panicle; floret.

Fig. 65. *Agrostis exarata.* Panicle; glumes
and floret.

Fig. 66. *Polypogon monspeliensis.* Plant;
glumes and floret.

Gould (1975), but otherwise the plants resemble *A. stolonifera*. Spike bentgrass is a tufted perennial.

21. POLYPOGON   Desf.

Annuals and perennials. Culms erect or decumbent, often rooting at lower nodes. Leaves with membranous ligules, the ligule margins extended as sheath margins. Inflorescence a panicle, contracted, dense. Spikelets 1-flowered; disarticulating below glumes; glumes subequal, 1-nerved, apexes awned from between two lobes, or apex tapering to the awn; lemmas thin, broad, smooth and shiny, usually 5-nerved, much shorter than the glumes, awnless or with a short, weak awn, apices often minutely toothed.

A genus of about 18 species in damp places of warm temperate regions of the world, and on mountains in the tropics. Three species are reported for Texas. The genus name is from Greek *polus*, much, and *pogon*, beard, in reference to the congested panicles.

Key to the Species

1. Glume apices minutely toothed or lobed on either side of dorsal awn, or apex rounded; glume awns 5–10 mm long; panicles dense, spikelike, seldom interrupted, usually 2–15 cm long; annual   **1. *P. monspeliensis.***

1. Glume apices gradually tapering to an awn; glume awns 2–3 mm long; panicles contracted, branches clustered and densely flowered to the base, but usually spreading slightly, lending a semi-interrupted appearance, 15–30 cm long; perennial   **2. *P. elongatus.***

1. Polypogon monspeliensis (L.) Desf.   RABBITFOOT GRASS.   Fig. 66. Usually along streams or in ditches and waste places where water tends to stand. El Paso Co., along Rio Grande, 3–4 mi above El Paso; Franklin Mts. Culberson Co., Guadalupe Mts.; 12 mi SW Texline. Jeff Davis Co., Musquiz Swamp, 18 mi N Alpine; 4 mi N Fort Davis; Madera Spring; lower Madera Canyon. Presidio Co., San Estaban Lake; Capote Creek. Brewster Co., Leoncita Springs, Kokernot Ranch; Alpine Creek, in town; Hidden Valley, 17 mi S Alpine; 20 mi S Alpine; Cathedral Mt.; Glenn Springs, Big Bend Natl. Park; saline flats of Rio Grande, Sublett Ranch; Rio Grande at Boquillas; Black Gap Refuge. Pecos Co., Comanche Springs, Fort Stockton; Leon Springs, 8 mi W Fort Stockton; 30 mi E Fort Stockton; 3 mi W Bakersfield. Val Verde Co., Mile Canyon, Langtry; along Rio Grande between Langtry and mouth of Pecos River. 1,300–5,000 ft. Flowering Mar–Sep. Throughout most of TX. Introduced from Europe, now a widespread weed in North America.

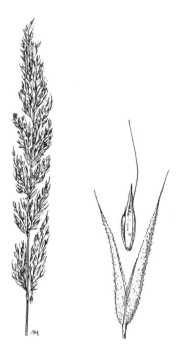

Fig. 67. *Polypogon elongatus*. Panicle;
glumes and floret.

The common name rabbitfoot grass alludes to the dense, spikelike panicles that bear some resemblance to the foot of a rabbit. This annual species is of little significance as a forage grass, but it probably is palatable to livestock and wildlife.

2. Polypogon elongatus H.B.K.   Fig. 67.   Sandy soil along a perennial stream. Brewster Co., under the Calamity Creek bridge, ca. 22 mi S Alpine, Hwy 118. 4,000 ft. Flowering Jun–Aug. AZ. Mexico to Argentina.

This species was recently discovered as new to Texas and the Trans-Pecos by Morden and Hatch (1981), who gave a thorough account of *P. elongatus* with respect to its known distribution and morphological distinctions from other taxa of *Polypogon*. At present the closest known localities for other *P. elongatus* are in Arizona, or in Chihuahua or Coahuila, Mexico. The species, with culms to near 1 m high, should be sought in other Trans-Pecos sites. The third Texas *Polypogon, P. interruptus*, a perennial with interrupted panicle and glume awns 2–4 mm long, is reported by Gould (1975) to have occurred in Texas only at the old Devils River bridge now inundated by Lake Amistad.

Fig. 68. *Gastridium ventricosum*. Plant;
glumes and floret.

22. GASTRIDIUM Beauv.

A European and North African genus of two species, one in Texas. The genus name is from Greek *gastridion*, a small pouch, in reference to the somewhat saccate glumes.

1. Gastridium ventricosum (Gouan) Schinz and Thell. NITGRASS. Fig. 68. Annual, tufted. Culms weak. Leaves essentially glabrous; ligules membranous, 3–4 mm long; blades flat, 2–6 mm wide, 3–11 cm long. Inflorescence a contracted, spikelike panicle. Spikelets 1-flowered; disarticulation above glumes; glumes lanceolate, 1-nerved, this scabrous, margins hyaline, first glume 3–5 mm long, second glume one-fourth shorter, apexes of both glumes tapering to a straight awn tip; lemma ca. 1 mm long, thin, hyaline, with appressed hairs, nerves indistinct, with an awn, straight or geniculate, 4–5 mm long; palea ca. 1 mm long, thin, hyaline, with appressed hairs, nerves indistinct, with an awn, straight or geniculate, 4–5 mm long; rachilla prolonged behind palea, forming a tiny hispid bristle.

Reported by Gould (1975) as an infrequent and casual weed in the Trans-Pecos. Flowering in spring. Native to the Mediterranean region. Of scattered distribution in the United States, most common in central and coastal CA.

23. PHALARIS   L.   CANARYGRASS.

Annuals or perennials. Culms of annuals weak, those of perennials stronger, often with rhizomes. Leaves mostly glabrous; ligules membranous; blades flat. Inflorescence a panicle, contracted and spikelike. Spikelets with one perfect floret and one or two rudimentary florets below the perfect one; disarticulation above glumes; glumes awnless, about equal, longer than the perfect floret, 3-nerved, laterally flattened and keeled dorsally, the keel often with a membranous wing; lemmas of perfect florets awnless, tough and shiny, usually appressed-pubescent, enclosing the palea.

A genus of about 15 species of the world temperate regions. Six species are reported for Texas (Gould, 1975). Certain perennial species provide excellent forage in early growth stages (Stubbendieck et al., 1992). The genus name, *Phalaris*, is an old Greek name for a grass. Hatch et al. (1990) listed the introduced species *P. aquatica* (harding grass) to occur in the Trans-Pecos.

Key to the Species

1. Panicle usually 2–7(–9) cm long, usually tapering to each end; culms usually 30–70 cm long; glume lateral, nerves glabrous, or scabrous with 5 or fewer spicules   **1. *P. caroliniana.***
1. Panicle usually 6–15 cm long, subcylindric; culms usually 60–150 cm long; glume lateral nerves scabrous with 9 or more spicules   **2. *P. angusta.***

1. Phalaris caroliniana Walt. CAROLINA CANARYGRASS. Fig. 69. Various habitats, usually at roadside, near springs or streams, or other sites of periodic standing water. El Paso Co., Franklin Mts. Reeves Co., 2 mi S Toyahvale. Jeff Davis Co., Musquiz Swamp, 18 mi N Alpine. Brewster Co., golf course, Alpine; Leoncita Springs, Kokernot Ranch. Pecos Co., 10 mi E Fort Stockton; 30 mi E Fort Stockton; 4 mi W Longfellow. Val Verde Co., 3 mi N Comstock. 1,600–4,800 ft. Flowering May–Jul. Throughout most of TX. Throughout much of the southern half of the United States, NE to VA, NW to OR. Northern Mex.

Carolina canarygrass is a seldom collected tufted annual of little forage value in the Trans-Pecos. It is related to *Phalaris canariensis* (canarygrass), the canarygrass that provides an important constituent in commercial birdseed.

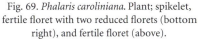

Fig. 69. *Phalaris caroliniana*. Plant; spikelet, fertile floret with two reduced florets (bottom right), and fertile floret (above).

Fig. 70. *Phalaris angusta*. Plant; spikelet.

2. Phalaris angusta Trin.   TIMOTHY CANARYGRASS.   Fig. 70.   Moist sites. Reported by Gould (1975) to occur in the Trans-Pecos. Flowering in the spring.

This is an annual species with thick, succulent stems.

Tribe 8. Bromeae

This tribe of three genera is dominated by *Bromus*, which includes all but about four of the species. Perhaps the most prominent distinguishing tribal feature of Bromeae is its simple, rounded starch grains of the endosperm (found elsewhere only in the Triticeae), whereas the endosperm starch grains in other Poaceae are compound or angular (Clayton and Renvoize, 1986).

24. BROMUS   L.   BROMEGRASS.

Annuals and perennials. Culms solitary or in clumps. Leaves with rounded sheaths, the margins fused at base to above the middle; ligule membranous, usually prominent; blades flat, thin. Inflorescence an open or contracted panicle (in our species). Spikelets pedicelled 1.3–4.5 cm long, with 4–numerous florets; disarticulation above glumes, between florets; glumes unequal, 1–5-nerved, usually acute and awnless; lemmas keeled or round on the back, 5–13-nerved, 2-toothed at apex, 1-awned from the notch of the bifid apex, or sometimes awnless; paleas large, fused to the grain. Caryopsis with tuft of hair at apex.

A temperate- and cool-region genus of about 150 species, with about 15 species occurring in Texas. Soderstrom and Beaman (1968) produced a useful treatment of *Bromus* in Mexico and Central America. *Bromus* is a cool-season genus in Texas with most species flowering from Jan to Jun, or with flowering extending into the summer months in species of the Trans-Pecos mountains. The brome grasses are, in general, palatable to all types of livestock, particularly so before the "seed heads" with awns reach maturity. The awns can cause problems in the eyes and other soft tissue near the mouth. The genus name is derived from *bromus*, an ancient Greek name for the oat.

Key to the Species

1. Spikelets strongly flattened laterally, the glumes and lemmas compressed and sharply keeled.
    2. Plants annual.
        3. Lemmas awnless, or with awns 1–3 mm long   **1. *B. catharticus.***
        3. Lemmas with awns 7–15 mm long   **2. *B. arizonicus.***
    2. Plants perennial; lemmas with awns 4–7 mm long   **3. *B. polyanthus.***
1. Spikelets not strongly flattened laterally, the glumes and lemmas rounded or rather flat across the back, not keeled.
    4. Plants perennial.
        5. Lemmas pubescent on margins only, or margins and base, hairs absent across the back   **4. *B. ciliatus.***
        5. Lemmas pubescent across the back as well as margins, sometimes hairs absent on upper half.
            6. Plants with leaf blades mostly 2–5 mm wide; lower leaf sheaths short-pubescent to glabrous; anthers ca. 2.5 mm long
                                                             5. *B. anomalus.*
            6. Plants with leaf blades 5–10 mm wide; lower leaf sheaths densely retrorsely villous or woolly; anthers 3.6–3.9 mm long
                                                             6. *B. lanatipes.*
    4. Plants annual.

Fig. 71. *Bromus catharticus.* Plant.

7. Awns of lemmas usually 3–6 cm long; second glume 2–3.5 cm long
7. *B. diandrus.*

7. Awns of lemmas usually less than 2.5 cm long; second glume usually less than 1.5 cm long.

   8. Panicles contracted, dense, usually 4–8 cm long, a "foxtail" appearance, whole panicle usually brownish or purplish at maturity
8. *B. rubens.*

   8. Panicles open, narrow to spreading with prominent pedicles, usually much exceeding 8 cm long, individual spikelets pale or purple-tinged.

      9. Spikelets usually with 4–6 florets; first glume usually 1-nerved (to 3-nerved), tapering to a slender, acuminate tip
9. *B. tectorum.*

      9. Spikelets with 6–11 florets; first glume 3–7-nerved, the tip obtuse, acute, or acuminate   **10. *B. japonicus.***

   1. Bromus catharticus Vahl. RESCUEGRASS. Fig. 71. [*Bromus unioloides* (Willd.) H.B.K.; *B. wildenowii* Kunth]. Abundant and widespread, in all types of disturbed areas including roadsides, vacant lots, lawns, and occasionally in pastures. El Paso Co., E and mid slopes, Franklin Mts. Culberson Co.,

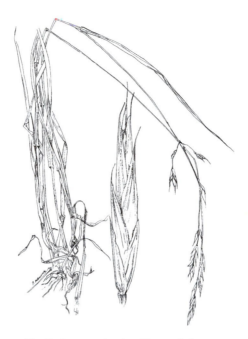

Fig. 72. *Bromus arizonicus.* Plant; spikelet.

1 mi above Nickle Creek Station. Reeves Co., Balmorhea Springs. Presidio Co., 22 mi S Marfa; Marfa; Childers Ranch. Jeff Davis Co., Haystack Mt. Brewster Co., Alpine and vicinity; 10 mi NE Alpine; Nine Point Mesa Ranch; Cattail Canyon, Chisos Mts. Pecos Co., Fort Stockton and vicinity. Terrell Co., Sanderson and Dryden and vicinities. 2,100–5,000 ft. Flowering Mar–Jun. Throughout TX. A native of South America, introduced as a forage grass into the United States, now frequent in most southern states and reported from as far W as OR and N to ND and NY.

As a cool-season weed, rescuegrass is one of the first grasses to flower in the spring. It is considered to be fair grazing for livestock and wildlife, and in places it is used as a cool-season pasture grass. Several names have been applied to rescuegrass, including *B. unioloides* (Gould, 1975) and *B. wildenowii* (Raven, 1960; Gould, 1962; Gould and Box, 1965). Here we follow Hitchcock (1935) and Pohl (1983) in using *B. catharticus.*

2. Bromus arizonicus (Shear) Stebbins   ARIZONA BROME.   Fig. 72. Reported from mid slopes of mountains of Trans-Pecos Texas (Gould, 1975). Flowering in the spring. Also W to AZ and southern CA. Baja CA, Mex.

Fig. 73. *Bromus polyanthus.* Plant; spikelets.

The author was not able to identify with certainty *B. arizonicus* among the specimens available at SRSU and with the keys and descriptions of Hitchcock (1951) and Gould (1975). The chief problem resides in distinguishing the annual *B. arizonicus* from the perennial *B. polyanthus* (Gould, 1975). Trans-Pecos specimens referable to one or the other of these species are usually described in collection labels as perennials, weak perennials, or annuals, and even as weak perennials and annuals in reference to the same collection. The Trans-Pecos plants exhibit awn lengths (4–7 mm) that are attributed to *B. polyanthus* (Gould, 1975). I have collected plants of this type and interpreted them as annuals, but the awn-length character still fits *B. polyanthus.*

3. Bromus polyanthus Scribn. POLYANTHUS BROME. Fig. 73. Mountains and canyons. Jeff Davis Co., Madera Canyon, scenic loop road; W ridge, Mt. Livermore; near top, Mt. Livermore; Rockpile; mid–Little Aguja Canyon. Brewster Co., Chisos Mts., trail to Boot Spring; Upper Boot Spring Canyon. 5,800–8,000 ft. Flowering Jun–Oct. Also W to MT, WA, CA. N Mex.

The Sul Ross specimens referred by their collectors to either *B. arizonicus* or *B. polyanthus*, but herein called *B. polyanthus*, were all collected in flower

Fig. 74. *Bromus ciliatus.* Plant; spikelet
and floret.

from Jun to Oct, while *B. arizonicus* is described as a species that flowers in
early spring and perishes after forming fruits (Hitchcock, 1951).

4. Bromus ciliatus L.   FRINGED BROME.   Fig. 74.   [*Bromus richardsonii* Link]. Mountains and canyons. Culberson Co., Pine Springs campground; North and South McKittrick canyons; near Bowl, top of Guadalupe
Mts. Jeff Davis Co., upper Madera Canyon, Mt. Livermore; Tobe's Gap, Mt.
Livermore; W ridge, Mt. Livermore. 5,000–8,000 ft. Flowering Jul–Sep. N
through Rocky Mts. to British Columbia, Can.; also southern NV, CA.

Although Gould (1975) recognizes the Trans-Pecos populations of this
taxon as *B. richardsonii*, Cronquist et al. (1977) and others have considered *B.
richardsonii* to be unworthy of specific status apart from *B. ciliatus*. *Bromus
ciliatus, B. anomalus*, and *B. lanatipes* appear to be closely related, they intergrade geographically and morphologically, and perhaps they are indistinct entities at least in the Trans-Pecos. It is difficult to decide which of the key characters presented by Gould (1975) is most useful in attempting to distinguish
B. ciliatus from *B. anomalus* and *B. lanatipes*. For purposes of this treatment,
plants with lemmas glabrous on the back, with hairs on the margins and base

Fig. 75. *Bromus anomalus*. Plant; spikelet with
two florets (three or more missing)
and floret (left).

Fig. 76. *Bromus lanatipes*. Spikelet;
lanate leaf sheath.

of the lemma, are assigned to *B. ciliatus*. Two collections from Mt. Livermore have lemmas without pubescence even on the margins.

5. Bromus anomalus Rupr. *ex* Fourn.   NODDING BROME.   Fig. 75. [*Bromus porteri* Nash]. Mountains and canyons. El Paso Co., Franklin Mts. (tentative, Worthington, pers. comm.). Culberson Co., South McKittrick Canyon; Bowl near old lodge. Presidio Co., Elephant Mt.; 10 mi NW Shafter, Cibolo Creek. Brewster Co., Chisos Mts., upper Boot Spring Canyon, Mt. Emory, upper ridge between Juniper and Pine canyons; Laguna; upper Green Gulch; Glass Mts., upper Jail Canyon; top of Goat Mt.; Mt. Ord. 4,500–7,500 ft. Flowering Jul–Sep. Also NM, CO, AZ. Mexico to Oaxaca, Michoacan. Baja CA.

Rather slender plants with sheaths glabrous to short-pubescent and lemmas hairy across the back were considered to be *B. anomalus*. The related species *B. pubescens* Mahl. *ex* Willd. may occur in the southeastern Trans-Pecos.

6. Bromus lanatipes (Shear) Rydb. WOOLLYSHEATH BROME. Fig. 76.   [*Bromus porteri* var. *lanatipes* Shear; *B. anomalus* var. *lanatipes* (Shear) Hitchc.]. Mountains and canyons. Culberson Co., W Dog Canyon

Fig. 77. *Bromus diandrus*. Spikelet.

area; upper Pine Springs Canyon. Presidio Co., Sierra Vieja Pass; High Lonesome, 10 mi S Capote Peak. Jeff Davis Co., near McDonald Observatory; upper Madera Canyon, Mt. Livermore; high meadow, old Friend Ranch, SE slopes Mt. Livermore; Sawtooth Mt.; Little Aguja Canyon; trail to Tricky Gap; Glass Mts., upper Jail Canyon; Toronto Pass, 3 mi W Alpine; Twin Peaks near Alpine; Chisos Mts., trail to Laguna, Lost Mine Peak. 4,200–7,800 ft. Flowering Jun–Oct. N through Rocky Mountains to British Columbia, S NV and S CA.

In this treatment *B. lanatipes* was distinguished from *B. anomalus* primarily by densely pubescent (pilose to lanate) sheaths of relatively robust plants. Both *B. ciliatus* and *B. lanatipes* reportedly occur in Jeff Davis County, particularly on Mt. Livermore, but specimens identified as *B. anomalus* were not seen from Jeff Davis County. *Bromus ciliatus* was not found to occur in the Chisos Mountains, but all three taxa were collected in the Guadalupe Mountains.

7. Bromus diandrus Roth   RIPGUT BROME.   Fig. 77.   I have not seen specimens of this species from Trans-Pecos Texas, but a map in Stubbendieck et al. (1992) suggests that it is to be found in far western parts of the region, perhaps in El Paso Co. Ripgut brome, a European species, is reported (Gould, 1975) to be a pesky weed in semiarid regions of the southwest, where it has gone under the name *B. rigidus* Roth.

One feature of ripgut brome, the long (3–6 cm), stout awns, influences the

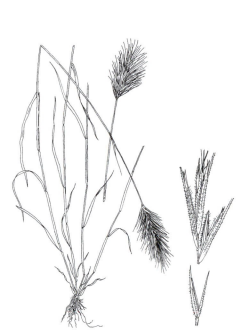

Fig. 78. *Bromus rubens*. Plant; glumes and florets.

Fig. 79. *Bromus tectorum*. Plant; spikelet and floret (above left).

forage value. The species reportedly is palatable in young vegetative stages, but the mature awned florets are injurious to livestock, often working into eyes, nostrils, and soft mouth tissue.

8. Bromus rubens L.   FOXTAIL BROME.   Fig. 78.   Various disturbed sites, frequently along highways. El Paso Co., Franklin Mts., lower slopes; McKelligon Canyon. Culberson Co., W of Van Horn. Reeves Co., 25 mi NW Pecos (in gypsum soil). Val Verde Co., 1 mi W Langtry. 1,900–4,200 ft. Flowering Mar–May. Also Edwards Plateau. A European species now naturalized over large areas of the western U.S., and occasionally in southern and eastern states.

The dense "foxtail" panicle easily distinguishes *B. rubens* from other Trans-Pecos species of *Bromus*.

9. Bromus tectorum L.   DOWNY BROME.   Fig. 79.   Usually disturbed sites. El Paso Co., Franklin Mts. Culberson Co., meadow N of the Upper Dog Canyon Ranger Station (Burgess and Northington, 1981). Flowering spring and early summer. E in TX to the Edwards Plateau, plains country, and Cross Timbers region. An introduced annual, native to Europe, now widely established in Canada, the U.S. (except the southeast), and part of northern Mex.

Fig. 80. *Bromus japonicus.* Partial plant.

According to Gould (1975), *B. tectorum* var. **tectorum** occurs in the Trans-Pecos. Another variety, *B. tectorum* var. *glabratus,* has about the same range as var. *tectorum* but is less common, and may eventually be found in the Trans-Pecos. The forage value of downy brome is fair before the inflorescence develops, after which palatability is severely reduced by the sharp awns, which may cause eye injury and jaw abscesses (Stubbendieck et al., 1992).

10. Bromus japonicus Thunb.   JAPANESE BROME.   Fig. 80.   Mostly in disturbed areas, particularly close to permanent water, or in areas where water may collect, if only periodically. El Paso Co., Franklin Mts.; pass in Hueco Mts. E of El Paso. Culberson Co., Guadalupe Mts., McKittrick Canyon; Frijole Spring. Brewster Co., 2 mi NE Marathon. 2,600–5,500 ft. Flowering May–Jun (occasionally summer). Throughout TX except for the Pineywoods. Introduced from the Old World where widespread, now established throughout the U.S.

This species is locally abundant at roadside, where in early vegetative stages it may provide food for wildlife, but it is of little or no significance as a range forage grass (Gould, 1978).

Tribe 9. Triticeae

The treatment of tribe Triticeae (barley, wildrye, wheatgrass, wheat, rye), including the key to genera, follows that of Barkworth and Dewey (1985).

The classical or traditional taxonomic treatments for this largely Asian tribe (including those in Hitchcock, 1951; Correll and Johnston, 1970; Gould, 1975) have been shown to be largely unnatural and are said not to represent a very accurate evolutionary picture for the taxa involved. In a series of recent works, Löve (1982; 1984), Dewey (1982; 1983a; 1983b), Barkworth and Atkins (1984), Barkworth and Dewey (1985), and others (summarized in Barkworth and Dewey, 1985) have attempted to clarify the taxonomy of the North American perennial Triticeae through the use of cytogenetic data, so that evolutionary ("genomic") relationships in the tribe are more accurately reflected. This has resulted in a series of new combinations and recombinations involving the transfer of a number of familiar species into several unfamiliar genera.

Instead of "splitting" the Triticeae and recognizing a number of smaller genera, Estes and Tyrl (1982) have recommended that all the native North American taxa be grouped into two genera, *Hordeum* and *Elymus*. The well-defended conservative taxonomic position advanced by Estes and Tyrl allows North American workers the use of familiar generic names. Admittedly, I am most comfortable with a taxonomy approaching that espoused by Estes and Tyrl. Other workers, however, including Watson et al. (1985) and Macfarlane (1987), continue to favor the more narrow generic views which are basically like the treatment (Barkworth and Dewey, 1985) presented here, except that in the former sources *Critesion* is combined with *Hordeum* and *Pseudoroegneria* is included in *Elytrigia*. Both Baum et al. (1987) and Kellogg (1989) presented strong arguments against the narrow genomic generic classification of Triticeae, while providing good reasons and evidence for using other characters in addition to genomic data in evaluating a taxonomic system for the Triticeae that best reflects the phylogeny. Kellogg (1989), however, ultimately suggested retaining most of the narrower genera treated here (e.g., *Pseudoroegneria, Elymus, Leymus, Pascopyrum*), while recommending that *Critesion* belongs with *Hordeum* and that *Aegilops* is distinct from *Triticum*. Hatch et al. (1990) recognized most of the narrow generic interpretations for Triticeae in the most recent checklist of Texas vascular plants. Johnston (1990) included the new combinations for Triticeae in his up-date of the *Manual of the Vascular Plants of Texas*. Clayton and Renvoize (1986) presented yet another taxonomic view. Perhaps the near future will hold a consensus of opinion regarding genera in the Triticeae. New molecular data, including those from chloroplast DNA, may be the best avenue for understanding phylogeny in the tribe (Kellogg, 1992).

For those accustomed to using Hitchcock (1935; 1951), Correll and Johnston (1970), and Gould (1975) to identify Triticeae of the Trans-Pecos, the following summary may be helpful: The familiar *Hordeum pusillum* and other hordeums can be found in *Critesion*; *Agropyron arizonicum* and *Sitanion* are in *Elymus*. *Elymus triticoides* is in *Leymus*; *Agropyron smithii* is in *Pascopyrum*; *Agropyron spicatum* is in *Pseudoroegneria*.

Key to the Genera of Triticeae

1. Spikelets 3 at each node, each with only 1 floret.
    2. Florets of the 2 lateral spikelets fertile; plants annual
                                          25. *Hordeum*, p. 106
    2. Florets of the 2 lateral spikelets sterile and highly reduced; plants annual
       or perennial   **26. *Critesion*, p. 108**
1. Spikelets 1–7 at each node, usually with more than 1 floret; all spikelets
   usually alike.
    3. Plants annual   **31. *Triticum*, p. 119**
    3. Plants perennial.
        4. Glumes 3–15 mm long, those of our species stiffly subulate from
           midlength or below and without evident veins above midlength; an-
           thers 3–6 mm long; lemmas acute, awnless or with awns less than
           7 mm long.
            5. Glumes lanceolate and prominently veined below, tapering to an
               awnlike tip, often appearing subulate in dried specimens; spikelets
               solitary at most or all nodes, sometimes 2 at central nodes
                                          29. *Pascopyrum*, p. 116
            5. Glumes of our species stiffly subulate from the base, not promi-
               nently veined; spikelets 1–7 per node   **28. *Leymus*, p. 115**
        4. Glumes more than 15 mm long (including the awn if present) or less
           than 15 mm long, lanceolate, and prominently veined over most of
           their length; anthers 2–7 mm long; lemmas obtuse to acute with
           awns more than 10 mm long.
            6. Spikelets solitary, shorter or slightly longer than the inter-
               nodes; anthers 3.5–5 mm long; plants cespitose or very shortly
               rhizomatous   **30. *Pseudoroegneria*, p. 118**
            6. Spikelets 1–4 per node, usually about twice as long as the inter-
               nodes; anthers 1.5–3 mm long in cespitose species, to 8 mm long
               in rhizomatous species.
                7. Glumes tapering to an acute tip from midlength; anthers 4–
                   6 mm long; plants rhizomatous   **29. *Pascopyrum*, p. 116**
                7. Glumes long-awned and awnlike, or acute but tapering only in
                   the distal third; anthers 2–3 mm long in cespitose species, 4–
                   6 mm long in rhizomatous species   **27. *Elymus*, p. 110**

25. HORDEUM   L.   BARLEY.

A genus of two species as treated by Barkworth and Dewey (1985). The
species are *Hordeum vulgare*, the cultivated Old World species that is now common throughout the cooler regions of the world, and in the subtropics as a

Fig. 81. *Hordeum vulgare*. Plant with inflorescence (upper center-right); group of spikelets
(lower right); floret (near center); and spike of
beardless barley (upper right).

cool-season grass (Gould, 1975), and *H. bulbosum* L., a Eurasian species not
found in North America. The other species that traditionally have been placed
in *Hordeum*, including three species that occur in Texas and in the Trans-Pecos
(Gould, 1975), have been transferred to *Critesion* (Barkworth and Dewey,
1985). The old Latin name for barley is *hordeum*.

1. Hordeum vulgare L.   BARLEY.   Fig. 81.   Annual. Culms thick, succulent, 50–120 cm long. Leaves with thin, rounded sheaths; ligules truncate,
usually 1.5–3 mm long; blades flat, usually 0.5–1 cm wide and with stiff
auricles at the base. Inflorescence a spike, 3–10 cm long excluding awns, ca.
1 cm thick, dense; rachis not disarticulating. Spikelets 3 at each node, these
sessile and fertile; glumes flattened, slightly broader at the base, glabrous or
pubescent, awned; lemmas shiny or glaucous, usually 8–12 mm long, usually
with an awn to 15 cm long.

Not persisting out of cultivation, found only at roadside and field borders.
Planted as a crop in many parts of TX. Flowering Apr–Jun.

26. CRITESION   Rafin.   BARLEY.

Perennials or annuals. Culms rather weak. Leaves with membranous ligules; blades soft, flat, auricles present or wanting. Inflorescence a spicate raceme, usually dense; inflorescence axis fragmenting at maturity, the short internodes falling with spikelets attached. Spikelets 1-flowered, 3 at each node, only the floret of the central spikelet perfect, the lateral spikelets of the threesome usually staminate or sterile and pedicelled; rachilla terminating in a bristle; lateral spikelets often of glumes only; glumes usually rigid, narrow, usually subulate or awned, resembling subtending bristles with rather broad bases; lemmas firm, rounded on back and dorsally flattened, 5-nerved, these often obscure, apexes usually with a stout awn; paleas barely shorter than lemmas.

A genus of about seven species in North America, with additional species in the Old World. Three species occur in Texas, all of these in the Trans-Pecos. The species of *Critesion* are considered generally to be of poor forage value, although most are grazed when the plants are young, usually in the spring. At maturity the plants may cause injury to the noses and mouths of grazing animals because of the sharp joints and stout awns of the inflorescences. According to Barkworth and Dewey (1985), *Critesion* is distinguished by its inflorescence, in which there are three spikelets at each node, with each spikelet exhibiting a single floret. Only the central spikelet has a fertile floret. Also plants of *Critesion* are smaller in overall size and in the size of the florets, as compared to *Hordeum* in the strict sense. Morphological and genomic differences between *Critesion* and *Hordeum* require further study, but there is mounting evidence that the species here treated as *Critesion* should remain with *Hordeum* (Kellogg, 1989).

Key to the Species

1. Spikelet threesome with lemmas of the lateral 2 spikelets absent or much smaller than lemma of the central spikelet; auricles wanting or only poorly developed at leaf bases.
   2. Awns, of glumes and lemmas, usually less than 1.5 cm long; glumes of fertile (central) spikelet dilated above the base; annual   **1. *C. pusillum.***
   2. Awns, of glumes and lemmas, usually 3.5 – 7.5 cm long; glumes of fertile spikelet slender and awnlike above the base; short-lived perennial
                                                        2. *C. jubatum.*
1. Spikelet threesome with lemmas of the lateral 2 spikelets as large as the lemma of the central spikelet; auricles prominent at leaf bases
                                          3. *C. murinum* subsp. *leporinum.*

   1. Critesion pusillum (Nutt.) A. Löve   LITTLE BARLEY.   Fig. 82. [*Hordeum pusillum* Nutt.]. Various disturbed sites including roadways and yards. El Paso Co., Hueco Tanks. Culberson Co., foothills of Guadalupe Mts.,

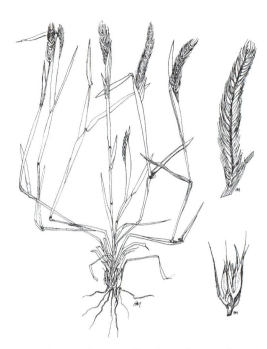

Fig. 82. *Critesion pusillum* (=*Hordeum pusillum*). Plant; spike (upper right); spikelets
(lower right).

15 mi N Frijole. Reeves Co., Balmorhea Springs; 5 mi E Pecos. Brewster Co.,
Alpine, golf course; along railroad tracks. 3,300–4,900 ft. Flowering Mar–May.
Throughout TX and the United States except in a few northern states. N Mex.

This is perhaps the most widespread and common *Critesion* in the Trans-
Pecos. It is quickly distinguished from the other barley species by its uni-
formly short awns. This taxon is recognized as *Hordeum pusillum* Nutt. in
Gould (1975).

2. Critesion jubatum (L.) Nevski FOXTAIL BARLEY. Fig. 83. [*Hordeum jubatum* L.]. Various disturbed sites but most commonly near canals and
other water sources. El Paso Co., 3 mi E Fabens; Rio Grande 4 mi above El
Paso; Rio Grande below El Paso. Hudspeth Co., 4 mi E Fort Hancock; 3 mi W
Fort Hancock. Reeves Co., 1 mi N Pecos. Pecos Co., Comanche Springs, Fort
Stockton. 2,500–3,900 ft. Flowering May–Jul. NW half of TX. Throughout
most of United States except the southeast. Alaska S to Mexico.

This species is possibly the only perennial *Critesion* in the Trans-Pecos
(Gould, 1975), but Barkworth and Dewey (1985) suggested that all North
American species are perennial. Like the other barleys it is of poor forage value

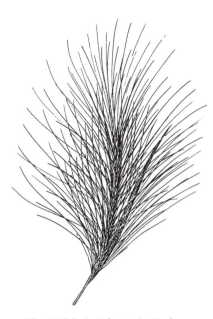

Fig. 83. *Critesion jubatum* (=*Hordeum jubatum*). Spike.

Fig. 84. *Critesion murinum* subsp. *leporinum* (=*Hordeum leporinum*). Spike.

except in the spring before spikelets mature. This taxon is recognized as *Hordeum jubatum* L. by Gould (1975).

3. Critesion murinum (L.) A. Löve subsp. **leporinum** (Link) A. Löve. HARE BARLEY. Fig. 84. [*Hordeum leporinum* Link]. Various disturbed areas including along roadways. El Paso Co., Franklin Mts., McKelligon Canyon; 2 mi W El Paso; Hueco Mts. Reeves Co., Balmorhea Springs. Brewster Co., N slopes of Twin Peaks. Pecos Co., N end of Glass Mts.; 10–25 mi S Fort Stockton; 4 mi W Longfellow. Terrell Co., 20 mi W Langtry; 7 mi W Langtry. 1,800–4,800 ft. Flowering Mar–Apr. Throughout much of TX except extreme E and S. Throughout much of the United States except infrequent in the central and eastern parts. N Mex.

The relative vegetative robustness of this species suggests that it might provide slightly better forage in early stages than most barleys. In Gould (1975) this taxon is treated as *Hordeum leporinum* Link.

27. ELYMUS   L.   WILDRYE.

Perennials, cespitose (in our species). Culms erect or decumbent. Leaves with membranous ligules; blades flat or folded; with slender, pointed auricles at the base. Inflorescence a spike, spikelets solitary or 2–3 spikelets at each node (in our species), perhaps with one spikelet at upper node(s), widely spaced (in *E. arizonicus*) or crowded. Spikelets 2–6-flowered; disarticulation above the glumes, between florets, or in nodes of rachis; glumes firm or soft, narrow and setaceous to wide and blunt, 1–several-nerved, awned or awnless; lemmas about equal to or longer than glumes, usually 5–7-nerved, rounded on back, awned or awnless; paleas nearly as long as lemmas.

A genus of perhaps 33 species in temperate North America and possibly as many more in South America. Gould (1975) included *Sitanion* Raf. species with long, divergent awns (one species in Texas) in *Elymus*, as do Barkworth and Dewey (1985). According to the latter authors, *Elymus* is by far the largest and most diverse genus in tribe. Most species of *Elymus* are cespitose, self-compatible species with short anthers (2–3 mm long). A few species now included in *Elymus*, those transferred from *Agropyron*, may have only one spikelet per node, and may be out-crossing, have long anthers (4–6 mm), and be rhizomatous (Barkworth and Dewey, 1985). The species of *Elymus* are in general good forage grasses, particularly in early growth stages, and taxa are often helpful in binding sand and other soil types. The caryopses of some species, including *E. canadensis*, have been used for food by Indians. The genus name is from *elumos*, a Greek name for a type of grain.

Key to the Species

1. Spikes flexuous, with spikelets rather widely spaced along the axis
                                                        1. *E. arizonicus.*
1. Spikes rather stiff, with spikelets usually densely crowded along the axis (spikelets perhaps somewhat spaced in *E. elymoides*, which has long awns).
    2. Glume awns 5–11 cm long; inflorescence rachis at maturity readily breaking apart at the nodes, the spikelets falling with sections of the rachis   **4. *E. elymoides.***
    2. Glume awns usually less than 3.5 cm long; inflorescence rachis at maturity not breaking into parts, with disarticulation above glumes and between florets.
        3. Glumes prominently bowed out at the base; the base thickened and shiny and usually measuring 1.2–2 mm wide   **3. *E. virginicus.***
        3. Glumes not bowed at the base, or only slightly so; the base usually of continuous texture and color, or perhaps slightly different at the base, measuring 0.2–1.2 mm wide   **2. *E. canadensis.***

1. Elymus arizonicus (Scrib. & Smith) Gould. ARIZONA WHEAT-GRASS. Fig. 85. [*Agropyron arizonicum* Scribn. & Smith; *Elytrigia arizonica* (Scribn. & Smith) Dewey]. Mountains and protected canyons. Culberson Co., Guadalupe Mts. Jeff Davis Co., Davis Mts., Mt. Livermore, upper and lower

Fig. 85. *Elymus arizonicus* (=*Agropyron arizonicum*). Spike.

Fig. 86. *Elymus canadensis.* Plant; spikelet (left) and floret.

Madera Canyon; Pine Canyon; Elbow Canyon. Brewster Co., top of Cathedral Mt.; Chisos Mts., between Boot Spring and South Rim; N slopes Mt. Emory; the Laguna. 5,500–7,800 ft. Flowering Jun–Sep. W to CA. N Mex.

Arizona wheatgrass probably should be called Arizona wildrye after the species was transferred to *Elymus* (Barkworth and Dewey, 1985) from *Agropyron*, where traditionally it has been included (Gould, 1975). The "new taxonomy" is based upon cytogenetic evidence of true genetic relationships.

2. Elymus canadensis L.   CANADA WILDRYE.   Fig. 86.   Usually protected habitats in canyons or along watercourses, or at roadside. El Paso Co., Rio Grande, 4 mi above El Paso. Culberson Co., Guadalupe Mts., Choisya Springs, South McKittrick Canyon. Jeff Davis Co., Haystack Mt.; 13 mi N Alpine; 18 mi N Alpine; 4 mi N Fort Davis. Brewster Co., Alpine Creek; Sul Ross campus; Kokernot Lodge; 3 mi N Alpine; 5 mi S Marathon, Fort Peña Colorado; Glass Mts., near Altuda Point; Gilliland Canyon; Iron Mt.; Doubtful Canyon, Mt. Ord. Pecos Co., Comanche Springs, Fort Stockton; 5 mi N Fort Stockton; 30 mi E Fort Stockton. Terrell Co., 30 mi N Sanderson, Big Canyon. Val Verde Co., 3 mi N Comstock. 1,600–5,900 ft. Flowering May–Sep. Throughout most of TX except southern South Plains. Throughout most of temperate North America.

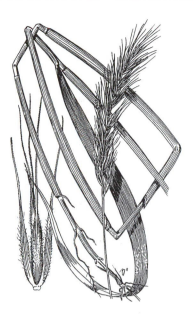

Fig. 87. *Elymus virginicus.* Plant; spikelet.

Gould (1975) recognized two varieties of *Elymus canadensis* L., the var. **canadensis** (Canada wildrye) and *E. canadensis* var. **interruptus** (Buckl.) Church (Texas wildrye). Hitchcock (1951) and Correll and Johnston (1970) treated var. *canadensis* and var. *interruptus* as distinct species. Reportedly these taxa hybridize rather freely among themselves and with *E. virginicus,* another taxon that perhaps should be merged with *E. canadensis.* The var. *canadensis* is distinguished by glumes flat at the base and 0.7–1.2 mm wide, while var. *interruptus* has glumes essentially terete at the base and only 0.2–0.5 mm wide (Gould, 1975). Trans-Pecos specimens distinctly referable to var. *interruptus* were collected in Jeff Davis County, Wild Rose Pass, Limpia Canyon, and Blue Hole Canyon (backside of Timber Mt.), and in the Guadalupe Mountains according to Burgess and Northington (1981). The distribution of var. *interruptus* extends in Texas to the Edwards Plateau, and then to New Mexico and Oklahoma (Gould, 1975). *Elymus canadensis* var. *canadensis* is one of the most common wildryes in the Trans-Pecos. Canada wildrye is a good forage species but its value declines as the plant matures. Barkworth and Dewey (1985) recognized *Elymus canadensis* L. and *E. interruptus* Buckl. as distinct species of *Elymus.*

3. Elymus virginicus L.   VIRGINIA WILDRYE.   Fig. 87.   Various habitats retaining considerable moisture. Val Verde Co., 3 mi N Comstock; San Felipe Creek. 960–1,500 ft. Flowering Apr–Jun. Throughout most of TX ex-

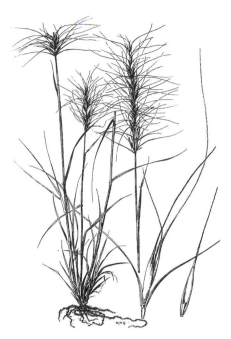

Fig. 88. *Elymus elymoides* (= *E. longifolius*).
Plant; spikelet and floret.

cept the High Plains and most of the Trans-Pecos. Throughout most of the United States except the extreme southwest.

Virginia wildrye possibly occurs only at the southeastern periphery of the Trans-Pecos as evidenced by the collections cited for Val Verde County. Two anomalous specimens from Cathedral Mountain in Brewster County (not cited above) have shiny glume bases similar to those characterizing *E. virginicus*. The glume trait could have resulted from hybridization between the varieties of *E. canadensis*, or simply represent genetic variability in the latter species. *Elymus virginicus* is recognized by Gould (1975).

4. Elymus elymoides (Rafin.) Swezey. LONGLEAF SQUIRRELTAIL. Fig. 88. [*Sitanion longifolium* J. G. Smith; *S. hystrix* (Nutt.) J. G. Smith; *Elymus longifolius* (Smith) Gould]. Usually in dry, open, disturbed areas, but also on mountain slopes and in canyons. El Paso Co., Franklin Mts.; Hueco Tanks; Hueco Pass; 5 mi W Hueco Mts. Hudspeth Co., N end Quitman Mts. Culberson Co., Guadalupe Mts., Dog Canyon, Shumard Canyon, McKittrick

Canyon, Smith Canyon, Guadalupe Canyon, Guadalupe Peak, the Bowl; Pine Spring Station; 2 mi W Texline; Sierra Blanca; Sierra Diablo, Victorio Canyon; Apache Mts.; 23 mi E Van Horn. Jeff Davis Co., Rockpile; lower Madera Canyon; Davis Mts. State Park; Mt. Locke; Wild Rose Pass; Musquiz Canyon. Presidio Co., W slopes Capote Mt.; Pinto Canyon; San Estaban Canyon; S slope Elephant Mt. Brewster Co., 11 mi S Alpine; Mt. Ord; Iron Mt.; Elephant Mt.; Goat Mt.; Cathedral Mt.; Cienega Mt.; 18 mi S Alpine; 20 mi NE Alpine; Altuda Pass; top Nine Point Mesa; Chisos Mts., Green Gulch; upper Cattail Canyon. Reeves Co., between Pecos and Fort Stockton. Pecos Co., 30 mi E Fort Stockton. 3,200–8,000 ft. Flowering Apr–Oct. In TX NE to Edwards Plateau, and plains country. Throughout much of the western United States. N Mex.

Longleaf squirreltail is perhaps the most common *Elymus* in the Trans-Pecos. It is easily distinguished from other species of the genus by its long awns. This species has little forage value. This taxon is recognized by Gould (1975) as *Elymus longifolius* (Smith) Gould.

28. LEYMUS   Hochst.   CREEPING WILDRYE.

A genus of about 16 species in North America as treated by Barkworth and Atkins (1984). Many authors traditionally have included the species of *Leymus* in *Elymus*. Additional species occur in Europe.

1. Leymus triticoides (Buckl.) Pilger CREEPING WILDRYE. Fig. 89. [*Elymus triticoides* Buckl.]. Perennial, strongly rhizomatous. Culms erect, 45–125 cm high, glabrous to pubescent. Leaves with truncate ligules, 0.2–1.3 mm long, blades flat to involute, 3.5–10 mm wide. Inflorescence a spike, 5–20 cm long, usually the nodes each with 2 spikelets, but varying from 1 to 3. Spikelets 10–22 mm long, 3–7-flowered; glumes slender, subulate, 5–16 mm long, widely separated; lemmas smooth or slightly scabrous, 5–12 mm long, acute or usually awn-tipped, the awn 3(–7) mm long.

Reported for the Trans-Pecos by Hitchcock (1951), but Correll and Johnston (1970) and Gould (1975) did not locate specimens to document the occurrence of this species in the Trans-Pecos. In the present study I also have not seen specimens of *L. triticoides* from the Trans-Pecos. Flowering in late spring and early summer. According to Barkworth and Atkins (1984), widespread throughout western North America, in dry to moist meadows, often in saline conditions.

Leymus triticoides is the most variable species of *Leymus* (Barkworth and Atkins, 1984), and is known to hybridize with several other species of the genus. Gould (1975) included *L. triticoides* in *Elymus*.

Fig. 89. *Leymus triticoides* (=*Elymus triticoides*). Partial plant, with rhizome.

29. PASCOPYRUM   A. Löve   WESTERN WHEATGRASS.

A monotypic genus where the one species, *P. smithii*, is an octaploid combining *Elymus* and *Leymus* genomes (Barkworth and Dewey, 1985). The wheatgrasses provide excellent forage for all classes of livestock and for wildlife, some being the most valuable forage grasses of the western United States (Hitchcock, 1951). This Trans-Pecos species is not abundant enough to furnish significant forage for cattle.

1. Pascopyrum smithii (Rydb.) A. Löve   WESTERN WHEATGRASS. Fig. 90.   [*Agropyron smithii* Rydb.; *Elymus smithii* (Rydb.) Gould; *Elytrigia smithii* (Rydb.) Nevski]. Perennial, with creeping rhizomes. Culms 30–90 cm long, slender, single or in clusters. Leaves glaucous; sheaths glabrous or puberulent, perhaps ciliate on upper margins, with or without pointed auricles; ligule ca. 1 mm long, truncate, ciliate; blades involute on drying, glabrous or scabrous-hispid, 2–7 mm wide, tapering to a slender tip. Inflorescence a spike, 6–20 cm long, usually dense. Spikelets 5–12-flowered, usually one per node, at lower and middle nodes perhaps paired; disarticulation above glumes; rachis internodes, flattened, thick, scabrous on margins, usually 7–10 mm long or longer. Spikelets 1.5–2.5 cm long, glaucous; glumes barely unequal, firm, lan-

Fig. 90. *Pascopyrum smithii* (=*Agropyron smithii*). Partial plant, with rhizomes.

ceolate, with 3–7 nerves, apex acuminate or short-awned, second glume usually equaling or exceeding the lowermost lemma; lemmas firm, pale, several-nerved, margins glabrous or pubescent; paleas scabrous or ciliate on keels.

Mountains, canyons, and flats where moisture is retained for long periods. Culberson Co., Sierra Diablo, Victorio Canyon; below Diablo Refuge headquarters; south of Bat Cave; Guadalupe Mts., McKittrick Canyon; trail to Smith Spring; near Mud Tank, top of Guadalupe Mts.; West Dog Canyon. Presidio Co., SW slope Elephant Mt. Reeves Co., Toyah Creek under I 10 bridge N Balmorhea. Brewster Co., Paradise Canyon, 4 mi W Alpine; Twin Peaks; W slopes Mt. Ord; Cienega Mt.; Glass Mts., Iron Mt.; top of Nine Point Mesa; Chisos Mts., in the Laguna area. 4,000–8,000 ft. Flowering May–Nov. In TX N and E to High Plains and Blackland Prairie. Throughout much of the United States except the southeast and extreme southwest, and Canada. N Mex.

Western wheatgrass is a significant forage grass in western North America, but it is of limited distribution and abundance in the Trans-Pecos. The morphological distinction between *Pascopyrum smithii* and *Pseudoroegneria spicata* in the Trans-Pecos is not clear, although these are regarded as "good" species. Some of the collections referred here to *Pascopyrum smithii* resemble *Pseudoroegneria spicata*, and vice versa. *Pascopyrum smithii* is recognized by Gould (1975) as *Agropyron smithii*.

Fig. 91. *Pseudoroegneria spicata* (=*Agropyron spicatum*). Plant; spikelet (left) and glumes (right).

30. PSEUDOROEGNERIA   (Nevski)
A. Löve.   WHEATGRASS.

A genus of about 15 species with only *P. spicata* occurring in the United States (Barkworth and Dewey, 1985). Members of this genus traditionally have been included in *Agropyron* (Gould, 1975), known commonly as the wheatgrasses, and generally regarded as excellent forage grasses. According to Barkworth and Dewey (1985) the genus *Pseudoroegneria* is best recognized by the characters cespitose habit, long inflorescence internodes compared to the florets, and long anthers.

1. Pseudoroegneria spicata (Pursh) A. Löve.   BLUEBUNCH WHEAT-GRASS.   Fig. 91.   [*Agropyron spicatum* (Pursh) Scribn. & Smith; *Elymus spicatus* (Pursh) Gould; *Agropyron inerme* (Scribn. & Smith) Rydb.; *Elytrigia spicata* (Pursh) Dewey]. Perennial, cespitose, occasionally with short rhizomes. Culms 50–80 cm long. Leaves with rounded, glabrous sheaths, these often with well-developed auricles; ligules membranous, 1–2 mm long; blades filiform, usually involute, 1–3 mm wide, yellowish or bluish-green, not glaucous. Inflorescence a stiff spike, usually 6–15 cm long, with 5–12 spikelets; rachis internodes usually 1–2 cm long; disarticulation above glumes. Spikelets awnless or with very short awns; glumes short, acute or obtuse, awnless in Texas plants (Gould, 1975); lemmas usually 0.8–1 cm long, weakly nerved, acute to minutely awned (in our plants); paleas equaling the lemmas.

Mountain slopes and canyons. Culberson Co., Guadalupe Mts., Smith Canyon; McKittrick Canyon; Pine Spring Canyon. Jeff Davis Co., Million Dollar Canyon, near Little Aguja Canyon. Brewster Co., Glass Mts., W slopes Old Blue Mt. 5,500–6,800 ft. Flowering Jun–Aug. Throughout much of the western United States.

The Trans-Pecos specimens furnishing the above localities are referred tentatively to *Pseudoroegneria spicata*. Some of the collections resemble *Pascopyrum smithii*, and the one from Million Dollar Canyon is anomalous. Those plants resembling *P. spicata* are not as widespread or common in the Trans-Pecos as the other wheatgrasses treated here. *Pseudoroegneria spicata* is included by Gould (1975) as *Agropyron spicatum*. Barkworth and Dewey (1985) recognize *P. spicata* A. Löve subsp. *spicata*, and *P. spicata* subsp. *inermis* (Scribn. & Smith) A. Löve, while Gould (1975) treated *Agropyron inerme* (awnless lemmas) as a synonym of *A. spicatum* (awned lemmas) because plants with awned and awnless lemmas are often found growing together.

31. TRITICUM   L.

Annuals. Culms glabrous, weak, erect or curving, branching at the base. Leaves with membranous ligules; blades thin, flat. Inflorescence a spike, this thick and bilateral, with spikelets single at the nodes; rachis continuous or disarticulating. Spikelets 2–5-flowered, flattened laterally and oriented flatside to rachis, or rounded and fitting close into rachis joints; glumes thick, nerves 3 or several, somewhat asymmetrical, apices toothed, mucronate, or 1–3-awned; lemmas keeled or rounded on back, awnless or with awns 3–6 cm or to 15 cm long.

A genus of 30 or more species native to southern Europe and western Asia, including *Aegilops* (Gould, 1975). There are many varieties of cultivated wheat. *Triticum* is the old Latin name for wheat. The genus name for *Aegilops* is from an old Greek name for a type of grass. Kellogg (1989) recommended that *Aegilops* be maintained as a separate genus.

Key to the Species

1. Spikelets flattened laterally   1. *T. aestivum.*
1. Spikelets essentially cylindrical   1. *T. cylindricum.*

1. Triticum aestivum L.   WHEAT.   Fig. 92.   Roadside weed, usually an escapee from cultivation. Brewster Co., 6 mi S Marathon. 3,800 ft. Flowering in May. A roadside weed throughout TX, usually in agricultural areas.

Fig. 92. *Triticum aestivum.* Plant with spikes awned (bearded wheat) and nearly awnless (beardless wheat); spikelet (lower right) and floret.

Fig. 93. *Triticum cylindricum* (=*Aegilops cylindrica*). Spike.

Widely distributed as a cultivated plant in cooler regions of the world, native to Eurasia.

2. Triticum cylindricum (Host) Ces., Pass., and Gib.   JOINTED GOAT-GRASS.   Fig. 93.   [*Aegilops cylindrica* Host]. Reported to occur as an occasional roadside weed in the Trans-Pecos (Gould, 1975). Flowering May–Jun. Throughout much of TX as a weed. Native to Europe.

SUBFAMILY IV. CHLORIDOIDEAE (ERAGROSTOIDEAE)

Tribe 10. Eragrosteae

The tribe Eragrosteae, or Eragrostideae (Clayton and Renvoize, 1986), is a large one with about 1,000 species in 77 genera. The species are widely distributed in tropical, subtropical, and warm temperate regions. Twenty-one genera of this tribe are recognized by Gould (1975) to occur in Texas, with 16 genera represented in the Trans-Pecos. Salient distinguishing characters of the Eragrosteae include the unspecialized, usually many-flowered spikelets and usually 3-nerved lemmas. Valdés-R. and Hatch (1991) reviewed subtribal classification in the Eragrosteae and presented new evidence for some subtribal relationships.

Key to the Genera of Eragrosteae

1. Spikelets 1-flowered; inflorescence a panicle.
    2. Ligule a line of hairs (or ciliate membrane); lemma usually 1-nerved; fruit wall free.
        3. Callus of floret bearded (the silvery hairs to 3–5 mm long)
                                        42. *Calamovilfa*, p. 156
        3. Callus of floret not bearded   45. *Sporobolus*, p. 184
    2. Ligule membranous; lemma 3-nerved (the lateral 2 perhaps faint); fruit wall adnate.
        4. Spikelets of 2 kinds, the upper perfect, the lower staminate or sterile (these deciduous in pairs)   43. *Lycurus*, p. 157
        4. Spikelets all alike.
            5. Palea villous (on and between the keels)
                                        46. *Blepharoneuron*, p. 194
            5. Palea not villous   44. *Muhlenbergia*, p. 160
1. Spikelets 2-or-more-flowered.
    6. Lemma apex entire, the nerves and margins glabrous (or the margin minutely ciliate); florets not bearded from callus.
        7. Inflorescence a panicle   32. *Eragrostis*, p. 122
        7. Inflorescence of 2 or more racemes (or spicate branches).
            8. Inflorescence digitate, with 1–2 branches arising 1–4 cm below the apical whorl; fruit 1–2 mm long, plump, transverse ridged or rugose, the thin pericarp loose   38. *Eleusine*, p. 146
            8. Inflorescence of racemose or spicate branches arranged singly along a central axis; fruit 1–2 mm long, more or less, subellipsoidal or cylindrical, usually laterally compressed, often grooved adaxially, smooth to reticulate, the pericarp adnate
                                        32. *Eragrostis*, p. 122
    6. Lemma apex emarginate to 2–3-lobed, or margins pubescent, or florets bearded from the callus.
        9. Awn pubescent; cleistogamous spikelets concealed within leaf sheaths
                                        34. *Triplasis*, p. 139
        9. Awn glabrous, if present, or absent; cleistogamous spikelets absent.
            10. Inflorescence of few to numerous spicate (or racemose) primary branches disposed along the main axis or clustered near the apex.

11. Ligule a line of hairs; branches of inflorescence ending in the branch tip or bristle　　32. *Eragrostis*, p. 122

11. Ligule membranous, the membrane perhaps ciliate; branches of the inflorescence ending in a spikelet

39. *Leptochloa*, p. 147

10. Inflorescence a panicle or with spikelets clustered and headlike.

12. Spikelets with the 2 lowermost florets staminate or sterile

41. *Blepharidachne*, p. 154

12. Spikelets with lowermost florets fertile.

13. Lemma 3-awned (plants usually dioecious, the male and female spikelets dissimilar, the lemmas of female spikelets with awns 5–10 cm long)　40. *Scleropogon*, p. 152

13. Lemma with a single awn, or awn absent, or the lateral nerves extending to a very short awn.

14. Leaf margins prominently cartilaginous.

15. Palea glabrous　　37. *Munroa*, p. 144

15. Palea pubescent.

16. Plants usually with stolons; spikelets in leafy fascicles, usually held among the leaves　　36. *Dasyochloa*, p. 143

16. Plants without stolons (in our plants); spikelets on a leafless floral axis above the leaves　　35. *Erioneuron*, p. 140

14. Leaf margins not cartilaginous.

17. Lemma apex emarginate to bidentate; lemma pubescence restricted to keel and nerves (except mostly glabrous in *T. albescens*)

33. *Tridens*, p. 135

17. Lemma apex entire; lemma pubescence on body and nerves (the hairs often tubercle-based)　　32. *Eragrostis*, p. 122

32. ERAGROSTIS　von Wolf　LOVEGRASS.

Annuals or perennials. Culms bunched, erect or decumbent. Leaves with ligules ciliate; sheaths with margins free; ligules ciliate; blades flat or involute. Inflorescence an open or contracted panicle. Spikelets laterally compressed, 2–many-flowered; disarticulation above the glumes, the paleas or rachilla perhaps persistent; glumes somewhat unequal, usually hyaline, 1-nerved, deciduous; lemmas usually membranous, 3-nerved, the lateral nerves perhaps obscure; paleas shorter than lemmas, hyaline, 2-keeled, usually ciliolate on keels. Grains usually reddish-brown and translucent, usually slightly compressed laterally, perhaps grooved on adaxial surface.

A genus of warm regions comprising perhaps 350 species. Gould (1975) recognizes 25 species in Texas, including several naturalized taxa that have been introduced into the southern United States, particularly in arid regions, as forage grasses and in revegetating denuded areas. The lovegrasses are considered to be of little forage value, although a few species such as *E. intermedia*, common in the Trans-Pecos, are said to provide good forage in semiarid rangelands. The genus name is derived from the Greek *eros*, love, and *agrostis*, a type of grass. Some annual and perennial taxa of *Eragrostis* are noted (Correll and Johnston, 1970; Gould, 1975; Hitchcock, 1951) for intergradation of characters and unclear taxonomic distinction. The Trans-Pecos lovegrasses require further study. Hatch et al. (1990) report the occurrence of *E. minor* Host (=*E. poaeoides* Beauv.) in the Trans-Pecos.

Key to the Species

1. Plants annual.
    2. Glumes and lemmas usually with glands in the keels; spikelets ovate, broadly lanceolate, to linear oblong, usually light greenish, perhaps turning darker green at maturity   **1. *E. cilianensis.***
    2. Glumes and lemmas without glands in the keels; spikelets lanceolate, linear, to narrowly ovate, usually dark greenish and turning purplish at maturity.
        3. Panicles with yellowish glandular band partially or completely around the axis and below branches of the panicle; spikelets linear   **2. *E. barrelieri.***
        3. Panicles without yellow bands below branches; spikelets usually lanceolate or narrowly ovate, perhaps linear in some.
            4. Culms usually with a partial or complete ring of yellow glands below the nodes; leaf sheaths and lower blades with small glandular pits on keels or near nerves; grains oblong, 0.5–1.0 mm long, flattened, with an adaxial groove   **3. *E. mexicana.***
            4. Culms usually without ring of glands below nodes; leaves without glandular pits; grains somewhat ellipsoidal, ca. 1 mm long, usually slightly flattened and without a groove, pyriform.
                5. Lateral pedicels on panicle branches appressed, rarely diverging as much as 20 degrees   **4. *E. pectinacea.***
                5. Lateral pedicels on panicle branches, at least in part, spreading at maturity   **5. *E. tephrosanthos.***
1. Plants perennial.
    6. Spikelets sessile or subsessile, the pedicels, if present, usually less or slightly more than 1 mm long (to 2 mm long in *E. lehmanniana*).
        7. Panicle branches simple (unbranched), straight, with spikelets remote and appressed on the stiff branches   **6. *E. sessilispica.***
        7. Panicles with at least some branchlets, at least some of the spikelets touching or overlapping, or spikelets crowded, perhaps appressed.

Fig. 94. *Eragrostis cilianensis*. Plant; spikelet
and partial spikelet (upper left).

8. Panicle branches densely flowered; spikelets 10–45-flowered, in
tightly imbricate groups, straw colored or often reddish
7. *E. secundiflora.*
8. Panicle branches loosely flowered; spikelets usually 6–12-
flowered.
   9. Spikelets appressed to stiffly spreading branchlets; branchlets
notably scabrous   **8. *E. curtipedicellata.***
   9. Spikelets spreading on short pedicels, perhaps somewhat appressed in *E. curvula*, the branches somewhat spreading and
flexuous.
      10. Culms commonly geniculate; leaf blades to 10 cm long;
rather stiffly spreading; lemmas ca. 1.6 mm long
9. *E. lehmanniana.*
      10. Culms not geniculate; leaf blades to 30 cm or more long,
arching over toward the ground; lemmas 2.2–2.6 mm long
10. *E. curvula.*
6. Spikelets pedicellate, the pedicels usually much more than 2 mm long.
   11. Spikelets 4–7 mm long; lemmas 1.6–2.2 mm long
11. *E. intermedia.*

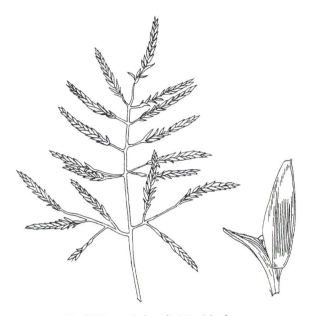

Fig. 95. *Eragrostis barrelieri.* Panicle; floret.

11. Spikelets 6.5–9(–13) mm long; lemmas 2.4–3 mm long
12. *E. erosa.*

1. Eragrostis cilianensis (All.) Janchen STINKGRASS. Fig. 94. [*Eragrostis megastachya* Link]. Usually disturbed habitats, soil of all types, commonly at sites of ephemeral moisture. El Paso Co., Franklin Mts.; 6 mi N El Paso; near Clint. Hudspeth Co., 10 mi E Hueco. Culberson Co., Guadalupe Mts. area. Presidio Co., Chinati Mts.; Sierra Vieja; 9 mi E Marfa; near Chispa; Old Ross Mine; 101 Ranch Hdq.; near Rio Grande below Candelaria; N slope, Elephant Mt. Jeff Davis Co., widespread in Davis Mts. area. Brewster Co., widespread in N half of county, and in Big Bend Natl. Park. Pecos Co., 30 mi E Fort Stockton. Terrell Co., 4 mi N Sanderson; 29 mi N Dryden; mouth San Francisco Canyon; Independence Creek. Val Verde Co., 5 mi NE Juno. Loving Co. 1,000–6,500 ft. Flowering Jun–Nov. All regions of TX. Native of Europe, widespread in North America, Central America, and into South America and West Indies.

The name stinkgrass probably came from the slightly pungent smell released when flowers are crushed. Perry and McNeill (1986) studied the nomenclature of *E. cilianensis.* This warm-season weed is of little or no forage value.

2. Eragrostis barrelieri Daveau MEDITERRANEAN LOVEGRASS. Fig. 95. Disturbed habitats, soils of most types. El Paso Co., Franklin Mts.,

Fig. 96. *Eragrostis mexicana.* Panicle; spikelet.

McKelligon Canyon; 10 mi E El Paso. Hudspeth Co., 10 mi E Hueco; 5 mi W Van Horn; 9 mi E Sierra Blanca; 20 mi N Sierra Blanca; 2 mi W Fort Hancock. Culberson Co., Guadalupe Mts.; between Kent and Van Horn; Pecos-Carlsbad Hwy. Jeff Davis Co., frequent in Davis Mts. area. Presidio Co., Marfa; old Marfa Air Base. Reeves Co., 5 mi S Pecos. Brewster Co., frequent in N half of county; also present S half to Big Bend Natl. Park. Pecos Co., 20–35 mi S Fort Stockton; 17 mi W Sanderson. Terrell Co., 6 mi E Sanderson. Val Verde Co., frequent in county. 1,100–5,800 ft. Flowering (Apr) Jun–Nov. Also Ward, Winkler, Loving, Crane, Ector counties; widespread in TX. Native of Mediterranean Basin, now from KS to NM and in FL; E and S Mex, to West Indies.

This is one of the most common weedy grasses in Alpine and other towns of the Trans-Pecos. Mediterranean lovegrass resembles *E. mexicana* and *E. diffusa* but is rather easily distinguished from these two similar taxa by the characters included in the key above.

3. Eragrostis mexicana (Hornem.) Link MEXICAN LOVEGRASS. Fig. 96. [*Eragrostis neomexicana* Vasey]. Various protected habitats including canyons and slopes, and on disturbed ground. Hudspeth Co., Beach Mts., 5 mi

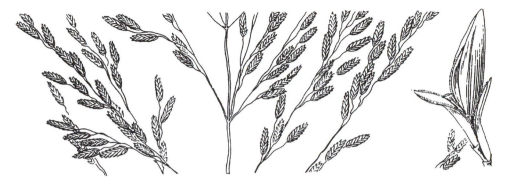

Fig. 97. *Eragrostis pectinacea.* Partial panicle; floret.

W Van Horn. Culberson Co., Victorio Canyon, Sierra Diablo; Guadalupe Mts., upper South McKittrick Canyon; upper Dog Canyon; wash E of Guadalupe Mts. Natl. Park. Jeff Davis Co., Mt. Livermore, high slopes and canyons; Madera Canyon on scenic loop road; Kent turnoff on scenic loop; 1 mi above Fort Davis, Limpia Canyon; Mt. Locke; near Sawtooth Mt.; Mitre Peak Girl Scout Camp. Brewster Co., sparse about Alpine. 4,100 – 8,000 ft. Flowering Jul–Oct. S CA to W TX; also Mex., Central America. N South America.

In the Trans-Pecos Mexican lovegrass apparently is centered in the Davis Mountains around Mount Livermore. Many of the specimens at Sul Ross are of the robust form (*E. neomexicana*, see Hitchcock, 1951; Correll and Johnston 1970; Koch and Sanchez V., 1985). This is a variable, weedy, annual species 10 – 130 cm tall that is similar in habit and difficult to distinguish superficially from the more widespread *E. diffusa*. Probably Mexican lovegrass is a fair forage grass for livestock where the plants are locally abundant. Koch and Sanchez V. (1985) have recently studied the *E. mexicana* complex, and they have subsequently recognized two subspecies, *E. mexicana* subsp. **mexicana**, the Trans-Pecos entity, and *E. mexicana* subsp. *virescens* (Presl) Koch & Sanchez V. of California and Nevada in North America and of South America.

4. Eragrostis pectinacea (Michx.) Nees SPREADING LOVEGRASS. Fig. 97. [*Eragrostis diffusa* Buckl.]. Various habitats including disturbed sites. El Paso Co., Franklin Mts., McKelligon Canyon; near Clint along canals; Hueco Mts. Hudspeth Co., 2 mi E, 9 mi N Sierra Blanca; 10 mi N Allamoore. Culberson Co., S McKittrick Canyon; Pratt Ranch; Pine Springs Canyon. Jeff Davis Co., widespread in Davis Mts. around Mt. Livermore; 18 mi N Alpine; Fern Canyon; Haystack Mt. Presidio Co., Chinati Mts., Sierra Vieja; 2 mi W San Jacinto Peak; 101 Ranch Hdq. Brewster Co., widespread in most mountain

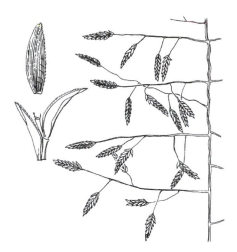

Fig. 98. *Eragrostis tephrosanthos.* Partial
panicle; floret.

systems from near Alpine south, including the high Chisos Mts., and 5 mi W
Study Butte in the desert. Val Verde Co. 1,700–8,000 ft. Flowering Jun–Nov.
Also Ward, Loving, and Crockett counties. Throughout most of TX except the
Pineywoods. E to ME, GA, N to ND, W to UT, S to CA. Mex. S to Cuba, Puerto
Rico, and Panama.

Koch (1974) presented good evidence that *Eragrostis diffusa* was synonymous with the widespread species *E. pectinacea.* According to Gould (1975)
E. diffusa intergrades with *E. pectinacea* (Michx.) Nees to the northeast of
Texas, and the latter species does not occur in Texas, but I suspect that Gould's
observations were made without the benefit of Koch's extensive work. Gould
(1975) treated *E. arida* as a form of *E. diffusa* with a more spreading panicle.
Eragrostis pectinacea, E. tephrosanthos, and *E. mexicana* are very similar in habit
and occupy overlapping ranges, particularly in the Davis Mountains, in the
Trans-Pecos. All three taxa are tufted annuals, but *E. pectinacea* and *E. tephrosanthos* commonly have more slender culms than the usually robust *E. mexicana.* Spreading lovegrass probably is fair forage where it is locally abundant.

5. Eragrostis tephrosanthos Schult.   Fig. 98.   [*Eragrostis arida* Hitchc.].
Various habitats including disturbed sites. Culberson Co., Guadalupe Mts., top
of South McKittrick Canyon. Presidio Co., Sierra Vieja, Vieja Pass; Chinati
Mts., Tigna Canyon; Wildhorse Canyon above Shely Ranch house. Jeff Davis
Co., Rockpile; Fern Canyon, Mitre Peak Girl Scout Camp; Musquiz Canyon.
Brewster Co., 8 mi N Alpine; 5 mi W Study Butte; Chisos Mts., Laguna; Upper

Cattail Canyon. Terrell Co., 6 mi E Sanderson. 2,200–8,000 ft. Flowering Jul–
Nov. E to FL, W to AZ. Throughout Mex. Central America. West Indies.

Eragrostis tephrosanthos is closely related to *E. pectinacea*, and the distributions and habitats of these taxa overlap in most of the southern portion of their
range. The single difference between these taxa is that the pedicels of the
spikelets borne laterally on the panicle branches are appressed in *E. pectinacea*,
while in *E. tephrosanthos* they are spreading to some degree (Koch, 1974).
According to Koch (1974) strongly spreading pedicels are never found in
E. pectinacea, but can be found on at least some part of the panicle in *E.
tephrosanthos*. Furthermore, even though *E. tephrosanthos* and *E. pectinacea*
occupy the same range and grow together, Koch (1974) did not find evidence
of hybridization between them, found that all of the plants had either spreading pedicels or appressed pedicels, and was convinced that the two very similar taxa should be recognized as distinct species. The conclusion by Reeder
(1986a), however, that *E. tephrosanthos* is synonymous with *E. pectinacea*,
where it should be recognized as *E. pectinacea* var. *miserrima* (Fourn.)
J. Reeder, ultimately may be the best way to represent the closely related taxa
in question. Correll and Johnston (1970) and Hitchcock (1951) treated the
E. arida as a separate species, but Koch (1974) presented good evidence that it
is synonymous with *E. tephrosanthos*. Gould (1975) considered *E. tephrosanthos* as perhaps a small form of *E. diffusa*. *Eragrostis tephrosanthos* is probably
of fair forage value where it is abundant.

6. Eragrostis sessilispica Buckl. TUMBLE LOVEGRASS. Fig. 99.
Sand and sandy clay. Ward Co. Winkler Co., Waddell Ranch. Andrews Co.,
17 mi SE Andrews. 2,600 ft. Flowering May–Oct. Scattered in TX from the
Gulf Prairies to Blackland Prairies across to the South Texas Plains and the
plains country. Also SW KS, W OK. N Tamaulipas, Mex.

Tumble lovegrass is easily recognized by its straight panicle branches lined
with sessile and appressed (usually purplish) spikelets. Whole panicles at maturity break away from the plants and tumble with the wind. This species is
infrequent to rare in the sandhill country adjacent to the Trans-Pecos and
probably is of no forage value.

7. Eragrostis secundiflora Presl. RED LOVEGRASS. Fig. 100.
[*Eragrostis beyrichii* J. G. Smith; *E. oxylepis* (Torr.) Torr.]. Deep sand to shallow
and mixed sandy habitats. Ward Co., 13 mi NW Monahans; 25 mi W Odessa.
Winkler Co., Waddell Ranch 12 mi E Kermit; 10 mi E Kermit. Andrews Co.,
15 mi W Andrews; 17 mi SE Andrews. Crane Co., 13 mi N Imperial. 2,600–
3,400 ft. Flowering May–Oct. Scattered throughout much of TX. E to FL; NM,
E CO. S to Veracruz, Mex.

Red lovegrass is easily recognized by its dense clusters of relatively large and

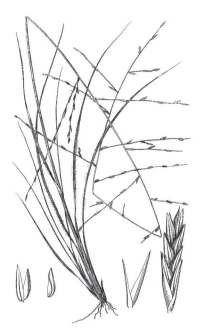

Fig. 99. *Eragrostis sessilispica*. Plant; glumes and spikelet (right), floret and palea (left).

Fig. 100. *Eragrostis secundiflora*. Panicle; floret.

usually reddish-tinged spikelets. This warm-season perennial species of the sandhill country is not abundant enough to be a good forage grass. Hitchcock (1951) and Correll and Johnston (1970) refer to this taxon as *E. oxylepis*, while my treatment follows that of Gould (1975).

8. Eragrostis curtipedicellata Buckl.   GUMMY LOVEGRASS.   Fig. 101. Various habitats including sand. Brewster Co., 3 mi S of Alpine; McIntire Hill S of Alpine. Ward Co., 5 mi E Monahans; between Imperial and Monahans; 2 mi S Imperial; 25 mi W Odessa. Winkler Co., 20 mi NW Monahans. Crane Co., 3–16 mi W Crane; 5–8 mi N Imperial. Loving Co., 5 mi NE Red Bluff Dam. Andrews Co., 15 mi W Andrews. 2,600–4,600 ft. Flowering May–Oct. Also Ector Co., Crockett Co. In all regions of TX. SE AR and S KS to E NM. Extreme NE Mex.

According to Gould (1975) gummy lovegrass appears to be close to or to intergrade with *E. spectabilis* (Pursh) Steud. (purple lovegrass) and *E. silveana* Swallen (Silveus lovegrass). Gummy lovegrass, a perennial species of little or no forage value, is the only one of these three taxa that is known to occur in the Trans-Pecos.

Fig. 101. *Eragrostis curtipedicellata.* Partial panicle; floret.

9. Eragrostis lehmanniana Nees   LEHMANN LOVEGRASS.   Fig. 102.
Disturbed habitats, particularly near highways. El Paso Co., 5 mi W Hueco;
Franklin Mts., McKelligon Canyon, recreation park. Hudspeth Co., 10 mi W
Sierra Blanca. Culberson Co., between Delaware Creek and Orla; ca. 10 mi N
Van Horn; 5 mi S Kent. Jeff Davis Co., Davis Mts. State Park; 4 mi S Fort Davis,
CDRI Landsite. Brewster Co., 9 mi S Alpine; roadside Big Bend Natl. Park.
Pecos Co., farms at Coyanosa Ward Co., 4 mi W Monahans. 2,600–5,100 ft.
Flowering Jul–Nov. Rio Grande Valley. Native of South Africa. OK, NM, AZ.
Sonora, Mex.

This introduced species has been widely used as a forage grass and as rapidly
establishing ground cover for denuded and root plowed areas. Lehmann lovegrass is readily established in the arid portions of Trans-Pecos Texas and is an
excellent choice for revegetating various habitats. It has been successfully used
for this purpose along denuded highway corridors. Success in establishing Lehmann lovegrass depends upon a seedbed of loose soil and good timing in
planting before rainfall. Once established this species persists and it probably
will become naturalized. Lehmann lovegrass is a good forage species with fair
food value.

10. Eragrostis curvula (Schrad.) Nees   WEEPING LOVEGRASS.
Fig. 103.   Disturbed habitats, cultivated and sandy. Reeves Co., near Pecos;

Fig. 102. *Eragrostis lehmanniana.* Partial plant; spikelet; panicle.

Fig. 103. *Eragrostis curvula.* Panicle; floret.

10 mi W Pecos; farms at Coyanosa. 2,600–3,800 ft. Flowering May–Oct. Throughout much of the northern two-thirds of TX, roadsides, fields, sandy habitats. Native of South Africa. Also southern United States where now spontaneous.

Weeping lovegrass reportedly was introduced as a forage grass, but its forage value is only fair for livestock. Evidently this species is readily established in areas with sufficient rainfall, but in the arid Trans-Pecos it is not as adaptable as is Lehmann lovegrass.

11. Eragrostis intermedia Hitchc. PLAINS LOVEGRASS. Fig. 104. Rocky slopes, canyons, and alluvial basins, various soil types. El Paso Co., Franklin Mts.; Hueco Tanks. Hudspeth Co., 20 mi E El Paso; Sierra Diablo; Eagle Mts., W slopes. Culberson Co., Guadalupe Mts., widespread; Sierra Diablo; Chispa Peak. Presidio Co., Sierra Vieja, widespread; Frenchman Hills ca. 22 mi S Marfa; 101 Ranch Hdq. Jeff Davis Co., Davis Mts., widespread; Musquiz Canyon; Fern Canyon; Haystack Mt.; 4 mi S Fort Davis, CDRI Landsite. Brewster Co., probably all the mountains and higher basins, throughout the county, including Packsaddle Mt., the Chisos Mts., and upper Tornillo Flats. Val Verde Co., near Langtry; near Comstock; Devils River area. 1,100–7,500 ft.

Fig. 104. *Eragrostis intermedia.* Partial panicle; floret.

Flowering Mar–Nov. Also Ward Co., Andrews Co. Throughout most of TX. W to S AZ; E to AR and AL. Mexico, Guatemala.

Plains lovegrass is a warm-season tufted perennial with culms to about 90 cm high. It is the most common and widespread lovegrass in the Trans-Pecos, where it provides good forage for livestock but poor grazing for wildlife. Plains lovegrass usually grows in mixed grassland communities with other per-ennials. According to Gould (1975) *Eragrostis intermedia* is related to a group of closely related taxa including *E. lugens* Nees (mourning lovegrass), *E. erosa* Scribn. (Chihuahua lovegrass), *E. palmeri* S. Wats. (Rio Grande lovegrass), *E. hirsuta* (Michx.) Nees (bigtop lovegrass), *E. trichocolea* Hack. & Arech. All these taxa occur in Texas except for *E. trichocolea*, which has been reported but not authenticated for the state. Only *E. intermedia* and *E. erosa* are commonly represented in the Trans-Pecos, although specimens resembling *E. palmeri* are known from Val Verde Co. One specimen resembling *E. trichodes* (Nutt.) Wood (sand lovegrass), which seems also related to this complex, is known from Winkler County. *Eragrostis lugens* has been reported from the Trans-Pecos, but Gould (1975) recognized this species as being restricted in Texas to extreme southeastern areas in mostly sandy habitats. Correll and Johnston (1970) recognized *E. lugens* and *E. intermedia* as conspecific, with *E. lugens* being the valid name. In the present treatment I follow Gould in recognizing *E. intermedia.* Intergradation between species of the *E. intermedia* complex is

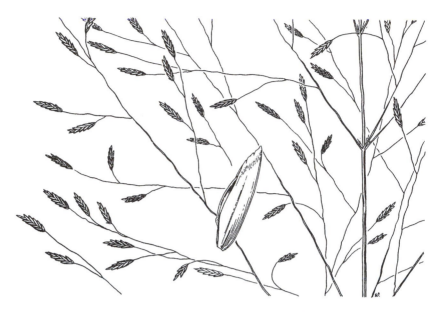

Fig. 105. *Eragrostis erosa*. Partial panicle; floret.

emphasized (Correll and Johnston, 1970) or implied (Gould, 1975). In the Trans-Pecos I have seen some indication of intergradation between *E. intermedia* and *E. erosa*, but for the most part these taxa are differentiated by lemma and spikelet size. Certain Trans-Pecos specimens match some of the characters attributed to *E. lugens* (Gould, 1975), but herein I have interpreted the Trans-Pecos specimens with small spikelets and short lemmas as either immature, staminate, or perhaps even sterile specimens of *E. intermedia*.

12. Eragrostis erosa Scribn. CHIHUAHUA LOVEGRASS. Fig. 105. Mountain slopes, canyons, and basins, various soil types. El Paso Co., Franklin Mts.; Hueco Tanks and Hueco Mts.; Sierra Diablo. Culberson Co., Guadalupe Mts., widespread; 1 mi S Texline. Jeff Davis Co., Limpia Creek near McIvor Hdq.; Mt. Locke, S slopes; Davis Mts. State Park; 2 mi N Bloys Encampment; Barbers Point, Kokernot Ranch; Haystack Mt., E slope. Presidio Co., Chinati Mts., big canyon above Shely Ranch house; Sierra Vieja, Capote Mt., S slopes. 3,500–8,000 ft. Flowering Apr–Nov. Also Edwards Plateau. W to NM and S AZ. N Chihuahua and Sonora, Mex.

Several Trans-Pecos specimens have spikelets longer than the measurements given by Gould (1975) for the species, 6–9 mm long. One collection from two miles north of Bloys Encampment has spikelets to 13 mm long. Chihuahua lovegrass, a tufted perennial to 1 m high, probably is good forage for livestock.

33. TRIDENS   Roem. & Schult.   TRIDENS.

Perennials. Culms erect. Leaves with flat blades; ligules membranous, glabrous or ciliate. Inflorescence a contracted or open panicle. Spikelets several flowered; disarticulation above the glumes, between florets; glumes membranous, thin, the first 1-nerved, the second 1–3(–5–7)-nerved; lemmas thin, relatively broad, back rounded, 3-nerved, pubescent on nerves of lower one-half or more (except glabrous or basally pubescent in *T. albescens*), midnerve and perhaps lateral nerves minutely mucronate, apex usually bidentate; palea equal to or slightly shorter than lemma. Caryopses dark brown.

A genus of about 18 species, distributed mostly in the southeastern United States and northern Mexico. The mostly warm-season Trans-Pecos species of *Tridens*, some often flowering as early as late spring, provide fair to good forage for livestock and wildlife. The genus name is derived from Latin, *tria*, thrice, and *dens*, tooth, in reference to the 3-toothed lemma of some species, but not in most Trans-Pecos taxa.

Key to the Species

1. Panicles contracted, the branches appressed (rarely spreading in *T. muticus*); the spikelets congested along the main axis or merely imbricate along the axis.
    2. Lemma nerves prominently pubescent (ciliate) from the base to near the middle of the lemma or above the middle; panicles slender and elongate, usually 4–9 mm wide; the spikelets linear-lanceolate, many or most of them along the panicle axis merely imbricate   **1. *T. muticus.***
    2. Lemma nerves glabrous or with a few hairs at the base on lateral nerves; panicles dense and congested, usually 8–18 mm wide; the spikelets ovate or elliptic and blunt at the apex, crowded on appressed branches
    2. *T. albescens.*
1. Panicles open, the branches spreading, the lowermost 3–12 cm long; the spikelets somewhat loose and imbricate or congested along the spreading branches.
    3. Spikelets 8–14 mm long; lemma lateral nerves usually extending beyond margin as short points   **3. *T. texanus.***
    3. Spikelets 4–7 mm long; lemma lateral nerves not (or very rarely) extending as short points   **4. *T. eragrostoides.***

1. Tridens muticus (Torr.) Nash   SLIM TRIDENS.   Fig. 106.   Various soil types, including gypsum, and habitats in desert and mountains, throughout much of the Trans-Pecos. El Paso Co., Franklin Mts. and foothills; Hueco Tanks. Hudspeth Co., 10 mi E Hueco; 40 mi N Sierra Blanca; Sierra Diablo, Victorio Canyon; 5–6 mi W Van Horn. Culberson Co., Guadalupe Mts.; 1 mi

Fig. 106. *Tridens muticus*. Partial panicle; floret
(two views).

S Texline; 10 mi N Mentone turnoff, Pecos-Carlsbad; Apache Mts., 2–10 mi
W Kent. Presidio Co., Bandera Mesa; near Shafter; Pinto Canyon; 6 mi N Can-
delaria; above Capote Falls; 13 mi SE Redford; Fresno Creek; Lajitas. Jeff Davis
Co., 2–12 mi S Kent. Brewster Co., from near Alpine to Black Gap Refuge and
Big Bend National Park, mountains and desert. Reeves Co., 22 mi NW Pecos.
Pecos Co., 10–35 mi S Fort Stockton; Comanche Springs, Fort Stockton;
3–6 mi N Fort Stockton; 20 mi W Sanderson; Sierra Madera; 13–30 mi E Fort
Stockton. Terrell Co., 30 mi N Sanderson; 6–9 mi E Sanderson; 9 mi W Dryden; mouth San Francisco Canyon. Val Verde Co., abundant in county.
1,100–5,800 ft. Flowering (Apr) May–Nov (Dec). Throughout most of TX
except the Pineywoods. W to CA, NV, and S UT. Central and NW Mex.

According to Gould (1975) two varieties of *T. muticus* occur in Texas. The
var. **muticus**, distinguished by second glumes typically ca. 5 mm long with one
nerve and leaf blades typically 1–2 mm wide, is the most widespread in Texas
and is the Trans-Pecos entity. The var. *elongatus* (Buckl.) Shinners [*Tridens
elongatus* (Buckl.) Nash], widespread in north-central Texas, is distinguished
by second glumes usually 6–8 mm long with 3–7 nerves, and leaf blades to
3–4 mm wide. A form of *T. muticus* (f. **effusus** M. C. Johnst.), discussed briefly
by Correll and Johnston (1970), occurs 20–21 miles south of Marathon. This

Fig. 107. *Tridens albescens.* Partial panicle;
floret (two views).

form is characterized by panicle branches spreading at near right angles,
2–2.8 cm long including spikelets, and in this trait is markedly distinct from
the typical *T. muticus.* Slim Tridens is by far the most widespread and abundant
Tridens of the Trans-Pecos, and is easily recognized by its slender spikelike
inflorescences and linear, near-terete spikelets.

2. Tridens albescens (Vasey) Woot. & Standl.   WHITE TRIDENS.
Fig. 107.   Various soil types and habitats, mountains and desert, usually in
canyons, arroyos, roadsides, and other places tending to collect water. Hud-
speth Co., Sierra Blanca. Culberson Co., 2 mi W Kent. Presidio Co., above
Capote Falls; Miller Ranch; Vieja Pass, Sierra Vieja. Jeff Davis Co., 27 mi W
Marfa; 5 mi S Kent; 13 mi N Alpine. Brewster Co., 20 mi NE Alpine; Chalk
Draw E of Santiago Peak; Black Gap headquarters; 10 mi W Marathon; Dog
Flats; Iron Mt., Glass Mts. Reeves Co., 10 mi E Balmorhea; 10 mi N Saragosa.
Pecos Co., Tunis Creek; 30 mi E Fort Stockton; 4 mi SW Imperial. Terrell Co.,
mouth of San Francisco Creek; 7 mi E Sanderson. Val Verde Co., Mile Canyon,
Langtry; Devils River. 1,300–4,500 ft. Flowering (Apr) Jul–Oct. Throughout
most of TX except the Pineywoods. N to OK, KS, CO, NM.

White Tridens is a tufted perennial with stems to 80 cm long. It is good
forage for livestock. The species is distinguishable by its contracted and dense
inflorescences of whitish, straw colored, to purplish spikelets.

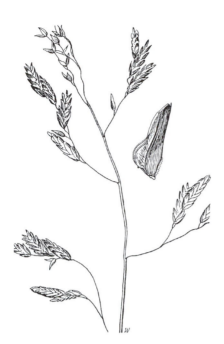

Fig. 108. *Tridens texanus.* Partial panicle; floret.

Fig. 109. *Tridens eragrostoides.* Plant; spikelets, glumes, and florets.

3. Tridens texanus (S. Wats.) Nash TEXAS TRIDENS. Fig. 108. Limestone or igneous alluvium, often in canyons or other protected habitats, and along roads. Brewster Co., highway shoulder, 15 mi E Marathon. Val Verde Co., Mile Canyon, Langtry; mouth of Pecos River; Seminole Canyon; Devils River; 8 mi W Del Rio; 10 mi N Del Rio. 1,300–4,500 ft. Flowering Apr–Sep. Southern TX. NE Mex.

Texas Tridens is restricted mostly to the eastern Trans-Pecos, although it may be found west to near Marathon along highways. Gould (1975) did not report *T. texanus* to occur in the Trans-Pecos. Its spikelets, 8–14 mm long, are the largest of the Trans-Pecos *Tridens* species.

4. Tridens eragrostoides (Vasey & Scribn.) Nash LOVEGRASS TRIDENS. Fig. 109. Igneous and limestone soils, canyons and other protected areas. Presidio Co., Fresno Canyon; Arroyo Secundo off Fresno Canyon. Brewster Co., 20–21 mi S Marathon; Sam Nail Ranch, Big Bend Natl. Park; Chisos Mts., Oak Creek Canyon below the Window; Black Gap Refuge, Cave Hill at Stairstep Mt.; Heath Canyon; road to Stillwell Crossing. Terrell Co., 8 mi

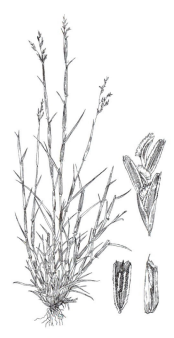

Fig. 110. *Triplasis purpurea.* Plant; spikelet,
floret, and cleistogamous spikelet.

N Dryden; 8 mi S Dryden; 1 mi E Sanderson. Val Verde Co., near mouth of
Pecos River. 1,200–4,800 ft. Flowering Mar–Nov. Southern Texas, frequent in
brushlands. E to FL and Cuba, W to AZ. N Mex.

Lovegrass Tridens is relatively widespread and rare in the Trans-Pecos. It
does resemble a lovegrass in its spreading inflorescence and macroscopic
spikelet appearance, although the spikelets are somewhat larger than are those
of the lovegrasses.

34. TRIPLASIS   Beauv.   SANDGRASS.

A genus of two North American species. Both species occur in Texas, but
only one of them in the Trans-Pecos. The genus name is from Greek, *triplasios,*
meaning triple, in reference to the apex of the lemma with two lobes and a
central awn.

1.   Triplasis   purpurea (Walt.)   Chapm.   PURPLE   SANDGRASS.
Fig. 110.   Strong annual. Culms 40–70 cm long, mostly erect, lateral culms
perhaps spreading or decumbent, the nodes hirsute; blades usually 4–8 cm

long, 1–3 mm wide, flat or involute, usually with marginal papilla-based hairs, the upper blades reduced; sheaths rounded, glabrous or with long hairs; ligules of white hairs. Inflorescence a panicle, 3–11 cm long, the lower spreading branches without spikelets on the lower one-half or more. Spikelets 6–10 mm long, florets 2–4, at least the upper one widely spaced; disarticulation between florets, also on culms with 1-flowered, cleistogamous spikelets in axils of enlarged sheaths; disarticulation with mature culm sections; glumes glabrous, 1-nerved, tapering to the apex, first glume ca 3 mm long, the second glume to 3.4 mm long; lemmas 3–4 mm long, 3-nerved, the nerves pubescent, the apex notched (0.5–1 mm deep) and usually with an awn, 0.5–1 mm long; palea narrow, with silky hairs ca. 0.5 mm long on the 2 nerves.

Usually in deep sand. Ward Co., 6 mi N Monahans; between Monahans and Imperial. Winkler Co., 22 mi SE Kermit; Waddell Ranch. Crane Co., 13 mi N Imperial. 2,600–3,600 ft. Flowering Jun–Sep. Scattered in sandy soils throughout much of TX. E to FL and N to ME, MN, and Ontario, Canada, NW to E CO; reported from Central America.

Purple sandgrass derives its name from purplish stems, leaves, and spikelets. The species is of little forage value, but it is useful in stabilizing sandy soil. Purple sandgrass is not known to occur in the Trans-Pecos proper, but might eventually be found in a sandy habitat west of the Pecos River.

35. ERIONEURON   Nash   ERIONEURON.

Perennials, low and tufted, some with stolons. Culms short. Leaves short; ligule a short, hairy membrane; blades short, narrow, folded lengthwise. Inflorescence a panicle, open or contracted, or a raceme. Spikelets several-flowered, the upper florets staminate or neuter; disarticulation between florets; glumes 1-nerved, membranous, subequal, glabrous, shiny, acute or acuminate; lemmas 3-nerved, rounded on the back, long-hairy on the nerves at least below, the central nerve often extended into a short awn, the two lateral nerves sometimes extended as small mucros near the margins, the apex narrowly margined, toothed, or 2-lobed; palea, barely shorter than lemma, keels ciliate, long-hairy below between the nerves. Caryopses oblong, translucent, glossy.

A genus of three species with seven varieties, native to the New World, occurring in the arid southwestern United States and northern Mexico. Hitchcock (1935; 1951) included the species of *Erioneuron* in *Tridens*, while Correll and Johnston (1970) and Gould (1975) treated *Erioneuron* as a separate genus. Valdés-R. (1985) removed *E. pulchellum* from *Erioneuron* and recognized it as the monotypic genus *Dasyochloa*. The genus name *Erioneuron* alludes to the hairy or "woollen" nerves of the lemmas. *Erioneuron* is distinguished in part from *Tridens* by its relatively short inflorescences and white-margined leaves in some species. *Erioneuron* is distinguished from *Dasyochloa* by its exserted inflorescences, conduplicate (folded) leaf blades, and inconspicuous stolons or no stolons. *Dasyochloa* has inflorescences included in and usually shorter than the fascicled leaves at the tips of short, naked culms, leaf blades involute, and slender stolons that are conspicuous, ascending or prostrate, and wiry. The species of *Erioneuron* are of little forage value. The key to the species and the treatment of *Erioneuron* is adapted from Valdés-R. (1985).

Key to the Species

1. Lemma apices entire or with a minute notch 0.5 mm or less deep; lemma midvein extending into an awn 0.5–2(–2.5) mm long; glumes shorter than lowermost floret of the spikelet   **1. *E. pilosum.***
1. Lemma apices with a notch 1–2.5 mm deep; lemma midvein extending into an awn 2–4 mm long; glumes, at least the second, as long as or longer than the lowermost floret of the spikelet.
   2. Lemma apex lobes obtuse to broadly acute; lemma notch 1–2 mm deep; lateral nerves not extending as small mucros; plants 10–30 cm high, commonly with stolons   **2. *E. avenaceum.***
   2. Lemma apex lobes rounded to truncate; lemma notch 1.5–2.5 mm deep; lateral nerves extending as small mucros to 0.5 mm long; plants 30–65 cm high, without stolons   **3. *E. nealleyi.***

1. Erioneuron pilosum (Buckl.) Nash   HAIRY TRIDENS.   Fig. 111. [*Tridens pilosus* (Vasey) Hitchc.]. Widespread and common in rocky desert or near-desert habitats, in every county of the Trans-Pecos. 1,300–6,000 ft. Flowering Mar–Nov. Throughout TX except extreme eastern portion. W to AZ and NV and UT, N to CO and KS. S to central Mex. Also Argentina.

Two varieties of *Erioneuron pilosum* occur in Argentina (Valdés-R., 1985). In addition to the key characters, hairy Tridens is usually distinguished by basal leaves and thus a scapose habit when in flower, but some plants of *E. avenaceum* and *E. nealleyi* also may exhibit this trait.

2. Erioneuron avenaceum (H.B.K.) Tateoka LARGEFLOWERED TRIDENS. Fig. 112. [*Tridens avenaceus* (H.B.K.) Hitch.; *T. grandiflorus* (Vasey) Woot. & Standl.; *T. nealleyi* (Vasey) Woot. & Standl.]. Mostly dry rocky slopes. El Paso Co., Franklin Mts.; Hueco Mts. Hudspeth Co., 2 mi N Allamoore. Presidio Co., 2 mi S Shafter. Jeff Davis Co., 2 mi S Kent. Brewster Co., Cienega Mt.; Elephant Mt.; Green Valley; Packsaddle Mt.; 5 mi S Marathon; 15 mi NE Marathon. 3,500–6,000 ft. Flowering Jul–Oct. W to AZ, NM. N Mex.

Gould (1975) recognized two varieties of *E. avenaceum*, the var. *grandiflorum* (Vasey) Gould and var. *nealleyi* (Vasey) Gould, while Valdés-R. treated

Fig. 111. *Erioneuron pilosum*. Plant; floret.   Fig. 112. *Erioneuron avenaceum*. Plant; floret.

var. *grandiflorum* as a synonym of *E. avenaceum* and *E. nealleyi* as a distinct species. Most of the Trans-Pecos specimens seemingly are of var. *nealleyi*, although some specimens matching the characters of *E. avenaceum* are also found in essentially the same localities. The two species recognized by Valdés-R. (1985) are not always easily distinguishable by the above characters and they do not appear to be geographically distinct in the Trans-Pecos.

3. **Erioneuron nealleyi** (Vasey) Tateoka NEALLY ERIONEURON. Fig. 113. [*Tridens nealleyi* (Vasey) Woot. & Standl.; *Erioneuron avenaceum* (H.B.K.) Tateoka var. *nealleyi* (Vasey) Gould]. Mostly rocky slopes. El Paso Co., Franklin Mts. Hudspeth Co., W slopes Eagle Mts. Culberson Co., Sierra Diablo, Victorio Canyon. Presidio Co., Sierra Vieja, above Capote Falls; 2 mi S Shafter; Chinati Mts., Ross Mine. Jeff Davis Co., Davis Mts., H. O. Canyon. Brewster Co., 20 mi NE Alpine, Cienega Mt.; Elephant Mt.; Glass Mts., W slopes Old Blue Mt.; Jail Canyon; 5 mi SW Marathon, Fort Peña Colorado; Del Norte Mts., Doubtful Canyon; Packsaddle Mt.; Chisos Mts., Boot Spring area; Ward Spring; Juniper Canyon. 3,000–7,000 ft. Flowering (May) Jul–Oct. Southern U.S. N Mex.

The two species distinguished by Valdés-R. (1985), *Erioneuron avenaceum*

Fig. 113. *Erioneuron nealleyi.* Glumes
and florets.

and *E. nealleyi*, appear to be very closely related and not always easily delimited
in Trans-Pecos populations.

36. DASYOCHLOA   Rydb.   FLUFFGRASS.

A monotypic genus native to North America and distributed mostly in arid
regions of the southwest United States and Mexico. The genus name is from
Greek *dasys*, hairy, and *chloe*, grass, alluding to the hairy and shaggy appearance of the plants with mature inflorescences.

1. Dasyochloa pulchella (H.B.K.) Rydb.   FLUFFGRASS.   Fig.   114.
[*Tridens pulchellus* (H.B.K.) Hitchc.; *Erioneuron pulchellum* (H.B.K.) Tateoka].
Perennial, tufted, low, strongly stoloniferous. Culms usually 4–10 cm long,
consisting of an elongated internode topped by a fascicle of leaves, these gradually bending to take root. Leaves with striate sheaths, these with scarious margins and a tuft of hairs (2 mm long) at the throat; ligules a fringe of hairs
3–5 mm long; blades strongly involute, 1–6 cm long, apex pointed, often
curved. Inflorescence a capitate panicle, or short raceme, 1–2.5 cm long,
1–1.5 cm wide, usually not exceeding the leaf blades of the panicle, light green

Fig. 114. *Dasyochloa pulchella* (=*Erioneuron pulchellum*). Plant; spikelet and floret.

or purplish when young, appearing white-woolly especially when mature, with 2–4 spikelets per branch. Spikelets (4–)6–10-flowered, 5–10 mm long, laterally compressed; disarticulation above the glumes; glumes persistent, subequal, glabrous, acuminate, 1-nerved, awn-tipped, as long as or longer than the florets, margins membranous; lemmas 3–5.5 mm long, prominently pilose toward the base, 3-nerved, the apex deeply cleft, the midnerve extending to an awn, 1.5–4 mm long; paleas long-pilose below, ciliate above the keels. Caryopses 1–1.5 mm long, translucent.

Desert flats and rocky slopes. One of the common desert grasses, in all counties of the Trans-Pecos. 2,000–6,000 ft. Flowering May–Nov. E to the Edwards Plateau, N to plains country in TX. W to AZ, UT, NV, CA. N Mex.

Fluffgrass is a widespread small grass characteristic of desert habitats in the Trans-Pecos. The "fluffy" appearance of the small clumps results from mature and fascicled spikelets with white hairs. As indicated in the synonymy, this taxon was until recently included with the genus *Tridens* or *Erioneuron*. Valdés-R. (1985) has presented good evidence that the taxon deserves recognition as a monotypic genus.

37. MUNROA   Torr.   FALSE BUFFALOGRASS.

Munroa is a genus of three to five species exhibiting continental disjunction, with most species in the dry plains of South America from Peru to Argentina

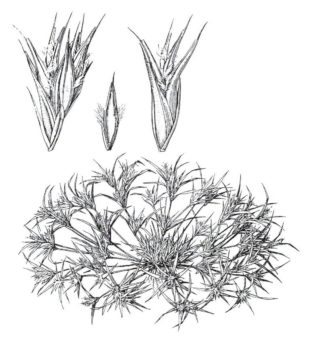

Fig. 115. *Munroa squarrosa.* Plant; group of
spikelets (upper left), floret, and spikelet.

and one in the western part of North America. The genus was named for
William Munro, an English agrostologist.

1. Munroa squarrosa (Nutt.) Torr.   FALSE BUFFALOGRASS.   Fig. 115.
Annuals, low, mat-forming, with stolons to ca. 8 cm long. Culms scabrous and
often minutely pubescent, branching, decumbent, or erect and to 10–13 cm
long. Leaves fascicled; sheaths 4–7 mm long; ligule a ring of hairs; blades
scabrous and often minutely pubescent, flat or folded, usually 1–5 cm long,
1–2.5 mm wide, with a stiff, pointed tip (subspinose). Inflorescence a cluster
of subsessile spikelets. Spikelets 7–10 mm long, usually 2–3-flowered; disarticulation between florets; glumes of lower spikelets equal, barely shorter than
the lemmas, 1-nerved, apex acute, glumes of upper florets unequal, the first
glume smaller or absent; lemmas 3-nerved, somewhat scabrous, those of lower
spikelets with marginal tufts of hair near the middle, with a scabrous awn 0.5–
1.5 mm long, the lateral nerves often extending beyond the margin; palea narrow. Caryopsis elliptic, dorsally compressed.

   Various alluvial habitats, also in sand, open sites including grasslands and
disturbed areas. El Paso Co., 10–15 mi E El Paso; between Ysleta and Hueco
Tanks. Hudspeth Co., 2 mi N Allamoore. Culberson Co., foothills Guadalupe
Mts. Presidio Co., Marfa; 3 mi W San Estaban Lake; 2 mi W San Jacinto Peak;

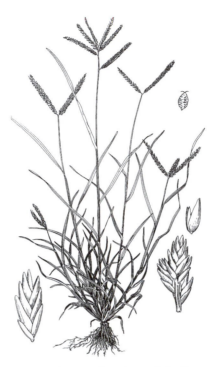

Fig. 116. *Eleusine indica.* Plant; spikelet (lower
left), group of spikelets (lower right), floret,
and seed (without pericarp).

5 mi E Chispa. Jeff Davis Co., Bloys Encampment; 3.5 mi S Fort Davis. Brewster Co., Paisano Campground; 8 mi S Alpine; Goat Mt.; Mt. Ord, 15 mi S
Alpine; Doubtful Canyon; Glass Mts. Pecos Co., 30 mi E Fort Stockton. 3,000–
5,500 ft. Flowering (May) Jun–Oct. Edwards Plateau and plains country,
common in the sand hills. N to Alberta, Canada, W to AZ. Chihuahua, Mex.

False buffalograss is of little forage value because it is small, low, and with
unpalatable stiff, sharp leaves.

38. ELEUSINE   Gaertn.

A genus of about nine species mostly in warm regions of the Old World,
one species native to South America, one species, *E. indica,* adventive in the
United States. The genus name is from Eleusis, the Old World city.

1. Eleusine indica (L.) Gaertn. GOOSEGRASS. Fig. 116.   Annual,
somewhat succulent. Culms to 75 cm long, erect or spreading, the lower ones

perhaps rooting at the nodes. Leaves essentially glabrous or long-hairy on the margins; sheaths laterally compressed, keeled; ligule membranous, ca. 1 mm long, lacerate-ciliate; blades 7–30 cm long, 3–8 mm wide, flat or folded. Inflorescence with usually 2–6 spreading, spicate branches, these digitate at culm apex, and often with 1–2 spicate branches 1–4 cm below the apical whorl of spicate branches, the branches usually 4–15 cm long, the rachis flattened, winged, with spikelets closely imbricate in 2 rows. Spikelets 3–6 mm long, 3–6-flowered; glumes glabrous, acute, the first glume 1-nerved, the second glume larger, 3–7-nerved, lemmas essentially glabrous, somewhat laterally compressed, keeled, acute or obtuse. Caryopses 1–2 mm long, transverse ridged, and rugose.

Apparently rare in the Trans-Pecos. Presidio Co., Capote Mt. 4,500 ft. Flowering November. Disturbed sites throughout TX; throughout most of the United States except perhaps the northwest.

39. LEPTOCHLOA   Beauv.   SPRANGLETOP.

Annuals and perennials, clumped. Culms leafy, 10–100 cm or more long. Leaves with blades flat or linear; ligules membranous, glabrous or ciliate. Inflorescence a panicle of numerous, ascending or erect, distinctly or indistinctly unilateral, spicate primary branches, these scattered along the main axis or clustered near the apex. Spikelets 1.5–12 mm long, 2–12-flowered, distant or imbricate on branches; disarticulation between florets; glumes thin, 1-nerved, acute, awnless or mucronate, the second glume usually longer than the first and perhaps 3-nerved; lemmas 3-nerved, rounded on the back or keeled, pubescent on the nerves or not, body of lowest lemma 1–5 mm long, apices acute, obtuse, or notched and awnless or awned; paleas well-developed. Caryopses somewhat elliptical or triangular in section, grooved on one side or not.

A genus of perhaps 50 species found throughout tropical Africa, Asia, Australia, and the Americas, and extending into temperate North America. McNeill (1979) recognized *Leptochloa* and *Diplachne* as separate genera, and also presented a taxonomic history regarding the taxa. The treatment here follows Hitchcock (1935; 1951), Gould (1975), Clayton and Renvoize (1986), and other workers who have combined *Diplachne* with *Leptochloa*. The present treatment also follows the recommendation of Estes and Tyrl (1982), who contended that the two taxa should remain united as one genus, pending further investigation. About nine species of *Leptochloa* occur in Texas, five of these in the Trans-Pecos. Only one species of *Leptochloa*, *L. dubia*, is known as an important forage grass (Hitchcock, 1951). The genus name *Leptochloa* is from Greek *leptos* and *chloa*, respectively meaning slender and grass, in reference to the slender, spikelike primary branches of the panicles.

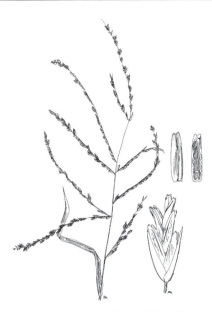

Fig. 117. *Leptochloa dubia.* Panicle; spikelet
and floret (two views).

Key to the Species

1. Plants perennial; lemmas broad, notched at the apex, the notch ca. 0.5 mm deep; lemma nerves glabrous   **1. *L. dubia.***
1. Plants annual; lemmas somewhat broad or acute, without a notch or notched at the apex, the notch less than 0.3 mm deep; lemma nerves pubescent.
   2. Spikelets 2–4-flowered, 1.5–3 mm long; lemmas strongly keeled   **5. *L. mucronata.***
   2. Spikelets 5–12-flowered, 3.5–10 mm long; lemmas rounded in section.
      3. Lemmas awnless (perhaps mucronate)   **3. *L. uninervia.***
      3. Lemmas awned.
         4. Lemmas viscid on the back; spikelets 3.5–5 mm long; 5–7-flowered   **2. *L. viscida.***
         4. Lemmas not viscid; spikelets 7–12 mm long; 6–12-flowered   **4. *L. fascicularis.***

     1. Leptochloa dubia (Kunth) Nees   GREEN SPRANGLETOP.   Fig. 117. [*Diplachne dubia* (Kunth) Scribn.]. Widespread and locally common, usually in deep soil, mixed with other grasses, commonly at roadside. El Paso Co., McKelligon Canyon, Franklin Mts.; 5–8 mi W El Paso. Hudspeth Co., 30 mi E El Paso, 1 mi W Hueco; Eagle Mts.; 5 mi W Van Horn. Culberson Co.,

Guadalupe Mts., Pine Spring Canyon area; Victorio Canyon, Sierra Diablo; between Texline and Orla. Presidio Co., Sierra Vieja; Chinati Mts.; mid–Pinto Canyon; 30 mi S Marfa; near Solitario Peak. Jeff Davis Co., Mt. Livermore; Rockpile; Haystack Mt.; Mitre Peak area; 13 mi NW Alpine. Brewster Co., widespread in alluvial valleys and mountains throughout the northern half of county; also Agua Fria, Packsaddle, Nine Point Mesa, Chisos Mts.; Tornillo Flats; Maravillas Creek, Brushy Canyon, Black Gap Refuge. Reeves Co., Hwy 290, 1 mi E of junct. Hwy 80. Pecos Co., 6 mi N Fort Stockton; 20–45 mi S Fort Stockton; 30 mi E Fort Stockton; Sierra Madera. Terrell Co., mouth of San Francisco Canyon; 6 mi E Sanderson; 14 mi W Sanderson; 14 mi N Dryden. 2,000–5,500 ft. Flowering May–Nov. Throughout most of TX except extreme E part. W to AZ, N to OK; also S FL. Also Argentina. Mex.

Green sprangletop is the only perennial species of *Leptochloa* in North America, and was placed in section *Ipnum* (of *Diplachne*) apart from the annuals, which were assigned to section *Diplachne* (McNeill, 1979). Plants of *L. dubia* form perfect cleistogamous spikelets in the axils of lower sheaths (Gould, 1975). Probably all of the *Leptochloa* species are fair forage when abundant enough, but *L. dubia* reportedly is an excellent forage grass in the Trans-Pecos and elsewhere. Unfortunately, green sprangletop characteristically is only locally abundant, and it seems to have difficulty competing with other, more hardy grasses in range pastures. In the Trans-Pecos, green sprangletop is most commonly seen at roadside, along fence lines, and in other somewhat protected and non-grazed areas. The plants are highly palatable and apparently they are selectively grazed by livestock.

2. **Leptochloa viscida** (Scribn.) Beal VISCID SPRANGLETOP. Fig. 118. [*Diplachne viscida* Scribn.]. Among rocks in canyons. El Paso Co., Hueco Tanks. Jeff Davis Co., Limpia Canyon, Wild Rose Pass. 4,000–4,800 ft. Flowering May. NM, AZ. N Mex.

Plants of *L. viscida* are small annuals 10–30 cm high, freely branching at the base forming spreading stems, and with leaves and panicles somewhat viscid (Hitchcock, 1951). Also the lemmas are somewhat viscid on the back, with an awn 0.5–1.5 mm long, panicles 2–10 cm long with main branches 1–2.5 cm long (McNeill, 1979). *Leptochloa viscida* was not reported for Texas by Gould (1975), but two collections in the Sul Ross Herbarium exhibit at least some of the characters of this species. Plants of both collections possibly are depauperate *L. fascicularis*, and thus the occurrence of this species in the Trans-Pecos requires verification.

3. **Leptochloa uninervia** (C. Presl) Hitchc. & Chase MEXICAN SPRANGLETOP. Fig. 119. [*Diplachne uninervia* (C. Presl) Parodi]. Along streams, including the Rio Grande, and irrigation canals, and around springs and marshes. El Paso Co., near El Paso. Brewster Co., Mariscal Canyon; Boquillas Canyon; lower Oak Creek Canyon, Chisos Mts.; Glenn Springs;

Fig. 118. *Leptochloa viscida.* Plant; spikelet and floret (two views).

Fig. 119. *Leptochloa uninervia.* Partial panicle; floret (two views).

mouth of Tornillo Creek; Comanche Springs between Terlingua and Lajitas. Pecos Co., 5 mi NE Coyanosa. Terrell Co., between Reagan Canyon and Sanderson Canyon, along Rio Grande. Val Verde Co., Mile Canyon, Langtry; mouth of the Pecos River. 1,300–3,900 ft. Flowering Apr–Dec. Edwards Plateau and south Texas. Southern and southwestern United States, West Indies. South America. Mex.

Mexican sprangletop requires abundant moisture and thus is not very widespread or of significant forage value in the Trans-Pecos. Superficially the species resembles *L. fascicularis,* but *L. uninervia* is easily distinguished under magnification by the blunt lemma apexes without awns.

4. Leptochloa fascicularis (Lam.) A. Gray   BEARDED SPRANGLETOP. Fig. 120.   [*Diplachne fascicularis* (Lam.) Beauv.]. Canyons, along streams and canals, around stock tanks and springs, usually in wet (muddy) soils. El Paso Co., Franklin Mts.; 15 mi N Ysleta; Hueco Mts. Hudspeth Co., 2 mi E Sierra Blanca. Culberson Co., South McKittrick Canyon, Guadalupe Mts.; Delaware Creek; 5 mi W Kent. Presidio Co., Brack's Canyon, Sierra Vieja. Jeff Davis Co., Timber Mt.; Little Aguja Canyon; 1 mi above Fort Davis, Limpia Canyon; 22 mi W Fort Davis; near McDonald Observatory, Brown Canyon; Musquiz Canyon; Mt. Livermore. Brewster Co., 5 mi W Alpine; 10 mi S Alpine; Iron Mt., Glass Mts.; 20 mi S Marathon; Cathedral Mt.; Nine Point Mesa; Chisos

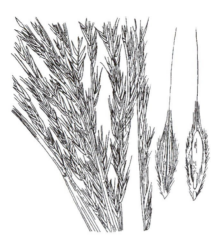

Fig. 120. *Leptochloa fascicularis.* Partial panicle;
floret (two views).

Mts., Upper Cattail Falls, above Boot Springs. Reeves Co., 15 mi S Pecos. Pecos Co., 13 mi E Fort Stockton. 2,800–6,000 ft. Flowering mostly Jun–Oct. Throughout most of TX. Throughout much of United States. Also Central and South America. Mex.

Bearded sprangletop is restricted usually to wet, muddy habitats and thus is not abundant enough to have forage value except perhaps for certain wildlife species. Other than the key characters *L. fascicularis* is distinguished by the lower glumes 1.3–2 mm long, upper glumes 2.2–3.5 mm long, and awned, acuminate lemmas.

5. Leptochloa mucronata (Michx.) Kunth RED SPRANGLETOP. Fig. 121. [*Eleusine mucronata* Michx.; *Festuca filiformis* Lam.; *L. filiformis* (Lam.) Beauv.]. Annual, weedy. Culms 10–80 cm long, slender, decumbent, spreading. Leaves glabrous, with few hairs, or prominently papillose-pilose usually on the sheaths; sheaths rounded on back; ligules 1–2 mm long, lacerate, ciliate; blades 2–10 mm wide, thin, flat, linear. Inflorescence a panicle, usually 9–36 cm long, the slender branches spreading or erect, usually numerous, and diffuse, 3–9(–12) cm long, 0.5–1.5 mm wide. Spikelets 1–2(–3) mm long, 2–4-flowered, spaced along the slender branches with some barely overlapping; glumes subequal, much exceeding the lowest floret, apices acute; lemmas (lower) usually 1–1.5 mm long, usually pubescent on nerves below middle, apexes obtuse or truncate. Caryopses triangular in section or with a longitudinal groove on one side.

Relatively rare in the Trans-Pecos, mostly on disturbed soils. El Paso Co., farm area near Ysleta. Brewster Co., 5 mi W Study Butte; Tornillo Flats; Wilson

Fig. 121. *Leptochloa mucronata.* Plant and
panicle; floret and spikelet.

Ranch. Terrell Co., mouth of San Francisco Canyon. 2,000–3,800 ft. Flowering
Aug–Oct. Throughout TX except the High Plains. SE United States, N to VA
and IN, W to AZ and S CA.

According to McNeill (1979), only *L. mucronata*, a weedy species, reaches
temperate North America, while the other Trans-Pecos species of *Leptochloa*
were treated by him as members of *Diplachne*. Clayton and Renvoize (1986)
recognized *L. mucronata* as a member of section *Leptochloa* (spikelets laterally
compressed, small, usually 1.5–5 mm long, usually imbricate on distinctly
unilateral branches), while the other Trans-Pecos members of the genus would
be members of their section *Diplachne* (spikelets round in section, large,
5–15 mm long, usually distant on indistinctly unilateral branches). Until recently (Snow and Davidse, 1993) *L. mucronata* was recognized as *L. filiformis*
(Lam.) Beauv.

40. SCLEROPOGON   Phil.   BURROGRASS.

A monotypic genus of North and South America. A recent study by Reeder
and Toolin (1987) confirmed that the genus is represented by a single species
despite its wide distribution on two continents. Burrograss is of little forage

Fig. 122. *Scleropogon brevifolius.* Pistillate and
staminate plants; staminate spikelet and floret
(lower left), pistil, and pistillate floret (upper
left) drawn with awn bases only.

value. The genus name is from Greek *skleros* and *pogon*, meaning hard and
beard, in reference to the hard awns of the female plants.

1. Scleropogon brevifolius Phil. BURROGRASS. Fig. 122. [*Scleropogon longisetus* Beetle]. Perennial, tufted, dioecious, sometimes monoecious,
with wiry stolons. Culms usually 10–25 cm long. Leaves mostly basal; sheaths
short, prominently nerved, upper ones glabrous, lower ones often pubescent;
ligule a fringe of hairs; blades stiff, flat or folded, usually 2–8 cm long, 1–2 mm
wide. Inflorescence mostly of pistillate and staminate flowers on separate
plants, sometimes on the same plant; perfect flowers occasionally produced.
Spikelets in spicate racemes or contracted panicles; the pistillate spikelets long-
awned, the staminate spikelets awnless. Pistillate spikelets usually with 3–5
perfect florets and 1–several awnlike rudimentary florets above, these disarticulating together; glumes unequal, lanceolate, awnless, usually 3-nerved,
perhaps with other delicate lateral nerves; lemmas firm, rounded on back,

3-nerved, the nerves leading into prominent awns 5–10 cm long, the awns (and florets) often cyanic, maturing straw colored, lowermost lemma with bearded, basal-pointed callus; paleas slender, with 2 nerves and 2 short awns. Staminate spikelets with 5–10(–20) florets; glumes and lemmas similar, thin, pale, lanceolate, usually 3-nerved, the first and second glumes separated by short internode, the florets separated on rachilla 1 mm or more, florets persistent.

Flat and dry alluvial soils, mountain basins and desert scrub, occasionally on slopes, one of the most common grasses in the Trans-Pecos, occurring in every county. 2,000–5,100 ft. Flowering (Apr) June–Dec, even in Jan. Edwards Plateau and plains country in TX. NW to CO and AZ. S to central Mex. Chile and Argentina.

Burrograss often occurs in dense stands, with pistillate plants often appearing more numerous in nearly pure stands. When the sun angle is right one can look out across the ranges and see large glistening patches of the straw colored or cyanic awns. Reportedly burrograss has low palatability, particularly after the stiff awns have developed on pistillate plants. The species is said to increase in areas that are heavily grazed by livestock, and it is a rapid colonizer of denuded and disturbed habitats. Seed dispersal in burrograss, including the function of awns on female spikelets, has been studied by Allred (1989).

41. BLEPHARIDACHNE   Hack.   DESERTGRASS.

A genus of three species, two in the United States, and one in Argentina. One species is found in Texas. *Blepharidachne kingii* occurs in the deserts of Utah, Nevada, and California. Plants of this genus are of no forage value. The genus name is from Greek *blepharis* and *achne*, meaning eyelash and chaff, in reference to the prominently ciliate lemmas.

1. Blepharidachne bigelovii (S. Wats.) Hack.   BIGELOW DESERT-GRASS.   Fig. 123.   Perennial, low, densely tufted, the base firm and tough. Culms 6–20 cm long, often branching, covered by the overlapping leaf sheaths. Leaves short and stiff; sheaths usually 0.5–1.3 cm long, often minutely pubescent on back; ligule membranous, small, fringed; blades firm, involute, densely short-pubescent, usually 1–3 cm long, curved, spine-tipped. Inflorescence a contracted, headlike panicle of 5–10 spikelets, these barely extending above upper leaves or elevated on short culms to ca. 6 cm above the leaves. Spikelets usually 5–7 mm long, with 4 florets, the first and second sterile, the third perfect, and the fourth reduced to a 3-awned rudiment; disarticulation barely above the glumes; glumes relatively large, thin, nearly equal to body of lower lemma, glabrous, except the nerve perhaps minutely scabrous, apexes acute; lemmas 3-nerved, 3-lobed, 3-awned, the awns plumose, deeply cleft be-

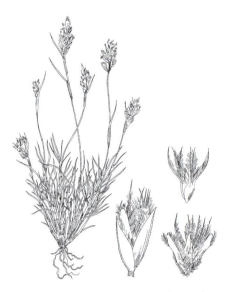

Fig. 123. *Blepharidachne bigelovii*. Plant; spikelet, sterile and fertile florets, and fertile floret
(above).

tween the nerves, the body ca. 2 mm long, long-hairy along central lobe and
lateral nerves; paleas of perfect floret barely longer than body of lemma, laterally compressed, paleas of lower floret reduced to slender membrane. Caryopsis ca. 1.5 mm long, subovate, with an inconspicuous double ridge on the
rounded edge.

Desert habitats, frequently in thin, rocky limestone substrates overlying
Cretaceous clays, endemic to the Trans-Pecos and adjacent Coahuila, Mexico.
Hudspeth Co., ca. 15 mi W Sierra Blanca, between Quitman Mts. and Rio
Grande. Presidio Co., 1 mi S Shafter; 2 mi E Lajitas. Brewster Co., ca. 40 mi S
Alpine; 2 mi SE Packsaddle Mt.; lower slopes, Packsaddle Mt.; 1 mi S Adobe
Wall Mt.; 50 mi S Marathon; near turnoff to Wilson Ranch, Big Bend Natl.
Park. Reeves Co., 10 mi E Balmorhea. Pecos Co., 20 mi E Fort Stockton toward
McCamey; 30 mi E Fort Stockton. Terrell Co., 5–10 mi E Dryden; 9.6 mi W
Dryden; 9–11 mi E Sanderson. 2,100–4,500 ft. Flowering Mar–Nov. Also ad-
jacent Coahuila, Mex.

Bigelow desertgrass is mostly, if not entirely, limited to certain limestone-
clay substrates in desert areas of the Trans-Pecos. The plants are often locally
abundant depending upon the extent of suitable substrate for growth. The stiff,
spine-tipped leaves of this species make it difficult to collect the plants without
receiving pricked fingers.

Fig. 124. *Calamovilfa gigantea*. Panicle; glumes
and spikelet.

42. CALAMOVILFA   Hack.   SANDREED.

A genus of four species, all in North America, often in dune sands or pine
barrens. Only one species occurs in Texas. The genus name is from Greek,
kalamos, meaning reed, and *Vilfa*, a genus of grasses.

1. Calamovilfa gigantea (Nutt.) Scribn. & Merr. BIG SANDREED.
Fig. 124.   Perennial, large and coarse, with stout, creeping rhizomes. Culms
1–2 m long, 0.5–1.4 cm thick near base, usually solitary at rhizome nodes.
Leaves large and coarse; sheaths rounded, glabrous or with small hairs near the
collar; ligule a ciliate fringe, 1–2 mm long; blades somewhat leathery at maturity, flat or folded, glabrous, 20–60 cm long, to 0.5–1.2 cm wide, tapering to
a narrow, involute apex. Inflorescence an open panicle, 30–60 cm long,
branches to near 20 cm long, stiff, spreading or ascending, longer branches
bare on lower 3–6 cm. Spikelets 1-flowered, awnless, usually 7–10 mm long,
on short pedicels, mostly aggregated toward branch tips; disarticulation above
glumes; glumes papery, glabrous, 1-nerved, acute, the first glume shorter than
the lemma, the second glume nearly equaling or exceeding the lemma; lemmas
papery, 1-nerved, tapering to an acute apex, the base with a prominent tuft of

whitish hairs to 3–5 mm long; paleas slender, perhaps exceeding the lemma.

Deep sand. Ward Co., 3 mi E of Monahans. Winkler Co., 3–8 mi E Kermit; 10 mi NE Kermit. Crane Co., 13 mi N Crane; 5 mi NE Grandfalls. 2,500–3,800 ft. Flowering mostly Jun–Oct. Also the plains country, W to NM, UT, and AZ, N to CO and KS.

Big sandreed occurs in the sand hills on the northeast periphery of the Trans-Pecos, but likely occurs at some sites west of the Pecos River. Probably these large, coarse plants are of limited forage value for livestock and wildlife, but more importantly they are of significance in binding sand.

43. LYCURUS   H.B.K.   WOLFTAIL.

Perennials, tufted or clumped. Culms 20–50 cm long, erect, weakly geniculate, or decumbent. Leaves mostly basal; sheaths shorter than internodes, compressed and keeled; ligule membranous, whitish, hyaline, acute to acuminate and 3–10 mm long, truncate and 0.5–1 mm long, or with sheath auricles and 1.5–3 mm long; blades 4–15 cm long, 0.5–3 mm wide, somewhat grayish-green, flat or folded and keeled, the midnerve and margins whitish. Inflorescence a dense spicate panicle, somewhat bristly-looking, 3–10 cm long, 4–7 mm wide. Spikelets 1-flowered, borne in pairs on short, unequal pedicels more or less fused at the bases; disarticulation at base of pedicels, the spikelets often falling together, perhaps later separating; spikelets perfect and fertile or staminate or neuter; glume bodies ca. 2 mm long, the first glume usually 2-nerved and 2-awned, the awns usually 3–5 mm long, the second glume 1-nerved, the nerve extending as a flexuous awn slightly longer than the body; lemmas 3-nerved, usually 3–4 mm long, minutely pubescent at least on margins, tapering to the apex, with one awn usually 1–3 mm long; paleas similar to lemmas but awnless. Caryopses linear, cylindrical, ca. 1.7 mm long.

A genus of about six species located in Argentina, South America, and in southwestern North America. Three species occur in North America, two species in Texas (Reeder, 1985). The genus name is from Greek, *lucos* and *oura*, wolf and tail, with reference to the wolftail-like (spikelike) panicles. The key to species is adapted from Reeder (1985).

Key to the Species

1. Leaves, at least the upper ones, terminating in a slender bristle to 10 mm long or more; ligules acute to acuminate (3–)5–6(–10) mm long; plants cespitose, culms erect   **1. *L. setosus.***
1. Leaves not terminating in a bristle, but often terminating in a short bristle-

Fig. 125. *Lycurus setosus*. Plant; glumes
and floret.

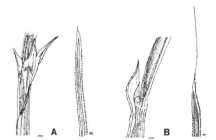

Fig. 126. (A) *Lycurus phleoides*; ligule (adaxial
view) and leaf blade tip. (B) *Lycurus setosus*;
ligule (side view) and leaf blade tip.

like point; ligules 1.5−2(−3) mm long, with evident auricles on either side; plants cespitose, culms ascending or lax, commonly geniculate

2. *L. phleoides.*

1. Lycurus setosus (Nutt.) C. Reeder BRISTLETIP WOLFTAIL. Figs. 125, 126. [*Pleopogon setosum* Nutt.; *Lycurus phleoides* var. *glaucifolius* Beal]. Abundant and widespread in mountain and basin grasslands, medium to higher elevations, alluvial basins and rocky mountain slopes. El Paso Co., Franklin Mts., McKelligon Canyon; 8 mi N El Paso. Hudspeth Co., Eagle Mts. Presidio Co., Sierra Vieja; Goat Mt. Jeff Davis Co., Davis Mts., Mt. Livermore and outlying mountains and basins. Brewster Co., common in mountains and basins, N part of county; also Chisos Mts. Reeves Co., 1 mi N junct. Hwy 290−80. Pecos Co., 6 mi N Fort Stockton; 20−40 mi SW Fort Stockton. 3,300−7,800 ft. Flowering (Apr) Jun–Nov. Also W Edwards Plateau and S High Plains. N to OK, CO, and UT, W to AZ. Baja CA Norte, Sonora, Chihuahua, Durango, Mex.

Lycurus setosus is the most widespread of the Trans-Pecos wolftail grasses. Traditionally only one wolftail grass was reported to occur in Texas, this being *L. phleoides* (Gould, 1975), but recently Reeder (1985) has recognized two species for the state, both of them occurring predominantly in the Trans-Pecos. *Lycurus setosus* is best recognized by its leaf blades tipped with slender bristles and ligules usually 5−6 mm long. *Lycurus setosus* appears to be an important forage grass for cattle and perhaps for wildlife.

2. Lycurus phleoides H.B.K. WOLFTAIL. Fig. 126. Infrequent to locally frequent, mountains and basin grasslands. Culberson Co., Guadalupe Mts., Guadalupe Peak; Bowl; South McKittrick Canyon; Upper Pine Spring Canyon; 10 mi S Texline; Sierra Diablo, Victorio Canyon; Apache Mts. Presidio Co., 30 mi S Marfa. Brewster Co., 5 mi S Marathon; Iron Mt.; Goat Mt.; Big Bend Natl. Park, Dead Horse Mts. Pecos Co., Sierra Madera. 3,800−7,500 ft. Flowering (May) Jun–Oct. Also E NM. Coahuila, Nuevo Leon, Tamaulipas, S Chihuahua, S to Oaxaca, Mex.

Lycurus phleoides in Texas is perhaps restricted to the Trans-Pecos (Reeder, 1985), and appears to be most common in Culberson County. The leaves of *L. phleoides* lack a slender bristle on the blade tips, but may exhibit a short point that often appears as if it is a reduced bristle. The hyaline ligules of *L. phleoides* are usually 1.5−2 mm long and prominently auriculate (Reeder, 1985). In observing herbarium specimens of some wolftails from the Trans-Pecos, it was often difficult to make a distinction between *L. phleoides* and *L. setosus* when the tips of leaf blades showed short bristles and the preserved leaves seemingly were not mature enough to show typical ligules. *Lycurus phleoides* should be palatable to livestock.

44. MUHLENBERGIA   Schreb.   MUHLY.

Perennials of diverse habits, some large and coarse, or annuals of diverse habits, some small and delicate, some perennials with creeping rhizomes. Culms branched or simple. Leaves of various sizes; ligule membranous; blades flat, folded, or involute. Inflorescence a panicle, from open and diffuse to partially or tightly contracted and spikelike. Spikelets 1-flowered (occasionally a second floret in some species); disarticulation usually above the glumes; glumes usually shorter than the lemma, mostly 1-nerved (or nerveless), rarely 3–5-nerved, apices obtuse to acuminate, or awned; lemmas 3-nerved (rarely 5-nerved), these distinct or inconspicuous, the apex with one awn, mucronate, or awnless, in some species the apex bifid with an awn between the minute lobes; paleas well developed. Caryopses elongate, subcylindrical, slightly flattened, or somewhat fusiform, usually persistent.

A large and variable genus broadly interpreted to include about 160 species distributed mostly from North America to South America, with some species in Asia. The center of distribution is in Mexico. Gould (1975) reports 41 species for Texas. At least 28 species occur in the Trans-Pecos, establishing *Muhlenbergia* as the largest grass genus in the region. In western North America many of the species comprise a significant part of the grass flora and are important forage grasses. The genus is named after G. H. E. Muhlenberg, a pioneer botanist from Pennsylvania. *Muhlenbergia pungens* (sandhill muhly) of the High Plains and sands was not observed but is expected to occur in the Trans-Pecos. Gould (1975) and Hatch et al. (1990) report *M. racemosa* (Michx.) B.S.P. (green muhly) to occur in El Paso County of the Trans-Pecos. Worthington (1989) does not list this species for El Paso County. In addition to the species included below perhaps still other species of the widespread and variable genus *Muhlenbergia* will be found to occur in the Trans-Pecos.

Key to the Species

1. Plants annual.
    2. Inflorescence contracted, dominated by wavy, olive-green awns 8–18 mm long; first glume acute, second glume 3-toothed
                                                              1. *M. crispiseta.*
    2. Inflorescence spikelike or open and diffuse, awns straight and mostly appressed in the "spike" if 1 cm or longer; first and second glumes otherwise.
        3. Inflorescence spikelike; first glume bidentate, 2-nerved; plants 5–12 cm high.
            4. Glumes about half as long as lemma; awn of lemma 9–18 mm long; spikelets 4–6 mm long   **2. *M. brevis.***

      4. Glumes about as long as lemma; awn of lemma 1–8 mm long;
          spikelets 2.5–3.5 mm long   **3. *M. depauperata.***
   3. Inflorescence spreading, diffuse, with small spikelets on delicate
      branches.
      5. Lemmas awned, the awn 1.5–3.5 mm long; lemmas 1.3–2.5 mm
          long.
         6. Awns 1.2–3.5 mm long; lemmas (1.7–)1.9–2.5 mm long; ped-
            icels 1–2(–3) mm long   **4. *M. eludens.***
         6. Awns 0.1–1.0(–2.0) mm long; lemmas 1.3–2.0 mm long; ped-
            icels 2–7 mm long   **5. *M. texana.***
      5. Lemmas awnless (perhaps with a mucro less than 1 mm long);
          lemmas 0.8–1.5 mm long.
         7. Glumes short-pilose to villous near the apex; ligules without
            prominent auricles   **6. *M. minutissima.***
         7. Glumes glabrous, or minutely scabrous near the apex; ligules
            with auricles 1.5–2.5 mm long   **7. *M. fragilis.***
1. Plants perennial.
   8. Rhizomes present, these creeping, scaly, perhaps branching.
      9. Leaf blades 2–4(–5) mm wide, flat   **8. *M. andina.***
      9. Leaf blades 2 mm wide, or less, mostly involute and short.
         10. Panicles open; spikelets on delicate pedicels, usually 0.4–2 cm or
            more long.
           11. Leaf blades with thickened white midnerve and margins; lig-
              ules with auricles 1–2 mm long; plants of dry habitats
                                   9. *M. arenacea.*
           11. Leaf blades without thickened white midnerve and margins;
              ligules without auricles; plants of moist habitats
                                 10. *M. asperifolia.*
         10. Panicles contracted to condensed; spikelets on short pedicels,
            usually much less than 0.4 cm long.
           12. Plants usually 15–40 cm or more tall, with appearance of
              tufted grasses; leaf blades 3–12 cm long, 1–2.5 mm wide.
              13. Lemmas awned, the awns 10–20 mm long; leaf blades
                 ca. 1 mm wide   **11. *M. polycaulis.***
              13. Lemmas awnless, mucronate, or with an awn 1.5–3 mm
                 long; leaf blades 2–2.5 mm wide   **12. *M. glauca.***
           12. Plants usually 10–20 cm tall (sometimes taller), with ap-
             pearance of turfgrass; leaf blades 1–2 cm long (to 4–5 cm in
             some floriferous shoots); 0.5–1(–2) mm wide.
              14. Lemmas pubescent on lower half   **13. *M. villosa.***
              14. Lemmas glabrous, perhaps minutely scabrous near the
                 apex.

            15. Lemmas 2.8–3.5 mm long, usually lead colored; plants of dry habitats   **14. *M. repens.***

            15. Lemmas 1.6–2 mm long, usually pale-greenish; plants of moist habitats   **15. *M. utilis.***

8. Rhizomes absent.

    16. Plants large, coarse, densely cespitose, culms (50–)100–150 (–200) cm long.

        17. Panicles spikelike, dense along the axis, 0.5–1 cm wide; sheaths rounded   **16. *M. rigens.***

        17. Panicles somewhat contracted and densely flowered, but plumose and not at all spikelike, 4–7 cm wide; sheaths laterally compressed and keeled   **17. *M. emersleyi.***

    16. Plants smaller, not so coarse, and usually with shorter culms.

        18. Culms decumbent, often geniculate below and rooting at the nodes   **18. *M. pauciflora.***

        18. Culms spreading or erect, not rooting at the nodes.

            19. Second glume 3-nerved and 3-toothed   **19. *M. montana.***

            19. Second glume usually 1-nerved and usually acute or awned, but not distinctly 3-toothed.

                20. Panicles open, widely spreading or somewhat narrow, but loosely flowered, usually 3–10 cm or more wide; panicle branches naked near the base.

                    21. Culms much-branched and spreading, wiry; persisting under spiny shrubs in grazed areas   **20. *M. porteri.***

                    21. Culms not much-branched and spreading, usually erect.

                        22. Leaf blades usually short and clustered at the base.

                            23. Leaf blades usually rather straight, usually 5–8 cm long, 1–2 mm wide, flat or folded; panicles usually exceeding 20 cm long   **21. *M. arenicola.***

                            23. Leaf blades strongly curved, 1–3.5 cm long, 1 mm or less wide, involute; panicles usually less than 15 cm long   **22. *M. torreyi.***

                      22. Leaf blades elongated.

                            24. Lemmas straw colored, smooth; glumes 1.5–2.2 mm long   **23. *M. setifolia.***

                            24. Lemmas purple, minutely scabrous near the apex; glumes 1–1.3 mm long   **24. *M. rigida.***

    20. Panicles contracted, narrow or spikelike, densely flowered, usually less than 2 cm wide; panicle branches usually with spikelets to the base or nearly so.

        25. Lemma awns usually less than 1 cm long, or awnless.

            26. Panicles dull greenish to gray, to 1 cm wide; glumes 2–3 mm long   **25. *M. dubia.***

            26. Panicles purplish, to 2 cm wide; glumes 1.5–2 mm long   **26. *M. metcalfei.***

        25. Lemma awns 1–4 cm long.

            27. Lemmas pubescent with straight spreading hairs on lower half; glumes usually acute or short-awned, usually exceeding 1.5 mm long   **27. *M. tenuifolia.***

            27. Lemmas uniformly scabrous, often with a few appressed hairs at the base; glumes obtuse, usually 0.5–1 mm long   **28. *M. parviglumis.***

1. Muhlenbergia crispiseta Hitchc. Fig. 127. Rocky habitats, slopes and drainages, sandy roadsides, calcareous mesas, pine-oak and pinyon-juniper woodlands with *Arctostaphylos* in Mexico (P. M. Peterson, pers. comm.), riparian woodland in igneous Chisos Mts. In the United States known only from one locality, Brewster Co., Chisos Mts., Big Bend National Park, lower part of Cattail Canyon. 4,500–6,500 ft. Flowering Aug–Oct. Chihuahua, Durango, San Luis Potosí, Zacatecas, Sonora, Mex.

This rather inconspicuous slender, tufted, annual species was collected for the first time in the United States by B. H. Warnock (*BHW 21268*, SRSC) on 7 Oct 1967. The species is easily distinguished from the other annual muhlys known to occur in the Trans-Pecos. Characters of *M. crispiseta* in addition to those listed in the key are: leaves with membranous ligules 1.3–2.0 mm long; blades flat or involute, 1–5 cm long, 0.7–1.4 mm wide, short-pubescent on upper surface; inflorescence 1.8–4.5 cm long, 1.5–3.0 cm wide, pedicels ascending and often curved; the acute first glume 1.2–1.6 mm long, the 3-toothed second glume 1.6–1.8 mm long; lemmas 1.7–2.2 mm long, lanceolate, plump near middle, mottled-greenish on lower half, densely pilose on lower half or two-thirds, glabrous above, the apex minutely bifid, the crisped and curled, olive-green awns arising from the dorsal surface of the lemma just below the apex. The identification of this species, the description, and other information was provided by P. M. Peterson of the U.S. National Herbarium (also see Peterson and Annable, 1991).

2. Muhlenbergia brevis C. O. Goodding SHORT MUHLY. Fig. 128. Known in the Trans-Pecos only from near the top of Mt. Livermore, Davis

Fig. 127. *Muhlenbergia crispiseta*. Plant; glumes and floret.

Fig. 128. *Muhlenbergia brevis*. Plant; glumes and floret.

Mts., Jeff Davis Co. 8,100 ft. Flowering Aug–Sep. Also W to AZ, CO, UT. N Mex.

Short muhly is closely related to *M. depauperata*.

3. Muhlenbergia depauperata Scribn.   SIXWEEKS MUHLY.   Fig. 129. Rare in protected canyons, often in moist habitats. El Paso Co., Hueco Mts. Culberson Co., Sierra Diablo, opposite Bat Cave. Presidio Co., Chinati Mts., big canyon above Shely Ranch house. Jeff Davis Co., Fern Canyon, Mitre Peak Girl Scout Camp. Brewster Co., Tarzan Falls, ca. 18 mi S Alpine; Chisos Mts., Laguna; upper Boot Canyon, Boot Spring area, ridge between Juniper and Pine canyons; Lost Mine Peak; near Green Gulch. 3,500–7,300 ft. Flowering Jul–Oct. W to NM, AZ, CO. N Mex., S to Oaxaca.

Both *M. depauperata* and *M. brevis* are remarkable low annuals which are unlike any other Trans-Pecos muhlys in their short habits. As pointed out by Correll and Johnston (1970) and Peterson and Annable (1991), these species have many characters in common with *Lycurus*.

4. Muhlenbergia eludens C. G. Reeder   Fig. 130.   Mountain slopes and canyons at medium to higher elevations. Jeff Davis Co., Davis Mts., N slope

Fig. 129. *Muhlenbergia depauperata.* Plant; glumes and floret.

Fig. 130. *Muhlenbergia eludens.* Plant; glumes and floret.

Mt. Livermore; Madera Canyon, roadside park 20 mi N Fort Davis; Fern Canyon, Mitre Peak Girl Scout Camp. Brewster Co., Chisos Mts., Boot Spring area, upper Boot Canyon toward South Rim. 4,800–7,500 ft. Flowering Jul–Oct. W to NM, AZ. S to central Mex.

Of the four delicate annuals with open panicles in the Trans-Pecos, *M. eludens* is the most uncommon species. It is like the other three species, *M. fragilis, M. texana,* and *M. minutissima,* in habit but is easily distinguished by its awned lemmas.

5. Muhlenbergia texana Buckley   Fig. 131.   [*Podosemum texana* (Buckley) Bush; *Muhlenbergia buckleyana* Scribn.]. Western Texas to El Paso, according to label data on the type specimen collected by Wright in 1849, but not otherwise cited for Texas or the Trans-Pecos (Peterson and Annable, 1991). Flowering probably in summer and fall. Also SW NM, SE AZ. NW Mexico.

I have not seen any Texas specimens of *M. texana.* Peterson and Annable (1991) recognize *M. texana* as a "transition taxon" linking *M. eludens* and *M. minutissima,* and include the following distinguishing characters of *M. texana:* lemma awns 0.1–1.0(–2.0) mm long, spikelets spreading from the inflorescence branches on pedicels 2–7 mm long, lanceolate-bidentate lemmas 1.3–2.0 mm long, paleas minutely pubescent between the nerves below, and cary-

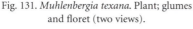

Fig. 131. *Muhlenbergia texana*. Plant; glumes
and floret (two views).

Fig. 132. *Muhlenbergia minutissima*. Plant;
spikelet (lower right) and floret; ligule
(upper left).

opsis 0.8–1.0 mm long. *Muhlenbergia eludens* has lemma awns 1.2–3.5 mm
long, spikelets appressed to inflorescence branches on pedicels ca. 2 mm long,
lanceolate-bidentate lemmas (1.7–)1.9–2.5 mm long, paleas glabrous, and
caryopsis 1.3–2.3 mm long. *Muhlenbergia minutissima* exhibits awnless lemmas, spikelets spreading on pedicels 2–7 mm long, lanceolate obtuse to
subacute lemmas 0.8–1.5 mm long, paleas glabrous or with short silky
hairs between the nerves, and caryopsis 0.6–0.9 mm long. The glumes of
M. minutissima are obtuse to acute, while those of *M. texana* and *M. eludens*
are acuminate.

Some Trans-Pecos specimens of *M. eludens* from the Davis Mountains and
the Chisos Mountains have spreading spikelets on pedicels 2–2.5 mm long,
but otherwise do not appear to have any traits of *M. texana*. The occurrence
and the distribution of *M. texana* in Trans-Pecos Texas needs to be verified.

6. Muhlenbergia minutissima (Steud.) Swallen LEAST MUHLY.
Fig. 132.   [*Muhlenbergia texana* Buckl.; *M. sinuosa* Swallen]. Rocky slopes and
canyons. Jeff Davis Co., Davis Mts., Mt. Livermore, NE slopes near Madera
Canyon; Upper Madera Canyon; Madera Canyon at roadside park; junction of
Madera Canyon and Elbow Canyon. Brewster Co., 8 mi W Alpine; 9 mi S
Alpine; Tarzan Falls ca. 18 mi S Alpine. 5,000–7,500 ft. Flowering Aug–Nov.
NW to MT, WA and W to AZ, CA. N Mex.

Fig. 133. *Muhlenbergia fragilis.* Plant; glumes
and floret (two views); ligule.

Least muhly is closely related to *M. eludens, M. texana,* and *M. fragilis.* Recent studies by Peterson and colleagues (Peterson and Rieseberg, 1987; Peterson, 1988; Peterson, 1989; Peterson and Annable, 1991) have greatly clarified these and other annual species of *Muhlenbergia.* Least muhly has chromosome numbers of $n = 30, 40$, while *M. eludens* is $n = 20$, *M. texana* is $n = 20$, and *M. fragilis* is $n = 10$ (Peterson and Annable, 1991).

7. Muhlenbergia fragilis Swallen DELICATE MUHLY. Fig. 133. Rocky slopes and canyons. El Paso Co., Franklin Mts. Presidio Co., Capote Mt., N slopes; Chinati Mts., Pinto Canyon, lower Tigna Canyon; La Mota Waterhole; N slope, Elephant Mt. Jeff Davis Co., Mt. Livermore; Merrill Canyon W side Mt. Livermore; Davis Mts. State Park; CDRI Landsite, 3 mi S Fort Davis. Brewster Co., 8 mi W Alpine; Doubtful Canyon, Del Norte Mts.; Iron Mt.; Glass Mts. 3,500–7,000 ft. Flowering Aug–Nov. W to NM and AZ. S to central Mex.

Delicate muhly is perhaps the most common of the delicate annual muhlys in the Trans-Pecos. In addition to the key characters it is identified by leaf blades with a thickened whitish midnerve and margins. All of the Trans-Pecos annual muhlys are too small to have significant forage value.

8. Muhlenbergia andina (Nutt.) Hitchc. FOXTAIL MUHLY. Fig. 134. According to Gould (1975) known in Texas only from a single collection (*W.*

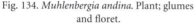

Fig. 134. *Muhlenbergia andina*. Plant; glumes and floret.

Fig. 135. *Muhlenbergia arenacea*. Plant; floret and glumes (bottom right).

A. *Silveus 3428*, TEX) from near Sierra Blanca, Hudspeth Co. Elsewhere in the United States, moist habitats, western U.S. E to western MT, eastern KS, western TX. Flowering Jul–Aug.

Foxtail muhly produces terminal densely flowered, contracted panicles that are silvery green or tinged with purple.

9. Muhlenbergia arenacea (Buckl.) Hitchc.   EAR MUHLY.   Fig. 135. Various soil types including sandy, dry habitats. El Paso Co., Franklin Mts.; 5 mi W Hueco. Hudspeth Co., 20 mi N Sierra Blanca; 9 mi N Sierra Blanca. Culberson Co., Apache Mts., 4 mi N Kent. Presidio Co., 2 mi W San Jacinto Peak. Brewster Co., between Alpine–Fort Davis; Alpine, Kokernot Lodge; N slopes Twin Peaks; Glass Mts., Bisset Hill; 20 mi NE Alpine; Chalk Draw E Santiago Peak; Green Valley; Black Gap Refuge, Norton Tank. Jeff Davis Co., 12 mi S Kent; 5 mi E Chispa; near Barrel Springs. Pecos Co., 3–5 mi N Fort Stockton; 3 mi WSW University Mesa; 20–30 mi S Fort Stockton; 30 mi E Fort Stockton. Terrell Co., 10 mi SE Sanderson. 2,700–5,100 ft. Flowering Jun–Nov. In TX also Edwards Plateau and High Plains. W to AZ, CO. S to Zacatecas, Mex.

The small plants of ear muhly are of very limited forage value.

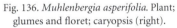

Fig. 136. *Muhlenbergia asperifolia.* Plant; glumes and floret; caryopsis (right).

Fig. 137. *Muhlenbergia polycaulis.* Plant; glumes and floret.

10. Muhlenbergia asperifolia Buckl. SCRATCHGRASS MUHLY. Fig. 136. Moist or marshy habitats. El Paso Co., 6 mi NW El Paso; 60 mi SE El Paso. Hudspeth Co., 4 mi E Fort Hancock. Culberson Co., Guadalupe Mts., Choisya Springs; 8 mi S Texline; Delaware Creek. Jeff Davis Co., Musquiz bog, 7 mi S Fort Davis. Brewster Co., Kokernot Springs, Alpine; Leoncita Springs, Kokernot Ranch; 3 mi S Alpine; Walnut Spring near Fresno Mine. Reeves Co., along canals, Balmorhea. Pecos Co., 5 mi N Fort Stockton. Terrell Co., Independence Creek. 2,500–6,000 ft. Flowering Jun–Dec. Also Edwards Plateau and plains country, TX. Throughout much of midwestern and western United States. British Columbia, Canada; Mex. Southern South America.

Gould (1975) uses the common name alkali muhly for this species. In the Trans-Pecos, some of its moist habitats are in alkaline soils. In the Trans-Pecos this species is too restricted in distribution to be of much forage value.

11. Muhlenbergia polycaulis Scribn. CLIFF MUHLY. Fig. 137. Mountain slopes and canyons. Culberson Co., Guadalupe Mts., upper Pine Spring Canyon, McKittrick Canyon. Presidio Co., Chinati Peak; High Lonesome, Brite Ranch. Jeff Davis Co., Davis Mts., Mt. Livermore, Madera Canyon, Goat Canyon, Elbow Canyon; Rockpile; Sawtooth Mt.; Musquiz Creek. Brewster Co., 8 mi W Alpine; 3 mi S Alpine; Mt. Ord, NE slopes and W slopes; Goat Mt.; Chisos Mts., Pine Canyon, Casa Grande, Boot Canyon, Green Gulch, N

Fig. 138. *Muhlenbergia glauca.* Plant; glumes
and floret.

branch Cattail Canyon. 4,000–8,200 ft. Flowering Jun–Oct. W to NM and AZ.
N Mex.

In addition to its rhizomatous base and flexuous lemma awns 10–20 mm
long, cliff muhly is distinguished by contracted and densely flowered panicles,
acuminate-awned glumes nearly as long as the lemmas, and lemmas villous on
the lower half. Cliff muhly evidently is palatable but of limited forage value
because of its distribution in medium to higher elevations.

12. Muhlenbergia glauca (Nees) Mez   DESERT MUHLY.   Fig. 138.
[*Muhlenbergia lemmonii* Scribn.]. Mountain slopes and canyons. Presidio Co.,
Capote Mt., S slopes; Elephant Mt., SW slope. Jeff Davis Co., Davis Mts., Mt.
Livermore, SE slopes, Madera Canyon; Sawtooth Mt., H. O. Canyon; upper
Limpia Canyon; Haystack Mt., N slope. Brewster Co., Mt. Ord, E side; Goat
Mt.; Elephant Mt.; Chisos Mts., Laguna. 4,500–7,500 ft. Flowering Jun–Nov.
W to southern CA. N Mex.

Desert muhly probably is palatable to grazing animals, but its distribution
in the mountains limits forage value except to wildlife. *Muhlenbergia glauca* is
similar to *M. polycaulis* but differs in its awnless to short-awned lemmas and
slightly broader leaf blades. Both species have pubescent lemmas on the lower
half.

Fig. 139. *Muhlenbergia villosa.* Plant; glumes and floret.

Fig. 140. *Muhlenbergia repens.* Plant; glumes and floret.

13. Muhlenbergia villosa Swallen HAIRY MUHLY. Fig. 139. Rare, desert flats and canyons, reported in alkaline conditions, but also in igneous non-alkaline soils. Culberson Co., Sierra Diablo, S fork of Victorio Canyon, 2 mi below Refuge Hdq. Hudspeth Co., Sierra Diablo, 15 mi N of Allamoore. Brewster Co., 6 mi S Alpine. 4,500–5,000 ft. Flowering Jul–Oct. Endemic to TX, reported also NW Edwards Plateau, southern High Plains.

Muhlenbergia villosa is closely related to *M. villiflora* Hitchc. of northern Mexico and might be treated as synonymous with the latter. However, in recent anatomical studies of the *Muhlenbergia repens* complex, to which *M. villosa* belongs, Morden and Hatch (1987) found a few anatomical differences between *M. villosa* and *M. villiflora* and suggested that the two be maintained as "distinct entities," but not necessarily different species.

14. Muhlenbergia repens (Presl) Hitchc. CREEPING MUHLY. Fig. 140. [*Muhlenbergia abata* I. M. Johnst.]. Open areas, usually alluvial flats or slopes in mountain basins, locally abundant. Hudspeth Co., Hueco Mts., 5 mi E Hueco. Culberson Co., Guadalupe Mts., McKittrick Canyon; 2 mi S state line, Road 1108. Presidio Co., Elephant Mt. Jeff Davis Co., Madera Springs Resort; Limpia Creek near Davis Mts. State Park; Point of Rocks; Fern Canyon, Mitre Peak Girl Scout Camp; Musquiz bog. Brewster Co., Alpine golf

Fig. 141. *Muhlenbergia utilis*. Plant; glumes
and floret.

course; Kokernot Lodge; 3 mi W Alpine; 8 mi W Alpine; Twin Peaks, lower N
slopes; 10 mi S Alpine; 18 mi S Alpine; Marathon; Altuda Point; Chisos Mts.,
Laguna. Pecos Co., Glass Mts. 20–40 mi S Fort Stockton; Sierra Madera.
3,200–6,500 ft. Flowering Apr–Nov. W to AZ. Mex.

Muhlenbergia repens is related to *M. villosa* and *M. utilis*, and is the most
abundant of the three taxa in the Trans-Pecos. Creeping muhly forms rather
extensive stands or "mats" in some areas and often resembles a lawn turfgrass
where the mats are low and thick. At the Point of Rocks in Jeff Davis County,
creeping muhly is mowed by roadside park caretakers to form an attractive
lawn. Most descriptions of *M. repens* report the leaf blades up to 2 cm long,
while leaf blades to 4 cm long were found in a population 10 mi S Alpine.
Vegetative apomixis has been reported for *M. repens* by Morden and Hatch
(1986). Creeping muhly is not reported to be of forage value but it should be
palatable.

15. Muhlenbergia utilis (Torr.) Hitchc.   APAREJOGRASS.   Fig. 141.
Along streams and in marshy or moist habitats. Brewster Co., 20 mi S of Al-
pine, at a seep, forming dense mats. 4,500 ft. Flowering Jun, probably through
Oct. Edwards Plateau. W to NV and southern CA. NW Mex.

Fig. 142. *Muhlenbergia rigens*. Plant; spikelet
and floret (left), and glumes and floret (right).

Muhlenbergia utilis is most similar in habit to *M. repens* (Gould, 1975), but *M. utilis* differs by its slender leaf blades usually less than 1 mm wide, spikelets ca. 2 mm long, glumes about half as long as the lemma, and lemmas 1.6–2 mm long with the apex merely acute or pointed (not awned). Aparejograss probably occurs at more Trans-Pecos localities than previously reported, but it is not abundant enough to be of forage value.

16. Muhlenbergia rigens (Benth.) Hitchc. DEERGRASS. Fig. 142. [*Muhlenbergia marshii* I. M. Johnst.]. Usually moist mountain canyons, in and along rocky and gravel washes, particularly ones with ephemeral or some permanent water. Presidio Co., Chinati Mts., Oso Creek; Solitario, Lower Shut-up. Jeff Davis Co., Elbow Canyon junct. Madera Canyon; Mt. Livermore, Merrill Canyon, Goat Canyon; Limpia Creek; Davis Mts. State Park; Fern Canyon, Mitre Peak Girl Scout Camp; Lower Madera Canyon; Little Aguja Canyon; Musquiz Creek, 13 mi N Alpine. Brewster Co., 7–8 mi W Alpine; Ranger Canyon; 9 mi S Alpine; 20 mi NE Alpine; Glass Mts., near Altuda Point; Iron Mt.; Walnut Springs near Fresno Mine; Dripping Springs, Paint Gap Hills, Big Bend Natl. Park. 2,500–5,100 ft. Flowering Jul–Dec. TX, one population in W Travis Co. (Johnston, 1988; 1990). W to southern CA. N Mex.

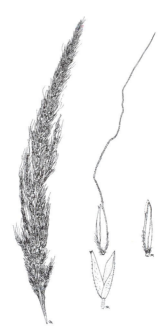

Fig. 143. *Muhlenbergia emersleyi*. Panicle;
glumes, floret awned, and floret awnless.

Deergrass is a large, coarse, densely clumped grass that is easily distinguished by its prominent, dense, spikelike panicles, usually 10–40 cm long,
0.5–1 cm wide, elevated above the leaves. Trans-Pecos plants are variable in
glumes and lemmas awnless or with awns 0.5–1 mm long. The plants of
M. rigens are too coarse to be highly palatable, and too restricted in distribution
to be of much forage value. Perhaps a better common name would be deer
muhly.

17. Muhlenbergia emersleyi Vasey BULLGRASS. Fig. 143. Rocky,
usually grassy mountain slopes and canyons, medium to high elevations. El
Paso Co., Franklin Mts.; Hueco Mts. Hudspeth Co., Sierra Diablo. Culberson
Co., Guadalupe Mts.; Sierra Diablo. Presidio Co., Capote Mt.; Chinati Mts.;
101 Ranch. Jeff Davis Co., Timber Mt.; Lower Madera Canyon; Mt. Livermore,
H. O. Canyon, Madera Canyon, Limpia Canyon; Rockpile; Mt. Locke; Davis
Mts. State Park; Haystack Mt.; Musquiz Canyon; Mitre Peak Girl Scout Camp.
Brewster Co., 5–7 mi W Alpine; 9 mi S Alpine; Mt. Ord; Cathedral Mt.; Goat
Mt.; Cienega Mt.; Elephant Mt.; Chisos Mts.; Dead Horse Mts.; Glass Mts.
Pecos Co., 30 mi E Fort Stockton. 3,200–7,500 ft. Flowering Apr–Nov. W to
AZ. Mex. S to Oaxaca.

Bullgrass, also known as bull muhly, is a large, coarse, densely clumped

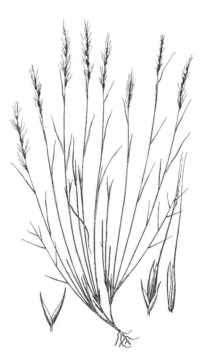

Fig. 144. *Muhlenbergia pauciflora*. Plant;
glumes (left), and spikelet and floret (right).

grass that is easily distinguished by its size and large feathery panicles arching above the leaves. The panicles are variable in being more or less contracted, and the lemma awns are 1.5 cm long, perhaps readily deciduous, or absent. The awn, when present, arises from just below the bifid apex of the scabrous lemma. The panicles may vary in color from pale gray or brown to purplish. Bullgrass is not considered to be a good forage species, possibly because it is coarse and not highly palatable.

18. Muhlenbergia pauciflora Buckl. NEW MEXICO MUHLY. Fig. 144. Mountain slopes and canyons, medium to high elevations. El Paso Co., Franklin Mts. Hudspeth Co., Diablo Mts., top, Buck Ridge, Victorio Canyon. Culberson Co., Guadalupe Mts., common, mid-canyons and slopes to the top. Jeff Davis Co., Davis Mts., Mt. Livermore, Madera Canyon, Goat Canyon; Sawtooth Mt.; Haystack Mt. Brewster Co., Chisos Mts., Laguna, Boot Spring Canyon; Packsaddle Mt. Pecos Co., 40–45 mi SE Fort Stockton. 3,200–8,000 ft. Flowering Jul–Oct. W to AZ, NW to CO and UT. N Mex.

New Mexico muhly is distinguished by its subequal, lanceolate glumes, lemmas 3–4.5 mm long and glabrous or scabrous, with awns 0.7–2.5 cm long,

Fig. 145. *Muhlenbergia montana.* Plant; glumes (two views) and florets (two views).

Fig. 146. *Muhlenbergia porteri.* Plant; spikelet and floret.

and decumbent, somewhat geniculate stems rooting at the lower nodes. New Mexico muhly is seemingly palatable and abundant enough in the Guadalupe Mountains to be a useful forage species.

19. Muhlenbergia montana (Nutt.) Hitchc. MOUNTAIN MUHLY. Fig. 145. Mountain slopes and canyons, medium to higher elevations. Culberson Co., Guadalupe Mts., top of South McKittrick Canyon. Jeff Davis Co., Davis Mts., Mt. Livermore, Madera Canyon and near peak; Sawtooth Mt. 6,000–8,200 ft. Flowering Aug–Oct. W to CA, N to MT. SW Mex. to Guatemala.

Mountain muhly is mostly a higher elevation species, in the Trans-Pecos most common on Mt. Livermore, with flexuous awns 0.6–2.5 cm long. Its most distinguishing character is microscopic, in that the second glume is 3-nerved and prominently 3-toothed. Mountain muhly is palatable and locally good forage mostly for wildlife. Flavonoid studies by Herrera A. and Bain (1991) compared *M. montana* with related species, and suggested that the annual *M. crispiseta* was not closely related to the *M. montana* complex.

20. Muhlenbergia porteri Scribn. *ex* Beal BUSH MUHLY. Fig. 146. Chihuahuan desertscrub, upper slopes and flats, usually in alluvium, various soil types, commonly protected by shrubs and cacti. El Paso Co., Franklin Mts.;

Fig. 147. *Muhlenbergia arenicola.* Plant; glumes
and floret.

Hueco Mts. Culberson Co., Guadalupe Mts. Jeff Davis Co., 12 mi S Kent; Mitre
Peak Girl Scout Camp. Brewster Co., 7 mi W Alpine; Twin Peaks; 20 mi NE
Alpine; Cathedral Mt.; 40 mi S Alpine; Steam Boat Mesa; Elephant Mt.; Pack-
saddle Mt.; Black Gap Refuge; Big Bend Natl. Park, Kit Mt., Smokey Creek,
Burro Mesa, Onion Spring in Paint Gap Hills, near Fresno Spring. Pecos Co.,
5 mi N Fort Stockton; 12 mi NW Fort Stockton; 25–40 mi SW Fort Stockton;
30 mi E Fort Stockton. Terrell Co., near mouth San Francisco Canyon; 8 mi N
Dryden. Val Verde Co., 40 mi W Del Rio. 2,100–5,500 ft. Flowering (May)
Jun–Nov. Edwards Plateau, S portion of High Plains. W to AZ and S CA, NW
to NV and CO. S to central Mex.

Bush muhly is an excellent forage grass named after its tendency to be sus-
tained in the protection of shrubs, cacti, and other plants in grazed pastures.
The plants are distinguished by the much-branched, wiry, geniculate culms
usually 40–70 cm long, lacerate, membranous ligules 1–5 mm long, panicles
that are open, terminal, 4–11 cm long and about as wide, usually purplish
lemmas 3–4 mm long with an awn 5–12 mm long.

21. Muhlenbergia arenicola Buckl.   SANDY MUHLY.   Fig. 147.   Open
grasslands and mesas, various soil types, sandy to clay alluvium. El Paso Co.,
Hueco Mts. Hudspeth Co., 5–8 mi NE Sierra Blanca; 9 mi E Sierra Blanca;

Fig. 148. *Muhlenbergia torreyi*. Plant; glumes
and floret.

6 mi W Salt Flats; 8 mi W Van Horn; near Baylor Mts. Culberson Co., Gua-
dalupe Mts. foothills; Apache Mts. Presidio Co., La Mota. Jeff Davis Co., 15 mi
E Chispa; Barrel Springs; Davis Mts. State Park; top of Fern Canyon; Musquiz
Canyon. Brewster Co., Alpine and vicinity; 30–43 mi S Alpine; Goat Mt.; Cie-
nega Mt.; Elephant Mt.; 20 mi NE Alpine; Glass Mts.; 15 mi N Marathon; Nine
Point Mesa; 5 mi SW Marathon. Reeves Co., 25 mi NW Pecos; Toyah. Pecos
Co., 3–5 mi N Fort Stockton; 25 mi SW Fort Stockton; 30 mi E Fort Stockton.
Terrell Co., 6 mi E Sanderson; 44 mi N Dryden. 2,600–5,100 ft. Flowering
May–Nov. Also Edwards Plateau and plains country. N to KS and CO, W to
AZ. N Mex.

Sandy muhly is also called sand muhly. This is one of the most common
muhlys in the Trans-Pecos, and it is reported to have fair palatability. Sandy
muhly is distinguished by its relatively short leaves and rather large, open panicles 13–30 cm long and 6–15 cm wide, and lemmas with a slender awn 0.5–
3.5 mm long.

22. Muhlenbergia torreyi (Kunth) Bush RING MUHLY. Fig. 148.
Dry, rocky hills, alluvial flats, and dry meadows, rare in the Trans-Pecos. El
Paso Co., Hueco Mts., 5 mi W Hueco; 5 mi E Hueco; 8 mi E Hueco. Hudspeth
Co., 8 mi NE Sierra Blanca; Moor Ranch 60 mi E El Paso. Culberson Co., West

Fig. 149. *Muhlenbergia setifolia.* Plant; glumes
and floret.

Dog Canyon SW of Coyote Peak; reported from Delaware Mts. 4,100–5,900 ft.
Flowering May–Oct. Also Edwards Plateau and plains country (Gould, 1975).
W to AZ, N to CO and KS. N Mex.

Ring muhly, also known as ringrass muhly, is apparently rare or at least
uncommon in the Trans-Pecos. In typical form it is distinguished by its leaves
that are in a short, basal cushion 2–5 cm high, with the blades involute or
folded, 1–4 cm long, slender, strongly curved, and pointed. *Muhlenbergia torreyi* is similar to *M. arenicola* and may intergrade with the latter species. Some
Brewster County collections identified as *M. arenicola* approach *M. torreyi*
(e.g., 2 mi N Marathon) in leaf form. Another possible locality for *M. torreyi* is
in Presidio Co., lower Musgrave Canyon, Sierra Vieja. The common name ring
muhly is taken from the basal growth habit of old plants that progressively
over years die in the center leaving a ring of plants to several feet in diameter.
Ring muhly is palatable to cattle when green, although it is low in forage
production.

23. Muhlenbergia setifolia Vasy CURLYLEAF MUHLY. Fig. 149.
Mostly in limestone soils, rocky hills, slopes, mountain canyons. El Paso Co.,
Franklin Mts. Hudspeth Co., Hueco Mts.; Sierra Diablo. Culberson Co., Gua-
dalupe Mts.; 10 mi W Kent. Jeff Davis Co., 2 mi S Kent. Brewster Co., 5 mi SW
Marathon; Glass Mts.; Iron Mt.; Del Norte Mts.; Cienega Mt. (limestone); Chi-

Fig. 150. *Muhlenbergia rigida.* Partial panicle; glumes and floret; ligule.

sos Mts., Lost Mine Trail, upper Cattail Canyon; Black Gap Refuge, Rock Heads Canyon. Pecos Co., between Iraan and Fort Stockton; 25–40 mi S Fort Stockton. 2,600–6,000 ft. Flowering (Apr) Aug–Nov. Rare W Edwards Plateau. Also NM. Coahuila, Mex.

Curlyleaf muhly is characterized by its tightly involute and often curled leaf blades, these 6–22 cm long, and only 0.2–0.7 mm wide and inrolled, panicles usually 8–22 cm long, 2–4 cm wide, glumes irregularly truncate and 1.5–2.3 cm long, yellowish lemmas that are glabrous and shining except for a few short hairs at the base, and lemma awns 1–2.8 cm long. The panicles and lemmas sometimes are purplish, at least when immature. *Muhlenbergia setifolia* occurs mostly in calcareous soils, except for the collections in the Chisos Mountains where igneous soils predominate. The Chisos Mountains plants may prove to be different in that their leaves do appear to be larger than those of typical plants. Plants of curlyleaf muhly are fairly large, 50–80 cm high, and should present good forage.

24. Muhlenbergia rigida (H.B.K.) Kunth   PURPLE MUHLY.   Fig. 150. Rocky mountain slopes, canyons, and alluvial valleys at medium to high elevations. El Paso Co., Franklin Mts. Presidio Co., Capote Mt., S slopes; 3 mi S Menzies Ranch house; Chinati Mts., upper Tigna Canyon; Elephant Mt., E slope. Jeff Davis Co., Davis Mts., Mt. Livermore, Pine Mt., Mt. Locke; trail to Tricky Gap; CDRI Landsite; Mitre Peak Girl Scout Camp; Musquiz Canyon; Kokernot Ranch, 18 mi N Alpine. Brewster Co., Kokernot Lodge, Alpine; Mt. Ord; Goat Mt.; Cathedral Mt.; Chisos Mts., Lost Mine Trail, Casa Grande, N branch Cattail Falls Canyon, Boot Spring, Laguna. 4,500–7,300 ft. Flowering Jun–Nov. In TX found only in the Trans-Pecos. W to AZ. Mex.

Purple muhly is characterized by its usually deep purple panicles. As pointed out by Gould (1975), the panicles may be rather contracted, 2–4 cm

Fig. 151. *Muhlenbergia dubia*. Plant; glumes
and floret.

wide, or somewhat open and to 9–10 cm wide. These panicle forms are evident at least in the Davis Mountains populations.

25. Muhlenbergia dubia Fourn. *ex* Hemsley   PINE MUHLY.   Fig. 151. [*Muhlenbergia acuminata* Vasey]. Rocky mountain slopes and canyons. Culberson Co., Guadalupe Mts., Guadalupe Peak, upper Pine Spring Canyon, Pine Top, top S McKittrick Canyon, lower Pipe Line Canyon, lodge in S McKittrick Canyon. Reeves Co., 24 mi E Balmorhea. Presidio Co., Solitario. Jeff Davis Co., Davis Mts., Mt. Livermore, upper Madera Canyon. Brewster Co., 10 mi NE Alpine; Glass Mts., Jail Canyon, Gilliland Peak; Cathedral Mt., N side; Cienega Mt. (limestone); Goat Mt.; Elephant Mt.; Chisos Mts., Lost Mine Trail, Chinese Wall. 3,900–8,000 ft. Flowering Jul–Dec. Also NM. N Mex.

Gould (1975) and Hitchcock (1951) recognized *M. dubia* as a species distinct from *M. metcalfei* that is confined in Texas to the Guadalupe Mountains. Correll and Johnston (1970) and Martin and Hutchins (1980) recognized *M. metcalfei* as synonymous with *M. dubia*. In summary of character differences, *M. dubia* has panicles usually greenish or gray, panicle branches to 2 cm long, panicles to 1 cm wide, glumes 2–3 mm long, and lemma awns 4 mm long (or rarely longer). *Muhlenbergia metcalfei* has panicles purplish, panicle branches

Fig. 152. *Muhlenbergia metcalfei.* Partial
panicle; glumes and floret.

Fig. 153. *Muhlenbergia tenuifolia.* Plant;
glumes and floret.

to 5 cm long, panicles to 2 cm wide, glumes 1.5–2 mm long, and lemma awns
(3–)5–10 mm long. Herein the species are treated as distinct, albeit tentatively
so, with *M. dubia* being recognized to occur in certain mountain systems south
of the Guadalupes, as far as the Chisos Mountains. Pine muhly should be a
good forage grass where abundant.

26. Muhlenbergia metcalfei M. E. Jones METCALFE MUHLY.
Fig. 152.   Mountain slopes and canyons. El Paso Co., Franklin Mts. Culber-
son Co., Guadalupe Mts., Guadalupe Peak; S McKittrick Canyon; McKittrick
Canyon; between Texline and Pine Springs. Brewster Co., Cathedral Mt.; Glass
Mts., Gilliland Peak. 4,000–7,000 ft. Flowering Aug–Nov. Also NM.

Plants matching the morphotypes (discussed above) named *M. dubia* and
M. metcalfei are indeed present in the Trans-Pecos, but it is difficult to defend
specific status for such close entities with sympatric distribution. Herein the
two species are recognized tentatively pending further studies.

27. Muhlenbergia tenuifolia (H.B.K) Kunth   MESA MUHLY.   Fig. 153.
[*Muhlenbergia monticola* Buckl.]. Mountain slopes and canyons. El Paso Co.,
Franklin Mts.; Hueco Mts. Culberson Co., Guadalupe Mts.; Sierra Diablo;

Fig. 154. *Muhlenbergia parviglumis*. Partial
panicle; floret and glumes.

Apache Mts. Presidio Co., Capote Mt.; Sierra Vieja; Chinati Mts.; Panther Can-
yon; Eagle Crag; Elephant Mt. Jeff Davis Co., Mt. Livermore and throughout
Davis Mts.; Musquiz Canyon. Brewster Co., Lizard Mt.; 3 mi W Alpine; Goat
Mt.; Cathedral Mt.; Elephant Mt.; Agua Fria Mt.; Packsaddle Mt.; Glass Mts.;
Chisos Mts.; Dead Horse Mts.; Black Gap Refuge, Brushy Canyon. Pecos Co.,
Sierra Madera; 20–45 mi S Fort Stockton. Terrell Co., 29 mi N Dryden. 1,500–
7,800 ft. Flowering (May) Jun–Nov. W portion Edwards Plateau. Also W to
NM and AZ. N Mex.

Mesa muhly is one of the most widespread and common muhlys in the
Trans-Pecos. Among its distinguishing traits are panicles contracted, narrow,
interrupted, glumes unequal and acute, lemmas 2.5–3.5 mm long, pubescent
with spreading hairs on the lower half, and with flexuous awns 10–20 mm
long. Some Trans-Pecos collections tentatively assigned to *M. tenuifolia* (Dorr
and Peterson, 1993) have less contracted, more open panicles and might prove
to be of a separate taxon. Mesa muhly should be an excellent forage grass.

28. Muhlenbergia parviglumis Vasey   LONGAWN MUHLY.   Fig. 154.
Mountain slopes and canyons. El Paso Co., Franklin Mts. Culberson Co., Guadalupe Mts., Bear Canyon, Smith Canyon, N McKittrick Canyon. Presidio Co.,

Chinati Mts., Tigna Canyon; Elephant Mt., SW slope. Jeff Davis Co., Fern Canyon, Mitre Peak Girl Scout Camp; Limpia Canyon, 12 mi below Fort Davis; Little Aguja Canyon; Mt. Livermore. Brewster Co., Twin Peaks; Glass Mts., Jail Canyon; Mt. Ord; Goat Mt.; Packsaddle Mt.; Chisos Mts., upper Green Gulch, trail to Lost Mine Peak. Terrell Co., 29 mi N Dryden. Val Verde Co., Goodenough Springs. (1,500) 2,600–8,000 ft. Flowering Jul–Nov. Elsewhere in TX, NM. N Mex. Cuba.

Longawn muhly is characterized by panicles contracted and dense but usually not interrupted, glumes usually obtuse, 0.5–1 mm long (the specific epithet means small glumes), lemmas evenly scabrous, 3–4 mm long, with appressed hairs on the base and awns only slightly flexuous and 20–40 mm long. Longawn muhly should be a good forage grass where abundant.

45. SPOROBOLUS R. Br. DROPSEED.

Perennials, of diverse habits, some large and coarse cespitose, or rhizomatous, or annuals. Leaves mostly basal, the linear blades flat, folded, or involute; ligule usually a ciliate or densely pilose membrane. Inflorescence a panicle, open or contracted, often partially or mostly enclosed in sheaths. Spikelets 1-flowered, in some species, the size variable in same panicle; disarticulation above the glumes, glumes 1-nerved, typically unequal, at least the first glume usually shorter than the lemma; lemmas 1-nerved, thin, awnless; paleas about as long as the lemma or slightly longer, perhaps splitting at maturity exposing the grain. Caryopses often laterally flattened, obovate, perhaps asymmetric, usually small and falling from the lemma and palea.

A large genus of about 160 species distributed in tropical and temperate regions of both hemispheres. About 23 species of *Sporobolus* occur in Texas. *Sporobolus* is distinguished from the related *Muhlenbergia* by its usually ciliate ligules, 1-nerved, thinner, awnless lemmas, and obovate, flattened grains with a free pericarp (fruit wall). The grain of *Sporobolus* is thus not a true caryopsis, because the seed coat is not adnate to the fruit wall, and the grain characteristically falls readily from the spikelet at maturity. The genus name is from Greek *spora*, seed, and *ballein*, to throw, in reference to the free seeds. Most of the dropseed species are palatable, and several species are abundant enough in the Trans-Pecos to be good forage grasses. Reportedly seeds of the Trans-Pecos species *S. cryptandrus* and *S. flexuosus* have been used as food by Indians. Several species of *Sporobolus*, including *S. asper*, in addition to those listed below, eventually might be found to occur in the Trans-Pecos area. In general the Trans-Pecos taxa of *Sporobolus* seem to be weakly delimited. I suspect that hybridization might occur between several species, including *S. cryptandrus, S. contractus*, and *S. flexuosus*.

Key to the Species

1. Plants annual   **1. *S. pulvinatus.***
1. Plants perennial.
   2. Pedicels of spikelets 5–20 mm or more long   **2. *S. texanus.***
   2. Pedicels of spikelets 4 mm or less long.
      3. Panicles spikelike, exposed portions usually 0.4–1.5 cm wide, to 2.5 cm wide.
         4. Mature panicle 0.4–0.7 cm wide; culms 45–110 cm long, 1.5–3.5 mm wide at base   **3. *S. contractus.***
         4. Mature panicle 0.8–2.5 cm wide; culms 100–200 cm long, 2–7 mm wide at base   **4. *S. giganteus.***
      3. Panicles open, exposed portions 3–30 cm wide.
         5. Mature panicles less than 10 cm wide.
            6. Lower panicle branches in whorls; mature panicles pyramidal   **5. *S. pyramidatus.***
            6. Lower panicle branches not in whorls; mature panicles ovate to somewhat pyramidal.
               7. Tufted perennial from a knotty base, culms 10–40 cm long; leaf blades 2–7 cm long, 1–1.5 mm wide, stiff, spreading, becoming involute; panicles 3–10 cm long when exposed, often mostly sheathed   **6. *S. nealleyi.***
               7. Cespitose perennial, culms 40–120 cm long; leaf blades mostly 9–25 cm long, 2–5 mm wide, not stiffly spreading, flat or drying involute; panicles 10–40 cm long   **7. *S. flexuosus.***
         5. Mature panicles more than 10 cm wide.
            8. Sheath collars with tufts of long white hairs **8. *S. cryptandrus.***
            8. Sheath collars glabrous or with a few pilose hairs at the corners.
               9. Panicle branchlets naked below, pedicels 0.5–2 mm long and spreading so that spikelets are not or only rarely touching or overlapping; leaf blades mostly involute   **9. *S. airoides.***
               9. Panicle branchlets densely flowered to the base, pedicels usually less than 0.5 mm long and appressed so that spikelets usually touch or overlap; leaf blades mostly flat   **10. *S. wrightii.***

1. Sporobolus pulvinatus Swallen   Fig. 155.   Rare in desert habitats, sand, gravel, loam, and clay. Reported from El Paso Co. Brewster Co., near Study Butte. 2,500–3,700 ft. Flowering Sep–Oct. Also S AZ.

Correll and Johnston (1970) referred the annual dropseeds from near El Paso to *Sporobolus patens* Swallen, but Johnston (1988; 1990) cited John Reeder in reporting that *S. patens* does not occur in Texas and that the Texas

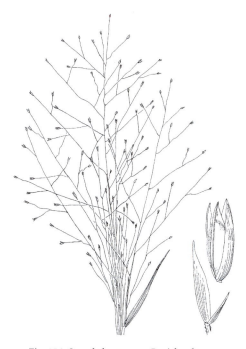

Fig. 155. *Sporobolus pulvinatus.* Panicle;   Fig. 156. *Sporobolus texanus.* Panicle; glumes
         glumes and floret.   and floret.

specimens alluded to by Correll and Johnston (1970) are actually *S. pulvinatus.* Gould (1975) also recognized the tufted annuals from El Paso County as *S. pulvinatus. Sporobolus patens* is reported to occur in southern Arizona (Hitchcock, 1951). The panicles of *S. pulvinatus* are ovate in outline and purplish in color, but with whorled lower branches as in *S. pyramidatus.*

   2. Sporobolus texanus Vasey.   TEXAS DROPSEED.   Fig. 156.   Occasionally frequent but otherwise scattered and uncommon. El Paso Co., along Rio Grande ca. 3 mi above El Paso. Presidio Co., near Screw Bean (Gould, 1975). Pecos Co., ca. 6 mi N Fort Stockton on road to Grandfalls. Ward Co., between Wink and Pyote. 2,600–4,000 ft. Flowering Jul–Nov. Also the plains country in TX. N to KS and CO, W to NM and AZ.

   Texas dropseed is either rare or poorly collected in the Trans-Pecos. The species is most easily recognized by its relatively long pedicels and open panicle which lends to this character the aspect of certain species of *Muhlenbergia* and *Panicum*, and *Digitaria cognata.* Texas dropseed has glabrous sheath collars, ligules less than 1 mm long, and spikelets 2.3–3.3 mm long.

   3. Sporobolus contractus Hitchc.   SPIKE DROPSEED.   Fig. 157.   Infrequent to locally common mostly in sandy soils but also limestone and igneous

Fig. 157. *Sporobolus contractus.* Panicle; glumes and floret. Fig. 158. *Sporobolus giganteus.* Panicle; glumes and floret.

alluvium in desert or semidesert habitats. El Paso Co., Franklin Mts.; 5 mi W Hueco; near El Paso. Hudspeth Co., 10 mi E Hueco; 4 mi W Sierra Blanca; 5–9 mi N Sierra Blanca; 10 mi SE Sierra Blanca. Culberson Co., foothills of Guadalupe Mts.; sand dunes E of Van Horn. Presidio Co., above Capote Falls, Sierra Vieja; Marfa. Jeff Davis Co., 5 mi E Chispa; 2 mi S Kent. Brewster Co., N slope Elephant Mt.; 56 mi S Alpine; lower slopes Nine Point Mesa; Cedar Springs, Christmas Mts.; Study Butte; Tornillo Flats, Big Bend Natl. Park. Ward Co., 6 mi N Monahans. 3,000–4,600 ft. Flowering Jun–Dec. Also TX plains country. N to CO, W to SE CA. Adventive in ME. Sonora, Mex.

Burgess and Northington (1981) reported hybridization between *Sporobolus contractus* and *S. flexuosus* in the sandy areas west of the Guadalupe Mountains, and remark that such hybrids key to *S. cryptandrus.* Spike dropseed can be distinguished from *S. cryptandrus* by its narrow spikelike panicle that may extend to 50 cm long. Spike dropseed probably is good forage where plants are abundant.

4. Sporobolus giganteus Nash   GIANT DROPSEED.   Fig. 158.   Infrequent to frequent in deep sand, occasionally in gypsum. El Paso Co., lower valley W of Clint; 6–7 mi NE El Paso. Culberson Co., loose gypsum dunes. Winkler Co., 3–26 mi E Kermit; 5 mi N Kermit. Ward Co., 3–4 mi E Mona-

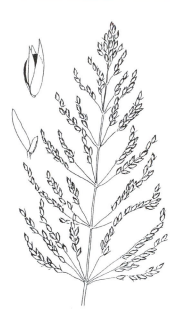

Fig. 159. *Sporobolus pyramidatus.* Panicle;
glumes and floret.

hans; 9 mi NE Monahans. Crane Co., 5–8 mi N Imperial. 2,500–3,800 ft. Flowering Jun–Nov. Also TX High Plains. N to OK, CO; W to AZ.

Giant dropseed is distinguished from spike dropseed by its larger culms. Both species have tufted sheath collars. Giant dropseed is an excellent binder of sandy soils and is excellent forage where abundant.

5. Sporobolus pyramidatus (Lam.) Hitchc.   WHORLED DROPSEED. Fig. 159.   Mostly in desert clay soils, frequently saline or gypseous, but also in other soil types, usually disturbed conditions. Brewster Co., golf course creek bottom; near Agua Fria Spring; Terlingua; 1 mi S Hen Egg Mt.; 7 mi N Study Butte; in and near Study Butte; Big Bend Natl. Park, 2 mi W Santa Elena Canyon, between Todd Hill and Burro Mesa, Glenn Spring, Tornillo Flats, Boquillas Canyon, Chisos Pens. Val Verde Co., Comstock. 1,800–4,400 ft. Flowering Apr–Oct. Throughout most of TX except the Pineywoods. Also N to KS and CO, E to LA and S FL, W to AZ. Throughout tropical America.

The smallish, yellow-green, pyramidal panicles and whorled lower panicle branches allow identification of whorled dropseed. In the Brewster County population at least, plants of this species often appear to be annual. Correll and Johnston (1970) recognized *Sporobolus pulvinatus* Swallen as a synonym of *S. pyramidatus*, while Gould (1975) considered *S. pulvinatus* to be a distinct annual species occurring in Texas only on sand and gravel slopes near El Paso.

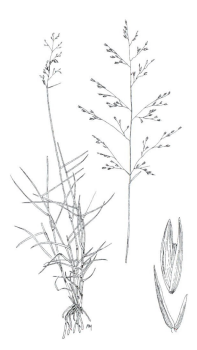

Fig. 160. *Sporobolus nealleyi.* Plant; panicle;
glumes and floret.

6. Sporobolus nealleyi Vasey GYPGRASS. Fig. 160. Seemingly restricted to gypsum habitats where it is a dominant species at least in some
gypsum substrates of northern Culberson Co. Hudspeth Co., SE of Malone
Mts. Culberson Co., 35 mi N Van Horn; 25 mi NW Kent; Delaware Creek
between Texline and Orla; 2 mi S Texline. Reeves Co., 7 mi SE Pecos, mouth
of Toyah Lake; 10 mi S Pecos. Pecos Co., hill above Comanche Springs, Fort
Stockton. Ward Co., 5 mi N Monahans. Crane Co., 5–8 and 15–20 mi N
Imperial; 3–16 mi W Crane. 2,500–4,300 ft. Flowering May–Nov. Also W to
NM, AZ, and NV. Mex. S to San Luis Potosí.

Gypgrass has culms 10–30(–40) cm long with the base having been described as a cluster of knotty rhizomes. Gypgrass is one of the most easily
distinguished dropseeds because of its restriction to gypsum habitats and its
short, stiff, involute leaf blades that spread at right angles to the culms. The
small panicles (3–10 cm long) of this species are often mostly enclosed in
sheaths. In the field I have observed whole culms disarticulating near the base,
resulting in culms and panicles tumbling away with the wind, suggesting a
mechanism of seed dispersal similar to that ascribed to *Schedonnardus paniculatus* and some other grasses. Gypgrass probably is good forage in its limited
habitats.

Fig. 161. *Sporobolus flexuosus.* Plant; glumes
and floret.

7. Sporobolus flexuosus (Thurb.) Rydb.   MESA DROPSEED.   Fig. 161.
Mostly sandy soils but also in various alluvial substrates. El Paso Co., 6 mi NE
El Paso; 2 mi W El Paso; 2 mi W Tornillo; 2 mi NE Ysleta; between Ysleta and
Hueco; Hueco Mts.; S of Hueco Tanks; 5 mi W Hueco. Hudspeth Co., 6 mi W
Fort Hancock; 9 mi E Sierra Blanca; 4 and 32 mi W Sierra Blanca. Culberson
Co., foothills Guadalupe Mts., quartz sand; 10 mi E Van Horn; 10 and 21 mi
W Kent. Presidio Co., along Rio Grande below Candelaria; Capote Falls; 6 mi
below Redford; Marfa, old Fort D. A. Russell. Jeff Davis Co., Point of Rocks;
stream in Fort Davis. Brewster Co., Study Butte; Big Bend Natl. Park, near
Castolon, River Road, between Castolon and Smokey Creek, Tornillo Flats,
between San Vicente and Lindsey Mine, between Santa Elena Canyon and Cas-
tolon, between Todd Hill and Burro Mesa, Dominguez Spring of Sierra Quemada, Dead Horse Mts., head of Boquillas Canyon; Black Gap Refuge, Maravillas Creek, Sheep Pasture, along Rio Grande. Reeves Co., 23 mi NW Pecos.
Terrell Co., mouth of San Francisco Canyon. Loving Co., between Wink and
Mentone; 4 mi NE Red Bluff dam; 18 mi W Kermit. Ward Co., Winkler Co.,
Crane Co. 2,200–5,100 ft. Flowering May–Nov. Also TX High Plains and W
Edwards Plateau. W to S UT, S CA. N Mex.

Sporobolus flexuosus has the general habit of *S. cryptandrus* and *S. airoides*
except that in *S. flexuosus* the main panicle branches are deflexed or arcuately
reflexed with spikelets on pedicels ca. 1 mm long with spikelets not appressed

Fig. 162. *Sporobolus cryptandrus.* Plant; glumes
and floret.

to the branchlets, and panicles that are only about three times as long as broad.
Mesa dropseed is abundant enough especially in sandy areas that it is probably
an important forage grass.

8. Sporobolus cryptandrus (Torr.) A. Gray   SAND DROPSEED.   Fig.
162.   Widespread and common in various soil types and habitats, including
the mountains. El Paso Co., Franklin Mts.; 6 mi N Fabens; 15 mi N Ysleta; 3 mi
E Fabens; W of Clint; 30 mi E El Paso. Hudspeth Co., 5 mi E Hueco; 4 mi E
Fort Hancock; 9 mi E Sierra Blanca; 30 mi N Sierra Blanca; Beach Mts.; Sierra
Diablo, Victorio Canyon. Culberson Co., lower slopes Guadalupe Mts.; be-
tween Delaware Creek and Orla; 6 mi W Kent; Apache Mts. Presidio Co., Sierra
Vieja, Vieja Pass; Capote Falls; Bandera Mesa; Solitario. Jeff Davis Co., 5 mi E
Chispa; Lower Madera Canyon; Davis Mts. State Park; Mitre Peak Girl Scout
Camp; Haystack Mt. Brewster Co., vicinity of Alpine south to Big Bend Natl.
Park and Black Gap, mountain systems, basins, and canyons. Reeves Co., 25 mi
NW Pecos; 15 mi N Saragosa. Pecos Co., 3 mi N Fort Stockton; Comanche
Springs; 13 mi E Fort Stockton; 6 mi S Sheffield; 30 mi E Fort Stockton; 20 mi
W Sanderson; 20–35 mi S Fort Stockton. Terrell Co., mouth of San Francisco
Canyon; upper Big Canyon, 30 mi N Sanderson. Val Verde Co., Mile Canyon,
Langtry. 1,300–6,500 ft. Flowering May–Nov. Throughout TX except for the

Fig. 163. *Sporobolus airoides*. Plant; spikelet
and floret.

Pineywoods. Throughout most of the United States, except the southeast, N to
Canada. Also Mex.

Sand dropseed is the most widespread dropseed in the Trans-Pecos, and it
is one of the most common roadside perennial grasses in Texas. Reportedly
this species provides fair grazing for livestock and poor forage for wildlife, but
it still ranks as an important forage grass because of its abundance. Sand dropseed is commonly found in sandy habitats, but in the Trans-Pecos other dropseed species are actually more characteristic of sandy soils, while *S. cryptandrus*
is found on a wide range of soil types. *Sporobolus cryptandrus* is distinguished
by its spreading, straight main panicle branches with spikelets on short pedicels
and appressed to the branchlets. The panicles are 15–30 (–40) cm long.

9. Sporobolus airoides (Torr.) Torr. ALKALI SACATON. Fig. 163.
Low slopes, flats, and basins, in sand, gravel, or clay, particularly in saline or
alkaline habitats. El Paso Co., lower valley W of Clint; 6 mi N El Paso; Franklin
Mts.; 7 mi W El Paso. Hudspeth Co., Salt Flats. Culberson Co., Guadalupe Mts.
foothills, creosote flats, and salt basin; 6 mi W Kent; between Texline and Orla.
Presidio Co., 6 mi N Candelaria; alkali flats, Jones Ranch, S Davis Mts. Brew-
ster Co., Glass Mts.; Packsaddle Mt.; 20 mi NE Alpine; W slopes Mt. Ord; Iron
Mt.; vicinity of Alpine; between Alpine and Fort Davis; 10 mi N Terlingua;

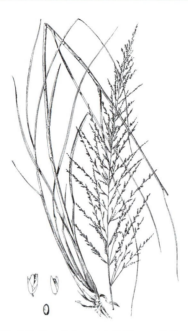

Fig. 164. *Sporobolus wrightii*. Plant; spikelets
and caryopsis.

Study Butte; Big Bend Natl. Park. Reeves Co., 9 mi E Pecos; 10 mi S Pecos. Pecos Co., 5–6 mi N Fort Stockton. Terrell Co., margin of Chandler Lake. Ward Co., alkaline flat near Pecos River. 2,500–4,400 ft. Flowering May–Nov. Plains country and Edwards Plateau in TX. N to NE, MO, and SD, W to WA and CA. Mex. S to San Luis Potosí.

Alkali sacaton is rated as having fair grazing value for livestock and poor value for wildlife, but it is still regarded as a good forage grass in alkaline areas where this large grass is likely to predominate. *Sporobolus airoides* is weakly distinguished from the related *S. wrightii* by its panicle branches naked on the lower parts and spikelets separated on short pedicels so that they are not or only rarely touching in a panicle that is less crowded than in *S. wrightii*.

10. Sporobolus wrightii Scribn. BIG ALKALI SACATON. Fig. 164. [*Sporobolus airoides* (Torr.) Torr. var. *wrightii* (Munro *ex* Scribn.) Gould]. Sandy, gravel, clay, or gypseous, saline or alkaline habitats, particularly on the margins of salt flats or basins and in large washes. Hudspeth Co., 5 mi W Van Horn, Beach Mts. Culberson Co., Guadalupe Mts., foothills, lower elev. streambeds. Presidio Co., above Capote Falls; Jones Ranch, S Davis Mts.; 1 mi NE Solitario Peak. Jeff Davis Co., Rockpile, Davis Mts.; Musquiz Creek, 12 mi N Alpine; Haystack Mt.; Fern Canyon. Brewster Co., Glass Mts.; Mt. Ord; Alpine; Goat Mt.; Elephant Mt.; Green Valley; Neville Ranch; Nine Point Mesa;

Packsaddle Mt.; Cottonwood Canyon; between Todd Hill and Burro Mesa; Boquillas. Reeves Co., 10 mi S Pecos; 10 mi E Balmorhea. Pecos Co., 5 mi N Fort Stockton; 30 mi E Fort Stockton; Grandfalls. Terrell Co., along Pecos River 2 mi above White Ranch house. Ward Co., 3 mi W Pyote. Crane Co., 13 mi N Imperial. 1,500–6,200 ft. Flowering May–Dec. South Texas Plains and Edwards Plateau. N to OK, W to CA. N Mex.

Big alkali sacaton is distinguished from alkali sacaton by its panicle branchlets densely flowered at the base and spikelets appressed and mostly touching or overlapping. The whole plants and panicles of *Sporobolus wrightii* are perhaps larger than are those of *S. airoides*. Big alkali sacaton is only a fair forage grass, but it is of greater value in areas where it is abundant and dominant.

46. BLEPHARONEURON   Nash   PINE DROPSEED.

A North American genus of two species. One species occurs in Texas and the other species is an annual from Chihuahua and Durango, Mexico (Peterson and Annable, 1990). The genus name is from Greek *blepharis*, eyelash, and *neuron*, nerve, referring to the densely short-pubescent nerves of the lemma.

1. **Blepharoneuron tricholepis** (Torr.) Nash PINE DROPSEED. Fig. 165. Perennial, tufted. Culms 20–60 cm long, nodes glabrous. Leaves mostly basal; sheaths rounded, glabrous; ligule membranous, ciliate, 0.3–2.0 mm long; blades glabrous or scabrous, filiform, involute, arcuate, 3–15 cm long, ca. 2 mm wide. Inflorescence a panicle, 5–17 cm long, usually loosely contracted and 1–3 cm wide, to somewhat open and to ca. 9 cm wide. Spikelets 1-flowered, 2.5–3.7 mm long, (the glumes) dark green to lead colored, borne on slender pedicels and branchlets; disarticulation above the glumes; glumes glabrous, back rounded, apex obtuse to broadly acute and perhaps minutely apiculate, the first glume weakly 5-nerved, about as long as the second, the second glume weakly 3-nerved, about as long or barely longer than the lemma; lemma awnless, 2.0–3.8 mm long, grayish-green, perhaps purple-tinged, 3-nerved, the nerves densely white-puberulent to above the middle or higher, the apex rounded, perhaps apiculate; palea as long or slightly longer than lemma, with a single band of dense, short hairs like those on nerves of the lemma. Caryopsis 1.2–1.4 mm long, light brownish, fusiform to elliptic, with a dorsal ridge.

Relatively common on medium to mostly upper elevations on slopes in pine woodland, on and near the three highest peaks of the Trans-Pecos. Culberson Co., Guadalupe Mts., Pine Top Mt., Bowl, upper South McKittrick Canyon. Jeff Davis Co., Mt. Livermore, upper slopes and near the peak, upper Madrone Canyon. Brewster Co., Chisos Mts., Boot Spring Canyon, Chinese Wall, upper Pinnacles Trail, Mt. Emory, Pine Canyon, upper Cattail Canyon, Wade Canyon. 5,400–8,000 ft. Flowering Jun–Oct. NW to NM, CO, AZ, UT. N Mex. S to Puebla and Tamaulipas, and in Baja CA (Peterson and Annable, 1990).

Fig. 165. *Blepharoneuron tricholepis*. Plant;
glumes and floret.

Blepharoneuron tricholepis is also known as hairy dropseed. Young plants are reported to be highly palatable to all classes of livestock.

Tribe 11. Chlorideae

Clayton and Renvoize (1986) recognized this tribe as Cynodonteae, with 59 genera and about 300 species. The distribution of the tribe is mostly tropical, extending into temperate North America. The Chlorideae are closely related to the Eragrosteae. Gould (1975) recognized 10 genera of Chlorideae in Texas, with nine of these genera being represented in the Trans-Pecos.

Key to the Genera of Chlorideae

1. Lemma of fertile floret 3-awned, or with 3 triangular lobes, with or without short other lobes; inflorescence of 1 – several spicate branches.
    2. Inflorescence branches reduced to a cluster of 3 spikelets (the upper one a perfect floret, the lower 2 with staminate or sterile florets)
        52. Cathestecum, p. 220

2. Inflorescence branches of more than 3 spikelets (fewer in some *Bouteloua*, but then not in dimorphic clusters).

    3. Inflorescence bisexual (disarticulation at base of spicate branch, or above the glumes)   **51. *Bouteloua*, p. 206**

    3. Inflorescence unisexual (the staminate of 1–4 spicate branches and elevated above the leaves, the pistillate in burlike clusters among the leaves)   **53. *Buchlöe*, p. 222**

1. Lemma of fertile floret with or without a single awn and the lemma entire to bilobed, or 3-awned with either the spicate branches subdigitate or the lemma deeply 2-lobed.

    4. Spikelike branches of inflorescence deciduous, or spikelets falling entire.

        5. Spikelets 2–several-flowered (with 1 perfect floret and 1–3 staminate or sterile florets above)   **51. *Bouteloua*, p. 206**

        5. Spikelets 1-flowered.

            6. Inflorescence of few to several spicate branches with closely placed, sessile spikelets (spikelets 1-flowered)   **54. *Spartina*, p. 223**

            6. Inflorescence a slender dense spike, the spikelets in 3's at each node (spikelets dissimilar, 2 lateral ones 2-flowered, staminate, the central one 1-flowered, perfect)   **55. *Hilaria*, p. 225**

    4. Spikelike branches of inflorescence persistent; spikelets breaking apart at maturity.

        7. Lemma concealed by both glumes closed around the floret (margins of lemma densely ciliate with hairs ca. 1 mm long)
                                                48. *Microchloa*, p. 198

        7. Lemma exposed by one or both glumes shorter than florets, or if longer then glumes divergent.

            8. Lemma conspicuously awned; spikelets 2–several-flowered (1–2 perfect, 2–3 reduced)   **50. *Chloris*, p. 200**

            8. Lemma not awned, or with a minute awn; spikelets 1-flowered.

                9. Spicate branches of inflorescence scattered along the axis
                                    47. *Schedonnardus*, p. 196

                9. Spicate branches of inflorescence digitate **49. *Cynodon*, p. 199**

47. SCHEDONNARDUS Steud. TUMBLEGRASS.

A monotypic genus distributed from Canada through the central United States and into Mexico, and also in Argentina. The genus name is taken from Greek *schedon*, near, and *Nardus*, a grass genus. The common name is derived from the tendency of disarticulated whole panicles to tumble before the wind as with a tumbleweed.

    1. Schedonnardus   paniculatus (Nutt.) Trel. TUMBLEGRASS. Fig. 166. Perennial, low and tufted. Culms 8–40 cm long, curving-erect or

Fig. 166. *Schedonnardus paniculatus*. Plant;
spikelet and floret.

decumbent and spreading basally. Leaves glabrous; sheaths compressed laterally and keeled, the hyaline margins broad; ligule usually 1–3 mm long, the
continuation of hyaline sheath margins; blades 2–12 cm long, 0.5–3 mm wide,
margins scabrous, usually folded and twisted at maturity. Inflorescence a panicle, the main axis usually curved and extending above the leafy culms, the axis
with a few widely spaced branches, these spicate and 2–15 cm long. Spikelets
sessile, 3–4 mm long, slender, appressed to the channeled branchlets and tip
of panicle axis, the spikelets usually spaced apart, not at all overlapping; disarticulation above the glumes and at panicle base; glumes 1-nerved, usually nar-
row-lanceolate and acuminate, the first glume shorter than lemma, the second
glume about equal to lemma; lemmas 3-nerved, glabrous or scabrous, slender,
stiff-acute or minutely awned; paleas glabrous, about equaling lemma. Caryopsis slender, mostly terete, 2.5–3.5 mm long.

Infrequent to common, mountain slopes and grassland basins. Hudspeth
Co., Sierra Diablo, head of Victorio Canyon. Culberson Co., Guadalupe Mts.,
Indian Meadow NE of Upper Dog Canyon ranger station (Burgess and Nor-
thington, 1981). Presidio Co., 20 mi W Marfa; 9 mi E Marfa. Jeff Davis Co.,
Scenic Loop above Fort Davis; Mt. Locke, near observatory. Brewster Co., 6 mi
N Alpine; 9–11 mi S Alpine. Pecos Co., 20 mi S Fort Stockton; 30 mi E Fort

Fig. 167. *Microchloa kunthii*. Plant; glumes
and floret.

Stockton. Ward Co., 5 mi NW Monahans. Crane Co. 3,000–6,500 ft. Flowering May–Oct. Throughout most of TX. Canada south through the central United States, probably into Mex. Reported from Argentina.

Tumblegrass is usually considered to be poor forage because typically not much herbage is produced from the short-tufted grass. *Schedonnardus* probably is more common in the Trans-Pecos than the few localities (above) would suggest. Certainly it forms locally dense patches in the hills and basins near Alpine.

48. MICROCHLOA   R. Br.

A genus of perhaps six species of mostly tropical Old and New World distribution. The genus name is from Greek *micros*, small, and *chloa*, grass.

1. Microchloa kunthii Desv.   Fig. 167.   Perennial, low, tufted. Culms 10–30 cm long, slender, erect. Leaves with sheaths, except lowermost, much shorter than internodes and minutely scabrous; ligule 1–1.5 mm long, ciliate; blades 1–6 cm long, 1–1.5 cm wide, usually folded, firm, with thick margins, these scabrous. Inflorescence a spike, 6–15 cm long, sickle-shaped, the rachis ciliate, the spikelets appressed, closely spaced, and overlapping about halfway. Spikelets awnless, 2.5–3.5 mm long; glumes 1-nerved, acute, subequal, longer than the lemma; lemma 1.8–2.5 mm long, wedge-shaped, 3-nerved, midnerve pilose, margins ciliate with hairs to 1 mm long; palea slightly shorter than lemma. Caryopsis fusiform, ca. 1.2 mm long.

Not previously reported for Texas. One collection known for Trans-Pecos Texas, Jeff Davis Co., igneous soil, above pool at head of Fern Canyon, Mitre Peak Girl Scout Camp. *E. Keough 255*, 30 Sep 1964. Reported from Huachuca Mts., AZ. Also Mex. and Guatemala.

The single collection of *Microchloa kunthii* was discovered among Sul Ross specimens of *Schedonnardus paniculatus*, to which the former taxon bears strong resemblance. The small size and local distribution of *M. kunthii* suggests that it has very limited forage value.

49. CYNODON   Pers.

A genus of about 10 species in warm regions of the Old World, with one species, bermudagrass, widely distributed in all warm regions of the world. The genus name is from *kuon*, dog, and *odous*, tooth, in reference to the "toothlike" scales of the rhizome.

1. Cynodon dactylon (L.) Pers.   BERMUDAGRASS.   Fig. 168.   Perennial, low, mat-forming, with stolons and stout, creeping rhizomes. Culms 10–40 cm long, mostly weak and stoloniferous with only flowering stems erect. Leaves with rounded, glabrous sheaths except for tufts of hair at the ligule margins; ligule membranous, ciliate, 0.2–0.5 mm long; blades glabrous, flat or folded, 3–12 cm long, 1–4 mm wide. Inflorescence a panicle, of usually (2–) 3–5(–7) spicate branches arising from the culm apex (digitate), the branches 2–6 cm long, with spikelets closely imbricated in 2 rows all along the flattened or triangular, narrow rachis. Spikelets awnless, with 1 perfect floret, the rachilla extending beyond the palea and perhaps bearing a rudimentary floret; glumes 1-nerved, nearly equal, lanceolate, shorter than lemma by one-third; lemmas usually 2–2.5 mm long, awnless, firm, shiny, 3-nerved, laterally compressed, keeled, midnerve minutely pubescent or scabrous; palea somewhat shorter than lemma. Caryopsis ovate-oblong, flattened.

Throughout the Trans-Pecos, grown as a lawn grass, common in vacant lots and along roads, also a weed in ditches, along streams, in pastures, in low areas and near marshes. Flowering May–Nov. Widespread and common in the S United States, extending NE and to Canada, less common or absent in NE, WI, MT, WA. Native to warm regions in Africa, now widespread throughout the world in warm regions.

Bermudagrass is one of the most important forage grasses in the United States. It is excellent for livestock and good to poor for wildlife. In the Trans-

Fig. 168. *Cynodon dactylon*. Plant; spikelet and
floret (two views).

Pecos it is often abundant enough to be useful forage. Bermudagrass is often
cultivated as a pasture grass in Texas and elsewhere.

50. CHLORIS   Swartz   FINGERGRASS.

Perennials, cespitose, rhizomatous, or stoloniferous, or annuals. Culms
erect. Leaves with sheaths rounded to flattened; ligule absent or a ciliate fringe.
Inflorescence a panicle of few to several one-sided spicate branches, these arranged at the apex (digitate) or near apex of the culm. Spikelets with 1 perfect
floret (rarely 2) and 2–3 reduced florets, the spikelets imbricate or spaced
apart on the rachis, usually pale in color, perhaps brown; disarticulation above
glumes; glumes lanceolate, glabrous with scabrous nerves, usually unequal,
shorter than lemma, apex acute or acuminate; lemma of lower (perfect) floret
3-nerved, lanceolate, awned from apex or between 2 teeth, margins pubescent,
internerves glabrous to scabrous, nerves usually scabrous; reduced florets perhaps 2–3 in number, in appearance either cylindrical, inflated-obovoid, or rudimentary, the apex acute to truncate, awned or awnless. Caryopses brown,
ovoid to three-angled. [Includes *Trichloris* Fourn.].

A genus of 56 species (Anderson, 1974) distributed in tropical, subtropical,
and warm temperate regions of both hemispheres. Fifteen species occur in

Texas. The genus is named for Greek *Chloris*, the goddess of flowers. Several species of *Chloris* provide good forage for livestock. *Chloris gayana* Kunth (rhodesgrass) is an important cultivated grass in the southwestern United States, including South Texas and the Gulf Coast where it also is common at roadside. Rhodesgrass probably is native to Africa. *Chloris subdolichostachya* Muller (shortspike windmillgrass) occurs on the Edwards Plateau and in Val Verde Co. about 10 mi N of Del Rio and eventually may be found in the Trans-Pecos, although Gould (1975) pointed out that this taxon appeared to be of hybrid origin and is in need of additional study.

Key to the Species

1. Plants annual, variable in size from ca. 10 cm to 1 m or more tall, usually tufted and robust; panicle branches 4–20, borne at the apex (digitate), mostly erect; lemma of lower (perfect) floret swollen and with upper margins long-ciliate (to 2 mm long), with an awn 0.5–1.5 cm long
   1. *C. virgata*.
1. Plants perennial, slender and few-stemmed to tufted and robust to 1 m tall; panicle, lemma, and awn characters different.
   2. Plants tufted, robust, to 1 m tall; panicle branches mostly erect; lemma of lower floret with 3 awns.
      3. Lateral awns of lower lemma usually 7–10 mm long, central awn 8–15 mm long **2. *C. crinita*.**
      3. Lateral awns of lower lemma usually 0.5–2 mm long, central awn 8–12 mm long **3. *C. pluriflora*.**
   2. Plants weakly tufted, 15–70 cm tall; panicle branches at right angles to verticil axis, with some branches erect; lemma of lower floret with 1 awn or awnless.
      4. Lower (perfect) lemma and sterile lemma awnless or with a very short awn **4. *C. submutica*.**
      4. Lower lemma and sterile lemma awned.
         5. Panicle branches usually in several whorls along an upper axis 2 cm or more long; lower (perfect) lemma 2–3.5 mm long, with an awn 4.5–9 mm long **5. *C. verticillata*.**
         5. Panicle branches in several whorls, these crowded near the apex of panicle axis; lower lemma 1.5–2 mm long, with an awn 0.3–1.5 mm long **6. *C. cucullata*.**

1. Chloris virgata Sw. SHOWY CHLORIS. Fig. 169. Various disturbed sites particularly at roadside, throughout most of the Trans-Pecos. 2,000–5,500 ft. Flowering May–Nov. Throughout TX as a roadside and disturbed-site weed. Also distributed worldwide in warm regions.

Showy chloris, also known commonly as feather fingergrass, is very abun-

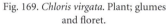

Fig. 169. *Chloris virgata*. Plant; glumes and floret.

Fig. 170. (A) *Chloris crinita*; plant; glumes and florets. (B) *Chloris pluriflora*; glumes and florets.

dant in the Trans-Pecos depending upon rainfall patterns. The plants usually are 30–70 cm high, but may become robust and exceed 1 m high under good moisture conditions. Showy chloris is palatable to livestock and might be developed as rangeland forage.

2. Chloris crinita Lag. FALSE RHODESGRASS. Fig. 170. [*Trichloris crinita* (Lag.) Parodi]. Usually in clay and alkaline soils of desert and semidesert habitats in depressions, basins, or near watercourses. El Paso Co., along canals W of Clint. Presidio Co., Capote Falls; 6 mi N Candelaria; between Ruidosa and Presidio; 30 mi S Marfa. Brewster Co., Packsaddle Mt.; 10–15 mi N Terlingua; Big Bend Natl. Park, Sam Nail Ranch E of Burro Mesa; Wilson Ranch; W of Castolon toward Santa Elena Canyon. Reeves Co., near Pecos; 5 mi S Pecos; mouth of Toyah Lake, 7 mi SE Pecos; Toyahvale. Pecos Co., Comanche Springs, Fort Stockton; near Imperial, near Pecos River; 13 mi E Fort Stockton, University Mesa; 30 mi E Fort Stockton. Val Verde Co., W side Pecos River Canyon. 1,200–4,000 ft. Flowering May–Nov. Uncommon in Edwards Plateau region and rare elsewhere in TX. W to NM and AZ. Coahuila, Chihuahua, and Durango, Mex. Also South America.

False rhodesgrass is the largest *Chloris* (with *C. pluriflora*) and one of the largest grasses (excluding river cane) in the Trans-Pecos. At maturity the whit-

Fig. 171. *Chloris submutica.* Plant; spikelet.

ish panicles are very showy on glistening culms to more than 1 m high. *Chloris crinita* has not been much collected in the Trans-Pecos, but I have observed the plants to be somewhat more common in heavy clay and alkaline soils than previous collections would suggest. False rhodesgrass probably is palatable in young stages but becomes coarse at maturity. Correll and Johnston (1970) treated *Trichloris* as a distinct genus, while the present work follows Gould (1975).

3. Chloris pluriflora (Fourn.) Clayton   MULTIFLOWERED FALSE RHODESGRASS.   Fig. 170.   [*Trichloris pluriflora* Fourn.]. Rare in the Trans-Pecos, although frequent at only known collection site. Terrell Co., deep wash sand at mouth of San Francisco Canyon. 2,000–2,100 ft. Flowering Jun–Oct. Gulf Coast and Prairies to South Texas Plains. Mex. Central and South America.

Chloris pluriflora is abundant in south Texas and elsewhere. This species is rated as good to excellent grazing for cattle. *Chloris pluriflora* resembles *C. crinita*, but is usually somewhat taller, to 1.5 m high, and is easily distinguished by the much shorter lateral awns on the lower lemmas.

4. Chloris submutica H.B.K.   Fig. 171.   Of restricted occurrence, alluvial bottomlands near watercourses and disturbed roadsides. Jeff Davis Co., near McGuire Ranch ruins, meadow alluvium near Limpia Creek, Davis Mts. Re-

Fig. 172. *Chloris verticillata*. Partial panicle; florets.

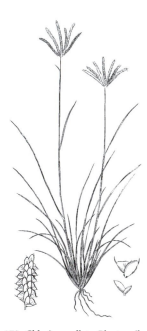

Fig. 173. *Chloris cucullata*. Plant; spikelets on
panicle branch (lower left); glumes and florets.

sort; city limits Fort Davis; S edge Fort Davis; 0.5 mi S Fort Davis. 5,000–5,600 ft. Flowering Jul–Oct. In TX known only in the Trans-Pecos. Extensively collected in Mex. Also Guatemala; Venezuela, Colombia, South America. Also known from Doña Ana Co., NM (Hitchcock, 1951; Anderson, 1974).

According to specimens in the Sul Ross Herbarium, *Chloris submutica* was first collected in Texas by Barton H. Warnock in 1955 from just south of Fort Davis. In 1979 R. D. Worthington discovered the species in the Davis Mountains Resort area and had the identity of the specimen verified by D. E. Anderson, who published a taxonomic study of *Chloris* in 1974. I have observed *Chloris submutica* to be abundant in the localities cited above, but not known to occur elsewhere in the Trans-Pecos. *Chloris submutica* somewhat resembles *C. verticillata* in habit, except that the plants of *C. submutica* seem to be taller and the panicle branches are a little shorter and more congested near the culm apex. *Chloris submutica* may be a recent introduction to the Davis Mountains area.

5. Chloris verticillata Nutt. WINDMILLGRASS. Fig. 172. Usually gravel, loam, or sandy soils, usually disturbed sites especially at roadside. Culberson Co., El Paso–Carlsbad Hwy, highest point above Guadalupe Pass. Presidio Co., 4 mi SW Valentine. Jeff Davis Co., Point of Rocks; Davis Mts. State Park; Mitre Peak Girl Scout Camp. Brewster Co., 8 mi N Alpine; 20 mi NE Alpine. Reeves Co., 10 mi S Pecos. Pecos Co., 3 mi N Fort Stockton; city limits of Fort Stockton. Val Verde Co., 20 mi N Del Rio. 2,500–5,100 ft. Flowering Apr–Sep. Also plains country, Edwards Plateau, and Cross Timbers and Prairies in TX. N to CO, NE, IA, W to NM and AZ.

Chloris verticillata is reported to hybridize extensively with *C. cucullata* (Correll and Johnston, 1970; Anderson, 1974; Gould, 1975) wherever the two species occur together. In the Trans-Pecos these species overlap in general distribution, but they are not often seen growing together and possibly do not hybridize as extensively as is reported elsewhere in Texas. Windmillgrass provides only fair to poor grazing for livestock and wildlife.

6. Chloris cucullata Bisch. HOODED WINDMILLGRASS. Fig. 173. Occasional to locally common particularly at roadside and in other disturbed habitats. Hudspeth Co., 5 mi E Sierra Blanca. Culberson Co., lower South McKittrick Canyon; North McKittrick Canyon. Brewster Co., Black Gap Refuge; just E of Tesnus; 5 mi S Marathon. Reeves Co., 25 mi NW Pecos; 1 mi S Pecos. Pecos Co., 30 mi E Fort Stockton; 3 mi N Fort Stockton. Terrell Co., 20 mi E Dryden; 6 mi E Sanderson; along Pecos River. 1,500–6,000 ft. Flowering May–Sep. Plains country, Edwards Plateau, South Texas Plains, and Gulf Prairies in TX. W to NM. Nuevo Leon and Tamaulipas, Mex.

Hooded windmillgrass is fair grazing for livestock and wildlife. *Chloris cucullata* hybridizes with *C. verticillata* and other species of *Chloris* (Anderson, 1974).

51. BOUTELOUA   Lag.   GRAMA.

Perennials and annuals, mostly tufted, some with stolons or rhizomes. Culms stiffly erect to weak and decumbent. Leaves mostly basal; ligule usually a ring of hairs; blades usually narrow, flat or folded. Inflorescence a panicle, of 1–numerous branches from a main axis, the branches short, spicate, closely or distantly spaced. Spikelets sessile, arranged in 2 rows along margins of a flattened or angular rachis (spicate branch), the spikelets 1–numerous; spikelets with 1 perfect floret and 1–3 staminate or sterile florets above; disarticulation at base of branch rachis, or above glumes; glumes 1-nerved, lanceolate, awnless or short-awned, nearly equal to unequal; lemmas 3-nerved, the midnerve often prolonged into an awn, the lateral nerves perhaps short-awned; paleas membranous, the 2 nerves awn-tipped in some. Caryopses 2–7 times as long as broad.

A genus of about 40 species mostly North American in distribution, centered in Mexico, with several species in Central and South America. Clayton and Renvoize (1986) segregated the genus *Chondrosum* Desv. (also spelled *Chondrosium*), including *Bouteloua gracilis*, from *Bouteloua*. About 17 species occur in Texas, with 14 species in the Trans-Pecos. The gramas are among the most valuable forage grasses in the western United States, with *Bouteloua gracilis*, *B. curtipendula*, *B. hirsuta*, *B. eriopoda*, and *B. barbata*, all species of the Trans-Pecos, being among the most prominent in forage value. Gould (1979) recognized two subgenera of *Bouteloua*, the subgenus *Bouteloua*, characterized by whole inflorescence branches disarticulating at maturity, the spikelets falling with branches, and spikelets usually 1–16 per branch, and subgenus *Chondrosum* (Desv.) Gould, distinguished by persistent inflorescence branches with spikelets disarticulating above the glumes, and spikelets usually 20–60 per branch, except in *B. eriopoda* and *B. kayi* with 6–20 spikelets per branch. "Grama" is a Spanish word for grass, and some other grass species have the common name grama associated with them. *Bouteloua rigidiseta* (Steud.) Hitchc. (Texas grama) and *B. repens* (H.B.K.) Scribn. & Merr. (slender grama) occur at least as close to the Trans-Pecos as the Edwards Plateau and Val Verde County and eventually may be found in the Trans-Pecos.

Key to the Species

1. Inflorescence branches as a whole, with their spikelets, falling at maturity; spikelets usually 1–12 on each branch.
    2. Inflorescence branches with 1 spikelet (rarely 2)   **1. B. uniflora.**
    2. Inflorescence branches with 2–12 spikelets, rarely more.
        3. Inflorescence branches 15–80 on each culm, if less than 15 branches then the branches with spikelets less than 1 cm long.

    4. Leaf blades, the largest ones at least, exceeding 2.5 mm wide; some plants (var. *curtipendula*) with rhizomes; anthers usually red-orange or yellow, less often blue to purple   **2. *B. curtipendula.***

    4. Leaf blades 1–2(–2.5) mm wide; plants without rhizomes; anthers dark purple   **3. *B. warnockii.***

  3. Inflorescence branches 1–13 on each culm, if more than 13 branches then the branches with spikelets 1.5 cm or more long.

    5. Plants annual; spikelets 2–5 per branch   **4. *B. aristidoides.***

    5. Plants perennial; spikelets 8–12 per branch **5. *B. chondrosioides.***

1. Inflorescence branches persistent, spikelets disarticulating above glumes; spikelets usually 20–60 on each branch (6–20 on each branch in *B. eriopoda* and *B. kayi*).

  6. Plants annual.

    7. Inflorescence a single spicate branch (rarely 2) at culm apex

                                      6. *B. simplex.*

    7. Inflorescence of 2–9 spicate branches arranged along culm axis

                                      7. *B. barbata.*

  6. Plants perennial.

    8. Second glume of at least some spikelets with papilla-based hairs.

      9. Rachis of spicate branches projecting well beyond attachment point of last (terminal) spikelet   **8. *B. hirsuta.***

      9. Rachis of spicate branches not projecting beyond attachment point of last spikelet   **9. *B. gracilis.***

    8. Second glume glabrous or pubescent, but without papilla-based hairs.

      10. Culm internodes, especially the lower ones, densely woolly-pubescent or covered with a white, chalky bloom.

        11. Culm internodes woolly-pubescent; spikelets 9–20 on each spicate branch   **10. *B. eriopoda.***

        11. Culm internodes with a waxy white bloom; spikelets 30–40 on each spicate branch   **11. *B. breviseta.***

      10. Culm internodes, even the lower ones, not covered with woolly pubescence or a white bloom.

        12. Spicate branches of inflorescence usually 3–20 along the culm axis.

          13. Spicate branches 3–7   **13. *B. trifida.***

          13. Spicate branches 8–20   **14. *B. kayi.***

        12. Spicate branches of inflorescence usually 2 (1–4) along culm axis.

          14. Base of plant knotty and semi-woody; culms with 4–5 nodes   **12. *B. ramosa.***

          14. Base of plant tufted, perhaps knotty, not semi-woody; culms with 2–3 nodes   **9. *B. gracilis.***

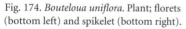

Fig. 174. *Bouteloua uniflora.* Plant; florets (bottom left) and spikelet (bottom right).

Fig. 175. *Bouteloua curtipendula.* Plant; spikelet and florets.

1. Bouteloua uniflora Vasey   NEALLEY GRAMA.   Fig. 174.   Limestone slopes and canyons and limy soils, relatively infrequent and localized to rare in the Trans-Pecos. Hudspeth Co. Culberson Co., Guadalupe Mts., North Mc-Kittrick Canyon. Brewster Co., Glass Mts., Altuda Point, W lower slopes Old Blue Mt., Jail Canyon, Gilliland Peak, Sibley Ranch. Pecos Co., 20–25 mi S Fort Stockton. 3,100–6,000 ft. Flowering (May) Jul–Nov. Frequent in TX Edwards Plateau. W to NM, possibly S UT. N Coahuila, Mex.

Nealley grama should be highly palatable to all classes of livestock, but in the Trans-Pecos this species is not often abundant enough to be useful forage, except perhaps in the Glass Mountains. Nealley grama resembles sideoats grama and is distinguished, as the specific epithet implies, by its panicle branches with one spikelet. Gould (1979) recognized two varieties of *B. uniflora*, the var. **uniflora** to which all Texas plants belong, and the var. *coahuilensis* Gould & Kapadia of Coahuila, Mexico.

2. Bouteloua curtipendula (Michx.) Torr. SIDEOATS GRAMA. Fig. 175.   Perhaps the most widely distributed of all grama grasses in the Trans-Pecos, most soil types, mountains and basins to desert habitats. Widespread to abundant in all counties of the Trans-Pecos. 2,000–6,900 ft. Flow-

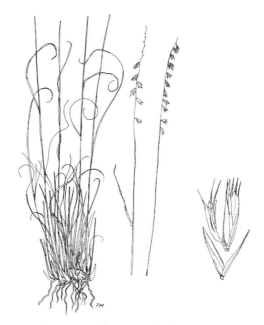

Fig. 176. *Bouteloua warnockii.* Plant; glumes
and florets.

ering mostly Jun–Nov. Throughout most of TX. Widespread in North
America, from Canada S to Mex. Also South America (Gould, 1979).

Three varieties of *B. curtipendula* are recognized (Gould, 1979), with two of
these, *B. curtipendula* var. **curtipendula** and *B. curtipendula* var. **caespitosa**
Gould & Kapadia, occurring in the Trans-Pecos. Plants of the var. *curtipendula*
are distinguished by creeping rhizomes, while in the var. *caespitosa*, stolons or
creeping rhizomes are not developed. Observation of herbarium specimens at
Sul Ross suggests that var. *caespitosa* is most common in the Trans-Pecos. Sideoats grama is one of the best forage grasses in the Trans-Pecos, being palatable
to livestock and wildlife. In the Trans-Pecos sideoats grama has been favored
in rangeland improvement efforts, particularly after root plowing in more arid
sites.

3. Bouteloua warnockii Gould & Kapadia WARNOCK GRAMA.
Fig. 176. Infrequent to rare in rocky limestone slopes, mesas, and ledges. El
Paso Co., Franklin Mts., McKelligon Canyon; recreation park N of McKelligon
Canyon; Hueco Mts. Hudspeth Co. Culberson Co., foothills of Guadalupe
Mts.; 10 mi W Kent. Jeff Davis Co., 2 mi S Kent. 3,500–4,800 ft. Flowering
Jun–Oct. Also Doña Ana Co., NM. Coahuila, Mex.

Warnock grama was described in 1962 in honor of the distinguished Sul

Fig. 177. *Bouteloua aristidoides*. Plant; glumes
(lower right), florets (lower left), and lemma
of fertile floret (above).

Ross botanist Barton H. Warnock. According to Gould (1979) *B. warnockii* is similar to *B. vaneedenii* Piger *ex* Urban of the Caribbean region. *Bouteloua warnockii* is also similar to *B. curtipendula* var. *caespitosa*, with which it hybridizes perhaps throughout the range of *B. warnockii* (Gould, 1979). Warnock grama should be a good forage grass in places where it is of sufficient abundance.

4. **Bouteloua aristidoides** (H.B.K.) Griseb. NEEDLE GRAMA. Fig. 177.   Usually desert habitats, limestone or igneous soils, slopes and flats, often along dry watercourses and in disturbed sites. El Paso Co., Franklin Mts., McKelligon Canyon; 6 mi N El Paso; between Ysleta and Hueco; Hueco Mts. Hudspeth Co., 19 mi W Sierra Blanca; Quitman Mts., 4 mi W Sierra Blanca; 5–8 mi W Van Horn; Beach and Baylor mts. Presidio Co., 6 mi N Candelaria; Pinto Canyon; Vieja Pass; 10 mi NW Shafter; 1 mi W Presidio; 10–15 mi N Lajitas; 30 mi S Marfa; 2 mi W San Jacinto Peak; La Mota waterhole; 101 Ranch Hdq. Jeff Davis Co., Mt. Livermore; H. O. Canyon; Kent turnoff from Scenic Loop; Point of Rocks; Davis Mts. State Park; 13 mi N Alpine; Fern Canyon. Brewster Co., 4 mi W Alpine; 8 mi S Alpine; Cienega Mt.; Nine Point Mesa; 02 Ranch, Cottonwood Spring; 2 mi W Study Butte; Chisos Mts., lower Green

Fig. 178. *Bouteloua chondrosioides*. Plant;
spikelet (left), lemma and palea of fertile
floret, and rudimentary floret (right).

Gulch; head of Boquillas Canyon. Reeves Co., 10 mi S Pecos. Val Verde Co.,
canyon of Rio Grande, Langtry. Winkler Co., 10 mi N Kermit. 1,200–5,200 ft.
Flowering Jun–Nov. In TX W Edwards Plateau and N South Texas Plains. W
to CA. Through Mex. to Oaxaca. Dry parts of South America.

In the Trans-Pecos the "sixweeks annual" needle grama usually flourishes
after good summer rains. Texas plants of this species belong to var. **aristidoides**, which is also the most widespread variety of the species. Another variety,
var. *arizonica* M. E. Jones, occurs in New Mexico, Arizona, and northern Mexico (Gould, 1979). Needle grama, as a short-lived annual, is of little forage
value. Reportedly the plants are detrimental in sheep country because the mature seed-bearing "heads" get into wool and diminish its value.

5. **Bouteloua chondrosioides** (H.B.K.) Benth. *ex* Wats. SPRUCETOP
GRAMA. Fig. 178. Dry canyons, slopes, grassland basins. Presidio Co., N
slope, Elephant Mt.; 101 Ranch Hdq.; 25 mi S Marfa, Frenchman Hills; Russell
Menzies Ranch; Pinto Canyon above Shely Ranch house; Vieja Pass. Jeff Davis
Co., Mt. Livermore, Goat Canyon; Barrel Springs; Davis Mts. State Park; CDRI
Landsite, 3 mi S Fort Davis; Musquiz Canyon; Fern Canyon. Brewster Co.,
vicinity of Alpine, common on Sul Ross Hill and other hills; 3 mi W Alpine;

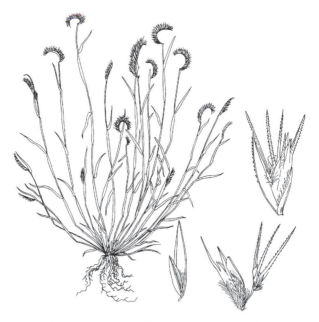

Fig. 179. *Bouteloua simplex*. Plant; spikelet (above) and florets.

Twin Peaks, N slopes; 3 mi S Alpine; Goat Mt., E slopes; Cathedral Mt., N side. Pecos Co., 20 mi SW Fort Stockton. Ward Co., 3 mi NE Royalty. 3,500–5,500 ft., mostly above 4,000 ft. Flowering (Mar) Jun–Oct. AZ. Throughout Mex. to Honduras and Costa Rica.

Sprucetop grama is highly palatable and is an excellent forage species where abundant enough. The species appears to be most common on slopes with relatively shallow soil above dominant blue grama habitats in deep alluvial grassland basins. The common name, sprucetop grama, was inspired by the "sprucelike" inflorescences which also exhibit exserted orange anthers in early floral stages.

6. Bouteloua simplex Lag.   MAT GRAMA.   Fig. 179.   Infrequent to frequent, medium to high elevation canyons, slopes, and small meadows. Culberson Co., Guadalupe Mts., Ranger Station. Jeff Davis Co., Mt. Livermore, Madera Canyon, H. O. Canyon; Mt. Locke, road to observatory. 5,100–6,100 ft. Flowering Jul–Oct. In TX only in the Trans-Pecos. NW to NM, CO, UT. Through Mex. to Hidalgo. W South America.

Mat grama is a tufted annual with usually weak, decumbent, spreading culms, or sometimes weakly erect culms, 3–30 cm long. The plants are distinguished by their single, apical, spicate branches of the panicle. In the Trans-Pecos mat grama is of no forage value.

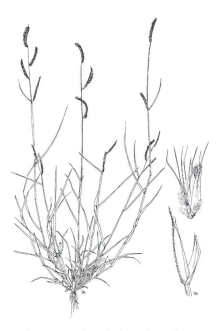

Fig. 180. *Bouteloua barbata.* Plant; glumes
(below) and florets.

7. Bouteloua barbata Lag.   SIXWEEKS GRAMA.   Fig. 180.   Dry usually desert habitats, various soil types, often in disturbed sites. El Paso Co., 6 mi N El Paso; 2 mi NE Ysleta; 10–15 mi E El Paso; between Ysleta and Hueco Tanks. Hudspeth Co., 6 mi W Fort Hancock; 2 mi N Fort Hancock; 4 mi W Sierra Blanca; 9–20 mi N Sierra Blanca; 10 mi SE Sierra Blanca. Culberson Co., Guadalupe Mts. desert slopes; between Texline and Orla; 4 mi N Kent. Presidio Co., Vieja Pass; Capote Falls; Pinto Canyon; 30 mi S Marfa; vicinity San Jacinto Peak; 10 mi N Lajitas; 101 Ranch Hdq. Jeff Davis Co., 5 mi E Chispa; 1 mi NW Valentine; Mt. Locke; Kent turnoff from Scenic Loop; Goat Canyon, Mt. Livermore; Musquiz Canyon; Fern Canyon; Haystack Mt. Brewster Co., 4 mi S Alpine; N lower slopes Mt. Ord; Elephant Mt.; Goat Mt.; 02 Ranch; Cathedral Mt.; Black Gap Refuge; Packsaddle Mt.; Rosillos Mts.; Chisos Mts.; Oak Creek Canyon, Green Gulch; Tornillo Flats; Mariscal Mt.; between Todd Hill and Burro Mesa. Reeves Co., 23 mi N Pecos; 10 mi S Pecos. Ward, Loving, Winkler, Crane counties. 2,200–6,500 ft. Flowering Apr–Nov. High Plains, Edwards Plateau, South Texas Plains, occasionally elsewhere in TX except Pineywoods and Post Oak Savannah. W to CO, UT, NV, CA. Through Mex. to Oaxaca. Argentina.

The Texas specimens of *Bouteloua barbata* are var. **barbata.** Gould (1979) recognized three varieties for the species, with the other two taxa occurring

Fig. 181. *Bouteloua hirsuta*. Plant; panicle;
glumes and florets.

west of Texas and in Mexico. Sixweeks grama usually is abundant after good summer rains especially in the desert, but its short-lived life form reduces its forage value. *Bouteloua barbata* occasionally may be confused with young plants of the perennial *B. trifida*, but there are numerous differences between the species (Gould, 1979).

8. Bouteloua hirsuta Lag.   HAIRY GRAMA.   Fig. 181.   Widespread and common in mountains, canyons, basins, various soil types. Present in all counties of the Trans-Pecos, most abundant in the basin grasslands along with blue grama over 4,000 ft. 2,200–6,500 ft. Flowering Jun–Nov. Throughout most of TX. Widespread in North America, Canada through Mex. to Chiapas.

Hairy grama occurs commonly in the same habitats with blue grama, and these species are similar in appearance. Hairy grama is easily distinguished from blue grama by the beaklike extension of the rachis of inflorescence branches. Hairy grama exhibits good palatability but is usually rated as fair forage for livestock and wildlife. Hairy grama is seldom abundant in the Trans-Pecos except in basin grasslands, and it is reported to have a weak root system that supports relatively little forage growth. Gould (1979) recognized two varieties of *Bouteloua hirsuta*, var. **hirsuta** the most widespread entity and the one that occurs in the Trans-Pecos, and var. *glandulosa* (Cerv.) Gould of Arizona south through Mexico to Guatemala. Vegetative apomixis has been reported to occur in *B. hirsuta* (Hill, 1982).

Fig. 182. *Bouteloua gracilis.* Plant; glumes
and florets.

9. Bouteloua gracilis (H.B.K.) Lag. *ex* Steud.   BLUE GRAMA.   Fig. 182.
Abundant and dominant in mountains, canyons, basins, often in pure stands,
especially in alluvial mountain basins. Present in all counties of the Trans-
Pecos. 2,000–8,200 ft. Flowering Jun–Nov. In TX, Edwards Plateau N through
the plains country, and Cross Timbers and Prairies. Throughout much of the
North American prairie, in extensive pure stands and in mixed grass associations, Canada through Mex. Argentina, probably introduced.

Blue grama is a good forage grass for all classes of livestock and for wildlife.
Blue grama is one of the most important forage grasses in western Texas and
throughout the plains regions of North America, where along with sideoats
grama it provides a large share of the native forage consumed by domesticated
animals. It is reported that blue grama withstands close grazing, but that it
benefits when rested every two or three years during the growing season. *Bouteloua gracilis* hybridizes occasionally with *B. hirsuta* (Gould, 1979). Plants
identified here as *B. gracilis* at higher elevations in the Guadalupe and Davis
mountains may exhibit shorter culms, wider leaves, and larger spicate branches
of the inflorescence.

10. Bouteloua eriopoda (Torr.) Torr.   BLACK GRAMA.   Fig. 183.   Frequently common and abundant, mountains, canyons, particularly on rocky
slopes above alluvial basins. Present in all counties of the Trans-Pecos. 2,500–

Fig. 183. *Bouteloua eriopoda*. Plant, with
woolly internode of stolon; spikelet.

6,500 ft. Flowering Jun–Nov. Edwards Plateau and plains country in TX. W to
AZ, CO, UT, N to OK, WY. N Mex.

Black grama is another grama grass with major forage significance throughout the year in the Trans-Pecos and elsewhere. Black grama is highly palatable
and is frequently abundant. Heavy grazing tends to reduce stands of black
grama except in the protection of shrubs and other plants. The best characters
for identifying *Bouteloua eriopoda* are the woolly pubescent internodes of
lower culms and of stolons, and the rather slender spicate branches of the panicle. In the central Trans-Pecos region, the location of black grama is assured by
looking on rocky slopes of mountain systems.

11. Bouteloua breviseta Vasey   GYP GRAMA.   Fig. 184.   Locally abun-
dant in gypsum and gypsum-alkaline habitats, most commonly below the
Guadalupe Mts. Hudspeth Co., 6 mi E Salt Flat station. Culberson Co., N end
Rustler Hills; Texline; near Delaware Creek between Texline and Orla; 5 mi W
Orla; 38–50 mi N Van Horn; 25 mi NW Kent; 10 mi beyond turnoff to Men-
tone, from Pecos-Carlsbad Hwy. Brewster Co., between Alpine and Fort Davis.
Reeves Co. Ector Co., 6 mi E Penwell. 2,500–4,500 ft. Flowering (May) Jun–
Sep. Otera Co., Chaves Co., Eddy Co., NM.

Bouteloua breviseta seemingly is restricted to gypsum or to gypseous soils,
and the Brewster County collection site (specimen annotated by J. R. Reeder)
needs to be confirmed. I suspect an error in the locality, because *B. breviseta*

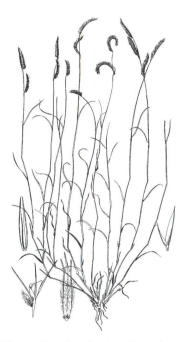

Fig. 184. *Bouteloua breviseta*. Plant; glumes
(right), rudimentary and fertile florets, and
palea of fertile floret (above).

appears to be an obligate gypsophile, and there are no known gypsum outcrops
between Alpine and Fort Davis. Gould (1975; 1979) treated *B. breviseta* and *B. ramosa* as conspecific. The present work follows Reeder and Reeder (1980) and
Correll and Johnston (1970), who regard *B. breviseta* and *B. ramosa* as distinct
species. Reeder and Reeder (1980) conducted a study of the two taxa and have
enumerated important characters by which the two species can be distinguished, including that *B. breviseta* is diploid ($2n = 20$), while *B. ramosa* is
tetraploid ($2n = 40$). Gyp grama is of modest significance as a forage grass.

12. Bouteloua ramosa Scribn. *ex* Vasey   CHINO GRAMA.   Fig. 185.
Often the dominant grass species, desert habitats, rocky and gravel slopes and
flats, limestone and igneous soils. Brewster Co., abundant on lower mountain
slopes, mesas, and some flats between the desert mountains, southern desert
portion of the county, around the Chisos Mts. Presidio Co., southern desert
portion of the county, and below the "rimrock" on the western desert region.
Hudspeth Co., Quitman Mts. Culberson Co., Baylor Mts. N of Van Horn; reported, but not confirmed, from Patterson Hills. Terrell Co., mouth of San
Francisco Canyon; 10 mi E Sanderson; 9 mi W Dryden. 1,800–4,500 ft. Flowering May–Oct. Chihuahua, Coahuila, Nuevo Leon, Durango, Mex.
    Chino grama, also known as chinograss, is exceedingly abundant in some

Fig. 185. *Bouteloua ramosa.* (above) Hillside dotted with characteristic clumps of chino grama, near Castolon in Big Bend National Park. (below) Plant; glumes and florets.

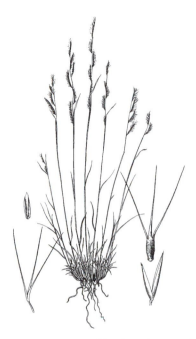

Fig. 186. *Bouteloua trifida.* Plant; glumes and
fertile floret (right), rudimentary floret (left),
palea of fertile floret (above).

areas of the southern Trans-Pecos, including on Black Mesa near Terlingua and
in Big Bend National Park. The species offers considerable forage potential.
Reeder and Reeder (1980) presented specific localities for *B. ramosa,* and they
list additional characters by which *B. ramosa* can be distinguished from *B. breviseta.* Reeder (1986b) studied the typification of *B. ramosa.*

13. Bouteloua trifida S. Wats.   RED GRAMA.   Fig. 186.   Dry, rocky, cal-
careous slopes and mesas, occasionally in gypsum, desert habitats. Hudspeth
Co., 1.5 mi E Indian Hot Springs, Quitman Mts. Culberson Co., Baylor Mts.;
probably Guadalupe Mts. Presidio Co., Capote Creek; near Shafter; Bandera
Mesa; near Lajitas. Brewster Co., 3 mi S Marathon near Peña Blanca; 40 mi S
Alpine; Packsaddle Mt.; Paint Gap Hills; Glenn Spring; 4 mi W Hot Springs;
Tornillo Flats; near Lone Mt. Pecos Co., 25–40 mi S Fort Stockton; 13 mi E
Fort Stockton; 30 mi E Fort Stockton. Reeves Co., 22 mi NW Pecos. Terrell
Co., 10 mi above mouth San Francisco Canyon; 1–6 mi E Sanderson; 4–9 mi
W Dryden; 20–23 mi E Dryden; 8–29 mi N Dryden; Big Canyon 30 mi N
Sanderson. Val Verde Co., Pumpville turnoff near Hwy 90; Mile Canyon, Lang-
try. 1,300–4,200 ft. Flowering Mar–Nov. Reported from most regions of TX
except Pineywoods and Blackland Prairies. W to NM, AZ, UT, NV, CA. N Mex.

Fig. 187. *Bouteloua kayi.* Plant; glumes
and florets.

Red grama is a relatively small (10–30 cm high) perennial grama, but it is a drought-resistant species that provides fair forage during early season growth.

14. Bouteloua kayi Warnock   KAY GRAMA.   Fig. 187.   Known only from the area of the type locality along and near Maravillas Creek, Black Gap Refuge, southern Brewster Co., dry limestone flats, slopes, and rocky ledges. Brewster Co., Cave Hill along Stairstep Mt.; bluffs of Maravillas Creek; Brushy Canyon; flats on Maravillas Creek. 2,200–3,700 ft. Flowering May–Nov.

Bouteloua kayi is closely related to *B. trifida* (Correll and Johnston, 1970; Gould, 1975; 1979) but differs in having stronger, erect culm bases, fewer expanded culm internodes and elevated nodes; the spicate branches of the panicle are more numerous and longer, the lemma awns are somewhat shorter, and the lemma is longer. Kay grama probably is very drought-resistant.

52. CATHESTECUM   Presl

A genus of about five species limited to Mexico, with one species also in the United States. The genus name is from Greek *kathestekos,* meaning stationary, but with unknown application.

1. Cathestecum erectum Vasey & Hack.   FALSE GRAMA.   Fig. 188. Perennial, low, tufted. Culms erect and flowering, to 25 cm long, and spread-

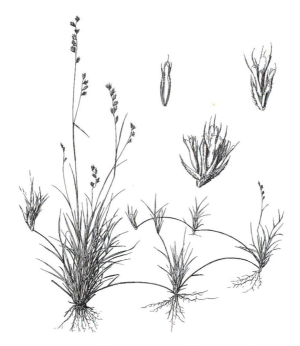

Fig. 188. *Cathestecum erectum*. Plant; group of
spikelets, central spikelet, and fertile floret.

ing, wiry-stoloniferous. Leaves with sheaths rounded on back, basal ones paperlike and somewhat woolly, upper ones mostly glabrous except perhaps for
upper margins; ligule a ring of hairs, ca. 0.5 mm long; blades flat or folded, 2–
10 cm long, ca. 1.4 mm wide. Inflorescence a panicle, with usually 4–8 spicate
branches, the branches 4–7 mm long with a short rachis. Spikelets in tight
clusters of 3 on each branch, the upper one with a perfect floret, the lower 2
spikelets with staminate or neuter florets, sometimes a fourth rudimentary
spikelet present; disarticulation of branch rachis near base, with a short stub
remaining on main axis; upper spikelet with 1 perfect floret and 1 or more
reduced florets above; glumes unequal, 1-nerved, the second much the longest;
second glume usually hairy on back, apex truncate or notched and with a short
awn; lower 2 spikelets of cluster with one large neuter floret below, one smaller
staminate floret above, these 2–3 mm long; lemmas similar in all spikelets,
somewhat papery, usually 3-nerved, sometimes 5–7-nerved, apex rather
deeply lobed, with nerves extending into short awns; paleas somewhat shorter
than lemmas, usually short-awned from the 2 nerves. Caryopses (in one plant)
lanceolate and flattened, 1.8 mm long.

Infrequent to abundant, lower desert, particularly south of the Chisos Mts.,
and in Terlingua area, rocky or gravel hills and slopes, gravel and clay mounds,
limestone or igneous alluvium. Presidio Co., Rooney Ranch, 6 mi N Cande-

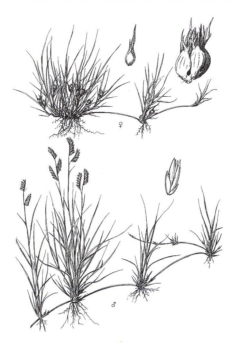

Fig. 189. *Buchlöe dactyloides*. Pistillate and
staminate plants; pistillate spike and floret;
staminate spikelet.

laria; 101 Ranch SW of Alpine. Brewster Co., 02 Ranch, Cottonwood Spring;
10 mi N Terlingua; 5 mi W Terlingua Creek; 2 mi W Study Butte; 5 mi N
Study Butte; 15 mi S Panther Junction toward Boquillas; Muskhog Spring;
McKinney Springs, Dead Horse Mts.; head of Boquillas Canyon; Talley Mt.,
N side; Hot Springs area. 1,800–4,500 ft. Flowering May–Oct. In TX only in
southern Trans-Pecos. Also S AZ. N Mex.

Cathestecum erectum was collected on the 101 Ranch in Presidio County in
1931 at an elevation of 4,500 ft. This locality is unusual, because *C. erectum*
otherwise seems to be restricted to the "lower" desert habitats in southern
Brewster and Presidio counties. False grama usually flourishes after good late
spring and summer rains, but is usually not abundant or widespread enough
to afford useful forage.

53. BUCHLÖE   Engelm.   BUFFALOGRASS.

A monotypic genus of North America. The genus name was derived from
Greek *boubaos*, buffalo, and *chloe*, grass, after the well-established common
name for this grass species. Buffalograss is a dominant short grass species over
much of the Great Plains or "short grass country" of the United States, where
it has been and is one of the most important forage grasses of the region. This

sod-forming species was used to make the sod houses of early westerners. Various biological aspects of buffalograss are discussed by Quinn (1991).

1. **Buchlöe dactyloides** (Nutt.) Engelm. BUFFALOGRASS. Fig. 189. Perennial, tufted, low, mat-forming with extensive wiry stolons, usually dioecious, sometimes monoecious. Culms spreading. Leaves with sheaths rounded, glabrous except at the collar; ligule membranous, ciliate, 0.5 mm long; blades flat, glabrous, or weakly pubescent, 2–12(–20) cm long, 1–2.5 mm wide. Inflorescence a panicle; in staminate plants with 1–4 spicate, unilateral branches, usually 6–14 mm long, elevated above basal leaves on slender culms usually 8–23 cm tall; in pistillate plants burlike clusters of spikelets on a short rachis, somewhat hidden among leaves. Staminate spikelets 2-flowered, usually 4–5.5 mm long, usually 6–12 spikelets on each narrow, flattened branch rachis; glumes unequal, broad, shorter than lemmas, 1–2-nerved, the nerves sometimes extended as short awns; lemmas awnless, 3-nerved, glabrous; anthers in both spikelets, orange-red. Pistillate spikelets 1-flowered, 3–5(–7) in the burlike clusters, the bur enclosed in a bractlike leaf sheath; at maturity the bur dehiscing as a unit with hardened rachis fused with the hardened second glumes of the collective spikelets; glumes unequal, glabrous or minutely hairy, the first glume reduced, the second glume broad, hard on lower part, apically narrowed to 3 sharp lobes; lemmas 3-nerved, firm, glabrous, apex with 3 awned lobes; paleas similar to lemmas. Caryopsis brown, ovate or oblong, usually 2–2.5 mm long.

Infrequent to frequent, usually in dense patches, gentle slopes to alluvial flats, clay, loam, or sand, commonly calcareous substrates, often in depressions or at roadside. Brewster Co., Alpine city limits; between Alpine and Fort Davis; Twin Peaks, N slopes; Glass Mts.; 10 mi NE Alpine; 20 mi NE Alpine; 10 mi E Marathon; 15 mi NE Marathon; 5 mi S Alpine; Chalk Draw E of Santiago Peak. Presidio Co., Marfa. Pecos Co., between Fort Stockton and Sheffield; 10–30 mi E Fort Stockton; 25 mi S Fort Stockton; 4 mi W Longfellow. Val Verde Co., near mouth of Pecos River. 1,600–4,800 ft. Flowering Apr–Dec. Occasional in all regions of TX. N to MT and MN, W to AZ, and NV. N Mex.

Buffalograss provides good grazing for livestock and fair forage for wildlife. The sod-forming perennial cures to furnish nutritious feed during winter. In the Trans-Pecos buffalograss is of marginal forage value because of its patchy distribution. Strains of buffalograss are being developed for recreational and landscape turf uses and for revegetation in arid regions because of its drought-resistant qualities once established. Low-growing strains of buffalograss also do not require frequent mowing.

54. SPARTINA   Schreb.   CORDGRASS.

A genus of about 16 species, most American in distribution, but extending to the Atlantic coasts of Europe and Africa. Six species occur in Texas, most of them along the Gulf Coast and in other moist areas. *Spartina* species with

Fig. 190. *Spartina pectinata.* Plant; spikelet
and floret.

rhizomes often grow in extensive, nearly pure stands and function in binding
soil in coastal and interior marshes. In general the cordgrasses are coarse and
unpalatable at maturity, but they may afford fair to poor forage for cattle in
young stages. The genus name is from Greek *spartine*, a cord made from
Spartium, probably in reference to the strong leaves of *Spartina*.

1. Spartina pectinata Link   PRAIRIE CORDGRASS.   Fig. 190.   Perennial, with spreading rhizomes. Culms solitary or in clumps, usually 1.5–2.5 m
long. Leaves with smooth sheaths; ligule a ring of hairs, 1–3 mm long; blades
flat, involute at maturity, to 1.5 cm wide. Inflorescence a panicle, usually
with 8–35 branches bearing numerous, closely spaced, sessile spikelets, the
branches 4–15 cm long, appressed to spreading; disarticulation below glumes.
Spikelets 1-flowered, flattened laterally, usually 1–2.5 cm long including
awns; glumes unequal, the keel hispid-scabrous, 1-nerved, or the second
glume with 2–3 nerves, apically tapering, the tip scabrous-awned, the first
glume 5–10 mm long, the second glume 10–25 mm long including the awn
that is 4–10 mm long; lemmas glabrous, keeled, 1–3 strong nerves, tapered
apex awnless but deeply bilobed and usually apiculate; paleas slightly longer
than lemmas, apically bilobed.

One collection, Pecos Co., sparse at Comanche Springs in Fort Stockton,
2,950 ft., 10 Sep 1949, *B. H. Warnock 9012*. Comanche Springs is essentially
dry and the *Spartina* is probably no longer growing at this locality. Also the

High Plains, Blackland Prairies, and Cross Timbers and Prairies regions in TX. Northern and central United States to southern Canada, also NC, AR, W in NM.

55. HILARIA   H.B.K.

Perennials, mostly with rhizomes or stolons. Culms from a hard, firm base or not, 10–75 cm long. Leaves with blades usually short and narrow, flat or involute; ligules membranous, the membrane lacerate and often ciliate. Inflorescence a spike, the spikes bilateral, dense, slender, the rachis zigzag with spikelets in clusters of 3 at each node; disarticulation of whole spikelet clusters. Spikelets of each cluster dissimilar, the central one 1-flowered, perfect, the 2 lateral ones 2-flowered, staminate; glumes usually asymmetrical, firm, flat, with an awn on one side arising near the middle; lemmas 3-nerved, thin, awned or awnless; paleas similar to lemmas in length and texture.

A genus of nine species mostly distributed in southern North America, with one species extending south to Venezuela. All the species of *Hilaria* are important range grasses that can resist close grazing. The genus is named for Auguste St. Hilaire.

Key to the Species

1. Plants forming dense clumps, 30–75 cm tall, the bases thick and hard, with scaly rhizomes; stolons absent; leaf blades somewhat thick, flat, or involute.
    2. Glumes of lateral spikelets flabellate, i.e., fan-shaped or broadly wedge-shaped, broadly rounded or truncate at the apex; tuft of hairs at spikelet cluster base 2–3 mm long   1. *H. mutica.*
    2. Glumes of lateral spikelets usually narrowing from middle to apex, not flabellate; rounded, lacerate, or acute at the apex; tuft of hairs at spikelet cluster base 3.5–5 mm long   2. *H. jamesii.*
1. Plants forming tufts 10–35 cm tall, the bases not thick and hard, without rhizomes; stolons usually present, some arching above ground; leaf blades thin and flat.
    3. Glumes dark, to the unaided eye, at least below the middle, densely covered with minute black dots (glands); spikelet clusters 6.5–8 mm long
                                                                    3. *H. swallenii.*
    3. Glumes pale, without black dots or with a few scattered or basal dots; spikelet clusters 5–6 mm long   4. *H. belangeri.*

1. Hilaria mutica (Buckl.) Benth.   TOBOSA.   Fig. 191.   Most abundant in basins with clay soil, also on dry slopes. El Paso Co., Franklin Mts., N McKelligon Canyon; 5 mi W Hueco; 2 mi W El Paso. Hudspeth Co., clay-gypsum E Finley; W Sierra Blanca; Sierra Diablo, head of Victorio Canyon; 2 mi N Allamoore. Culberson Co., 2 mi S Texline; Apache Mts., 3–4 mi N

 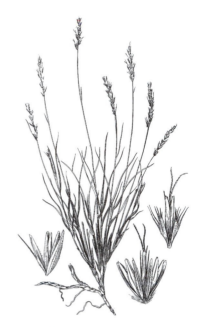

Fig. 191. *Hilaria mutica.* Plant; group of spikelets (below), staminate spikelet, and fertile
spikelet (above).

Fig. 192. *Hilaria jamesii.* Plant; group of spikelets (lower right), fertile spikelet, and staminate spikelet (lower left).

Kent. Presidio Co., W end Capote Mt.; 101 Ranch Hdq. Jeff Davis Co., 8 mi W
Valentine; 5 mi S Kent; Forbidden Mt.; Mt. Livermore; Barrel Springs; Hay-
stack Mt.; Mitre Peak Girl Scout Camp. Brewster Co., Sul Ross Hill, Alpine;
Mt. Ord; 20 mi NE Alpine; 15 mi NE Marathon; Cathedral Mt.; Goat Mt.; O2
Ranch; Packsaddle Mt.; Terlingua area; Dow Crossing, Black Gap Refuge; Big
Bend Natl. Park, Kit Mt., Tornillo Flats, between Alamo Spring and Burro
Spring, Glenn Springs, between Todd Hill and Burro Mesa. Reeves Co., 10 mi
E Balmorhea. Pecos Co., 3 mi N Fort Stockton; 20–35 mi S Fort Stockton;
30 mi E Fort Stockton. Terrell Co., 6 mi E Sanderson; 8 mi N Dryden; 2–
10 mi N Sanderson. Val Verde Co., near mouth of Pecos River. 1,600–5,500 ft.
Flowering Apr–Nov. W half of TX, South Texas Plains N through plains coun-
try. NW to WY, NV. N Mex.

   Tobosa is relatively common in all counties of the Trans-Pecos, but it is most
abundant in alluvial basins and rangeland depressions where it forms extensive, nearly pure stands known in the region as "tobosa flats." When relatively
young and green, tobosa is of fair forage value to cattle and horses. It is mostly
unpalatable when mature.

   2. Hilaria jamesii (Torr.) Benth.   GALLETA.   Fig. 192.   Infrequent to
rare on dry slopes and alluvial flats. Presidio Co., Sierra Vieja, one small area

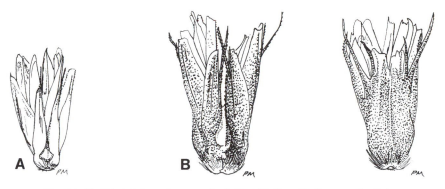

Fig. 193. (A) *Hilaria belangeri*; group of spikelets. (B) *H. swallenii*, group of spikelets (two views).

ca. 20 mi S Valentine; Chinati Mts., above Oso Creek 18 mi NW Shafter; Bunton Flat, road from Marfa-Presidio Hwy to McCraken Ranch. 3,600–4,800 ft. Flowering May–Nov. Plains country in TX. NW to WY and NV, W to AZ, S CA.

Galleta is seemingly rare in the Trans-Pecos, probably not forming the extensive stands characteristic of its look-alike, tobosa. Galleta is rated as good forage when relatively young and green.

3. Hilaria swallenii Cory SWALLEN CURLYMESQUITE. Fig. 193. Often abundant in alluvial flats and on rocky slopes. Presidio Co., S slopes Capote Mts.; Pinto Canyon; 25 mi S Marfa; 101 Ranch. Jeff Davis Co., Davis Mts., Rockpile; Barrel Springs; between Madera Canyon and observatory; 2 mi W Mt. Locke; 3 mi S Fort Davis, CDRI Landsite; E slope Haystack Mt. Brewster Co., between Alpine and Fort Davis; between Lizard Mt. and Twin Peaks 2 mi W Alpine; 3 mi W Alpine; 9 mi S Alpine; Cathedral Mt. 3,500–6,200 ft. Flowering Jun–Nov. Also N Coahuila, Mex.

Hilaria swallenii is much more common in the Trans-Pecos than is *H. belangeri*. These two species are similar in appearance and both species are drought-resistant and produce good forage throughout the year where abundant.

4. Hilaria belangeri (Steud.) Nash COMMON CURLYMESQUITE. Fig. 193. Uncommon, rocky slopes and brushy flats. Reported from the S Hueco Mts., El Paso Co. Val Verde Co., Comstock; 35 mi W Del Rio. 1,800 ft. Flowering Apr–Nov. Throughout most of TX except far E parts. W to AZ. N Mex.

Hilaria belangeri is the more widespread of the two curlymesquite species. It has been described as the dominant "short grass" of the Texas Plains and thus is a significant forage species.

Tribe 12. Zoysieae

Clayton and Renvoize (1986) recognized this group as a subtribe of the tribe Cynodonteae (tribe Chlorideae as treated here). Only the genus *Tragus* of this group occurs in Texas (Gould, 1975) and in the Trans-Pecos. *Zoysia*, with mat-forming perennial species, has provided cultivars that have become popular turfgrasses in the southern United States.

56. TRAGUS   Haller

Annuals. Culms weak, 5–30(–40) cm long. Leaves with glabrous sheaths usually shorter than internodes; ligule membranous, fringed with soft woolly hairs; blades usually flat, short, the margins usually coarsely pubescent. Inflorescence a spikelike raceme 4–10 cm long; itself a bristly cylinder, with clusters of 2–5 bristly spikelets ("burs"), these burs closely spaced on axis; disarticulation at base of spikelet cluster. Spikelets 1-flowered; first glume reduced and thin or absent; second glume of lowermost spikelets (of each cluster) prominent, firm, convex with usually 3 rows of stout, hooked spines on raised nerves of the back and one row of spines on each margin; lemmas of lowermost spikelets thin, flat; the two second glumes of lower spikelets forming the bur, upper 1–3 spikelets reduced, sterile, or absent. Caryopses elliptic, flattened, one side convex, to 1.5 mm long.

A genus of about seven species native to tropical and subtropical regions of the Old World. These weedy annual species are not native to the United States, but two species are introduced. The genus name is from Greek *tragos*, he-goat, here used by Plinius in reference to a plant. The key to the species was adapted from Wipff (1992).

Key to the Species

1. Spikelets in clusters of 2(3); second glume 5-veined   **1. *T. berteronianus.***
1. Spikelets in clusters of 3–6; second glume 7-veined   **2. *T. racemosus.***

1. Tragus berteronianus Schult.   SPIKE BURGRASS.   Fig. 194.   Infrequent to rare, usually in disturbed sites. El Paso Co., Franklin Mts., McKelligon Canyon; Hueco Mts. Culberson Co., lower slopes, Guadalupe Mts.; top of S McKittrick Canyon. Presidio Co., Sierra Vieja, Vieja Pass; 10 mi N Shafter, hills along Cibolo Creek, near Cieneguita; 4 mi SSE San Jacinto Mt.; Solitario; 101 Ranch. Jeff Davis Co., H. O. Canyon, Mt. Livermore; 20 mi S Kent; Scenic Loop above Fort Davis; Musquiz Creek. Brewster Co., college pasture, Alpine; Big Hill, 6 mi S Alpine; Chisos Mts., Green Gulch; Ward Spring; Wilson Ranch. 3,700–5,500 ft. Flowering Jun–Nov. Also South Texas Plains and Edwards Plateau. W to S NM, and AZ. Mex. Also in South America.

Fig. 194. *Tragus berteronianus*. Plant; bur and
spikelet (above).

Fig. 195. *Tragus racemosus*. Partial plant.

Spike burgrass is an Old World species now well-established in North
America and Texas, although it is not frequently collected in the Trans-Pecos.
The chromosome number reported for *T. berteronianus* is $2n = 20$. Burgrass
does not offer significant forage in the Trans-Pecos.

2. Tragus racemosus (L.) All.   STALKED BURGRASS.   Fig. 195.   Reported for the Trans-Pecos by Gould (1975) but not documented for this region by specimens at Sul Ross. Flowering Aug–Sep. Gulf Prairies and Marshes
in TX; reportedly in much the same habitats as *T. berteronianus* but less often
collected (Gould, 1975). Also AZ (Reeder and Reeder, 1978). Native to the Old
World. Stalked burgrass has a chromosome number reported as $2n = 40$.

Tribe 13. Aeluropodeae

Clayton and Renvoize (1986) included *Distichlis* and *Allolepis* in the subtribe Monanthochloineae of tribe Eragrostideae, the tribe herein referred to as
Eragrosteae. Gould (1975) recognized three genera of Aeluropodeae in Texas,
with two genera in the Trans-Pecos.

Fig. 196. *Distichlis spicata* var. *stricta*. Plant;
pistillate panicle and floret, staminate spikelet
and floret.

Key to the Genera of Aeluropodeae

1. Plants with strong rhizomes (usually without stolons); lemma faintly 7–11-nerved; leaf blades stiff, distichous   **57. *Distichlis*, p. 230**
1. Plants with long, thick stolons (usually with rhizomes); lemma 3(–5)-nerved; leaf blades flat, not distichous   **58. *Allolepis*, p. 231**

57. DISTICHLIS   Raf.   SALTGRASS.

A genus of about five species found in North and South America and in Australia. In general the species have fair to poor forage value except in areas where it is the only grass available for cattle and horses. The genus name is from Greek *distichos*, 2-ranked, in reference to the distichous (two vertical rows) leaves.

1. Distichlis spicata (L.) Greene   SALTGRASS.   Fig. 196.   Perennial, with creeping rhizomes, dioecious, rarely monoecious. Culms with short internodes, 10–55 cm long. Leaves overlapping, distichous, 2-ranked, the lower ones reduced sheaths; sheaths rounded, glabrous or minutely pubescent; ligule membranous, less than 0.5 mm long; blades drying involute, 2–8 (–17) cm long, 1–4 mm wide. Inflorescence a contracted panicle or spikelike raceme 2.5–8 cm long, the spikelets on short pedicels and branches. Pistillate and staminate panicles similar. Spikelets usually 5–15-flowered, laterally flattened, 6–18 mm long or more, awnless; disarticulation above glumes, between florets. Glumes somewhat unequal, glabrous, firm, 3–9-nerved, the lateral nerves often obscure, apex acute; lemmas similar to glumes, somewhat longer and wider, laterally compressed and keeled, usually 3–6 mm long, 5–11-nerved, apex acute; paleas about as long as lemmas.

Often common, frequently in wet saline or alkaline habitats. El Paso Co., along the Rio Grande, 3–4 mi above El Paso; 7 mi W El Paso; 3 mi E Fabens, along water canals. Hudspeth Co., 4 mi E Fort Hancock, canals; bank of Rio Grande near Little Box Canyon. Presidio Co., near Candelaria; Sierra Vieja, just above Capote Falls; near Casa Piedra. Jeff Davis Co., E entrance, Davis Mts. State Park. Brewster Co., Cienega Mt.; Fort Peña Colorado; near Terlingua Creek, 9 mi N Terlingua. Pecos Co., 4 mi N Fort Stockton; between Grandfalls and Coyanosa, along Pecos River; 11 mi N Fort Stockton. 2,800–4,500 ft. Flowering May–Oct. Also Edwards Plateau and plains country in TX. W United States.

Gould (1975) recognized two weakly delimited varieties of *Distichlis spicata*, the var. *spicata* (coastal saltgrass), limited to coastal areas, and (inland saltgrass) var. **stricta** (Torr.) Beetle of various inland habitats, and distinguished from var. *spicata* by having shorter culms that are more slender and erect, slightly longer leaf blades, and less crowded panicles. Inland saltgrass provides useful forage in some Trans-Pecos saline areas where it is abundant.

58. ALLOLEPIS   Soderstrom & Decker

A monotypic genus of North America, only recently (Soderstrom and Decker, 1965) distinguished from *Distichlis*.

1. **Allolepis texana** (Vasey) Soderstrom & Decker   Fig. 197.   [*Distichlis texana* (Vasey) Scribn.; *Poa texana* Vasey]. Perennial, dioecious, with long stolons, to 3–17 m long. Culms glabrous, ascending or spreading, 24–63 cm long. Leaves with sheaths rounded, glabrous except at the collar; ligule a ciliate membrane, 0.5–1.4 mm long; blades flat or somewhat folded, 30 cm or more long, 2.5–6 mm wide, essentially glabrous except scabrous on the margins and tips. Inflorescence a panicle, this contracted, usually 5–20 cm long, the appressed branches 1–6 cm long, with spikelets to the base; disarticulation very tardy, spikelets persisting. Spikelets (staminate) ovate-lanceolate, shiny, 0.9–2.3 cm long, 3–8 mm wide, with 4–14(–20) florets; glumes ovate, hya-

Fig. 197. *Allolepis texana*. Panicle; lemma
and palea.

line, glabrous; first glume 1-nerved, 4–5 mm long; second glume 1–3-nerved, slightly longer than first; lemmas of lower florets glabrous, shiny, 3-nerved, 5–5.5 mm long. Spikelets (pistillate) terete or compressed slightly, 1–2 cm long, 2.5–3.5 mm wide, florets 8–9; glumes leathery, with wide scarious margins; first glume 7–9 mm long; second glume slightly longer than first; lemmas of lower florets leathery, broadly ovate, 7.5–10 mm long.

Infrequent and highly localized, deep silty or sandy soil. Presidio Co., along the Rio Grande at Presidio; mouth of Cibolo Creek between Presidio and the international bridge, where abundant. Jeff Davis Co., Davis Mts., Limpia Canyon, 10 mi NE Fort Davis; Wild Rose Pass; 12 mi NE Fort Davis; Limpia Valley, cattle guard to Jeff Ranch, hwy from Fort Davis to Balmorhea. 2,300–4,900 ft. Flowering Jul–Oct. Coahuila, Chihuahua, Durango, Mex.

Allolepis is distinguished from *Distichlis* in habit by its long stolons, leaves that are flat, wider, and not distichous, and non-alkaline habitat. *Distichlis* has scaly rhizomes and involute leaf blades (at maturity), and occurs in alkaline or saline habitats. Additional features serving to delimit these genera are discussed by Soderstrom and Decker (1965). *Allolepis* has been so infrequently collected and observed in the field that more information is needed about its habit and habitat.

Tribe 14. Pappophoreae

With primary distribution in the tropics, tribe Pappophoreae is represented by five genera and about 41 species. Three genera of this tribe occur in Texas, all of them in the Trans-Pecos. The tribe is distinguished by its many-nerved glumes and lemmas with many nerves and awns.

Key to the Genera of Pappophoreae

1. Lemma awns 9, subequal in length, plumose; lemma body with 9 strong nerves, the apex not lobed   **60. *Enneapogon*, p. 236**
1. Lemma awns 11 or more, unequal in length, scabrous or glabrous; lemma body with 9–11 or more nerves, the apex lobed.
   2. Glumes 1-nerved; florets falling together   **59. *Pappophorum*, p. 233**
   2. Glumes 7–13-nerved; florets falling separately   **61. *Cottea*, p. 237**

59. PAPPOPHORUM   Schreb.   PAPPUSGRASS.

Perennials, cespitose, erect. Culms 0.5–2 m long, glabrous. Leaves with sheaths having a tuft of hairs at sides of collars; ligule a ring of short hairs, but longer hairs (2–4 mm long) at base of leaf blade above ligule; blades flat or involute, 10–30 cm long, 1.5–5 mm wide. Inflorescence of contracted, slender, spikelike panicles, these bristly in aspect because of lemma awns and whitish to purplish. Spikelets 3–6-flowered, 6–8 mm long, with only lower 1–3 spikelets perfect; disarticulation above glumes, florets falling together; glumes subequal, 1-nerved, membranous, usually 3–4 mm long; lemmas rounded on back, many-nerved, these indistinct, pubescent on margins and midnerve from base to middle, the nerves extending to 11–15 awns, these glabrous or scabrous; paleas nearly equal in length to lemma body.

A genus of eight species (Reeder and Toolin, 1989) distributed in North and South America. The genus name is from Greek *pappos*, pappus, and *phoros*, bearing, in reference to the pappuslike awns of the lemma (pappus is a structure characteristic of fruits of the sunflower family). The key to the species is adapted from Reeder and Toolin (1989).

Key to the Species

1. Lemma body 3–4 mm long, oblong; awns usually not more than 1.5 times as long as lemma body, usually not spreading at right angles; inflorescence axis, branchlets, and pedicels perhaps with small sunken glands

1. *P. bicolor.*

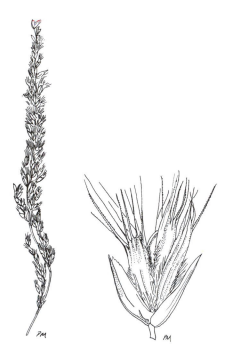

Fig. 198. *Pappophorum bicolor*. Panicle;
spikelet.

1. Lemma body 3–3.2 mm long, rather obovate, broadest above the middle;
   awns about twice as long as lemma body, or slightly less, usually spreading
   at near right angles at maturity; inflorescence not glandular

   2. P. vaginatum.

    1. Pappophorum bicolor Fourn. *ex* Hemsl. PINK PAPPUSGRASS.
Fig. 198.   Often common especially at roadside in moist depressions and in
disturbed sites, not widespread in the Trans-Pecos. Brewster Co., 40 mi S
Marathon near boundary to Big Bend Natl. Park; Black Gap Refuge, Cave Hill,
Big Brushy Canyon, Bear Creek, Heath Gorge, 4 mi S Hdq.; 10 mi N Terlingua;
Chisos Mts., Basin campground; Glenn Spring; Sierra Quemada near Dominguez Spring. Pecos Co., 5 mi N Fort Stockton near Corral Hill. Terrell Co.,
mouth of San Francisco Canyon; banks of Persimmon Creek, 20 mi SE Sanderson; 5–10 mi E Dryden. Val Verde Co., Pumpville turnoff from Hwy 90;
Mile Canyon, Langtry; 5 mi W Langtry; near mouth of Pecos River. 1,100–
4,500 ft. Flowering Apr–Nov. Southern plains country in TX S to near the Gulf
Coast. W to AZ. N Mex.
    In the Trans-Pecos *Pappophorum* species are erect, vigorous grasses to 80 cm
or more tall. The two species can be distinguished by the key characters and

Fig. 199. *Pappophorum vaginatum.* Plant;
spikelet and perfect floret (above).

tentatively by the inflorescences, usually purplish in *P. bicolor* and brownish-yellow to whitish (rarely purple-tinged) in *P. vaginatum.* Although pink pappusgrass is a reasonably large grass, it is reported to furnish only fair forage for cattle and poor grazing for wildlife.

2. Pappophorum vaginatum Buckl.   WHIPLASH PAPPUSGRASS. Fig. 199.   [*Pappophorum subbulbosum* Arechav.; *P. mucronulatum* auct., not Nees]. Often common especially at roadside in moist depressions, disturbed sites, and on low, rangeland hills. Presidio Co., vicinity of old San Carlos below Presidio. Brewster Co., between Alpine and Fort Davis; 5 mi S Marathon, Fort Peña Colorado; 45 mi S Alpine; Nine Point Mesa, lower slopes; 10 mi N Terlingua; Grapevine Hills, Big Bend Natl. Park; Chisos Mts., Oak Canyon, Chisos Pens, Basin campground; Black Gap Refuge, Big Brushy Canyon. Pecos Co., 3 mi N Fort Stockton toward Grandfalls; 3 mi S Imperial; 30 mi E Fort Stockton. Reeves Co., 10 mi N Saragosa. Terrell Co., 9 mi W Dryden. 2,400–5,000 ft. Flowering May–Nov. South Texas Plains. AZ. N Mex.

The somewhat confused synonymy of *Pappophorum vaginatum* is clarified by Reeder and Toolin (1989). This species has gone under the name *P. mucronulatum* (Correll and Johnston, 1970; Hitchcock, 1951), but *P. mucronulatum* Nees is a species restricted to South America. In the Trans-Pecos, *P. vaginatum*

Fig. 200. *Enneapogon desvauxii.* Plant; spikelet,
perfect floret, and cleistogamous floret
(above).

more commonly exhibits whitish than tawny inflorescences, and a tinge of
purple is also seen especially in immature inflorescences. Whiplash pappusgrass is abundant at roadside in southern Brewster County, where the plants
can be recognized from a moving vehicle by their feathery, whitish, spikelike
panicles to about 20 cm long. Whiplash pappusgrass probably is of at least fair
forage value for cattle.

60. ENNEAPOGON　　Desv. *ex* Beauv.

A genus of about 28 species in warm regions of the world, especially Australia and Africa, with one species in North and South America. The genus name
is from *ennea*, nine, and *pogon*, beard, in reference to the nine awns of the
lemma that are plumose or "bearded."

1. Enneapogon desvauxii Beauv.　FEATHER PAPPUSGRASS.　Fig. 200.
[*Pappophorum wrightii* S. Wats.]. Perennial, tufted. Culms 10–40(–50) cm
long, usually pubescent, densely pilose at the nodes. Leaves with rounded
sheaths, these usually pilose and shorter than internodes; ligule a ring of hairs,
0.5 mm long; blades involute or folded at maturity, filiform, pubescent, usually

2–13 cm long, 0.5–2 mm wide. Inflorescence a narrow, spikelike panicle, at maturity this 2.5–8 cm long, 6–12 mm wide, densely contracted, gray or lead colored. Spikelets usually 3-flowered and 5–7 mm long, 1 floret, the lower one, perfect; glumes subequal, the first 3–5 mm long, 5–7-nerved, lanceolate, membranous, minutely pubescent, second glume slightly narrower than the first, perhaps with fewer nerves, 3–4-nerved in some; lemmas shorter than glumes, the body usually 1.5–2 mm long, rounded on back, firm, pubescent, 9-nerved and 9-awned, these usually 3–4 mm long, equal in length and plumose; paleas nearly equal to lemma.

Often common, mountain slopes, canyons, and flats, various soil types. El Paso Co., Franklin Mts., McKelligon Canyon; E slopes Franklin Mts.; 8 mi N El Paso. Hudspeth Co., 10 mi W, 20 mi N Sierra Blanca; 5 mi W Van Horn; 10 mi E Hueco; Guadalupe Mts., lower W slopes. Culberson Co., 1 mi SW Pine Spring along Hwy 62–180; between Texline and Orla; Sierra Diablo, S of Hdq.; 10 mi W Kent. Presidio Co., N Chinati Mts.; 1 mi W Marfa; 3 mi W San Estaban Lake; 101 Ranch; La Mota waterhole; 4 mi SE San Jacinto Peak; just NW Solitario Peak; Eagle Crag Canyon S Redford. Jeff Davis Co., 20 mi S Kent; Davis Mts. State Park, Musquiz Canyon. Brewster Co., Paisano campground; Sul Ross campus, Alpine; Cathedral Mt.; Goat Mt.; Elephant Mt.; 15 mi NE Marathon; 20 mi NE Alpine; 5 mi SW Marathon; Nine Point Mesa; Packsaddle Mt.; 10 mi W Terlingua; Black Gap Refuge, Heath Canyon, Venado Tank, 10 mi S Hdq., Maravillas Creek; Big Bend Natl. Park, head of Boquillas Canyon, Dead Horse Mts. Reeves Co., 23 mi NW Pecos. Pecos Co., 20 mi W Sheffield. Terrell Co., 8 mi N Dryden; 2–10 mi N Sanderson; 6 mi E Sanderson. 1,800–6,500 ft. Flowering Apr–Nov. Plains country and Edwards Plateau in TX. W to UT and AZ. Mex. Bolivia, Peru, Argentina.

Although feather pappusgrass is widespread and often abundant, it is not regarded as an important forage grass, because the plants form relatively small tufts and do not produce much herbage. *Enneapogon desvauxii*, also known as spike pappusgrass, is easily recognized by its usually lead colored, spikelike inflorescences.

61. COTTEA Kunth

A monotypic genus of North and South America. The genus was named for Heinrich Cotta.

1. Cottea pappophoroides Kunth Fig. 201. Perennial, tufted, weak and short-lived. Culms rather uniformly leafy, 30–70 cm long, erect or somewhat geniculate and spreading, pilose, with glandular hairs especially below nodes. Leaves with pilose, rounded sheaths; ligule a minute ring of hairs; blades 8–20 cm long, 3–6 mm wide, usually flat below and involute toward tips, finely pilose. Inflorescence a panicle, the panicles loosely contracted, 10–20 cm

Fig. 201. *Cottea pappophoroides.* Plant; spikelet, floret, and cleistogamous floret.

long, 4–6 cm wide, branches stiff, erect-spreading, with dense, glandular
hairs, the hairs longer and shorter, spreading, the glands minute at hair tips;
cleistogamous spikelets often produced in reduced panicles in axils of lower
leaves. Spikelets usually 7–10 mm long, 4–6 mm wide, with 6–10 florets, the
upper 1–2 usually sterile; disarticulation above glumes and between florets;
glumes subequal, minutely pubescent, broadly lanceolate, about as long as
lemmas, 7–13-nerved, the midnerve often extended as a short awn; lemmas
broad, the margins irregularly lobed, long-hairy on lower part, 9–13-nerved,
the nerves prominent and extended into awns of unequal lengths but usually
1–3.5 mm long; palea somewhat longer than lemma body. Caryopsis oblong,
ca. 1.5 mm long.

Infrequent to rare, rocky slopes and canyons, desert habitats. Presidio Co.,
South Canyon, Bandera Mesa; Closed Canyon, 14 mi SE Redford; Panther
Canyon near Big Hill near Rio Grande. Brewster Co., "slick sides mountain,"
Big Bend Natl. Park. Terrell Co., mouth of San Francisco Canyon; 30 mi NE
Sanderson on Sheffield road. 2,100–4,200 ft. Flowering Jul–Nov. W to AZ. S
to central Mex. Ecuador to Argentina and Peru.

Cottea is not abundant enough in the Trans-Pecos to be of any forage value,
but the plants evidently are palatable to livestock and to wildlife.

Tribe 15. Aristideae

Traditionally the Aristideae has been considered to be a small tribe of three genera and about 300 species distributed mostly in the tropics and subtropics. By far the largest genus is *Aristida*, the only genus of this tribe in Texas. Recent evidence suggests that Aristideae might be recognized as a monotypic tribe with *Aristida* its only member (Esen and Hilu, 1991).

62. ARISTIDA   L.   THREEAWN.

Perennials and annuals, small to medium sized, lacking rhizomes or stolons. Culms erect or spreading. Leaves with blades narrow, usually involute; ligule a ring of hairs or a minute ciliate membrane. Inflorescence a panicle, open or contracted. Spikelets 1-flowered, disarticulation above glumes; glumes lanceolate, thin, central nerve prominent, 2 lateral nerves present or absent; lemma hardened, terete, 3-nerved, the base with a pointed, sharp, hard, usually minutely bearded callus, above the middle tapering to an awn column (beak) bearing usually 3 stiff awns, in a few species the lateral awns reduced only slightly or almost totally to minute points; palea enclosed by lemma. Caryopses long, slender, permanently enclosed by lemma.

A genus of about 250 species distributed throughout the warmer regions of the world. Gould (1975) recognized 23 species of *Aristida* for Texas. About 11 species occur in the Trans-Pecos. In general the threeawn grasses are considered to be poor forage because of the wiry inflorescences, stiff awns, and hard, sharp-pointed lemmas. The plants supposedly are palatable before inflorescences mature, mostly in the spring and early summer. I have observed a goat pasture in Alpine where in winter the only grasses left standing are aristidas. The fruits are disseminated by wind because of the awns, and by animals because of the awns and sharp calluses on the lemmas. The genus name is from Latin *arista*, awn. *Aristida* is noted for its taxonomic difficulty. Many described species complexes are comprised of closely related entities that might be recognized by different authors as conspecific, or as distinct species, or as varieties. Some populations apparently intergrade or hybridize. Considerable taxonomic work has been directed at *Aristida*. Allred (1984) has produced extensive clarification of the *A. purpurea* complex, and Trent (1985) and Trent and Allred (1990) have studied the divaricate threeawns of the southwestern United States. Allred is involved in ongoing studies of the genus. The present treatment of Trans-Pecos threeawns is tentative.

Key to the Species

1. Plants annual.
    2. Lemmas 1.8–2.6 cm long; awns 3–7 cm long   **1. *A. oligantha.***

    2. Lemmas 0.6–0.9 cm long; awns 0.7–2 cm long   **2. *A. adscensionis.***
1. Plants perennial.
    3. Lateral awns of lemma much reduced, 1–2 (rarely more) mm long, or minute to apparently absent.
        4. Panicle branches appressed.
            5. First glume 6.5–8 mm long, including a short awn; second glume 10–11 mm long; lemma ca. 10–11 mm long; sparse hairs or glabrous at leaf collars   **3. *A. brownii.***
            5. First glume ca. 5–6 mm long, awnless; second glume slightly longer than first glume; lemma ca. 5 mm long; cobwebby hairs at leaf collar edges   **4. *A. gypsophila.***
        4. Panicle branches stiffly spreading throughout or loosely contracted except for lower branches spreading at maturity.
            6. Awn column strongly twisted   **5. *A. schiedeana.***
            6. Awn column straight or slightly twisted
                6a. *A. ternipes* var. *ternipes.*
    3. Lateral awns of lemma more than 3 mm long, usually more than one-third as long as central awn.
        7. Panicle open, the main branches spreading at right angles or somewhat ascending (especially in *A. pansa*).
            8. Panicle branches ascending   **7. *A. pansa.***
            8. Panicle branches spreading at right angles, or perhaps reflexed at panicle base.
                9. Pedicels of spikelets and branchlets mostly spreading
                        8. *A. havardii.*
                9. Pedicels of spikelets and branchlets mostly appressed.
                    10. Awn column not twisted, or only slightly so, the column usually short and stout   **6b. *A. ternipes* var. *hamulosa.***
                    10. Awn column strongly twisted, usually slender and 2–5 mm long   **9. *A. divaricata.***
        7. Panicle contracted and narrow, the main branches appressed or ascending (perhaps somewhat spreading in *A. purpurea*).
            11. Leaf blades relatively broad and flat, usually curled at maturity; medium to upper woodland habitats, usually at slightly higher elevations than the *A. purpurea* complex   **10. *A. arizonica.***
             11. Leaf blades narrow, usually strongly involute; medium to lower woodland to desert habitats   **11. *A. purpurea.***

    1. Aristida oligantha Michx. OLDFIELD THREEAWN. Fig. 202. A weedy species in various soil types, usually disturbed habitats. Indicated by Gould (1975) as being present in the Trans-Pecos, but no Trans-Pecos specimens of oldfield threeawn are in the Sul Ross Herbarium. Flowering Aug–Nov. Reported from all regions of TX, most common in central and southern parts.

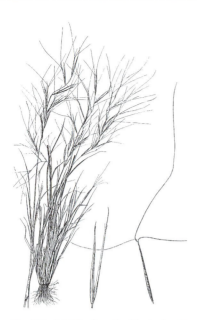

Fig. 202. *Aristida oligantha.* Plant; glumes and floret.

Fig. 203. *Aristida adscensionis.* Plant; glumes and floret.

Throughout much of the E United States, N to SD; reported from CA and other western states.

2. Aristida adscensionis L.   SIXWEEKS THREEAWN.   Fig. 203.   Widespread, common, often abundant, a weed in various soils, frequently disturbed sites, every county of the Trans-Pecos. 1,100–7,000 ft. Flowering mostly Jun–Nov. Also South Texas Plains, Edwards Plateau, and southern plains country. N to MO and KS, W to NV, CA. Mex. South America. Also Africa.

This very common "sixweeks annual" is extremely variable in size (culms 15–50 cm long), growth habit (erect or spreading), and longevity (more or less than six weeks). The glumes are unequal, lemmas 6–9 mm long to awn base, and the awns are flattened at the base with the central awn 7–20 mm long.

3. Aristida brownii Warnock   BROWN THREEAWN.   Fig. 204.   Reportedly widespread on limestone slopes and ridge tops, Del Norte Mts., elev. 4,600 ft. or more, and also in the Glass Mts. and Chisos Mts. At present known only from the type collection made in Jun 1981 (Warnock, 1982) and from four or five populations in W Texas and one population in S New Mexico (Kelly Allred, pers. comm.). A Sul Ross specimen from the W slopes of Old Blue, Glass Mts., 4,700 ft., has been identified by K. Allred as *A. brownii.* The

Fig. 204. *Aristida brownii.* Glumes (first one short-awned) and floret.

Fig. 205. *Aristida gypsophila.* Plant; cobwebby hairs at leaf collar edges; spicate panicle; glumes and floret.

Chisos Mts. collection, also identified by Allred, is from the upper slopes of Cattail Canyon W of Laguna Meadow, ca. 6,800 ft.

Allred (1984) commented about the possible relationship of *Aristida brownii* to *A. arizonica* and *A. schiedeana.* But during his ongoing and recent studies, Allred (pers. comm., 1992) has concluded tentatively that *A. brownii* is most closely related to *A. purpurea* var. *wrightii.* Warnock (1982) noted that *A. brownii* resembles *A. wrightii* in habit and ecological association. According to Johnston (1988; 1990), *A. brownii* is a synonym of *A. pansa.* Additional collection and study of the rarely collected *A. brownii* morphotypes should allow further evaluation of its relationship in the genus. Brown threeawn is reported by Warnock (1982) to be of minor importance as a forage grass, except like most threeawns, before the lemmas and awns develop.

4. Aristida gypsophila Beetle   GYP THREEAWN.   Fig. 205.   A Mexican species recently identified to occur in Texas in at least two localities (K. Allred, 1992, pers. comm.). Presidio Co., head of Hot Spring Creek, below Tierra Vieja Mts. rimrock; Solitario formation, W side above Fresno Creek. 3,500–4,200 ft. Flowering Jul–Oct. W Coahuila, Mex.

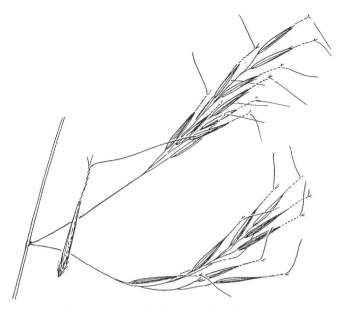

Fig. 206. *Aristida schiedeana.* Partial panicle; floret.

As suggested by the specific epithet, *Aristida gypsophila* was described as endemic to certain gypsum habitats (Beetle, 1981) at sites in Coahuila, Mexico. The two Trans-Pecos localities listed above apparently are not gypseous. Allred (pers. comm., 1992) has found *A. gypsophila* on non-gypseous (limestone) substrates in Mexico. *Aristida gypsophila* closely resembles *A. brownii* with its filiform and curved leaves, spicate panicles, and rudimentary to short (1–2 mm) lateral awns. Through initial work with the species, Allred (pers. comm., 1992) observed that *A. gypsophila* may be distinguished from *A. brownii* by mostly involute leaf blades (mostly flat or folded in *A. brownii*), distinctive cobwebby hairs at leaf collar edges, pulvini in primary axils of the panicle, subequal glumes that are a distinctive brown in color, and a more slender habit. According to Allred, *A. gypsophila* is related to *A. pansa*. Both *A. schiedeana* and *A. ternipes* var. *ternipes*, the other two Trans-Pecos aristidas with short lateral awns, usually can be distinguished by flat or involute leaf blades, spreading panicle branches, and other characters. Gyp threeawn has limited forage value in the Trans-Pecos.

5. Aristida schiedeana Trin. & Rupr. SINGLEAWN THREEAWN Fig. 206. [*A. orcuttiana* Vasey]. Infrequent in moist canyons and protected mountain slopes, often among trees, medium to high elevations. El Paso Co., Franklin Mts., 8 mi N El Paso. Jeff Davis Co., Davis Mts., Mt. Livermore, near Tobe's Gap; Goat Canyon; 1–2 mi N Bloys Campground; Davis Mts. State

Fig. 207. *Aristida ternipes* var. *ternipes*. Partial
panicle; glumes and floret.

Park; Rockpile; trail to Tricky Gap and Little Aguja Canyon; mid–Little Aguja
Canyon; Timber Mt.; 3.5 mi S Fort Davis, CDRI Landsite; Fern Canyon, top of
mesa, Mitre Peak Girl Scout Camp. Brewster Co., Chisos Mts., Big Bend Natl.
Park. 4,600–7,200 ft. Flowering Jul–Oct. W to S CA. NW Mex.

Singleawn threeawn is a tufted perennial with culms to 100 cm long, curled
leaves, stiffly spreading main branches of the panicle, much reduced lateral
awns, and twisted awn column. Reportedly this is the best threeawn forage
species in North America, although it is not considered to be abundant anywhere. *Aristida schiedeana* resembles *A. divaricata* in habit and in the spreading
panicles, but typical *A. divaricata* has subequal awns. Both have strongly
twisted awn columns. The correct name, *A. schiedeana*, for this taxon (Johnston, 1988; 1990) replaced a traditional name (*A. orcuttiana*) that is well known
to botanists in the region. According to Trent (1985), *A. schiedeana* may be
related to a Mexican species, *A. laxa* Cav., in that both share the long, twisted
awn column, drooping habit, and "woodshaving"-like leaves.

6a. Aristida ternipes Cav. var. **ternipes** SPIDERGRASS. Fig. 207.
Infrequent to common, rocky slopes, mesas, and canyons. El Paso Co., Frank-
lin Mts., McKelligon Canyon; 8 mi N El Paso. Hudspeth Co., Beach Mts., 8 mi
W Van Horn. Presidio Co., Sierra Vieja, Vieja Pass; above Capote Falls; Chinati
Mts., big canyon N side; near Shafter; Panther Canyon, near Big Hill and Rio
Grande; Eagle Crag Canyon; 101 Ranch; Elephant Mt., W slope. Jeff Davis Co.,

Mt. Locke, S slopes; Davis Mts. State Park; Lower Madera Canyon; Fern Canyon. Brewster Co., 4–8 mi W Alpine, Paradise Canyon, Sunny Glen; Sul Ross Hill; Kokernot Lodge, Alpine; 10 mi NE Alpine; Goat Mt.; Cienega Mt.; Cathedral Mt.; Nine Point Mesa; 10 mi N Lajitas near Big Hill; Chisos Mts., trail to Laguna, base of Bailey Peak, Basin, Green Gulch, Oak Canyon below the Window; Paint Gap Hills; Sierra Quemada near Dominguez Spring; Boquillas Canyon, nearby hills; Black Gap Refuge, Stairstep Mt. Ward Co., 7 mi NW Monahans. 1,900–6,600 ft. Flowering May–Oct. W to NM and AZ. Mex. S to N South America. West Indies.

A traditional species, *Aristida ternipes*, with its short lateral awns, was considered by Gould (1975) to be closely related to *A. hamulosa*, which is distinguished in its typical form by lateral awns about equal to or somewhat shorter than the central awns. *Aristida ternipes* is also similar to *A. schiedeana* in that both have short lateral awns and spreading panicles, but they are distinguished partly by the straight or only slightly twisted awn columns and subequal glumes in *A. ternipes*. In *A. schiedeana* the awn columns are strongly twisted and the glumes are unequal in length.

Considerable preliminary taxonomic information concerning certain *Aristida* species has been provided through the thesis work by J. S. Trent (1985). Trent studied the traditional species *A. ternipes, A. hamulosa, A. schiedeana, A. divaricata, A. havardii, A. pansa,* and *A. dissita.* In general Trent concluded that distinct forms of most of these taxa are recognizable, but that certain taxa also are linked by forms with intermediate characters. In the case of the "species pair" *A. ternipes* and *A. hamulosa*, Trent (1985) concluded that there are intermediates in awn length and other traits, and that *A. ternipes* and *A. hamulosa* are possibly conspecific. Later Trent and Allred (1990) formally merged the two taxa and recognized them as varieties. There are "spreading" and "appressed" forms of these two taxa where spikelet pedicels and branchlets are spreading from the panicle branches or they are appressed to the branches.

6b. Aristida ternipes Cav. var. **hamulosa** (Henr.) Trent HOOK THREEAWN. Fig. 208. [*Aristida hamulosa* Henr.]. Infrequent to common, rocky slopes, mesas, canyons, and basins, or plains. El Paso Co., Franklin Mts. Hudspeth Co., Quitman Mts., 10 mi W Sierra Blanca; 6 mi W Van Horn. Presidio Co., 25 mi S Marfa; 101 Ranch. Jeff Davis Co., 5 mi E Chispa; Madera Canyon; Barrel Springs; Davis Mts. State Park; Musquiz Canyon, 12–13 mi N Alpine; Fern Canyon. Brewster Co., between Alpine and Fort Davis; 2 mi N Alpine; Kokernot Lodge, Alpine; Sul Ross campus, Alpine; N slopes Twin Peaks; 6 mi S Alpine; 11 mi S Alpine; Goat Mt. Ward Co., 4 mi W Pickett; Monahans. 3,500–6,500 ft. Flowering Jun–Oct. W to southern CA. S to Guatemala.

As discussed above, the traditional *Aristida hamulosa* is considered to be conspecific with *A. ternipes* (Trent and Allred, 1990). *Aristida ternipes* var. *ha-*

Fig. 208. *Aristida ternipes* var. *hamulosa*.
Partial panicle; glumes and floret.

mulosa also resembles *A. divaricata*, which has, unlike *A. ternipes* var. *hamulosa*, a strongly twisted awn column. Both var. *hamulosa* and var. *ternipes* are more widely distributed and more common in the Trans-Pecos than is *A. schiedeana*, but all are fair forage grasses only prior to development of inflorescences.

7. Aristida pansa Woot. & Standl.   WOOTON THREEAWN.   Fig. 209. [*Aristida dissita* I. M. Johnst.]. Infrequent to frequent on rocky slopes and in alluvial basins. El Paso Co., Franklin Mts.; Hueco Mts. Hudspeth Co., 10 mi W Sierra Blanca; W side Van Horn Mts. Culberson Co., Guadalupe Mts., North McKittrick Canyon; Salt Flat Station; 21 mi N Kent. Presidio Co., 4 mi SW Valentine; 3 mi W San Estaban Lake; 2 mi S Shafter. Jeff Davis Co., 2 mi S Kent. Brewster Co., 20 mi NE Alpine; Glass Mts., Old Blue; 45 mi S Alpine, near Buckhill Mt.; 56 mi S Alpine; 2 mi SE Packsaddle Mt.; 5 mi W Study Butte. Reeves Co., Hwy 90, 1 mi E junct. Hwy 80. Pecos Co., 20–35 mi S Fort Stockton. Terrell Co., 12 mi S Sanderson. 2,300–5,600 ft. Flowering May–Nov. W Edwards Plateau, S plains country. W to NM, AZ. N Mex.

Correll and Johnston (1970) treated *Aristida dissita* as distinct, while Gould (1975) recognized it as synonymous with *A. barbata* (*A. havardii*). Trent

Fig. 209. *Aristida pansa*. Panicle.

Fig. 210. *Aristida havardii*. Plant; glumes and floret.

(1985) concluded that *A. pansa* and *A. dissita* intergrade to such an extent that distinct entities cannot be recognized. Kelly Allred (pers. comm., 1992) recognized the intergradation of *A. pansa* and *A. dissita*, and furthermore contended that *A. pansa/dissita* occasionally hybridizes with *A. purpurea*. The "hybrids" are generally distinguished by spreading panicle branches supporting spikelets with unequal glumes and long awns. Johnston (1988; 1990) listed *A. brownii* as synonymous with *A. pansa*, and retained *A. dissita* as a separate species, while adding *A. pansa* var. *dissita* (I. M. Johnst.) Beetle as a synonym of *A. dissita*.

8. Aristida havardii Vasey   HAVARD THREEAWN.   Fig. 210.   [*Aristida barbata* Fourn.]. Infrequent to common, mountain slopes, canyons, alluvial basins. El Paso Co., Franklin Mts. Hudspeth Co., 10 mi NE Sierra Blanca. Culberson Co., 2 mi W Van Horn. Presidio Co., Sierra Vieja, Capote Mt.; N Chinati Mts. Jeff Davis Co., 5 mi S Kent; Barrel Springs; Davis Mts. State Park; Musquiz Canyon. Brewster Co., 6 mi W Alpine; Mt. Ord; Glass Mts., Sibley Ranch; 10 mi S Alpine; Cathedral Mt.; Goat Mt.; Elephant Mt.; Chisos Mts.; Green Gulch, near top of Mt. Emory. Ward Co., 4 mi E Monahans. 3,500–7,500 ft. Flowering May–Oct. Southern High Plains. W to AZ. S to central Mex.

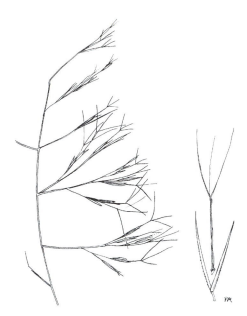

Fig. 211. *Aristida divaricata*. Partial panicle;
glumes and floret.

Aristida havardii is recognized by some workers as *A. barbata*, but according to Trent (1985) the correct name by nomenclatural priority is *A. havardii*. Havard threeawn in typical habit is a relatively low, hemispherical threeawn, 15–40 cm high, commonly with densely spreading panicles, but also with an "appressed" form. The key characters (above) are for identifying distinct forms of the respective taxa. Trent (1985) has concluded that *A. havardii* and *A. divaricata* are closely related, with many intermediate forms in panicle spreading and other traits.

 9. Aristida divaricata Willd. POVERTY THREEAWN. Fig. 211. Rocky mountain slopes and canyons. El Paso Co., 6 mi N El Paso. Hudspeth Co., 2 mi N Allamoore. Presidio Co., Capote Mt., S slopes; Chinati Mts., Tigna Canyon; big canyon above Shely Ranch house, N side; Elephant Mt.; 10 mi W Marfa. Jeff Davis Co., Davis Mts., Friend Ranch S of Livermore; Davis Mts. State Park; top of Fern Canyon. Brewster Co., Sul Ross campus, Alpine; 10 mi S Alpine; Goat Mt.; Chisos Mts., upper Cattail Canyon, above Boot Spring, lower Pine Canyon. 3,800–7,000 ft. Flowering Jul–Nov. Also southern High Plains in TX. N to KS, W to CA. Mex. Guatemala.

 The collection sites listed above include those for some specimens intermediate between *Aristida divaricata* and *A. havardii*. The culms of *A. divaricata*

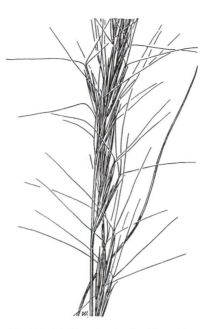

Fig. 212. *Aristida arizonica*. Partial panicle.

usually are longer (25–70 cm long) than are those of *A. havardii*. Gould (1975) discussed other classic distinctions between *A. divaricata* and *A. havardii*, including usually larger panicles with longer main branches, and appressed spikelet pedicels and branchlets in *A. divaricata*. Trent (1985) found, however, that *A. divaricata* exhibits both "appressed" and "spreading" forms, as does *A. havardii*. Plants of *A. divaricata* in typical form are larger, with larger panicles, and well-developed, twisted awn columns, but the intergradation of these characters with those of *A. havardii* suggests that eventually the two entities might be merged. Hitchcock (1951), Correll and Johnston (1970), and Gould (1975) noted the resemblance of *A. divaricata* to *A. hamulosa*, the two differing mostly by the twisted awn column in *A. divaricata*.

10. Aristida arizonica Vasey   ARIZONA THREEAWN.   Fig. 212.   Infrequent on medium to higher elevation mountains, slopes, woodland habitats. Jeff Davis Co., Davis Mts., Mt. Livermore; Sproul Ranch; Lower Madera Canyon. Brewster Co., Chisos Mts., Boot Spring area, trail from Boot Spring to Laguna, South Rim, upper Green Gulch. 5,000–8,200 ft. Flowering Jun–Oct. N to CO, W to AZ. Mex.

Gould (1975) observed that *A. arizonica* is a distinct species closely related to *A. glauca*, which also has twisted awn columns, and tends to occupy drier

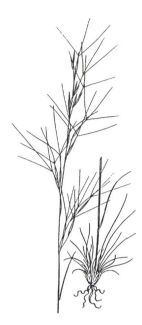

Fig. 213. *Aristida purpurea.* Partial plant.

habitats at medium to lower elevations. Plants of *A. arizonica* also have narrow panicles, subequal glumes, and flat, curled (resembling wood shavings) lower leaf blades. Allred (1984) reported the relationship of *A. arizonica* to be with a group of Mexican and Central American species, but he also viewed *A. arizonica* as a link between the Mexican–Central American species and the *A. purpurea* complex, which includes *A. glauca*, and is abundant in the Trans-Pecos.

11. Aristida purpurea Nutt.   PURPLE THREEAWN.   Fig. 213.   Common in various habitats, mountain slopes and canyons, alluvial basins, desert slopes, mesas, and flats, sometimes abundant at roadside and in other disturbed sites. Present in all counties of the Trans-Pecos. 1,000–6,500 ft. Flowering Apr–Nov. Throughout most of TX. Central and W United States. Southern British Columbia. N Mex.

The present treatment follows the work of Allred (1984), who merged seven or eight somewhat weak and controversial (but traditional) taxa with one species, *Aristida purpurea*. This included six species Gould (1975) recognized as distinct, although Gould also fully recognized the morphological intergradation and subsequent weak distinction between most of the taxa concerned. In the Trans-Pecos and elsewhere in the range of these traditional species, *A. purpurea, A. roemeriana, A. longiseta, A. fendleriana, A. glauca,* and *A. wrightii* are difficult to identify except where key characters had been devised by Hitchcock

(1951), Correll and Johnston (1970), Gould (1975), and others to facilitate recognition of typical forms. The extensive study by Allred (1984) resulted in the recognition of the single species *A. purpurea* and seven varieties which he characterized as "meaningful recognizable morphological units" that should be recognized taxonomically. Five of these varieties of *A. purpurea* occur in the Trans-Pecos. The key to varieties is adapted from Allred (1984).

Key to the Varieties of Aristida Purpurea

1. Awns 4–10 cm long.
    2. Apex of the lemma 0.1–0.3 mm wide; awns delicate, at the base usually 0.2 mm or less wide, 4–6 cm long; second glume usually shorter than 16 mm   **A. var. *purpurea.***
    2. Apex of the lemma 0.3–0.8 mm wide; awns usually stout, at the base more than 0.2 mm wide, 4–10 cm long; second glume 14–25 mm long   **B. var. *longiseta.***
1. Awns 1–3.5 cm long (to 4 cm long in var. *fendleriana*).
    3. Apex of lemma often narrowed to a slender awn column, usually less than 0.2 mm wide; awns delicate, at the base usually less than 0.2 mm wide.
        4. Panicle branches and pedicels in an "S" or "U" shape   **A. var. *purpurea.***
        4. Panicle branches and pedicels stiff, erect, sometimes spreading   **D. var. *nealleyi.***
    3. Apex of lemma usually not narrowed into a definite awn column, the apex usually more than 0.2 mm wide; awns stout, at the base usually more than 0.2 mm wide.
        5. Panicle branches and pedicels slender and curving in an "S" or "U" shape   **A. var. *purpurea.***
        5. Panicle branches usually stiff and straight, erect or less often spreading.
            6. Panicles usually 3–14 cm long   **C. var. *fendleriana.***
            6. Panicles usually 15–30 cm long   **E. var. *wrightii.***

The following synopsis includes the varieties of *Aristida purpurea* that are believed to occur in the Trans-Pecos, and synonymy pertinent to the Trans-Pecos taxa. For a more complete account of *A. purpurea*, see Allred (1984).

A. *Aristida purpurea* Nutt. var. **purpurea** PURPLE THREEAWN. Fig. 214. [*Aristida roemeriana* Scheele, ROEMER THREEAWN]. Distributed from TX E to LA, N to AR and KS, W to UT, NV, and CA. N Mex. Also Cuba. Allred (1984) considered var. *purpurea* to be a "catch-all" taxon including plants intermediate between the typical var. *purpurea* and var. *wrightii*, and the plants Gould (1975) and others have referred to *A. roemeriana*.

Fig. 214. *Aristida purpurea* var. *purpurea* (=*A. roemeriana*). Partial panicle.

B. *Aristida purpurea* var. **longiseta** (Steudel) Vasey RED THREEAWN. Fig. 215. [*Aristida longiseta* Steudel]. Distributed from TX N to IA, ND, and S British Columbia, NW to OR and WA. N Mex. Allred (1984) regarded var. *longiseta* to be one of the most variable varieties within *A. purpurea*, including relatively tall plants with cauline leaves and long panicles to short plants with basal leaves and short panicles. The var. *longiseta* differs from var. *purpurea* and var. *fendleriana* by its longer awns and glumes and wider lemma apexes and awn bases.

C. *Aristida purpurea* var. **fendleriana** (Steudel) Vasey FENDLER THREEAWN.   Fig. 216.   [*Aristida fendleriana* Steudel]. Trans-Pecos collections: Hudspeth Co., 5 mi E Hueco, Hueco Mts. Jeff Davis Co., Timber Mt. Distributed from TX N to ND and MT, W to NV and S CA. N Mexico and Baja CA. The var. *fendleriana* is distinguished from var. *longiseta* by its shorter awns (1.8–4 cm long) and more slender lemma apexes and awn bases. The var. *wrightii* differs from var. *fendleriana* by its longer leaf blades, longer panicles, and usually shorter awns (Allred, 1984). *Aristida fendleriana* classically has been identified as plants with short, basal leaves, short panicles, and relatively long awns (Gould, 1975), but as Allred (1984) pointed out, many plants with just these characters may also belong with var. *longiseta*.

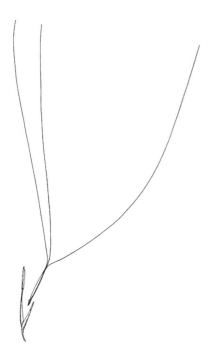

Fig. 215. *Aristida purpurea* var. *longiseta.* Glumes and floret.

Fig. 216. *Aristida purpurea* var. *fendleriana.* Plant.

D. *Aristida purpurea* var. **nealleyi** (Vasey) Allred NEALLEY THREEAWN. Fig. 217. [*Aristida glauca* (Nees) Walp.; BLUE THREEAWN. *Aristida nealleyi* Vasey. *Aristida stricta* var. *nealleyi* Vasey]. Trans-Pecos collections: El Paso Co., Franklin Mts.; Hueco Mts. Culberson Co., Guadalupe Mts.; Apache Mts. Brewster Co., Terlingua Creek near Agua Fria Mt. Crane Co., 3–16 mi W Crane. Distributed from TX N to OK, W to UT, NV, and CA. N Mex. According to Allred (1984), var. *nealleyi* is a relatively distinct taxon, with tight foliage and straw colored panicles, but it does intergrade morphologically with the *roemeriana* form of var. *purpurea*. The panicles of var. *nealleyi* are much like those of var. *wrightii*, but in var. *nealleyi* the awns are smaller and the lemmas are more slender. Gould (1975), who recognized the well-known *A. glauca* as a species, considered it to be a catch-all taxon. Allred (1984) pointed out that while *glauca* would have been a more familiar name for this variety of *A. purpurea*, by nomenclatural priority it must be var. *nealleyi*.

E. *Aristida purpurea* var. **wrightii** (Nash) Allred WRIGHT THREEAWN. Fig. 218. [*Aristida wrightii* Nash]. Distributed from TX N to OK, and NW to CO and S UT, W to CA. N Mex. The var. *wrightii* and var. *purpurea* are similar

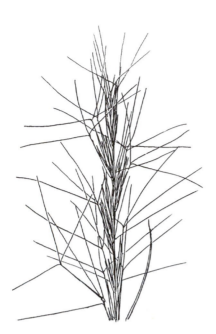
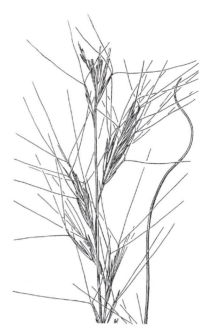

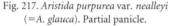

Fig. 217. *Aristida purpurea* var. *nealleyi*   Fig. 218. *Aristida purpurea* var. *wrightii.*
(=*A. glauca*). Partial panicle.   Partial panicle.

in several characters including lemma shape, but var. *wrightii* usually has panicles tan to brown (fading to straw colored), while panicles of var. *purpurea* usually are purplish. The var. *wrightii* and var. *nealleyi* both have narrow panicles but appear to be less closely related to each other than to other taxa of the *A. purpurea* complex (Allred, 1984).

SUBFAMILY V. PANICOIDEAE

Tribe 16. Paniceae

The Paniceae is a very large tribe in the grass family with about 2,000 species in about 101 genera (Clayton and Renvoize, 1986). The tribe is pantropical in distribution, with many elements extending into temperate North America. Gould (1975) recognized 18 genera of Paniceae for Texas. Some of them are merged with *Panicum* in the treatment of nine genera presented herein for the Trans-Pecos area. Important characters of the Paniceae include the indurated upper floret which encloses the fruit. The lower floret is often reduced to an empty lemma, and the glumes also usually are thin, with the lower (or first) glume often rudimentary. Much biological information about Paniceae is included by Crins (1991) in his generic treatment of this tribe for the southeastern United States. Crins discusses numerous taxa that also occur in the Trans-Pecos.

Key to the Genera of Paniceae

1. Spikelets surrounded by bristles or flattened spines that may be fused to form subtending involucres (burs) that disarticulate with the enclosed 1–4 spikelets.
   2. Bristles or flattened, hard spines fused together, at least at the base
   71. *Cenchrus*, p. 308
   2. Bristles, some of them whitish and plumose, not fused together
   70. *Pennisetum*, p. 307
1. Spikelets not enclosed in bristly or spiny involucres that fall with the spikelets, if bristles present these persistent in the inflorescence.
   3. Spikelets subtended by 1–several bristles (at least those spikelets near branchlet apexes)   **69. *Setaria*, p. 296**
   3. Spikelets not subtended by bristles.
      4. Inflorescence with spikelets sunken on one side in a flattened, fleshy articulated rachis (introduced lawn grass, St. augustinegrass)
      64. *Stenotaphrum*, p. 262
      4. Inflorescence not as above.
         5. Second glume awned; first glume and lemma of lower (sterile) floret awned or awnless (awn reduced to a short point in *E. colona*)
         68. *Echinochloa*, p. 291
         5. Second glume, first glume, and lower lemma awnless.
            6. Lemma of upper (fertile) floret with thin hyaline margins overlapping the palea, the fertile lemma usually dark colored
            63. *Digitaria*, p. 256
            6. Lemma of upper floret with margins inrolled and not readily visible over the palea, the lemma usually whitish or pallid.
               7. First glume present on all spikelets   **66. *Panicum*, p. 266**
               7. First glume absent on some or all of the spikelets.
                  8. Rachis at base of spikelet with a ringlike or cuplike callus; lemma of upper floret mucronate or short-awned
                  65. *Eriochloa*, p. 264
                  8. Rachis at base of spikelet without a ringlike callus; lemma of upper floret not mucronate or awned
                  67. *Paspalum*, p. 286

63. DIGITARIA Haller CRABGRASS, COTTONTOP.

Perennials and annuals. Culms erect to decumbent and spreading. Leaves with membranous ligules; blades usually thin, flat. Inflorescence a panicle, with spikelike primary branches crowded at the apex or within a few cm of apex of main axis, the spikelike branches unbranched or sparingly branched near the base, the axis (rachis) of spikelike branches flat or 3-angled and perhaps winged, with spikelets in 2 rows, subsessile or short-pedicelled. Spikelets 2-flowered, with silky hairs or not, the upper floret perfect, the lower one staminate or neuter; disarticulation below the glumes; glumes unequal, the first one minute or absent, the second glume usually shorter than lemma of lower floret, but well-developed; lemma of upper (perfect) floret narrow, firm, and cartilaginous, but not hard, the margins thin, flat, not inrolled over the palea, apex acute or acuminate. [*Trichachne* Nees; *Leptoloma* Chase].

A genus of about 220 species found in both tropical and temperate regions of the world, with about 22 taxa in North America (Webster, 1988). The treatment here follows Gould (1975) and other authors in submerging *Trichachne* Nees, a small taxon with about 15 species in Australia and warmer regions of the Americas, in the larger genus *Digitaria*. The submerged genus name *Trichachne* was taken from Greek *trich-*, hair, and *achne*, chaff, in reference to the long-silky spikelets of the species belonging to this group. The genus name *Digitaria* is from Latin *digitus*, finger, in reference to the digitate spikelike branches of the panicles. Gould (1975) recognized 13 species of *Digitaria* for Texas. In general the species are good forage grasses.

Key to the Species

1. Annuals with weak culms frequently decumbent and rooting at the lower nodes; rachis of spikelike primary branches winged.
    2. Lower lemma with minute spicules (thus scabrous-hispid) on the lateral nerves; leaf blades usually with papilla-based hairs   **1. *D. sanguinalis.***
    2. Lower lemma without spicules on the lateral nerves; leaf blades usually without hairs, except perhaps at leaf blade base   **2. *D. ciliaris.***
1. Perennials with erect, tufted culms; rachis of spikelike primary branches not winged.
    3. Spikelets on short, appressed pedicels, these on only several spicate branches of the panicle.
        4. Sterile lemmas pubescent between all the nerves; spikelets 2.5–3 mm long, villous, the hairs grayish, 1 mm or less long; inflorescence slender, usually with only 3–6 branches   **3. *D. hitchcockii.***
        4. Sterile lemmas glabrous from midnerve to adjacent lateral nerves; spikelets 3–4 mm long, villous, the hairs silvery or purple-tinged, 2–4 mm long; inflorescence dense, usually with more than 3–6 branches   **4. *D. californica.***

Fig. 219. *Digitaria sanguinalis.* Plant; spikelet
(two views) and floret (above).

3. Spikelets on relatively long, slender pedicels in an open (at maturity)
panicle with spreading branches   **5. *D. cognata.***

1. Digitaria sanguinalis (L.) Scop. HAIRY CRABGRASS. Fig. 219.
Common weed, fields, gardens, lawns, golf courses, roadsides, and other cul-
tivated and disturbed sites, particularly where there is frequent moisture. El
Paso Co., Franklin Mts. Presidio Co., Chinati Mts., bog in Tigna Canyon. Jeff
Davis Co., Madera Canyon roadside park; Mt. Livermore, upper spring, Ma-
dera Canyon; upper Goat Canyon; Davis Mts. State Park; Mitre Peak Girl Scout
Camp, Fern Canyon; Haystack Mt. Brewster Co., yards and gardens, Alpine.
4,400–7,500 ft. Flowering Jul–Nov. Throughout most of TX and the United
States into Canada. Mex. Reportedly adventive from Europe.

Digitaria sanguinalis is one of the six species of *Digitaria* section *Digitaria*
(Webster, 1987), a group of species commonly known as crabgrass. In the large
genus *Digitaria* numerous other sections (about 30) are recognized (Henrard,
1950). The section *Digitaria* includes annual species with paired spikelets occurring on winged primary spicate branches. These weedy species have near
worldwide distribution. In North America it is not uncommon to find more
than one species at the same site. *Digitaria sanguinalis* is distinguishable from
D. ciliaris only by microscopic examination, except to the extent that hairs

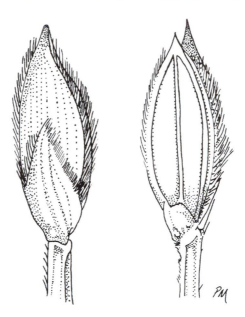

Fig. 220. *Digitaria ciliaris.* Spikelet (two views).

can be seen with the naked eye on upper leaf blade surfaces in *D. sanguinalis.* In *D. sanguinalis* the lower lemmas have tiny, forward-projecting spicules, or short, curved hairs, extending from the lateral margins, particularly the anterior margins, and usually the spikelets are otherwise mostly glabrous (Webster, 1987). In *D. ciliaris* the leaves are without hairs except perhaps at the leaf blade base, and the lower lemma margins have silky, often appressed, rows of hairs but no spicules on the lemma margins. Occasional intermediates occur (Webster, 1987). I have observed intermediates in Alpine, Texas, where *D. ciliaris* seems to be the prominent crabgrass species, but in the Trans-Pecos *D. sanguinalis* and *D. ciliaris* usually are distinguishable by the microscopic key characters discussed above. Hairy crabgrass is palatable to livestock and is good forage where abundant enough.

   2. Digitaria ciliaris (Retz.) Koel.   SOUTHERN CRABGRASS.   Fig. 220. [*Digitaria adscendens* (H.B.K.) Henr.; *D. sanguinalis* var. *ciliaris* (Retz.) Parl.]. Locally common weed in various disturbed sites with frequent moisture. Presidio Co., Chinati Mts., big canyon above Shely Ranch house, NE side. Jeff Davis Co., Davis Mts., Limpia Canyon, 1 mi above Fort Davis; 2 mi above Fort Davis; springs, Merrill Ranch; 12–15 mi N Alpine. Brewster Co., Alpine city limits; Sul Ross campus; Del Norte Mts., Doubtful Canyon; Chisos Mts., lower Green Gulch; Government Springs, Big Bend Natl. Park; Rio Grande at Boquillas. Terrell Co., Pecos River. 1,500–5,200 ft. Flowering Jun–Nov. Throughout most of TX. E half of United States, through Mex., Central America, to South America. Introduced from Old World.

In the Trans-Pecos *D. ciliaris* appears to be more common at intermediate and lower elevations while *D. sanguinalis* seems to be more restricted in the central mountains. The two taxa do occur together in Alpine and probably other sites in the central mountains. The Sul Ross specimens of *D. ciliaris* all exhibit the silky hairs in rows between the veins on the margins of lower lemmas, although in this species the hairs may be present or absent (Webster, 1987). Another widespread and similar crabgrass species, *D. bicornis* (Lam.) Roemer & Schultz, is suspected but not yet documented to occur in the Trans-Pecos. In Texas *D. bicornis* does occur in the adjacent South Texas Plains as well as elsewhere in the United States. *Digitaria bicornis* is most like *D. ciliaris* in its lower lemma characters, with the silky hairs usually on the marginal interspaces (Webster, 1987). But *D. bicornis* differs in that the plants are yellow-green in color, the very short first glume is cleft to rounded (rarely acute as in *D. ciliaris* and *D. sanguinalis*), and the nerves on the back of the lower lemma are equidistant from midrib to margins instead of being wider from the midrib and crowded at the margins as in *D. sanguinalis*. All of the crabgrass species are highly palatable.

3. Digitaria hitchcockii (Chase) Stuck. SHORTLEAF COTTONTOP. Fig. 221. [*Trichachne hitchcockii* (Chase) Chase]. Relatively rare, rocky slopes, canyons, mesas. Culberson Co., Guadalupe Mts., between Pratt Ranch house and McKittrick Canyon. Jeff Davis Co., Fern Canyon, Mitre Peak Girl Scout Camp. Pecos Co., Sierra Madera, main canyon on NE side, 25 mi S Fort Stockton. Terrell Co., 9 mi E Sanderson. Val Verde Co., near Pecos River Canyon, 1 mi W of bridge. 1,700–4,600 ft. Flowering May–Nov. Also South Texas Plains. Adjacent Mex.

Reportedly shortleaf cottontop is palatable to livestock and would be a good forage species except that it is not widespread and it is rarely abundant enough to be useful. The leaf blades of *D. hitchcockii* are 2–5 cm long and 2–3 mm wide, as compared to blades 2–12 cm long and 2–5(–7) mm wide in the common California cottontop. *Digitaria hitchcockii* is easily distinguished from *D. californica* in habit by its slender, few-branched inflorescences that are merely grayish at maturity, and microscopically by the short rows of hairs between veins on the back of the lower lemma, and relatively short marginal hairs (less than 1 mm) on the lower lemma. The common name cottontop is applied to *Digitaria* species that have been included in a separate genus, *Trichachne* (Hitchcock, 1951; Correll and Johnston, 1970).

4. Digitaria californica (Benth.) Henr. CALIFORNIA COTTONTOP. Fig. 222. [*Trichachne californica* (Benth.) Chase]. Mountain slopes, canyons, and on well-drained alluvial plains, usually infrequent but widespread and common throughout the Trans-Pecos; particularly in all major and minor

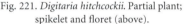

Fig. 221. *Digitaria hitchcockii.* Partial plant;
spikelet and floret (above).

Fig. 222. *Digitaria californica.* Plant; spikelets
(several views) and floret (two views).

mountain systems; probably more common in desert and semidesert habitats.
1,300–6,500 ft. Flowering May–Nov. Throughout much of TX. N to CO, W
to AZ. Mex.

California cottontop is palatable throughout the year and is regarded as
being good forage for livestock and fair forage for wildlife. The plants are tol-
erant of drought conditions and respond well after overgrazing. Plants with
mature inflorescences are recognizable for their dense, whitish to silvery panicles. The collective silvery appearance is furnished by dense hairs 2–4 mm long
on the margins of lower lemmas. The backs of the lower lemmas are glabrous.
A third cottontop species, *Digitaria insularis* (L.) Mez *ex* Ekmann (sourgrass),
is reported for the Trans-Pecos (Gould, 1975), but this species does not appear
to be represented among the numerous collections of Trans-Pecos *Digitaria* at
Sul Ross. Sourgrass is recognized by dense brownish hairs 2–4 mm long, usually on the backs as well as the margins of lower lemmas. Sourgrass is rather
frequent in the South Texas Plains, usually in ditches and along depressions,
and eventually may be found in the Trans-Pecos, particularly at roadside. In
Correll and Johnston (1970), sourgrass is listed as *Trichachne nutans* (L.)
Baum, although the name in reference to sourgrass should have been *T. insularis* (L.) Nees (Johnston, 1988; 1990). Johnston (1988; 1990) points out that

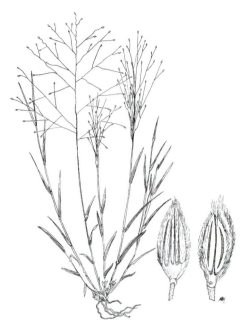

Fig. 223. *Digitaria cognata* var. *cognata* (=*Leptoloma cognatum*). Plant; spikelet (two views).

the name *T. nutans* (L.) Baum is a synonym of *Sorghastrum nutans* (L.) Nash (Veldkamp, 1984). The common name is in reference to the unpleasant odor, much like rotting lemons, produced at plant bases when foliage is crushed.

5. Digitaria cognata (Schult.) Pilg. var. **cognata**   FALL WITCHGRASS. Fig. 223.   [*Leptoloma cognatum* (Schult.) Chase]. Mountain slopes, canyons, mesas, and flats, mesic to desert habitats, widespread and abundant, occurring in all counties of the Trans-Pecos. Most commonly found in mountain systems. 1,200–6,500 ft. Flowering May–Nov. Throughout most of TX. E half of the United States into Canada; W to AZ. N Mex.

Many agrostologists including Gould (1975) have long recognized this taxon as belonging to the genus *Leptoloma*, but Webster (1988) has concluded that *Leptoloma* can be defined as a distinct genus only when compared with North American species of *Digitaria* and therefore should be combined with *Digitaria*. Gould (1975) recognized two varieties, var. *cognatum* (fall witchgrass), the widespread taxon and the one occurring in the Trans-Pecos, and var. *arenicola* (Swallen) Gould (sand witchgrass), seemingly restricted to coastal sands in Texas. The var. *arenicola* produces creeping rhizomes. The var. *cognatum* has a relatively weak roots system. Hatch et al. (1990) list *Digitaria cognata* subsp. **pubiflora** (Dewey) Wipff as the Trans-Pecos entity of this spe-

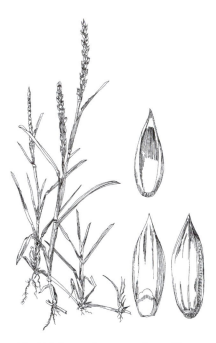

Fig. 224. *Stenotaphrum secundatum.* Plant;
spikelet (two views) and fertile floret.

cies. Fall witchgrass is generally rated as providing fair grazing for livestock and
for wildlife. The plants are relatively inconspicuous, on grassy mountain slopes
for example, but when in flower they are recognizable by the spreading panicles with silvery spikelets at the end of delicate pedicels.

64. STENOTAPHRUM   Trin.   ST. AUGUSTINEGRASS.

A genus of about seven species distributed mostly in tropical and subtropical regions of both hemispheres (Sauer, 1972). Only one species occurs in the
United States. The genus name is from Greek, *stenos*, narrow, and *taphros*,
trench, alluding to the cavities in the rachis.

1. Stenotaphrum secundatum (Walt.) Kuntze.   ST. AUGUSTINEGRASS.
Fig. 224.   Perennial, stoloniferous, mat-forming. Culms decumbent,
branched, creeping, flowering branches erect. Leaves essentially glabrous,
sheaths sparsely ciliate on upper margins; ligule a small fringed membrane;
blades thick, flat, 3–15 cm long, or longer, 4–10 mm wide, apex rounded.
Inflorescence spikelike, 5–10 cm long, with appressed branches each with
1–3 essentially sessile spikelets. Spikelets partly embedded in one side of thick,
flattened rachis; disarticulation at nodes of rachis, spikelets falling attached to

Fig. 225. *Axonopus compressus*. Plant; spikelet
(two views) and floret.

sections. Spikelets 2-flowered, 4–5 mm long, lower floret staminate or neuter, upper floret perfect; first glume short, rounded; second glume and lemma of lower floret about equal and similar; lemma of upper floret papery, ovate, awnless, acute, margins flat.

Used as a lawn grass in yards of Alpine, and elsewhere in towns of the Trans-Pecos. Flowering in the summer. In TX Edwards Plateau E throughout most of the state except the plains country, used as a lawn grass and also spontaneous in moist soils along streams, near lakes, and in low areas. E to SC, FL, and W to CA and possibly elsewhere in the U.S. Throughout much of the world tropics and subtropics.

The relatively broad-leaved, mat-forming St. augustinegrass is widely favored as a lawn grass in moist regions of Texas, where it is also called "carpetgrass." This species is used in Trans-Pecos lawns, where heavy watering is required to maintain lush growth. *Stenotaphrum secundatum* apparently is not native to the United States, but it was known in the Carolinas along the eastern coast before the year 1800 (Sauer, 1972). In many tropical areas of the world the species originally became established as a coastal pioneer. A variegated form of St. augustinegrass is used as a basket plant. St. augustinegrass is propagated by stolon joints, as is another lawn grass known commonly as carpetgrass, *Axonopus compressus* (Swartz) Beauv. (Fig. 225). *Axonopus compressus* does not occur in Texas, but two other species are found in eastern regions of the state, including *A. affinis* Chase (common carpetgrass), which is closely related to *A. compressus* (Gould, 1975). It is likely that both of these *Axonopus* species are to be found in eastern Texas lawns, but the extent of their use in lawns of the Trans-Pecos is not evident at the present time.

65. ERIOCHLOA H.B.K. CUPGRASS.

Perennials or annuals, tufted or not. Culms erect or decumbent. Leaves with rounded or laterally compressed sheaths; ligule usually a fringe of hairs from a basal minute rim; blades usually flat, linear. Inflorescence a panicle, contracted or with somewhat spreading primary branches, secondary branches appressed. Spikelets solitary or paired on pedicels and in two rows on one side of the narrow rachis, 2-flowered, the lower floret staminate or neuter (and resembling the second glume) with palea present, reduced, or absent, the upper floret perfect; disarticulation below the spikelet; glumes very different, first glume reduced and fused with rachilla tissue to form a usually discolored cuplike structure or ringlike disc (the "callus") at base of spikelet; second glume nearly equal and resembling lemma of lower (sterile) floret, both glume and lemma hispid or hirsute, apex acute, acuminate, or short-awned; lemma of upper (fertile) floret glabrous, indurated (hardened), finely rugose on the rounded back, margins slightly inrolled, apex apiculate or short-awned. Caryopses not grooved.

A genus of 25–30 species in warm regions of the world. Shaw and Webster (1987) reported that 15 species, eight perennial and seven annual, are represented in North and Central America, nine of these distributed in the southwestern United States and Mexico. Six species are represented in Texas (Shaw and Webster, 1987). Only three species are reported to occur in the Trans-Pecos (Shaw and Webster, 1987), but a fourth species, rather widespread in Texas, *E. sericea* (Scheele) Munro, occurs in Crockett County and eventually may be found in the Trans-Pecos. In general the cupgrass species are highly palatable but of limited forage value in Texas because the plants are either not sufficiently abundant or they do not survive well under grazing pressure. In the Trans-Pecos these plants are found mostly in disturbed areas. The common name "cupgrass" comes from the small, usually dark colored, cup or ring of (swollen) tissue, with remnants of the first glume, positioned immediately below each spikelet at the point of disarticulation (Shaw and Webster, 1987). The cuplike swellings contain lipids that may attract ants, which subsequently aid in the dispersal of caryopses (Davidse, 1987). The "cup" character is barely visible to the naked eye and becomes one of the best traits by which to distinguish the genus. The genus name is taken from Greek *erion*, wool, and *chloa*, grass, in reference to the long hairs on the spikelets and pedicels.

Fig. 226. *Eriochloa acuminata.* Plant; spikelet
(two views) and floret.

Key to the Species

1. Leaf blades glabrous to puberulent, usually 5–12 mm wide; lemma of fertile floret (the hardened floret) distinctly mucronate or awned.
   2. Lemma of the fertile floret mucronate, the mucro 0.1–0.3 mm long; spikelets typically 20–36 on primary branch; leaves glabrous or nearly so   **1. *E. acuminata.***
   2. Lemma of the fertile floret awned, the awn usually 0.5–0.8 mm long; spikelets typically 8–16 on primary branch; leaves pubescent
           2. *E. contracta.*
1. Leaf blades velvety-pubescent, 6–20 mm wide; lemma of fertile floret merely acute to rounded   **3. *E. lemmonii.***

1. Eriochloa acuminata (Presl) Kunth   SOUTHWESTERN CUPGRASS. Fig. 226.   An annual typically growing as a weed in disturbed habitats at roadside, near campsites, on golf courses, and elsewhere. Shaw and Webster (1987) recognized two varieties of *E. acuminata* to occur in the Trans-Pecos: *Eriochloa acuminata* var. **acuminata** [*E. gracilis* (Fourn.) Hitchc.; *E. lemmonii* Vasey & Scribn. var. *gracilis* (Fourn.) Gould] is distinguished by spikelets 4–6 mm long, acuminate or tapering to a short awn, and leaf blades usually glabrous but pubescent in some plants. Shaw and Webster (1987) cited specimens of this taxon from: El Paso Co., El Paso; Franklin Mts.; Hueco Mts. Culberson Co., 9K Ranch. Presidio Co., Marfa. Brewster Co., Alpine. *Eriochloa acuminata* var. **minor** (Vasey) Shaw [*E. punctata* (L.) Desv. *ex* Hamilt. var. *minor* (Vasey) Hitchc.] is distinguished by spikelets usually less than 4 mm long, merely acute, and leaf blades usually pubescent but glabrous in some plants. Shaw and Webster (1987) cited specimens of this taxon from: El Paso Co., El Paso; Hueco Tanks. Presidio Co., Marfa. Brewster Co., W of Alpine. Specimens housed in the Sul Ross Herbarium appear to be of *E. acuminata* var. *acuminata*, because of their acuminate and awned spikelets, but the spikelets are generally less than 4 mm long and the leaves of all but one specimen (from Marfa) are glabrous. Culberson Co., Delaware Creek. Presidio Co., Marfa. Jeff Davis Co., Rockpile; Mitre Peak Girl Scout Camp. Brewster Co., Kokernot Ranch road, 8 mi N Alpine; Alpine; Chalk Draw E of Santiago Peak. 3,700–6,000 ft. Flowering Jul–Nov. *Eriochloa acuminata* apparently is uncommon in TX outside the Trans-Pecos, but is reported to occur on the Edwards Plateau and Rolling Plains (Gould, 1975). Also a weed elsewhere in the U.S. and Mex. (Shaw and Webster, 1987).

2. Eriochloa contracta Hitchc.   PRAIRIE CUPGRASS.   Fig. 227.   An annual usually growing as a weed in various, often moist, disturbed sites. Reported by Shaw and Webster (1987) to occur in the Trans-Pecos in El Paso Co., El Paso. Gould (1975) reported the species from throughout TX, except the Trans-Pecos. Flowering Apr–Nov. N to NE and MO, E to LA, W to AZ. N Mex.

3. Eriochloa lemmonii Vasey & Scribn.   Fig. 228.   Reported to occur in El Paso Co. (Worthington, 1989). Not cited for TX by Shaw and Webster (1987). Also AZ. Chihuahua, Sinaloa, Sonora, Mex. Rare in canyons and on rocky slopes. In addition to key characters, *E. lemmonii* can be distinguished from *E. acuminata* by the usual presence of a palea in the lower floret and prominent nerves on the second glume and lower lemma. Shaw and Webster (1987) reported that *E. lemmonii* probably hybridizes with *E. acuminata*.

66. PANICUM   L.   PANICUM.

Perennials and annuals, habits diverse. Leaves of two types, those not prominently differentiated up the culms, and those where relatively short and broad basal ones form a rosette; ligule a fringe of hairs or membranous; blades cuneate or rounded at base. Inflorescence a panicle open or contracted, secondary branches spreading or appressed; rachis terminating in a spikelet. Spikelets solitary, awnless, 2-flowered, pubescent or glabrous, the lower floret staminate or neuter, the upper floret perfect; disarticulation below the glumes;

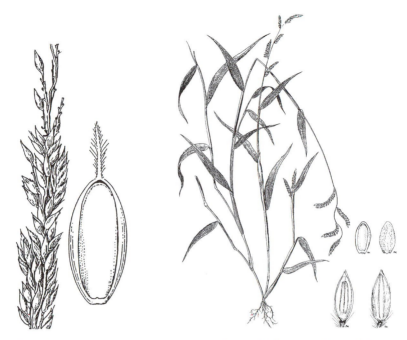

Fig. 227. *Eriochloa contracta.* Partial panicle; floret.

Fig. 228. *Eriochloa lemmonii.* Plant; spikelet (two views) and floret (two views).

glumes both present, first glume usually short, encircling spikelet base, blunt; second glume about equal to spikelet length; lower (sterile) floret similar to glumes in appearance, usually about equaling or longer than second glume, palea absent or developed; lemma of upper (fertile) floret shiny and glabrous, smooth or rarely rugose, indurate, white, brown, or yellow, clasping palea with inrolled margins, margins same in texture as body, apex blunt; palea of upper floret similar to lemma in texture. [*Dichanthelium* (Hitchc. & Chase) Gould; *Steinchisma* Raf.; *Brachiaria* (Trin.) Griseb., in part].

A genus of about 500 species (Webster, 1988) distributed throughout warm regions of the world. *Panicum* is by far the largest genus of the tribe Paniceae, and probably is the largest genus in the whole grass family. A number of sub-genera of *Panicum* have been recognized as separate genera, most notably in our region, including *Dichanthelium* (Hitchc. & Chase) Gould and *Brachiaria* (Trin.) Griseb. Gould (1975) recognized *Dichanthelium* and *Brachiaria*, while Correll and Johnston (1970) and Hitchcock (1951) included *Dichanthelium* with *Panicum* and recognized *Brachiaria*. Classical distinguishing features of *Brachiaria* as a genus apart from *Panicum* include racemose primary branches of the panicle, transversely rugose fertile lemmas (in some species), and spikelet orientation with the back of the fertile lemma away from the axis (as in *Eriochloa*, Correll and Johnston, 1970). Gould (1975) recognized *Dichanthelium* as a genus based upon several characters, but mainly that species of this group all produce a basal rosette of short, broad leaves during the winter. Webster (1988) analyzed the North American genera of the tribe Paniceae from a worldwide perspective and concluded that *Brachiaria* should comprise only the type species, with the rest of the species belonging with other genera including *Panicum*, and that *Dichanthelium* represents a strong subgenus of *Panicum* but a weak genus. The present treatment follows Webster (1988) in including the North American species of *Brachiaria* with *Panicum*. The present treatment also follows Webster (1988) and Morrone and Zuloaga (1991) in recognizing *Dichanthelium* as a subgeneric entity of *Panicum*.

A number of species of *Panicum* are important range grasses in the United States, including *P. virgatum* (switchgrass), *P. bulbosum* (bulb Panicum), *P. obtusum* (vine mesquite), and *P. texanum* (Texas Panicum). The seeds of many *Panicum* species were used as food by the Indians. *Panicum miliaceum* L. (proso millet), the "true millet" of the Romans, has been and still is cultivated widely in Europe, Russia, India, and elsewhere in the world, including in the United States (Great Plains region) to a limited extent, where it is known as a good hay grass and nutritious forage grain with up to 10% protein in the grains. This species has been grown in Texas, where it is known as broomcorn millet. The genus name, *Panicum*, is an old Latin name for the common millet (*Setaria italica*). Hatch et al. (1990) list *Panicum texanum* Buckl. (Texas Panicum) as *Brachiaria texana* (Buckl.) Blake for the Trans-Pecos.

Key to the Species

1. Second glume and lemma of lower floret densely villous on the margins, pubescent with shorter hairs on the back (*Brachiaria*)   **1. *P. ciliatissima.***
1. Second glume and lemma of lower floret glabrous or rarely evenly pubescent, without villous margins of glumes or lemmas.
    2. Plants annual.
        3. Lemma of perfect floret rugose; spikelets subsessile or on short pedicels, the primary branches racemose (*Brachiaria*).
            4. Spikelets glabrous, 2.5–3 mm long   **2. *P. fasciculatum.***
            4. Spikelets pubescent, 3.5–3.9 mm long   **3. *P. arizonicum.***
        3. Lemma of perfect floret smooth and shiny; spikelets on short or long pedicels in a panicle that is usually branching and open or slightly contracted.
            5. Spikelets usually 4.5–5 mm long; cultivated millet
                                                    4. *P. miliaceum.*
            5. Spikelets 3.9 mm long or less.

6. Axils of lower panicle branches with pubescent pulvini; panicles roughly less than 1–2 times as long as broad

5. _P. capillare._

6. Axils of lower panicle branches with glabrous pulvini; panicles roughly 2–10 times as long as broad   **6. _P. hirticaule._**

2. Plants perennial.

7. Basal leaves usually very different from the culm leaves, i.e., with a tuft or rosette of short, broad-bladed basal leaves developed during the winter; species usually flowering in early spring and again in summer or fall, with little viable seed production in spring (vernal); panicles that are terminal and larger, most seed apparently being formed in the later (autumnal) phase in reduced axillary panicles (_Dichanthelium_).

8. Spikelets 2.5–4.3 mm long.

9. Spikelets broadly elliptic to obovate; leaf blades tapering to the apex from the distal half (or less) of the blade

7. _P. oligosanthes._

9. Spikelets narrowly obovate, tapering to a narrow base; leaf blades gradually tapering from the base to an acuminate apex

8. _P. pedicellatum._

8. Spikelets 0.9–2.2 mm long.

10. Ligule absent, or present as a fringe of hairs ca. 1 mm long

9. _P. sphaerocarpon._

10. Ligule present, hairs 2–6 mm long (at least in upper leaves)

10. _P. lanuginosum._

7. Basal leaves similar to culm leaves; winter rosette absent; spikelets usually produced summer and autumn, rarely late spring, and spikelets usually all fertile.

11. First glume and second glume about equal, apex blunt; long stolons produced   **11. _P. obtusum._**

11. First glume shorter than second, acute or acuminate if nearly as long; stolons absent.

12. Spikelets usually 4–8 mm long; rhizomes developed.

13. Culms usually not formed in dense clumps; spikelets 6–8 mm long; usually growing in dune sand

12. _P. havardii._

13. Culms usually formed in dense clumps; spikelets (3–)4–5 mm long; growing in various habitats, widespread

13. _P. virgatum._

12. Spikelets less than 4 mm long; rhizomes absent.

14. Mature plants much-branched and bushlike, culms hard, somewhat "woody," 0.5–2(–3) m tall, with a knotty base; introduced   **14. _P. antidotale._**

Fig. 229. *Panicum ciliatissima* (=*Brachiaria ciliatissima*). Plant; spikelet (three views) and floret (two views).

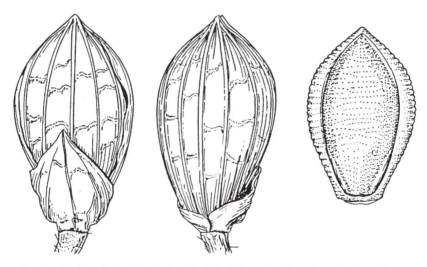

Fig. 230. *Panicum fasciculatum* (=*Brachiaria fasciculatum*). Spikelet (two views) and floret.

14. Mature plants not bushlike, with woody culms to 2 m high, and branching above.
  15. Lemma of fertile floret finely rugose; culm bases usually swollen and cormlike   **15. *P. bulbosum.***
  15. Lemma of fertile floret smooth and shiny; culm bases not cormlike.
    16. Spikelets not appressed, the panicle branches ascending or spreading, with few short-pedicelled spikelets near the ends of branches
                16. *P. diffusum.*
    16. Spikelets appressed, rather tightly clustered on primary panicle branches, or on short spur shoots (spikelets commonly on spreading, slender pedicels in *P. hallii* var. *filipes*).
      17. Plants tufted, strong perennials often with knotty bases and firm culms 60–135 cm tall; lemma of fertile floret slightly beaked at apex; introduced   **17. *P. coloratum.***
      17. Plants modest perennials without knotty bases, with rather slender culms 20–60 (–80) cm tall; lemma of fertile floret ovate-elliptic (usually brown), apex not beaked
                  18. *P. hallii.*

1. Panicum ciliatissima Buckl. FRINGED SIGNALGRASS. Fig. 229. [*Brachiaria ciliatissima* (Buckl.) Chase]. Mostly in sandy soil. Terrell Co., along Pecos River behind R. White Ranch house. Loving Co., 4 mi NE Red Bluff Dam; between Wink and Mentone. Ward Co., 2–6 mi N Monahans; 25 mi W Odessa; 10 mi SE Monahans. Winkler Co., 8 mi W Wink; 1–3 mi NE Kermit; 10 mi E Kermit. Crane Co., 3–16 mi W Crane. 1,500–3,600 ft. Flowering May–Nov. Central to S TX, occasionally in the Rolling Plains. Also OK, AR.

This stoloniferous perennial species is perhaps most easily recognized by the densely pubescent spikelets, specifically the silky margins of the second glume and the lemma. Fringed signalgrass is not a significant forage species, but the plants are palatable and of possible forage value particularly in the sand hills area.

2. Panicum fasciculatum Swartz BROWNTOP PANICUM. Fig. 230. [*Brachiaria fasciculatum* (Swartz) L. Parodi]. An annual weed, relatively rare, mostly present during moist periods in disturbed sites at roadside. Brewster Co., between Alpine and Fort Davis; Alpine; Sul Ross Hill; near Marathon; 10 mi W Marathon; Christmas Mts., 70 mi S Alpine; 5 mi W Study Butte; between St. Elena and Castolon. Val Verde Co., along hwy, near mouth of Pecos

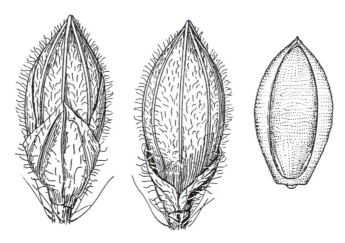

Fig. 231. *Panicum arizonicum* (= *Brachiaria arizonica*). Spikelet (two views) and floret.

Fig. 232. *Panicum miliaceum*. Plant; spikelet
(two views) and floret (two views).

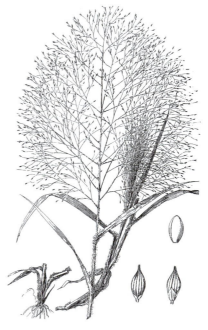

Fig. 233. *Panicum capillare*. Plant; spikelet
(two views) and floret.

River; 5 mi NE Juno. 1,600–4,600 ft. Flowering Aug–Sep. Throughout TX, except for the Pineywoods. Also AZ, NM, FL. S to N South America.

The common name is taken from the bronze-brown to yellowish-brown spikelets. The spikelets are appressed on simple branches, as is usual in the *Brachiaria* section of *Panicum*, and the second glume and lower lemma usually are reticulate with cross veins. According to Gould (1975) the Texas populations of *P. fasciculatum* are included in *P. fasciculatum* var. **reticulatum** (Torr.) Beal. Browntop Panicum is palatable but of limited forage value in the Trans-Pecos.

3. **Panicum arizonicum** Scribn. & Merr. ARIZONA PANICUM. Fig. 231. [*Brachiaria arizonica* (Scribn. & Merr.) S. T. Blake]. An annual weed, often common, mostly present during moist periods in various disturbed habitats. El Paso Co., reported by Worthington (1989) as *Brachiaria arizonica*. Hudspeth Co., Quitman Mts.; 8 mi W Van Horn. Presidio Co., 101 Ranch Hdq.; Chinati Mts., S side, mouth of Tinaja Prieta Canyon; 1 mi S Ross Mine; Pinto Canyon; Sierra Vieja, Vieja Pass; Knox Canyon; 6 mi N Candelaria, Rooney Ranch; Eagle Crag below Redford. Jeff Davis Co., Davis Mts., Mt. Livermore, Goat Canyon; Fern Canyon, Mitre Peak Girl Scout Camp. Brewster Co., Lizard Mt., 3 mi W Alpine; Nine Point Mesa; Black Gap Refuge, Maravillas Creek; Dead Horse Mts.; Christmas Mts., 10 mi N Study Butte; between St. Elena Canyon and Castolon; between Todd Hill and Burro Mesa; 1 mi E mouth Terlingua Creek; head of Boquillas Canyon; 4 mi W Hot Spring; Ward Spring, Chisos Mts. 1,850–5,200 ft. Flowering Jun–Nov. W to S CA. N Mex.

Arizona Panicum is similar in habit to browntop Panicum but has pubescent spikelets that are not reticulate. In Texas the weedy *Panicum arizonicum* is restricted to the Trans-Pecos, where it is a palatable plant of limited forage value.

4. **Panicum miliaceum** L. BROOMCORN MILLET. Fig. 232. A cultivated annual millet, probably not established anywhere in Texas, but occasionally escaping cultivation as a weed in disturbed sites. Reported in El Paso Co. (Worthington, 1989).

Broomcorn millet is introduced in cooler regions of the United States, where it has seen limited use as forage, and the grain is used as hog feed (other common names, hog millet, proso). This millet is more widely cultivated in Europe and western Asia, where the grain is used for human consumption.

5. **Panicum capillare** L. COMMON WITCHGRASS. Fig. 233. [*Panicum philadelphicum* Trin.; *P. flexile* (Gatt.) Scribn.; *P. hillmanii* Chase]. An infrequent annual weed usually in disturbed habitats. Jeff Davis Co., Davis Mts., Mt. Livermore, Goat Canyon; Limpia Canyon, 14 mi N Fort Davis; head of Fern Canyon, Mitre Peak Girl Scout Camp. Brewster Co., Kokernot Ranch,

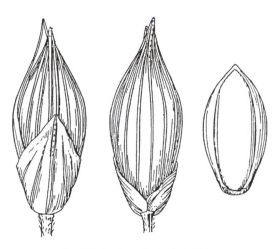

Fig. 234. *Panicum hirticaule.* Spikelet
(two views) and floret.

8 mi N Alpine; Sul Ross Hill; Iron Mt.; Chisos Mts., above Boot Springs; Boot
Springs. 4,100–7,000 ft. Flowering Mar, Jul–Nov. Throughout TX, except the
South Texas Plains, most common in N-central TX (Gould, 1975). Through-
out most of the United States. S Canada.

Gould (1975) and Hitchcock (1951) recognized *P. philadelphicum, P. flexile,*
and *P. hillmanii* as distinct, but they are treated here as synonyms of *P. capillare,*
as suggested by Johnston (1988; 1990) and by Gould (1975) regarding *P. hillmanii.* Of the three entities treated as synonyms here, only *P. hillmanii* would
occur in the Trans-Pecos. Common witchgrass is reported not to be a significant forage grass (Gould, 1978).

6. Panicum hirticaule Presl   ROUGHSTALK WITCHGRASS.   Fig. 234.
[*Panicum pampinosum* Hitchc. & Chase]. Common to infrequent annual in
various habitats including sandy soil. El Paso Co., 6 mi NE El Paso; between
Ysleta and Hueco Tanks. Culberson Co., Salt Flats; Apache Mts., 4 mi N Kent.
Presidio Co., above Capote Camp, above Candelaria; 2 mi W San Jacinto Peak.
Brewster Co., Elephant Mt., N slopes; Big Bend Natl. Park, near McKinney
Springs; Dead Horse Mts. Terrell Co., 2 mi S Dryden. 3,500–4,000 ft. Flower-
ing Jul–Oct. Also NM, AZ, CA. Mex. Argentina.

In Texas roughstalk witchgrass apparently is restricted to the Trans-Pecos.
The species probably is of little forage value.

7. Panicum oligosanthes Schult.   SCRIBNERS PANICUM.   Fig. 235.
[*Dichanthelium oligosanthes* (Schult.) Gould var. *scribnerianum* (Nash) Gould;

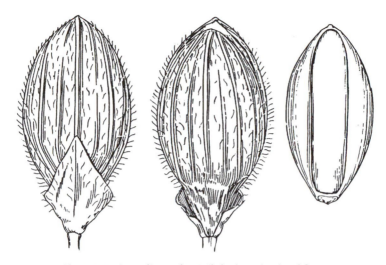

Fig. 235. *Panicum oligosanthes.* Spikelet (two views) and floret.

Panicum scribnerianum Nash; *P. helleri* Nash]. Infrequent perennial usually in loamy and often moist soil, sometimes on slopes, usually in canyons. Culberson Co., Guadalupe Mts., E escarpment. Jeff Davis Co., Little Aguja Canyon; Musquiz Canyon, 14 mi N Alpine; Fern Canyon, above the falls, Mitre Peak Girl Scout Camp. Brewster Co., Lane Ranch, 2 mi S Alpine; Wilson Ranch. 3,700–5,400 ft. Flowering Apr–Jun and Aug–Oct. Throughout Texas. Throughout most of the U.S., except FL, GA, and AL. Also in Mex.

The Trans-Pecos entity of this species is *Panicum oligosanthes* Schultz. var. **scribnerianum** (Nash) Fern., hence the common name Scribners Panicum. Gould (1975) recognized this taxon and relatives (the next three species in this treatment) that produce a winter rosette as belonging in a separate genus *Dichanthelium.* The dichantheliums are of much wider and more frequent occurrence in other parts of Texas than in the Trans-Pecos. Scribners Panicum is palatable but of limited forage value because of its sparse occurrence.

8. Panicum pedicellatum Vasey CEDAR PANICUM. Fig. 236. [*Dichanthelium pedicellatum* (Vasey) Gould]. Infrequent and sparse to common, mostly in canyons, sandbanks near watercourses, limestone areas. Culberson Co., Guadalupe Mts., Smith Canyon, North and South McKittrick Canyon. 5,000–6,500 ft. Flowering May–Jun and perhaps Aug–Oct. Val Verde Co., Edwards Plateau and in limestone outcrops in the Blackland Prairie and Cross Timbers regions of TX (Gould, 1975). N Coahuila, Mex.

Panicum pedicellatum is related to *P. oligosanthes*, which also has spikelets

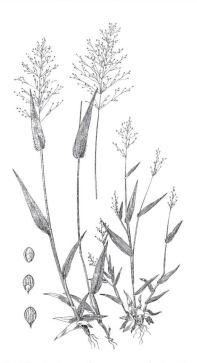

Fig. 236. *Panicum pedicellatum.* Plant; spikelet (three views) and floret (two views).

Fig. 237. *Panicum sphaerocarpon.* Plant; spike-let (two views) and floret.

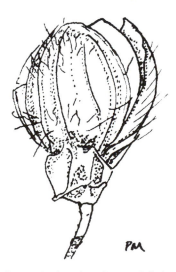

Fig. 238. *Panicum lanuginosum.* Spikelet.

over 2.5 mm long. The species is palatable but is too restricted in occurrence in the Trans-Pecos to be of forage value.

9. Panicum sphaerocarpon Ell.   ROUNDSEED PANICUM.   Fig. 237. [*Dichanthelium sphaerocarpon* (Ell.) Gould var. *sphaerocarpon*]. Moist low places between dunes in deep sand area. Ward Co., 8 mi N Monahans. Winkler Co., 4.5 mi N and then 7 mi E Kermit. Andrews Co. 2,800–3,400 ft. Flowering Apr–Jun and Aug–Oct. Throughout TX except in the plains country. Throughout eastern U.S., N to OK, MO, KS, and MI. S through Mex. to Venezuela.

Gould (1975) recognized two varieties of *Dichanthelium sphaerocarpon* and reported that var. **sphaerocarpon** is infrequent in the Trans-Pecos region. According to specimens at Sul Ross, the taxon is restricted to the sand dune areas at the NE periphery of the Trans-Pecos. The common name roundseed Panicum is taken from the roundish spikelets that are characteristic of this taxon (and certain related species). Roundseed Panicum is palatable but too limited in occurrence to be of much forage value in the sand dune area.

10. Panicum lanuginosum Ell.   WOOLLY PANICUM.   Fig. 238.   [*Panicum acuminatum* Swartz; *Dichanthelium lanuginosum* (Ell.) Gould var. *lanuginosum*; *D. acuminatum* (Swartz) Gould & Clark var. *acuminatum*; *Panicum lindheimeri* Nash; *Dichanthelium lindheimeri* (Nash) Gould; *Dichanthelium acuminatum* var. *lindheimeri* (Nash) Gould & Clark]. Infrequent, mostly in moist habitats in canyons and protected areas. Culberson Co., Guadalupe Mts., South McKittrick Canyon; Choisya Springs; 12 mi SW Texline. Jeff Davis Co., Little Aguja Canyon, near Calf Slide. Brewster Co., Chisos Mts., near Cattail Falls. 4,800–6,500 ft. Flowering May–Jun and Aug–Oct. At least occasional throughout TX except the High Plains, most common in deep E TX. Also the E United States, N to KS. Mex. to Guatemala.

Gould and Clark (1978) recognized eight varieties of *Dichanthelium acuminatum*, a species that is treated here as *Panicum lanuginosum*. According to Gould and Clark (1978), two of the taxa they recognized as varieties of *D. acuminatum* might occur in the Trans-Pecos, var. *acuminatum* and var. *lindheimeri*. Gould and Clark (1978) indicated that var. *lindheimeri* is common in the eastern two-thirds of Texas, but characters in their key to the varieties suggest that var. *lindheimeri* also occurs in the Trans-Pecos. In the Trans-Pecos the plants of *P. lanuginosum* cited above for Culberson and Jeff Davis counties are distinguished by leaf sheaths pilose on the back, perhaps woolly or merely pubescent, culm nodes bearded, and internodes pubescent. These are characters of *P. lanuginosum* var. **huachucae** (Ashe) Hitchc. (or *D. acuminatum* var. *acuminatum*, see synonymy Gould and Clark, 1978). The Trans-Pecos plants cited above for Brewster County (Chisos Mountains) are distinguished by leaf sheaths glabrous on the back, perhaps ciliate on the margins, culm nodes es-

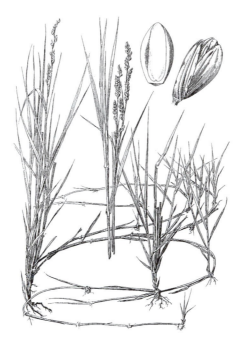

Fig. 239. *Panicum obtusum*. Plant; spikelet and floret.

sentially glabrous, with the internodes perhaps sparsely pubescent. These are traits of *P. lanuginosum* var. **lindheimeri** (Nash) Fern. (or *D. acuminatum* var. *lindheimeri*, see synonymy, Gould and Clark, 1978). Gould (1975) treated *P. lindheimeri* (as *Dichanthelium*) as a species weakly distinct from *P. lanuginosum*. Woolly Panicum is palatable but not abundant enough in the Trans-Pecos to be of much forage value.

11. Panicum obtusum H.B.K.   VINE MESQUITE.   Fig. 239.   Widespread and often abundant, periodically moist habitats, mostly clayey soils in ditches, swales, and low areas. Every county of the Trans-Pecos, perhaps most widespread and common in Jeff Davis, Brewster, and Pecos counties because of soil and habitat conditions. 2,200–6,500 ft. Flowering Mar–Oct (rarely to Jan). Throughout TX except for the deep east Pineywoods. N to MO and CO, W to AZ. N Mex.

Vine mesquite forms thick patches of vegetation where conditions allow the spreading of plants from tough rhizomes and long stolons. Plants of this species tolerate heavy grazing and furnish good grazing for livestock and fair for-

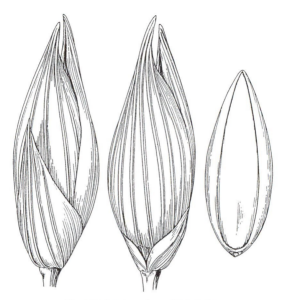

Fig. 240. *Panicum havardii.* Spikelet
(two views) and floret.

age for wildlife. Reportedly the Indians gathered the grains of vine mesquite and ground them to make flour.

12. Panicum havardii Vasey   HAVARD PANICUM.   Fig. 240.   Infrequent to frequent in deep sand, usually associated with dune formations. Ward Co., 3 mi E Monahans; 4 mi E Monahans; 25 mi W Odessa. Winkler Co., 10 mi NE Kermit; Waddell Ranch. Crane Co., 20–25 mi W Crane; 20 mi NE Grandfalls. Andrews Co., SW corner of county. 2,200–3,500 ft. Flowering (Jul) Aug–Oct. W Edwards Plateau in TX. S NM. N Chihuahua, Mex.

Havard Panicum is a tall, coarse grass with an extensive rhizome system developing in deep sand. The species is closely related to *Panicum virgatum* and *P. amarum* (Gould, 1975), and possibly is merely a dune ecotype of *P. virgatum* (Correll and Johnston, 1970). Havard Panicum is good grazing for livestock and fair for wildlife, but is too localized in the Trans-Pecos to be of much forage value. Palatability and nutrition may decline as stems mature in the summer.

13. Panicum virgatum L.   SWITCHGRASS.   Fig. 241.   Canyon bottoms, along watercourses, and generally moist habitats. Jeff Davis Co., Point of Rocks; Little Aguja Canyon; Musquiz bog; Kokernot Ranch, E slopes Major

Fig. 241. *Panicum virgatum*. Plant; spikelet
(two views) and floret.

Peak. Reeves Co., 1 mi W of Balmorhea. Brewster Co., Calamity Creek, 18 mi
S Alpine. Val Verde Co. 3,500–6,500 ft. Flowering Jul–Oct. Throughout TX in
moist lowlands. Throughout much of United States except Pacific Coast. SE
Canada; N Mex.; Cuba.

Switchgrass is a widespread, ecotypically variable, tall (to nearly 3 m) panicum in relatively moist habitats, with a resemblance in the Trans-Pecos to *Panicum bulbosum*. *Panicum virgatum* is distinguished from *P. bulbosum* by its
longer spikelets (to 5 mm long) with smooth upper florets and lack of bulbous
culms at the base. Switchgrass furnishes good and nutritious forage for all
classes of livestock and fair forage for wildlife. Nutrient content and palatability
are reported to decline as plants mature in late season.

14. Panicum antidotale Retz.   BLUE PANICUM.   Fig. 242.   An introduced species sometimes found at roadside and other moist, disturbed habitats. Culberson Co., Guadalupe Mts., corral at Frijole Ranger station. Brewster
Co., near Hwy 118, ca. 32 mi S Alpine; Big Bend Natl. Park, just W of Castolon.
Pecos Co., 10 mi N Fort Stockton. Val Verde Co., Pecos River bank near railroad bridge. 3,000–5,500 ft. Flowering May–Oct. Frequent in South Texas and

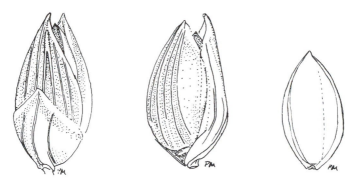

Fig. 242. *Panicum antidotale*. Spikelet (two views) and floret.

the Edwards Plateau, and from the Gulf Coast to the plains country. Also introduced and naturalized in AZ, and elsewhere in SW United States.

Blue Panicum is a native of India introduced in the southwestern United States, where it has been commonly used in reseeding ranges, especially following brush control in south-central Texas. The culms of this tall species are to 3 m long, firm to hard and perhaps glaucous, and the plants tend to persist for several years after being established, but in time the stands diminish. Blue Panicum provides good forage for livestock and wildlife, but supposedly can accumulate hydrogen cyanide under certain conditions and thus cause prussic acid poisoning in livestock.

15. Panicum bulbosum H.B.K.   BULB PANICUM.   Fig. 243.   [*Panicum plenum* Hitchc. & Chase; *P. bulbosum* var. *minus* Vasey]. Common on mountain slopes and in canyons, medium to high elevations. El Paso Co., Franklin Mts.; Hueco Tanks. Hudspeth Co., W slopes Eagle Mts.; Sierra Diablo, head of Victorio Canyon. Culberson Co., Guadalupe Mts., Bowl; McKittrick Canyon; Smith Canyon; near Delaware Creek; Sierra Diablo; Apache Mts. Presidio Co., Sierra Vieja; Chinati Mts.; Pinto Canyon. Jeff Davis Co., Davis Mts., Mt. Livermore and canyons; Mt. Locke; Limpia Canyon near Fort Davis; Point of Rocks; Wild Rose Pass; Davis Mts. State Park; Little Aguja Canyon and trail to Tricky Gap; CDRI Landsite; Musquiz Canyon; Fern Canyon; Haystack Mt. Brewster Co., mts. and canyons vicinity of Alpine, W to Paisano Peak; Calamity Creek; Cathedral Mt.; Cienega Mt.; Elephant Mt.; Cottonwood Spring, 02 Ranch; Chisos Mts., Boot Spring, Basin, Cattail Canyon, Lost Mine Trail; 20 mi NE Alpine; Mt. Ord; Glass Mts; Iron Mt.; 3.5 mi S Marathon; 20 mi S Marathon. Reeves Co., 1 mi W Balmorhea. 3,500–7,500 ft. Flowering Jun–Nov. In TX elsewhere one record from Crockett Co. (Gould, 1975). W to NM and AZ. Mex. S to Chiapas.

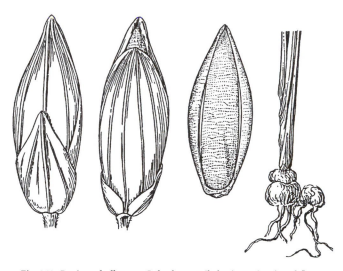

Fig. 243. *Panicum bulbosum.* Culm base; spikelet (two views) and floret.

Bulb Panicum is by far the most common large panicum in the Trans-Pecos, being present in all the major mountains, and is especially abundant in Jeff Davis and Brewster counties. The Trans-Pecos populations of this species, with narrow leaf blades, have been referred to *Panicum bulbosum* var. **minus** (Gould, 1975). Hitchcock (1951) and other authors have recognized *P. plenum* Hitchc. & Chase, which supposedly differs from *P. bulbosum* by its larger size, wider leaf blades, and absence of swollen culm bases, as distinct, although Gould (1975) and others consider these entities to be conspecific. Trans-Pecos populations of these plants exhibit considerable variation in plant size, leaf width, and in cormlike swellings at the culm bases. Both types have overlapping distributions in the Trans-Pecos and appear to represent but a single species, although further study of these plants is desirable. Bulb Panicum should provide good grazing for livestock and at least fair forage for wildlife.

16. Panicum diffusum Sw.   SPREADING PANICUM.   Fig. 244.   Disturbed habitats. Terrell Co., 4–5 mi N Sanderson. Ca. 3,600 ft. Flowering Jun. Throughout most of TX, usually roadsides, lawns, and other disturbed sites. E Mex. Brazil, West Indies, Cuba, Bahamas.

According to Gould (1975), spreading Panicum has often been included with *Panicum hallii* var. *filipes* (as *P. filipes*), but spreading Panicum is distinguished by its prostrate habit, green (not glaucous) leaves, sheath margins ciliate with ascending hairs, nodes spreading pilose, spikelets 2–2.8 mm long, and tetraploid ($2n = 36$) chromosome number. The distribution of *P. diffusum*

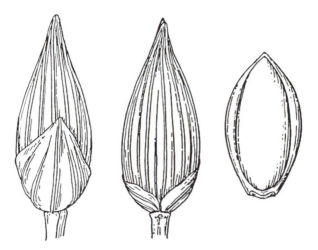

Fig. 244. *Panicum diffusum*. Spikelet (two views) and floret.

in the Trans-Pecos requires further study. It is perhaps not abundant enough to be of forage value.

17. Panicum coloratum L. KLEINGRASS. Fig. 245. A species native to Africa widely introduced as a forage grass in the warmer regions of the world including Trans-Pecos Texas and elsewhere in TX, particularly in S and central portions of the state. According to Gould (1975), kleingrass persists on the ranges of the Edwards Plateau. Probably kleingrass has not been widely used in the Trans-Pecos as a primary forage species, but its seeds have been mixed with native species in revegetating ranges after plowing the soil.

18. Panicum hallii Vasey HALLS PANICUM. The present treatment follows Gould (1975) in recognizing two varieties of *Panicum hallii*.

Key to the Varieties

1. Leaf sheaths with sparse to abundant stiff, papillose hairs, these usually evenly spaced; primary panicle branches usually less than 15, the spikelets not numerous, appressed near the ends of ascending branches

18a. *P. hallii* var. *hallii*.

1. Leaf sheaths glabrous or with a few stiff hairs near the apex; primary panicle branches usually exceeding 15, the spikelets numerous, perhaps appressed, but usually somewhat spreading on capillary pedicels

18b. *P. hallii* var. *filipes*.

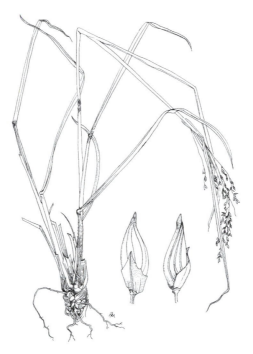

Fig. 245. *Panicum coloratum*. Plant; spikelet
(two views).

18a. Panicum hallii Vasey var. **hallii** HALLS PANICUM.   Fig. 246.
Widespread and often abundant in various soil types. El Paso Co., Franklin
Mts.; Hueco Mts. Hudspeth Co., Hueco Mts.; Quitman Mts.; Sierra Diablo;
Eagle Mts.; 10 mi NW Indian Hot Springs. Culberson Co., Guadalupe Mts.;
Sierra Diablo; 2 mi S Kent; 3.5 mi N Kent. Presidio Co., Sierra Vieja, Capote
Mt.; 6 mi N Candelaria; Chinati Mts.; 2 mi S Shafter; between Redford and
Lajitas; Elephant Mt. Jeff Davis Co., Davis Mts.; Musquiz Canyon; Fern Can-
yon. Brewster Co., mts. vicinity of Alpine; Mt. Ord; 20 mi NE Alpine; Altuda
Pass; Glass Mts.; Marathon Basin; Cienega Mt.; Goat Mt.; Cathedral Mt.;
Elephant Mt.; Buchhill Mt.; Nine Point Mesa; Packsaddle Mt.; Black Gap Ref-
uge; Big Bend Natl. Park, Chisos Mts., Smokey Creek, Hot Springs, Boquillas
Canyon. Reeves Co., 25 mi NW Pecos. Pecos Co., 4–6 mi N Fort Stockton;
10–30 mi S and E Fort Stockton. Terrell Co., vicinity of Sanderson; vicinity of
Dryden; Independence Creek. Val Verde Co., Mile Canyon, Langtry; Pumpville
turnoff Hwy 90; Comstock. 1,300–6,500 ft. Flowering Mar–Nov. Throughout

Fig. 246. *Panicum hallii* var. *hallii*. Plant;
spikelet (two views) and floret.

most of TX. N to OK and CO, W to NM and AZ. Coahuila, Durango, San Luis
Potosí, Mex.

Panicum hallii var. *hallii* is abundant in the Trans-Pecos, occurring in all
the counties, and it is much more commonly encountered than var. *filipes*. In
overall aspect var. *hallii* is usually recognized by curled leaf blades resembling
wood shavings (in mature plants) and smaller panicles with fewer branches and
spikelets (than in var. *filipes*). The warm-season perennial Halls Panicum is
regarded as providing fair forage for livestock and wildlife.

18b. Panicum hallii Vasey var. **filipes** (Scribn.) Waller FILLY PANI-
CUM. Fig. 247. [*Panicum filipes* Scribn.]. Scattered and often infrequent
mostly in semi-dry habitats. Presidio Co., Sierra Vieja, above Capote Falls.
Brewster Co., 65 mi S Alpine; 2 mi W Study Butte. Reeves Co., 15 mi S Pecos;
20 mi SE Pecos. Terrell Co., mouth of San Francisco Canyon. 2,100–3,800 ft.
Flowering Apr–Nov. Throughout most of TX. Mex. S to Guerrero.

In habit var. *filipes* can be distinguished from var. *hallii* by its rather straight
or lax leaves and larger panicles with more numerous spikelets spreading on

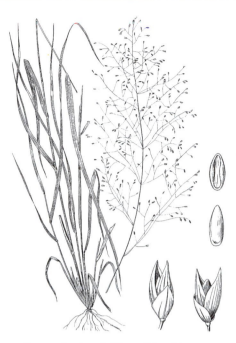

Fig. 247. *Panicum hallii* var. *filipes*. Plant;
spikelet (two views) and floret (two views).

more branchlets. In general the plants of var. *filipes* lack the papillose pubescence that is characteristic of var. *hallii*. A more thorough field survey is needed to find out if var. *filipes* is more widespread in the Trans-Pecos than is suggested by currently available collections.

67. PASPALUM L. PASPALUM.

Annuals or perennials (in our species), some with rhizomes or stolons. Leaves not conspicuously differentiated; ligule a membrane or fringe of hairs; blades usually flat, thin, cuneate or truncate at the base. Inflorescence a panicle, with 1 to several unilateral spicate branches, these scattered along the main axis or paired at the apex, the primary branches with appressed secondary branches, the spikelets arranged on one side of branch (unilateral). Spikelets 2-flowered, the lower floret staminate or neuter, the upper floret perfect; spikelets on short pedicels that are flat or convex at apex, solitary or paired on rachis, the rachis flattened, broadly winged in some, spikelets flat on one side, convex on other, oriented with rounded back toward rachis; disarticulation at the spikelet base; first glume normally absent (when present then a small nerveless scale); second glume and lemma of lower (sterile) floret usually about equal, broad, usually rounded at apex, rarely acute; lemma of upper (fertile) floret indurate, usually smooth, rarely striate, brown to yellow and dull or shiny, margins inrolled.

A genus of about 250 species distributed throughout the warmer regions of the world, with most species concentrated in the Americas (Webster, 1988). About 50 species occur in the United States (Hitchcock, 1951), with 29 species listed for Texas (Gould, 1975). Only about three of these taxa are known to occur in the Trans-Pecos, although several other taxa including *Paspalum urvillei* and *P. plicatulum* are known for the Edwards Plateau and eventually may be found west of the Pecos River. I have seen specimens of *P. urvillei* from the Devils River and Del Rio. The genus name is taken from Greek *paspalos*, a type of millet. Several species of *Paspalum* are regarded as good forage, including the introduced South American taxon, *P. dilatatum*, which is now widespread in Texas. In the southern states *P. distichum* has been used for erosion control because its creeping stolons allow extensive establishment especially along the banks of watercourses.

Key to the Species

1. Plants usually extensively creeping, with rhizomes and perhaps stolons, rooting at nodes; leaf blades 3–12 cm long; inflorescence branches 2, usually less than 1 cm apart at the culm apex, perhaps with 1–2 additional branches below   **1. *P. distichum.***
1. Plants usually tufted perennials, perhaps subrhizomatous; leaf blades 5–36 cm long; inflorescence branches usually 3 or more, the branches 1–2 cm or more apart.
   2. Spikelet margins ciliate with silky hairs 1–2 mm long   **2. *P. dilatatum.***
   2. Spikelet margins ciliate with short hairs usually 0.5 mm or less long, or nearly glabrous.
      3. Spikelets elliptic, pointed, usually ca. 3 mm long   **3. *P. pubiflorum.***
      3. Spikelets suborbicular, usually 2 mm long or less   **4. *P. setaceum.***

1. Paspalum distichum L.   KNOTGRASS.   Fig. 248.   [*Paspalum paspalodes* (Michx.) Scribn.]. Moist and wet habitats near watercourses, springs, seeps, ponds, roadsides, and other sites. El Paso Co., 15 mi N Ysleta; Hueco Mts. Culberson Co., Guadalupe Mts., Choisya Springs. Presidio Co., Chinati Mts., Tigna Canyon; 2 mi S Menzies Ranch house. Jeff Davis Co., Davis Mts., near Mt. Locke; Madera Springs; Davis Mts. State Park; Limpia Canyon, 14 mi N Fort Davis; 1 mi N Fort Davis; N above Fern Canyon, Mitre Peak Girl Scout

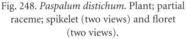

Fig. 248. *Paspalum distichum.* Plant; partial raceme; spikelet (two views) and floret (two views).

Fig. 249. *Paspalum dilatatum.* Plant; spikelet (two views) and floret.

Camp; Haystack Mt., N slope. Brewster Co., Alpine Creek near Kokernot Lodge; 8 mi W Alpine, Sunny Glen; lower slopes Nine Point Mesa. Pecos Co., 20 mi E Fort Stockton, Tunis Spring. 3,000–5,800 ft. Flowering Jun–Nov. Throughout TX. Throughout S United States, and E and W coasts. Widespread in warmer regions of world.

Gould (1975) recognized two varieties of *Paspalum distichum* for Texas, *P. distichum* L. var. **distichum** and *P. distichum* L. var. **indutum** Shinners. The var. *indutum* is distinguished by its lower leaf sheaths and perhaps the leaf blades as well as being strongly hirsute with papilla-based hairs. According to the pubescent character of the leaves, var. *indutum* occurs in Culberson, Jeff Davis, and Brewster counties, but var. *distichum* is decidedly the more widespread and common knotgrass in the Trans-Pecos area. Allred (1982) concluded that var. *indutum* represents merely an extreme pubescent form of *P. distichum* and should not be recognized as a taxonomic entity. Knotgrass is palatable but is limited in occurrence to wet areas and thus is not of major forage value in the Trans-Pecos.

2. Paspalum dilatatum Poir. DALLISGRASS. Fig. 249. Introduced and now naturalized, becoming established mostly in disturbed, protected

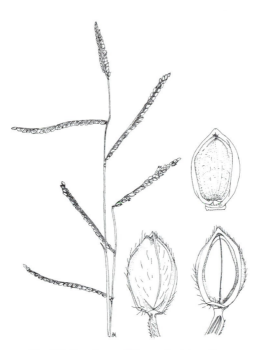

Fig. 250. *Paspalum pubiflorum*. Panicle; spikelet (two views) and floret.

habitats. El Paso Co. Presidio Co., Cibolo Creek at Shafter. Jeff Davis Co., Little
Aguja Canyon. Brewster Co., Alpine, SRSU campus; 20 mi S Marathon; Agua
Fria Ranch; Chisos Mts., drainage below Cattail Falls. Ward Co., 4 mi SW Im-
perial. 3,000–4,600 ft. Flowering Jun–Nov. Throughout most of TX except the
High Plains. S United States and scattered elsewhere in the U.S. Widely distrib-
uted in warmer parts of the world.

Dallisgrass is regarded as a good forage species for livestock and of fair value
for wildlife, but it requires somewhat moist and protected habitats and is thus
not abundant enough to be of significant forage value in the Trans-Pecos. Dallisgrass is introduced from South America, native to Uruguay and Argentina.
Reportedly the species has been widely seeded as a forage grass in the southern
states. It persists mostly in disturbed sites but seemingly is naturalized at least
in some areas including in the Trans-Pecos.

3. Paspalum pubiflorum Fourn.   HAIRYSEED PASPALUM.   Fig. 250.
Usually moist habitats along watercourses, near springs, in canyons. Presidio
Co., Sierra Vieja, above Capote Falls; Howard Canyon; Solitario, Lower Shut-
up. Brewster Co., 18 mi S Marathon; Chalk Draw; Terlingua Creek near Terlingua; Black Gap Refuge; Chisos Mts., Pinnacles; Paint Gap Hills. Terrell

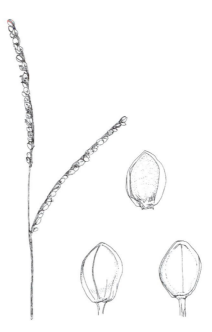

Fig. 251. *Paspalum setaceum*. Panicle; spikelet
(two views) and floret.

Co., mouth of San Francisco Canyon. Val Verde Co., near mouth of Pecos River. 1,600–5,100 ft. Flowering May–Oct. Throughout most of TX. E to LA. Mex. Also Cuba.

According to Gould (1975) *Paspalum pubiflorum* var. **pubiflorum** occurs in the Trans-Pecos. The var. *pubiflorum* has pubescent spikelets, which are characteristic of the Trans-Pecos plants of this species, while var. *glabrum*, which occurs elsewhere in Texas and in the eastern United States, exhibits glabrous spikelets. Hairyseed Paspalum should be palatable to livestock but is not abundant enough in the Trans-Pecos to be of much forage value.

4. Paspalum setaceum Michx.   THIN PASPALUM.   Fig. 251.   Frequent to infrequent in sandy soil, usually deep sand. Ward Co., 6 mi N Monahans. Winkler Co., 1–3 mi NE Kermit; 10 mi E Kermit; 22 mi SE Kermit; 8 mi W Wink. Crane Co., 5 mi N Crane; 13 mi N Imperial; 20 mi NE Grandfalls; 20–25 mi W Crane. 2,600–3,800 ft. Flowering Jun-Oct. Throughout most of TX except for counties W of the Pecos River. Central United States, Atlantic Coastal Plain, to SE AZ. Mex. Also West Indies, the Caribbean, and Central America.

Thin Paspalum appears to be restricted to sandy soils at the northeastern periphery of the Trans-Pecos region, although it might be expected west of the Pecos River. Gould (1975) recognized four varieties of the widespread and variable *Paspalum setaceum*. The variety found in Ward, Winkler, and Crane counties is *P. setaceum* var. **stramineum** (Nash) D. Banks. Thin Paspalum is distinguished by its slender inflorescence branches usually 4–10 cm long, with spikelets mostly suborbicular, 1.6–2.2 mm long, and pale yellow to light green. The plants of thin Paspalum are palatable and may be of forage value in the sand hills.

68. ECHINOCHLOA   Beauv.

Annuals (our species) and perennials. Culms mostly weak and rather succulent. Leaves not obviously differentiated; ligule a fringe of hairs or absent (in our species); blades usually broad, thin, flat, the base incised (Webster, 1988). Inflorescence a panicle, primary branches few to numerous, simple or with appressed branchlets, densely flowered. Spikelets on short pedicels, solitary or paired, in regular rows or in irregular clusters; disarticulation below the glumes; spikelet (glumes and lemma of lower [sterile] floret) scabrous or hairy, or glabrous; first glume present, encircling the spikelet base, acute or short-awned, much shorter than second glume; second glume and lemma of lower floret subequal, awned or awnless; lemma of upper (fertile) floret indurate, smooth, shiny to dull, margins inrolled, the apex differentiated, abruptly pointed; palea of upper floret similar to lemma but narrowed to pointed tip.

About 40 species distributed in warm regions of the world. Seven species are represented in the United States (Webster, 1988). Six species are known to occur in Texas (Gould, 1975), with four species in the Trans-Pecos. The genus name is from Greek *echinos*, hedgehog, and *chloa*, grass, in reference to the prickly spikelets. All species of *Echinochloa* are palatable to livestock, but usually they are not regarded as providing much forage value. The grains provide abundant and valuable food for various bird species. At least one species, *E. colona*, has been grown in tropical Asia and tropical Africa for its grains to be used as human food. *Echinochloa walteri* is known from the Devils River near Del Rio and may be expected west of the Pecos River. The Trans-Pecos species of *Echinochloa* are all annuals, some of them large and coarse plants, but still annual.

Key to the Species

1. Primary inflorescence branches usually 1–2 cm long, not rebranched; spikelets 2.5–3 mm long, awnless, crowded in 4 regular rows on branch rachis; leaf blades 3–6 mm wide   **1. *E. colona*.**

1. Primary inflorescence branches usually more than 2 cm long, often rebranched; spikelets 2.8–4.0 mm long, awned or awnless, in regular rows or not, usually not; leaf blades usually more than 5 mm wide.

Fig. 252. *Echinochloa colona*. Plant; spikelet
(four views) and floret (two views).

2. Apex of the upper (fertile) lemma with an acuminate, slender, membranous tip that is stiff and persistent, the green apex formed in gradual transition from the lustrous body; spikelets usually with papilla-based hairs; palea of lower floret well-developed   **2. E. muricata.**
2. Apex of the upper lemma with a broadly acute membranous tip that is more or less deflexed or withered, the green apex abruptly delimited from the lustrous body; spikelets with or without papilla-based hairs, hispid, or the hairs perhaps short and few; palea of lower floret well-developed, vestigial, or absent.
   3. Panicle branches with hairs as long as the spikelets; palea of the lower floret well-developed; spikelets usually variously hispid, perhaps with papilla-based hairs   **3. E. crusgalli.**
   3. Panicle branches with short hairs; palea of the lower floret absent, or vestigial; spikelets inconspicuously hispid   **4. E. cruspavonis.**

   1. Echinochloa colona (L.) Link JUNGLERICE. Fig. 252. Locally abundant weed in periodically or permanently moist, disturbed habitats, introduced and seemingly naturalized. El Paso Co., Franklin Mts.; Hueco Mts. Hudspeth Co., between Finlay and McNary. Presidio Co., Sierra Vieja, Vieja Pass; above Capote Falls; Chinati Mts., Woods Ranch; Solitario; Elephant Mt. Jeff

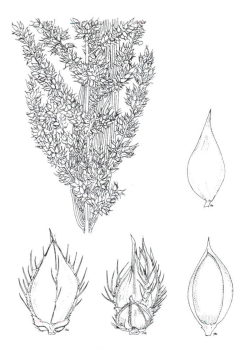

Fig. 253. *Echinochloa muricata.* Partial panicle;
spikelet (two views) and floret (two views).

Davis Co., near Rockpile; near Mt. Locke; upper Madera Canyon of Mt. Livermore; Davis Mts. State Park; Lower Madera Canyon; 3 mi S Fort Davis; Mitre Peak Girl Scout Camp. Brewster Co., between Alpine and Fort Davis; 9 mi S Alpine; 20 mi NE Alpine; 15 mi NE Marathon; Doubtful Canyon, Del Norte Mts.; 16 mi S Marathon; Elephant Mt.; Green Valley, 02 Ranch; Packsaddle Mt.; Nine Point Mesa; near Study Butte; near Lajitas; Black Gap Refuge, Horse Canyon; Chisos Mts., Oak Canyon, Wade Canyon; Paint Gap Hills, Onion Spring; Dog Flats. Reeves Co., 10 mi S Pecos; 20 mi SE Pecos. Pecos Co., between Grandfalls and Coyanosa, Pecos River. Terrell Co., mouth of San Francisco Canyon. 2,000–6,500 ft. Flowering Jun–Nov. Throughout TX. S and SE United States. Widespread in warm regions of both hemispheres.

Of the four species of *Echinochloa* that are reported to occur in the Trans-Pecos (Gould, 1975), *E. colona* is by far the easiest to recognize by its short primary inflorescence branches, crowded small spikelets in four regular rows, absence of awns, and relatively narrow leaf blades. Junglerice is rated as a poor forage species, but it is regarded as providing abundant bird seed.

2. Echinochloa muricata (Beauv.) Fern.   Fig. 253.   [*Echinochloa pungens* (Poir.) Rydb.; *E. microstachya* (Wiegand) Rydb.; *E. occidentalis* (Wiegand)

Rydb.; *E. crusgalli* (L.) Beauv. var. *mitis* (Pursh) Peterm.]. Infrequent to locally common in periodically moist habitats, frequently disturbed sites. El Paso Co., Hueco Tanks. Presidio Co., 6 mi N Candelaria; 101 Ranch Hdq. Jeff Davis Co., Davis Mts., Friend Ranch, near Point of Rocks, Madera Canyon, near Mt. Locke; Davis Mts. State Park; 1 mi N Fort Davis; Barilla Mts.; E of Timber Mt.; Musquiz Swamp. Brewster Co., between Alpine and Fort Davis; Leoncita Springs, Kokernot Ranch; Alpine; Calamity Creek; Big Bend Natl. Park, Dog Flat, Boquillas Canyon area. Terrell Co., Independence Creek. Val Verde Co., Mile Canyon near Langtry. 1,300–7,500 ft. Flowering (May) Jul–Nov. Throughout most of TX. E North America, midwest United States, also CA. N Mex.

Gould (1975) recognized two varieties of *Echinochloa muricata*; var. **muricata**, with spikelets 3.5 mm or more long, and var. **microstachya** Wiegand, with spikelets less than 3.5 mm long. Both varieties are reported by Gould to occur in the Trans-Pecos, and as near as can be determined, both varieties are represented among Trans-Pecos specimens housed at Sul Ross. In this treatment, however, I have chosen not to delimit the two varieties, because they do not appear to represent distinct populations in the Trans-Pecos. In fact, after studying Trans-Pecos specimens of *Echinochloa* it is evident that only *E. colona* is readily distinguished as a specific entity, while *E. muricata*, *E. crusgalli*, and *E. cruspavonis* do not appear to represent natural taxa, at least in this region of Texas. The characters used by Gould (1975) and others to separate *E. muricata*, *E. crusgalli*, and *E. cruspavonis*, including awns and pubescence of the spikelets, apex traits of the fertile lemma, lemma size and shape, and palea (well-developed to absent), seem to appear (in Trans-Pecos specimens) in numerous indistinct combinations of the sort that might be expected to result from extensive hybridization of the morphological types. It is possible that initially distinct taxa of these wetland plants have been widely dispersed, and over the years interspersed, by birds so that species boundaries have been blurred through hybridization. I have attempted to distinguish *Echinochloa muricata*, *E. crusgalli*, and *E. cruspavonis* for the current treatment, following mostly the morphological characters in Gould (1975) and Crins (1991), but I believe that this *Echinochloa* complex is in need of extensive study on a continental scale. The treatment of Crins (1991), however, suggests considerable confidence in the recognition of *E. muricata*, *E. crusgalli*, and *E. cruspavonis* as distinct species. Hitchcock (1951) included *E. muricata* var. *muricata*, *E. muricata* var. *microstachya*, and *E. cruspavonis* var. *macera* in the variable species *E. crusgalli*.

3. Echinochloa crusgalli (L.) Beauv. BARNYARDGRASS. Fig. 254. Infrequent, in moist habitats. El Paso Co., Franklin Mts.; Hueco Mts. Jeff Davis Co., Davis Mts., Mt. Livermore, near the peak, rooted in water; Davis Mts. State

Fig. 254. *Echinochloa crusgalli*. Plant (awned form); panicle branch (awnless form); spikelet (two views) and floret (two views).

Park. Brewster Co., just E of Alpine; 10 mi S Alpine; E side, Cienega Mt. 4,400–7,500 ft. Flowering Jun–Oct. Occasional throughout TX. Reportedly not native to North America but now widespread from Canada, throughout the United States, into Mex.

As interpreted by Gould (1975), the Trans-Pecos plants would be of *Echinochloa crusgalli* var. **crusgalli**. This introduced, weedy annual is considered to be of little forage value for livestock, but its grains are widely used by various bird species.

4. Echinochloa cruspavonis (H.B.K.) Schult.   Fig. 255.   Infrequent, in moist habitats. El Paso Co., 15 mi N Ysleta. Jeff Davis Co., Davis Mts., Davis Mts. State Park; Mitre Peak Girl Scout Camp. Brewster Co., Paradise Canyon, 4 mi W Alpine; Iron Mt.; Cathedral Mt., N side; Chalk Draw, Shuler Ranch. Presidio Co., 101 Ranch; Elephant Mt. 3,700–6,000 ft. Flowering Jun–Sep. Throughout TX except Pineywoods, according to Gould (1975) probably the most widespread *Echinochloa* in TX. E to MS, W to AZ, CA. N Mex.

According to Gould (1975) the Trans-Pecos entity of this species is *Echinochloa cruspavonis* var. **macera** (Wiegand) Gould. This introduced annual is

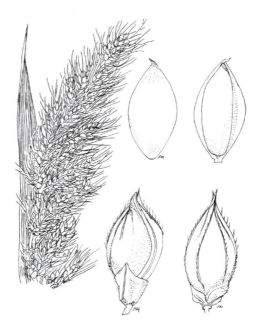

Fig. 255. *Echinochloa cruspavonis*. Panicle
branch (awned form); spikelet, awnless form
(two views), and floret (two views).

regarded as providing only low forage value for livestock, but its grains are of
value to birds.

69. SETARIA   Beauv.   BRISTLEGRASS.

Annuals and perennials, usually cespitose. Culms erect or geniculate. Leaves
not obviously differentiated; ligule a ciliate membrane or a fringe of hairs;
blades flat, thin, narrow to broad. Inflorescence a panicle, usually contracted,
spikelike, and often somewhat cylindrical, densely flowered and bristly. Spikelets on very short pedicels on main axis and on short branchlets; persistent
bristles subtending all spikelets or not; disarticulation below the glumes, above
the bristles. Spikelets solitary; first glume present, short; second glume equal
to or shorter than lemma of lower (sterile) floret. Lemma of upper (fertile)
floret indurate, transversely rugose, yellow, dull, the apex rounded, the margins involute; palea indurate.

A genus of about 100 species mostly distributed in tropical and subtropical
regions, with many species in Africa, but with some species on all continents.
About 22 species occur in the United States (Webster, 1988), and 16 species in

Texas (Gould, 1975), 11 of these in the Trans-Pecos. The genus name was taken from Latin *seta*, a bristle, in reference to the bristles of the panicle. *Setaria italica*, Italian or foxtail millet, has been cultivated since prehistoric times. One collection of *S. italica* is known from the Chisos Mountains, mid–Cattail Canyon at 6,000 feet elevation, where it possibly grew from seeds originally brought to the Chisos Basin to feed horses. In general the species of *Setaria* are palatable and provide fair to good forage value. Rominger (1962) has monographed the North American species of *Setaria*.

Key to the Species

1. Bristles present (usually) at base of terminal spikelet of each branchlet but not all spikelets along the branchlet; inflorescence spikelike but not contracted into a dense cylinder.
    2. Bristles, at least some of them, longer than the spikelets they subtend, the bristles to ca. 6 mm long; leaf blades to 13–20 cm long, usually tapering to a base narrower than the sheath apex, the blades often drying involute   **1. *S. reverchonii.***
    2. Bristles shorter than the spikelets they subtend; leaf blades usually 5–10(–13) cm long, not or only slightly narrowed at the base, the blades flat   **2. *S. ramiseta.***
1. Bristles present below all or most all spikelets; inflorescence contracted into a dense cylinder, except in *S. grisebachii*, where the panicle is interrupted.
    3. Bristles 4–12 below each spikelet, the collective bristles lending a caterpillarlike appearance to the inflorescence.
        4. Plants perennial, usually with short rhizomes   **3. *S. parviflora.***
        4. Plants annual   **4. *S. pumila.***
    3. Bristles 1–3 below each spikelet.
        5. Bristles retrorsely scabrous.   **5. *S. verticillata.***
        5. Bristles antrorsely scabrous.
            6. Plants annual, often robust with tall culms.
                7. Panicle loose, interrupted, with the main axis visible along most or part of the length, the panicles in some plants contracted above and loose below   **6. *S. grisebachii.***
                7. Panicle dense, with the main axis usually visible only below
                                                             7. *S. viridis.*
            6. Plants perennial.
                8. Spikelets 2.9–3.4 mm long   **8. *S. villosissima.***
                8. Spikelets 2.7 mm or less long.
                    9. Panicles 2–4(–6) cm long; spikelets 1.9–2.1 mm long; culms usually branching at upper nodes; herbage dark green
                                                             9. *S. texana.*

Fig. 256. *Setaria reverchonii.* Partial panicle; spikelet (two views) and floret.

    9. Panicles 6–20 cm or more long; spikelets 2.0–2.6 mm long; culms not often branching at upper nodes; herbage dark or light green.

        10. Leaf blades usually 2–5(–7) mm wide, flat or folded, usually glabrous; herbage light green or glaucous **10. *S. leucopila.***

        10. Leaf blades usually 9–20 mm wide, flat, usually pubescent; herbage dark green **11. *S. scheelei.***

    1. Setaria reverchonii (Vasey) Pilger   REVERCHON BRISTLEGRASS. Fig. 256.   [*Panicum reverchonii* Vasey]. Rocky limestone habitats, and in sand. Culberson Co., Guadalupe Mts. area, quartz sand. Brewster Co., 28 mi E Marathon. Reeves Co., 25 mi NW Pecos. Terrell Co., 7 mi E Longfellow; 1 mi E Sanderson; 20 mi E Dryden. Val Verde Co., 3 mi N Comstock. Loving Co., 12 mi N Mentone. Ward Co., between Monahans and Imperial; 5 mi N Monahans. Crane Co., 15–20 mi N Imperial. 1,600–3,500 ft. Flowering Mar–Jun (Jul–Aug). Throughout most of TX, except the Pineywoods and Blackland Prairies, most common on the Edwards Plateau. N to S OK.

    Both *Setaria reverchonii* and *S. ramiseta* were included in *Panicum* by Hitch-

Fig. 257. *Setaria ramiseta*. Plant; spikelet
(three views) and floret (two views).

cock (1951) and Correll and Johnston (1970), while Gould (1975) recognized
these taxa as *Setaria*. The bristle subtending terminal spikelets in the inflorescence is a character relating these species to *Setaria*, while the slender spikelike
panicles more closely resemble those in some species of *Panicum*. Reverchon
bristlegrass provides fair forage for livestock and wildlife in areas where it is
reasonably abundant.

2. Setaria ramiseta (Scribn.) Pilger Fig. 257. [*Panicum ramisetum*
Scribn.]. Rocky limestone habitats, and in sand. Brewster Co., Big Bend Natl.
Park, Glenn Spring, head of Boquillas Canyon, Dead Horse Mts. Pecos Co.,
near Iraan. Terrell Co., ca. 30 mi N Sanderson; Independence Creek; near Pe-
cos River. Val Verde Co., Mile Canyon, 2 mi below Langtry. Loving Co., 10 mi
E Mentone; 3 mi E Red Bluff Lake. Ward Co., between Wink and Pyote; 9 mi
SE Monahans. Crane Co., 3–16 mi W Crane; 20 mi S Odessa; 5 mi N Crane.
Winkler Co., 5 mi S Wink. 1,300–2,800 ft. Flowering May–Nov. South Texas
Plains and Edwards Plateau, also Rolling Plains, Cross Timbers, and Gulf Prai-
ries. NE Mex.

According to Gould (1975) *Setaria ramiseta* is closely related to *S. reverchonii*, differing mainly by the shorter, flat leaf blades not much narrowed at
the base, bristles shorter than spikelets, smaller spikelets, and more prominent

Fig. 258. *Setaria parviflora*. Plant; spikelet with
subtending bristles.

rhizome development in *S. ramiseta*. For the present treatment, Trans-Pecos
specimens could not be separated consistently according to the characters cited
above. For example, some specimens with bristles longer than the spikelets also
have short leaf blades that are not narrowed at the base. For purposes of the
current treatment, specimens cited for *S. reverchonii* and *S. ramiseta* were distinguished primarily by their bristle lengths, but it is clear that additional systematic study of these taxa is needed. *Setaria ramiseta* should provide only fair
forage value.

    3. Setaria parviflora (Poir.) Kerguelen   KNOTROOT BRISTLEGRASS.
Fig. 258. [*Setaria geniculata* (Lam.) Beauv.]. Moist habitats, various soil
types. El Paso Co. Jeff Davis Co., Davis Mts., Mt. Livermore, Madera Canyon;
5 mi W Mt. Locke; Musquiz Swamp. Brewster Co., Alpine; Peña Blanca, 5 mi
S Marathon; Big Bend Natl. Park, Hot Springs, banks of Rio Grande; head of
Boquillas Canyon. Pecos Co., 20–35 mi S Fort Stockton. Terrell Co., Independence Creek. 1,800–6,500 ft. Flowering Jun–Nov. Throughout TX. Widely distributed in the United States. Mex. Central America. Possibly the most widespread *Setaria* in North America (Gould, 1975).

    Knotroot bristlegrass provides only fair forage for livestock and wildlife. In
the Trans-Pecos this species is widespread but limited to moist sites where it
may be abundant or sparse.

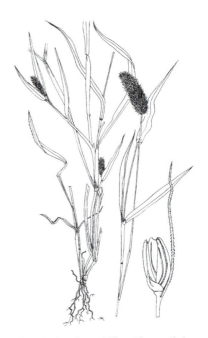

Fig. 259. *Setaria pumila*. Plant; spikelet
(two views) and floret.

Fig. 260. *Setaria verticillata*. Plant; spikelet
with subtending bristle.

4. Setaria pumila (Poir.) Roem. & Schult.   YELLOW BRISTLEGRASS.
Fig. 259.   [*Setaria lutescens* (Weigel.) F. T. Hubb.; *S. glauca* (L.) Beauv.]. In-
troduced from the Old World; protected canyons and various disturbed habi-
tats, frequently under periodically moist conditions. El Paso Co., W of Clint.
Culberson Co., Guadalupe Mts., South McKittrick Canyon. Jeff Davis Co.,
Davis Mts., Madera Canyon; Elbow Canyon; Barrel Springs; Davis Mts. State
Park; Limpia Canyon; 3 mi S Fort Davis; Musquiz Swamp; Pollard Ranch;
Fern Canyon. Brewster Co., Leoncita Springs; Alpine; Sul Ross campus; Glass
Mts., Gilliland Canyon; E side Mt. Ord; 5 mi S Marathon. Terrell Co., 9 mi
E Sanderson. Val Verde Co. Ward Co. 2,000–6,500 ft. Flowering Jun–Nov.
Throughout most of TX except the South Texas Plains. Throughout temperate
and subtropical regions of North America, occurring as a weed.

The common name yellow bristlegrass presumably was inspired by the yellowish inflorescences in mature plants. *Setaria pumila* is similar to *S. parviflora*
but is readily distinguished by its annual habit. Yellow bristlegrass is of limited
forage value.

5. Setaria verticillata (L.) Beauv.   HOOKED BRISTLEGRASS.   Fig. 260.
[*Setaria adhaerans* (Forssk.) Chiov.]. A common weedy annual of disturbed
habitats. El Paso Co., Worthington, 1989; 1 mi W El Paso. Presidio Co., Marfa.

Fig. 261. *Setaria grisebachii*. Plant; spikelet
(three views, one with subtending bristle)
and floret.

Brewster Co., Alpine; hwy between Alpine and Fort Davis. 3,800–4,700 ft. Flowering Jul–Oct. Also Edwards Plateau and South Texas Plains, Post Oak Savannah in TX. Throughout warm regions of the world, now established and widespread in southern North America. Also Bermuda, Cuba, Mex., Central America.

Hooked Bristlegrass is the only annual species in the Trans-Pecos with retrorse bristles that cause the detached inflorescences or "seed heads" to cling to clothing or animal fur. Apparently *S. verticillata* is now a rather common weed in towns of the central Trans-Pecos, as it is in Alpine, but it has not been much collected. Until recently *S. verticillata* and *S. adhaerans* were regarded as closely related but distinct species by some agrostologists (Gould, 1975), but Webster (1993) has combined *S. adhaerans* with *S. verticillata* after reviewing the taxonomy and nomenclature of *Setaria*.

6. Setaria grisebachii Fourn.   GRISEBACH BRISTLEGRASS.   Fig. 261. Infrequent to frequent in protected habitats mostly in canyons, on mountain slopes, and under trees, often in periodically moist sites. El Paso Co., Franklin Mts.; Hueco Mts. Culberson Co., Guadalupe Mts., Upper Dog Canyon. Presidio Co., Sierra Vieja, Joe Sitter's Canyon, Vieja Pass; W side High Lonesome;

Fig. 262. *Setaria viridis.* Plant; spikelet (three
views, one with subtending bristle) and floret.

Chinati Mts., Tigna Canyon; Cibolo Creek; 101 Ranch; Elephant Mt.; Paisano
Campground; Panther Canyon, near Big Hill on the Rio Grande. Jeff Davis
Co., Davis Mts., Mt. Livermore; Madera Canyon; Elbow Canyon; Sawtooth
Mt.; Barrel Springs; Rockpile; Davis Mts. State Park; Limpia Canyon; Little
Aguja Canyon; Musquiz Canyon; Mitre Peak Girl Scout Camp. Brewster Co.,
Paradise Canyon W of Alpine; Paisano Campground; Doubtful Canyon, Del
Norte Mts.; Iron Mt.; 30 mi S Marathon; 56 mi S Alpine; Packsaddle Mt.; Agua
Fria Springs; Chisos Mts., near Laguna Meadows; near Boot Springs; Ward
Spring; N branch of Cattail Canyon; Oak Springs. Val Verde Co. 2,300–
7,600 ft. Flowering Jun–Nov. In TX also South Texas Plains and W Edwards
Plateau. N to OK, W to AZ. Through Mex. to Central America.

Grisebach bristlegrass is a robust annual to 80 cm high with erect or genicu-
late-spreading culms. The most identifiable feature is the panicle, where widely
spaced branches reveal the panicle main axis for most of its length in typical
individuals. The plants of *Setaria grisebachii* should be palatable, but the species is of limited forage value because of its spotty distribution.

7. Setaria viridis (L.) Beauv.   GREEN BRISTLEGRASS.   Fig. 262.   Introduced, mostly infrequent, a weedy annual in protected habitats on mountain slopes, in canyons and basins. El Paso Co., Franklin Mts.; Hueco Mts.
Culberson Co., Guadalupe Mts., McKittrick Canyon; Sierra Diablo. Presidio

Fig. 263. *Setaria villosissima.* Plant; spikelet
(three views, one with subtending bristle)
and floret.

Co., Capote Mt.; Chinati Mts., Tigna Canyon; Pinto Canyon N Shely Ranch
house; Wildhorse Canyon, N side Chinati Peak; 101 Ranch. Jeff Davis Co., Da-
vis Mts., upper Madera Canyon; Mt. Locke; Pig Pen Canyon of Forbidden Mt.;
15 mi N Alpine. Brewster Co., Alpine, Sul Ross campus; Twin Peaks; Toronto
Pass; Elephant Mt.; Glass Mts., Gage Ranch; Sibley Ranch. Terrell Co., near
Pecos River, White Ranch. Val Verde Co. 1,500–6,500 ft. Flowering Jun–Nov.
Throughout much of TX except the E portions and S parts of the South Texas
Plains. Throughout temperate and some subtropical regions of the world.

Setaria viridis resembles *S. grisebachii* but is often even more robust; its
panicles are densely flowered and have the main axis obscured, and the panicle
bristles are green to purple, often turning purplish at maturity. The cultivated
foxtail millet, *S. italica*, is closely related to *S. viridis*.

8. Setaria villosissima (Scribn. & Merr.) K. Schum. HAIRLEAF
BRISTLEGRASS. Fig. 263. Rare on mountain slopes and in canyons. Jeff
Davis Co., Davis Mts., Kokernot Ranch, Major Peak; head of Wild Rose Pass.
4,800–5,000 ft. Flowering in August. Also Edwards Plateau, rare in South Texas
Plains. AZ. Coahuila and Sonora, Mex.

Hairleaf bristlegrass is a loosely clumped perennial with leaf blades densely

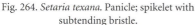

Fig. 264. *Setaria texana*. Panicle; spikelet with subtending bristle.

Fig. 265. *Setaria leucopila*. Plant; spikelet (three views, one with subtending bristle) and floret (two views).

pilose on both surfaces, panicles 8–20 cm long, and light green spikelets that are 2.9–3.4 mm long. This species is seldom collected and apparently rare in the Trans-Pecos.

9. Setaria texana W. H. P. Emery   TEXAS BRISTLEGRASS.   Fig. 264. Infrequent in shallow, rocky limestone soils, mesas, slopes, and canyons, and in sand. Brewster Co., near Rio Grande. Pecos Co., 6 mi N Fort Stockton; 20 mi SW Fort Stockton; 30 mi E Fort Stockton. Terrell Co., 30 mi N Sanderson; 29 mi N Dryden. Val Verde Co., Pumpville turnoff Hwy 90. Ward Co., 8 mi N Monahans; 4 mi E Monahans. Winkler Co., 10 mi NE Kermit. Crane Co., 5–8 mi N Imperial. 1,800–3,500 ft. Flowering Apr–Nov. South Texas Plains and S Edwards Plateau. Adjacent Mex. A taxon of limited distribution.

The collections herein referred to *Setaria texana* are tentative identifications. As pointed out by Gould (1975), *S. texana* is closely related to the wide-ranging *S. leucopila*, and *S. texana* is not easily distinguished from forms of *S. leucopila* with short panicles and smaller spikelets. Presumably *S. texana* is a reasonably good forage grass in areas where it occurs in sufficient abundance.

10. Setaria leucopila (Scribn. & Merr.) K. Schum.   PLAINS BRISTLE-GRASS.   Fig. 265.   Widely distributed and frequent, found in every county of the Trans-Pecos, in all mountain systems at low to mid elevations, in the

Fig. 266. *Setaria scheelei*. Partial plant; spikelet
with subtending bristle.

alluvial basins, and in the Chihuahuan Desert, including Big Bend Natl. Park
and Guadalupe Mountains Natl. Park. 1,200–6,500 ft. Flowering Mar–Nov.
Throughout the arid portions of TX, all regions except the Pineywoods, Post
Oak Savannah, and Blackland Prairies. N to S CO, W to NM and AZ. S to
central Mex.

Plains bristlegrass is regarded as an important forage species because it is
palatable to livestock and wildlife and it is both widespread and abundant
throughout most of its range. The species does not occur in extensive stands,
but it is frequent even in open, dry sites of the Trans-Pecos. Plains bristlegrass
has been recommended for reseeding mixtures after root plowing for brush
control. *Setaria leucopila* was once included under *S. vulpiseta* (Lam.) Roem.
& Schult. (=*S. macrostachya* H.B.K.), a species mainly of south Texas and
northern Mexico (Gould, 1975). *Setaria leucopila* is weakly delimited from *S.
texana*, as discussed above, and also from *S. scheelei*, as discussed below. Hybridization is suspected to occur between perhaps all of these closely related
bristlegrasses.

11. Setaria scheelei (Steud.) Hitchc.   Fig. 266.   Infrequent in protected
sites in canyons, along watercourses, and under shade trees. Jeff Davis Co.,
Gomez Peak. Brewster Co., Glass Mts., near Altuda Point; Big Bend Natl. Park,

River Road, ca. 29 mi E Castolon. Terrell Co., Independence Creek. Val Verde Co., Pecos River Canyon below the bridge on Hwy 90. 1,200–4,600 ft. Flowering Jun–Nov. Also the W half of TX. Possibly AZ. N Mex.

Setaria scheelei is weakly distinguished from *S. leucopila* by its wider, pubescent, flat leaf blades, culms usually geniculate and suberect, looser panicle typically tapering from base to apex, panicle bristles spreading and 1–3.5 cm long, and dark green herbage. There is some suspicion that *S. scheelei* might represent a shade form of the widespread *S. leucopila*, which is usually identified by narrower, usually glabrous, flat or folded leaf blades, culms usually stiffly erect, panicle usually columnar, panicle bristles usually appressed and 0.4–1.5 cm long, and light green or glaucous herbage. The *Setaria* complex involving *S. leucopila, S. scheelei, S. texana,* and *S. vulpiseta* deserves additional study.

70. PENNISETUM   L. Rich.   PENNISETUM.

A genus of about 100 species mostly in tropical and subtropical regions of the world. All North American species, six of them, are probably introduced (Webster, 1988). Two species are known for Texas. The genus name is from Latin *penna*, feather, and *seta*, bristle, in reference to the plumose bristles of some species, including *Pennisetum villosum* Fresen. of the Trans-Pecos. Numerous species of *Pennisetum* have economic value, including the famous *P. glaucum* (L.) R.Br. (pearl millet), widely cultivated in Africa and Asia for the grains which are used for human food. *Pennisetum villosum* and other species are used as ornamentals, while *P. clandestinum* Chiov. (Kikuyu grass), which has a tendency to become a noxious weed, is used for range improvement and soil stabilization. *Pennisetum* is closely related to *Cenchrus*, and was included in the latter genus by Correll and Johnston (1970), while Gould (1975) and Webster (1988) maintain *Pennisetum* as distinct.

1. Pennisetum villosum Fresen.   FEATHERTOP.   Fig. 267.   [*Cenchrus longisetus* M. C. Johnst.]. Perennial, somewhat rhizomatous. Cespitose, with culms to 70 cm long. Leaves not differentiated; ligule a ciliate membrane with hairs ca. 1 mm long; blades flat or folded, glabrous, usually 2–5 mm wide, 10–25 cm long. Panicles dense, usually 4–10 cm long, the bristles whitish, to 4–5 cm long, numerous in spreading fascicles; inner bristles of the fascicle long-plumose with silky hairs. Spikelets solitary in each fascicle of bristles, the spikelets 8–9 mm long; first glume small or vestigial; lemma and palea of upper (fertile) floret thin, firm, smooth, dull; lemma margins thin and flat, apex not differentiated.

Disturbed habitats about roads, streets, and yards. El Paso Co. Brewster Co., Alpine; Sul Ross campus; between Alpine and Fort Davis. 3,500–4,600 ft. Flowering Jun–Nov. Reportedly commonly grown as an ornamental through-

Fig. 267. *Pennisetum villosum.* Panicle; group
of spikelets and bristles, and spikelet (above).

out TX, and persisting for a short time as an escape. Native to Africa and widely
distributed in the world as an ornamental.

71. CENCHRUS   L.   SANDBUR.

Annuals and perennials. Culms erect, geniculate, or spreading, perhaps stoloniferous. Leaves not obviously differentiated; ligule a ciliate membrane or a
fringe of hairs; leaf blades cuneate or truncate at base. Inflorescence spikelike.
Spikelets enclosed in burs, with 1–8 spikelets in each bur; burs subsessile on a
short, angular, unbranched rachis, the burs formed by bristles or flattened
spines (modified branchlets) fused together at least at the base; bristles and
spines in most species retrorsely barbed or scabrous; disarticulation at base of
bur; callus at base of bur flared to form a discoid receptacle; glumes unequal,
thin, membranous; lemma of lower (sterile) floret thin, as long as or longer
than second glume; palea of lower floret about as long as the lemma; lemma
of upper (fertile) floret thin, membranous, tapering to a slender apex, the margins not inrolled. Caryopses elliptic to ovoid, dorsally flattened.

A genus of about 22 species native to warm regions of the Americas, Africa,
and Australia. Seven species occur in North America. Webster (1988) concluded that although *Cenchrus* and *Pennisetum* are similar, the two genera can

Fig. 268. *Cenchrus ciliaris*. Plant; group of
spikelets (bur) and spikelet (above).

be distinguished by the callus structure at the base of the inflorescence burs. In *Cenchrus* the callus is flared or swollen at the apex to form a wide receptacle, while in *Pennisetum* the callus is not flared or swollen. The genus name *Cenchrus* is from Greek *kenchros*, a type of millet.

Key to the Species

1. Plants strongly perennial; burs with bristles or spines but these not with flat bases and perhaps not hardened.
   2. Bristles prominently ciliate on the inner margins   **1. *C. ciliaris.***
   2. Bristles retrorsely scabrous or with minute retrorse barbs
                                                                2. *C. myosuroides.*
1. Plants annual, perhaps weakly perennial; burs with stiff, often hardened spines, at least some of them with flattened bases.
   3. Burs usually with 8–40 spines, the largest ones to 1.5 mm wide at the base; upper (fertile) floret 3.4–5.8 mm long   **3. *C. incertus.***
   3. Burs usually with 45–75 spines, the largest ones usually 1 mm or less wide at the base; upper floret 5.8–7.6 mm long   **4. *C. longispinus.***

   1. Cenchrus ciliaris L. BUFFELGRASS. Fig. 268. [*Pennisetum ciliare* (L.) Link]. Introduced perennial now common at roadside in the S Trans-

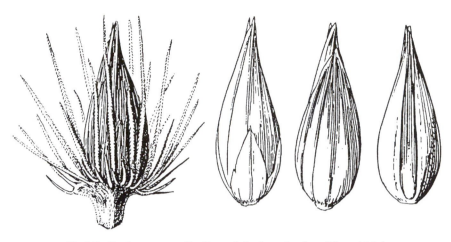

Fig. 269. *Cenchrus myosuroides.* Bur, spikelet (two views), and floret (right).

Pecos, particularly in low areas that collect water. Presidio Co., Chinati Mts., Pinto Canyon; 2 mi S Shafter. Brewster Co., Christmas Mts., Cedar Springs; near Terlingua; 40 mi S Marathon; Big Bend Natl. Park, Boquillas Canyon trail head. Val Verde Co. 1,850–3,600 ft. Flowering May–Nov. South Texas Plains, occasional in Edwards Plateau, Post Oak Savannah, and Gulf Prairies. Native to South Africa, perhaps India, widely introduced in warm regions.

Buffelgrass is regarded as an excellent forage grass. It was first introduced into south Texas in the 1940's (Hanselka, 1989), where it was hoped that this drought-resistant grass would be an answer to periodic droughts on the ranges of South Texas. Buffelgrass has deep roots that reach to 6–8(–10) ft. in deep soils, and the plants spread by seeds and rhizomes (Stubbendieck et al., 1992). Hanselka (1989) reports that the nutritional values of buffelgrass are generally greater than in most native grass species, and that the nutritional values are increased by burning. Buffelgrass is not frost-tolerant, which probably accounts for its southerly distribution in the Trans-Pecos. Perhaps the first collection of buffelgrass in the Trans-Pecos was in 1964 in Pinto Canyon, where the plants had probably escaped from an attempt to introduce the grass in pastures near that locality. The current distribution of buffelgrass in the Trans-Pecos suggests that this species has migrated extensively along the roadways in the southern desert region, or perhaps along the Rio Grande corridor, since the mid-1970's. The most helpful distinguishing feature of buffelgrass is the cylindrical spikes of purplish bristles 4–10 mm long, with the terete bristles long-ciliate on the inner margins. The bristles are slender and wavy at the distal half. The tough, clumped plants reach 1 m tall.

2. Cenchrus myosuroides H.B.K.   BIG SANDBUR.   Fig. 269.   Rare in canyons, near springs, and at roadside, often in clay or sand. Brewster Co.,

Fig. 270. (A) *Cenchrus incertus*; plant; bur,
spikelet (two views), and floret (right).
(B) *C. longispinus*; bur and floret.

30 mi S Marathon; Big Bend Natl. Park, Fresno Springs. Val Verde Co., Mile
Canyon below Langtry; mouth of the Pecos River. 1,200–3,500 ft. Flowering
May–Nov. S Edwards Plateau, South Texas Plains, and S Gulf Prairies. FL, West
Indies, Mex., Caribbean Islands, South America.

Big sandbur is regarded as a good forage grass in areas other than the Trans-
Pecos where it is abundant. The plants are most palatable before the burs mature with their stiff, retrorsely scabrous bristles that cling to wool and mohair.

3. Cenchrus incertus M. A. Curtis   SANDBUR, GRASSBUR.   Fig. 270.
[*Cenchrus pauciflorus* Benth.; *C. parviceps* Shinners]. A common weed of disturbed habitats including roadsides, vacant lots, lawns, ditches, in various soil
types, particularly in sand. Probably in every county in the Trans-Pecos, most
common in Jeff Davis, Presidio, Brewster, and Terrell counties, and in the
sandhill counties such as Loving, Ward, Winkler, and Crane. 1,300–5,500 ft.
Flowering mostly Jun–Nov. Throughout TX. Frequent in S and SE United
States, occasional on the W coast. Common in Mex., West Indies, Caribbean
region, Central America, and central South America.

Sandbur is an annoying weed that is familiar to most citizens. The hard,
sharp spines of the burs are retrorsely scabrous and difficult to extract from

Fig. 271. *Coelorachis cylindrica.* Plant; rachis
joint (two views) with fertile (below) and
sterile (above) spikelets.

the skin. Those acquainted with this painful species can appreciate the specific epithet "incertus." Sandbur is of no forage value.

4. Cenchrus longispinus (Hack.) Fern. LONGSPINE SANDBUR. Fig. 270. A weed of disturbed habitats. Reported for the Trans-Pecos by Gould (1975) and Correll and Johnston (1970), but no specimens were located among the collections of *Cenchrus* at the Sul Ross Herbarium. Certainly this species is infrequent in the Trans-Pecos. Throughout most of TX, especially north-central portions. Central and NE United States N to SE Canada. West Indies, Mex., Central America, and Venezuela. Adventive in W Europe, South Africa, and Australia.

Longspine sandbur is surely as annoying as is *C. incertus* in areas where it is common. This species is of little forage value.

Tribe 17. Andropogoneae

This tribe includes about 960 species in 85 genera, distributed especially throughout the savanna zone of the world tropics and into warm temperate regions (Clayton and Renvoize, 1986). Gould (1975) recognized 16 genera of Andropogoneae for Texas, with 12 of these genera occurring in the Trans-Pecos. Important tribal characters include the fragile racemes bearing paired spikelets, and in most taxa the sterile, usually smaller, pedicelled spikelet of the pair. *Coix lacryma-jobi* L. (jobstears), an Old World annual introduced in the Americas, has been cultivated on the Sul Ross campus, but is no longer found there. The beadlike grains are used in some places as beads for rosaries. *Coelorachis cylindrica* (Michx.) Nash [Fig. 271] (Carolina jointtail) occurs on the Edwards Plateau and Rolling Plains and may eventually be found in the Trans-Pecos.

Among the major genera of Andropogoneae in the Trans-Pecos are *Andropogon*, *Bothriochloa*, and *Schizachyrium*. The latter two genera formerly were included in *Andropogon* (Hitchcock, 1951). Many workers including Correll and Johnston (1970) and Gould (1975) have concluded that all three taxa should be recognized as separate but closely related genera.

Key to the Genera of Andropogoneae

1. Spikelets unisexual (pistillate and staminate spikelets conspicuously different; plants monoecious).
   2. Staminate spikelets in terminal panicles (tassels), pistillate spikelets axillary on "cobs" in modified leaves (ears); plants commonly known as corn or maize   **83. *Zea*, p. 340**
   2. Staminate and pistillate spikelets in the same inflorescence (spikelike racemes).
      3. Pistillate spikelets at maturity hardened and bony
             82. *Tripsacum*, p. 339
      3. Pistillate spikelets at maturity not hardened (the upper part of raceme disarticulating at maturity, lower part with pairs of staminate spikelets remaining intact)   **80. *Heteropogon*, p. 336**
1. Spikelets, at least the sessile one, mostly perfect.
   4. Spikelets all alike, and with perfect florets.
      5. Lemma awnless; spikelets 3–4 mm long   **72. *Imperata*, p. 314**
      5. Lemma awned; spikelets 6–8 mm long   **74. *Sorghastrum*, p. 317**
   4. Spikelets not all alike, at least some perfect (usually the pedicelled ones).
      6. Spikelets, each sessile one, sunken into a thickened, dorsally compressed, clavate internode of the rachis   **81. *Hemarthria*, p. 338**
      6. Spikelets not sunken in a thickened rachis.
         7. Pedicelled spikelet with pedicel thickened and appressed to thickened rachis joint; pedicelled spikelet well-developed; rachis joints and pedicels woolly   **79. *Elionurus*, p. 335**
         7. Pedicelled spikelet with pedicel and rachis joint otherwise; pedi-

celled spikelet well-developed or not; rachis joints and pedicels hairy or not.

8. Perfect spikelet the pedicelled one, the sessile spikelet sterile
78. *Trachypogon*, p. 334

8. Perfect spikelet the sessile one, the pedicelled spikelet sterile.

   9. Flowering culms much-branched above, the branches with numerous short, leafy branchlets above, the branchlets each with 1–6 spikelet clusters above the uppermost bract.

      10. Branchlets terminating in a panicle with 2–6 racemose branches; rachis joints slender, sometimes with a shallow groove on one side   **75. *Andropogon*, p. 319**

      10. Branchlets terminating in a spicate raceme; rachis joints cup-shaped or lobed at the apex
77. *Schizachyrium*, p. 330

   9. Flowering culms not much-branched above.

      11. Pedicels of pedicelled spikelets and usually the upper rachis internodes with a translucent groove or thin area in the center   **76. *Bothriochloa*, p. 324**

      11. Pedicels and rachis internodes flat or rounded and without a groove or thin area in the center
73. *Sorghum*, p. 315

72. IMPERATA   Cyr.   SATINTAIL.

A genus of about 8 species in warmer parts of the world. Two or three species occur in the United States, one of these in Texas. The genus is named after Ferrante Imperato.

1. Imperata brevifolia Vasey   SATINTAIL.   Fig. 272.   [*Imperata hookeri* Rupr. *ex* Hack.]. Perennial, with thick creeping rhizomes. Culms usually 1–1.5 m long. Leaves glabrous except for tuft of hairs near ligule; ligule a fringed membrane, short, truncate, often extended as sheath auricles; blades flat, usually 6–12 mm wide. Inflorescence a panicle, dense, contracted, elongate, 10–30 cm long, with dense, silky hairs obscuring the spikelets. Spikelets all the same, awnless, usually 3–4 mm long, with a tuft of silky hairs at the base, in pairs supported by pedicels of unequal length; disarticulation below the spikelet, the hairy callus falling with spikelet; glumes thin, equal to spikelet, the second glume with narrower and longer apex; lemma of lower floret, lemma and palea of upper floret all thin and hyaline.

Reported as rare in the mountains, S part of Hudspeth and Brewster counties (Correll and Johnston, 1970). One collection is known from Big Bend Natl. Park, Croton Peak, 3,500 ft., flowering in Aug. Gould (1975) also listed this species for the Trans-Pecos and for the W Edwards Plateau. Also Jackson Co.,

Fig. 272. *Imperata brevifolia.* Partial plant.

TX. Also NM, AZ, UT, NV, CA in desert mountains. Sonora, perhaps Chihua-hua, Mex.

The distribution of *Imperata brevifolia* in the Trans-Pecos and the extent of the current populations in the area are matters that require further investiga-tion. The species is seldom seen or collected and may be extremely rare. Satin-tail occurs in desert regions but may always grow near permanent water sources such as springs, ponds, or streams. Another species similar to *Imperata brevifolia*, but with a flaring panicle and not occurring in the Trans-Pecos, is the ornamental introduced from eastern Asia, *Miscanthus sinensis*.

73. SORGHUM   Moench   SORGHUM.

A genus of about 20 species distributed mainly in the warmer regions of the Old World, with two species native to Mexico and Central America. Probably two or three species occur in the United States and in Texas, all of these intro-duced. The genus name is from *Sorgho*, the Italian name for the plant. The cultivated annual sorghum, *Sorghum bicolor* (L.) Moench (synonym *S. vulgare* Pers.), is grown as a feed grain in the few farming areas of the Trans-Pecos, including the fields near El Paso, Pecos, Balmorhea, Presidio, Fort Stockton, and Coyanosa. These plants may occur as weeds at roadside and in other dis-turbed habitats, but they do not persist. There are numerous cultivated vari-

Fig. 273. *Sorghum halepense.* Plant; sessile
spikelet and two pedicelled spikelets (in back).

eties of sorghum in the world, including sorgo, milo, kafir, durra, shallu, and
broomcorn, but these are not recognized as formal taxa by most workers. Another variety of *S. bicolor* commonly cultivated in the United States as a hay
and pasture grass is Sudan grass, formerly known as *S. sudanense* (Piper) Stapf.
Sorghum almum Parodi, a tall (to 3–4 m) rhizomatous perennial native to
Argentina, has been used as a pasture grass particularly in fields taken out of
cultivation on the Edwards Plateau, South Texas Plains, and perhaps in the
Trans-Pecos.

   1. Sorghum halepense (L.) Pers.   JOHNSONGRASS.   Fig. 273.   Perennial, with extensive, creeping rhizomes. Culms to 1–2 m long, but often much
shorter. Leaves essentially glabrous; ligule a ciliate membrane; blades usually
flat, large, 0.8–2 cm wide. Inflorescence a panicle, open, branched, usually
15–35 cm long. Spikelets in pairs, one sessile and perfect, another pedicelled
and staminate or neuter, except at branch tips the sessile spikelet occurs with 2
pedicelled spikelets; sessile spikelets 4.5–5.5 mm long, awnless or awned, the
awn if present on the lemma geniculate, twisted below, delicate, 1.5 cm long,
readily deciduous; glumes of sessile spikelet broad, leathery, nerveless, and
shiny except at tip, pubescent at least on the margins; pedicelled spikelets usually awnless, lanceolate, about as long as sessile spikelets but more slender, with
more conspicuously veined glumes.

A common introduced weed in various disturbed habitats including at roadside. Found in every county of the Trans-Pecos. 2,000–6,500 ft. Flowering Apr–Nov. N to IA and MA, E to FL, W to S CA. Also common throughout the world in temperate, subtropical, and tropical regions. Apparently native to S Europe.

Johnsongrass has the reputation as a farmland and garden pest, difficult to eradicate because of its extensive rhizome system. Johnsongrass has been widely used as a forage grass where its drought resistance, once established, and persistent habit become an advantage. In the Trans-Pecos region, ranchers have seeded johnsongrass in "overflow areas," low range sites where water tends to collect after periodic rains, with the purpose of getting the grass established and allowing it to persist as forage in an arid region. Ranchers are aware that johnsongrass tends to accumulate cyanogenic glucosides in its herbage under certain conditions and that this can result in prussic acid poisoning in grazing animals. Recent studies have revealed important information about the accumulation of cyanogenic glucosides in johnsongrass (R. A. Hilsenbeck, pers. comm.). Hilsenbeck found that the cyanogenic compounds tend to accumulate rapidly within 24 hours after rains in new growth, and that cyanogenesis tends to drop after freezing, wilting, and several other measurable environmental factors. It has long been believed that cyanogenesis in johnsongrass was evident in new growth but also might follow various stressful conditions including frost damage. When cyanogenic glucosides are produced in the plant tissues, they are converted enzymatically to hydrogen cyanide (HCN), which acts as the poisonous principle in grazing animals. Enzymes that convert cyanogenic glucosides to HCN are sequestered in cell vacuoles until they are released mechanically as the plants are chewed and eaten. Cyanogenic glucosides may also be converted to HCN spontaneously after 24 hours even without the enzymes being present. In johnsongrass the cyanogenic glucosides are converted to parahydroxybenzaldehyde (an allelopathic substance), HCN, and glucose. The HCN can kill grazing animals in as little as 15 minutes if enough plant material is eaten. According to Hilsenbeck, many native range grasses in the Trans-Pecos also produce copious amounts of the cyanogenic glucosides, and these are produced in new growth after rains. This has been well documented in *Leptochloa dubia* (green sprangletop), one of the best forage grasses, and in numerous species of *Bouteloua*, the grama grasses, where cyanogenesis is particularly intense in inflorescences.

74. SORGHASTRUM Nash INDIANGRASS.

A genus of about 17 species distributed in warmer parts of the Americas and Africa. Three species are reported for the United States (Hitchcock, 1951). Two species occur in Texas (Gould, 1975). The genus name is from *Sorghum* and the Latin suffix *astrum*, meaning a poor imitation of, in reference to the

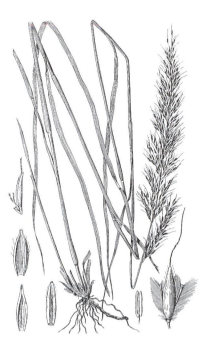

Fig. 274. *Sorghastrum nutans*. Plant; spikelet
with pedicel and rachis joint, and various
floret parts.

resemblance of *Sorghastrum* to *Sorghum*. Davila and Clark (1990) have found
that related groups of species in *Sorghastrum* can be recognized through scanning electron microscope studies of leaf epidermis structure.

   1. Sorghastrum nutans (L.) Nash   INDIANGRASS.   Fig. 274.   [*Andropogon nutans* L.; *Sorghastrum avenaceum* (Michx.) Nash]. Perennial, with
stiffly erect hairs. Leaves essentially glabrous; ligule a stiff membrane 2–5 mm
long, this exhibited at the sides as pointed sheath auricles; sheaths usually glabrous, rarely weakly hispid; blades flat, long, usually 5–10 mm wide, base narrow, apex attenuated. Inflorescence a panicle, 15–30 cm long, loosely or tightly
contracted, upper branchlets, pedicels, and glumes rather densely pubescent
with silvery hairs; disarticulation involving spikelet and section of rachis and
the pedicel(s). Spikelets usually in pairs of one sessile and perfect and one
pedicelled and rudimentary, in this case the pedicelled spikelet completely reduced, represented only by the hairy pedicel (2 pedicels at branched tips);
perfect spikelets 2-flowered, 6–8 mm long, glumes hard or leathery, subequal,
light brown or straw colored; lemma and palea of lower floret absent or
reduced; lemma of fertile floret thin, hyaline, the midnerve extending into

a stout, geniculate awn usually 11–18 mm long, twisted below and above the bend.

Infrequent mostly in mountain canyons and on protected slopes, usually mesic sites. Culberson Co., Guadalupe Mts., West Dog Canyon; Pine Top Mt.; trail to Guadalupe Peak; Pine Springs Canyon; South McKittrick Canyon; North McKittrick Canyon. Jeff Davis Co., Davis Mts.; 3 mi S Fort Davis, CDRI Landsite. Brewster Co., Lizard Mt., 1 mi W Alpine; Big Hill, 6 mi S Alpine; 9 mi S Alpine; Iron Mt.; Marathon; Big Bend Natl. Park, Chisos Mts., Wilson Ranch. 3,750–8,200 ft. Flowering Aug–Nov. Reportedly from all regions of TX, most frequent in the tall grass prairie areas of central and coastal TX (Gould, 1975). Throughout the United States E of Rocky Mts., N to south-central Canada. N Mex.

Sorghastrum is regarded as one of the "big four" tallgrass prairie grasses of the central United States, True Prairie Association (Gould, 1975). Other grasses of the big four are *Andropogon gerardii* (big bluestem), *Schizachyrium scoparium* (little bluestem), and *Panicum virgatum* (switchgrass). Indiangrass, also known as yellow indiangrass, provides good grazing for livestock and wildlife. It is palatable throughout the summer when it is green, but it loses palatability and forage value with maturity into the winter.

75. ANDROPOGON   L.   BLUESTEM.

Perennials, usually cespitose, some with rhizomes. Culms erect. Leaves with keeled sheaths; ligules membranous; blades flat or folded. Flowering culms in some species much-branched (broomlike), in other species unbranched or little-branched. Inflorescence a panicle; racemose branches of panicle 2 to several. Spikelets in pairs, one sessile and perfect, another pedicelled and staminate or neuter, absent or rudimentary in some; disarticulation involving the rachis, with the sessile (fertile) spikelet falling attached to pedicel and rachis part; spikelets 2-flowered, the lower (sterile) floret often vestigial; glumes hard, large, awnless; lemmas of lower and upper (fertile) florets thin and hyaline, the lemma of the upper floret awned or awnless.

In its strict sense this is a genus of about 100 species in warmer regions of the world, with about 17 species in the United States and about six species in Texas. In its broad sense *Andropogon* has been interpreted to include the closely related genera *Bothriochloa*, *Schizachyrium*, and *Dichanthium*. The genus name is from Greek *aner* (*andr-*), man, and *pogon*, beard, in reference to the hairy pedicels of the staminate or sterile spikelets, and accounting for one common name of the genus, beardgrass. Several species of *Andropogon* are regarded as important forage grasses, with *A. gerardii* being most significant, although the amount of prairie hay or wild hay in the United States has steadily decreased as cultivated fields have replaced prairie.

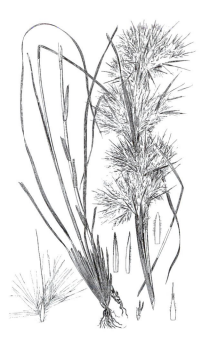

Fig. 275. *Andropogon glomeratus*. Plant; spikelet with rachis joint and pedicel, and various
floret parts.

Key to the Species

1. Flowering culms profusely branched and rebranched, the collective
   branches and villous inflorescences broomlike   **1. A. glomeratus.**
1. Flowering culms only moderately rebranched, not at all broomlike.
   2. Pedicelled spikelets well-developed, usually staminate; inflorescence of
      2–7 racemose branches   **2. A. gerardii.**
   2. Pedicelled spikelets much reduced, sterile; inflorescence of 2 racemose
      branches in V-shaped pairs at ends of inflorescence branches
                                                          3. A. spadiceus.

   1. **Andropogon glomeratus** (Walt.) B.S.P. BUSHY BLUESTEM.
Fig. 275.   Infrequent to rare in certain moist habitats. Culberson Co., Gua-
dalupe Mts., South McKittrick Canyon; Bear Canyon; Choisya Springs. Presi-
dio Co., Arroyo Secundo, Fresno Canyon. Brewster Co., Chisos Mts., lower
Cattail Falls drainage near the falls; Alamo Spring; moist drainage in gravel hills
NW of Chisos Mts. Terrell Co., Independence Creek. Val Verde Co., Devils
River. 1,500–6,500 ft. Flowering Aug–Nov. Scattered throughout most of TX.
E United States, OK, S NV, S CA. Mex.

Andropogon glomeratus is a densely cespitose perennial with coarse stems to 1.5 m tall. The plants are easily recognized by the dense, broomlike inflorescences influenced by much culm branching and rebranching and long-villous hairs of the small inflorescence branches. Bushy bluestem is regarded as a poor forage grass, but it does provide good cover for wildlife. The Texas plants of this species are included in *A. glomeratus* var. **pumilus** Vasey (Johnston, 1990; Campbell, 1983).

2. Andropogon gerardii Vitman   BIG BLUESTEM.   Three varieties of *A. gerardii* are recognized by Gould (1975) to occur in Texas and in the Trans-Pecos.

Key to the Varieties

1. Sessile (fertile) spikelet awnless, or rarely with a short awn; rhizomes well-developed   **A. *A. gerardii* var. *paucipilus*.**
1. Sessile spikelet with an awn 0.8–2 cm long; rhizomes well-developed, short, or absent.
   2. Hairs of rachis internodes dense, usually 3–4 mm long and golden yellow in color, sometimes whitish; rhizomes well-developed
                                          B. *A. gerardii* var. *chrysocomus*.
   2. Hairs of rachis internodes sparse to dense, usually 1–2 mm long and whitish; rhizomes absent or short   **C. *A. gerardii* var. *gerardii*.**

A. *Andropogon gerardii* var. **paucipilus** (Nash) Fern.   SAND BLUESTEM. Fig. 276. [*Andropogon hallii* Hack]. Infrequent to frequent in deep sand, rarely in gypsum sand. Hudspeth Co., gypsum dunes W of Guadalupe Mts. Ward Co., 3–4 mi E Monahans. Winkler Co., 8 mi W Wink; 3 mi and 10 mi E Kermit; 5 mi N Kermit; 10 mi NE Kermit. Crane Co., 20–25 mi W Crane; ca. 10 mi N Imperial. 2,300–2,800 ft. Flowering Aug–Nov. Plains country of TX. N to ND and E MT, W to AZ.

The large plants of sand bluestem exhibit well-developed rhizomes and culms to 2 m high. At the northeastern periphery of the Trans-Pecos, var. *paucipilus* appears to be restricted to deep sandy soils, as it probably is throughout much of its range in North America. Sand bluestem is easily distinguished by its awnless spikelets, and inflorescence of usually a pair of dark colored racemes. The plants offer good forage.

B. *Andropogon gerardii* var. **chrysocomus** (Nash) Fern.   GOLDEN BLUESTEM.   Fig. 277. [*Andropogon hallii* sensu Hitchcock (1951) and Gould (1969) in part]. Infrequent to frequent in mountains, canyons and upper slopes, limestone and igneous substrates. Culberson Co., Guadalupe Mts., W Dog Canyon; Pine Top; Guadalupe Peak; Smith Canyon; South McKittrick

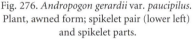

Fig. 276. *Andropogon gerardii* var. *paucipilus.*
Plant, awned form; spikelet pair (lower left)
and spikelet parts.

Fig. 277. *Andropogon gerardii* var. *chrysocomus.*
Plant; spikelet pair. This figure also depicts
A. gerardii var. *gerardii.*

Canyon. Jeff Davis Co., Davis Mts., Limpia Canyon near Mt. Livermore; NW slopes Mt. Locke; 2 mi N Bloys Encampment. Brewster Co., Del Norte Mts., Mt. Ord, E side; Chisos Mts., Upper Cattail Canyon. 5,000–8,100 ft. Flowering Jul–Nov. Plains country of TX. N to KS, W to NM and NE AZ.

Plants of var. *chrysocomus* supposedly produce well-developed rhizomes. The spikelets of this species are awned and the copious hairs of the inflorescence rachis internodes are usually golden or yellowish, less often whitish, hence the common name golden bluestem. Plants of var. *chrysocomus* are palatable and doubtless provide good forage where the abundance is sufficient.

C. *Andropogon gerardii* var. **gerardii** BIG BLUESTEM. Fig. 277. [*Andropogon provincialis* Lam.; *A. furcatus* Muhl.]. Seemingly rare in the Trans-Pecos, with one tentatively identified collection from Jeff Davis Co., Scenic Loop above Fort Davis, 5,000 ft. Throughout TX. N to S Canada, including AZ, CO, MT. N and central highlands of Mex.

Big bluestem is one of the "big four" most widespread and important forage grasses in the tallgrass prairie region of North America (Gould, 1975). The plants reach 2 m high, but rhizomes are short or absent. The spikelets of big

Fig. 278. *Andropogon spadiceus.* Racemes,
terminal in V-shaped pair; spikelet pair and
rachis joint.

bluestem are awned, and typically the inflorescence rachis internodes are sparsely to copiously pubescent with relatively short hairs (to 2 mm long).

3. Andropogon spadiceus Swallen   Fig. 278.   Dry limestone slopes in desert mountains. Brewster Co., Del Norte Mts., Altuda Mt., 15 mi E Alpine; Glass Mts., Sibley Ranch; Black Gap Refuge, upper Heath Canyon. 2,200–4,400 ft. Flowering Aug–Oct. Primarily a species of Coahuila, Mex. (Johnston, 1981).

According to Johnston (1981), *Andropogon spadiceus,* formerly known only from Coahuila, Mexico, is most closely related to *A. ternarius* Michx. Johnston noted that *A. spadiceus* superficially resembles the common little bluestem, *Schizachyrium scoparium* (Michx.) Nash, and that collectors thus might have passed by *A. spadiceus* without close observation. Superficially *A. spadiceus* can be distinguished by its racemes in V-shaped pairs at the ends of inflorescence branches, while *S. scoparium* exhibits racemes solitary at the ends of inflorescence branches. Additional collections of *A. spadiceus* should be sought in the limestone mountains from the Del Nortes south to the Rio Grande.

76. BOTHRIOCHLOA   Kuntze   BEARDGRASS.

Perennials (in our species) and annuals; culms cespitose or tufted, with stiffly erect culms, geniculate in some, perhaps decumbent in *B. ischaemum*. Leaves with membranous ligules; blades flat, long, and narrow. Inflorescence a panicle, whitish and "beardlike" in most native species. Spikelets in pairs on few to many primary branches, these rebranched in some species; disarticulation at base of spikelets, but with rachis joint and pedicel falling with the sessile spikelet; pedicels and upper rachis internodes with a central groove or broad membranous area; sessile spikelets perfect, usually awned, somewhat deltoid-lanceolate in outline; first glume dorsally flattened, second glume with rounded keel in middle; lemma of upper (fertile) floret reduced, thin and hyaline, midnerve stout, this usually extended into an awn, the awn geniculate and twisted; pedicelled spikelets awnless, well-developed, neuter or staminate.

A genus of about 35 species ranging throughout warmer regions of the world. The species of *Bothriochloa* are in general fair to good forage grasses. The genus name is from Greek *bothr*, hole or trench, and *chloe*, young shoots, presumably alluding to the central groove of rachis internodes in the inflorescence. Species of *Bothriochloa* other than those discussed below eventually could be found in the Trans-Pecos, including *B. edwardsiana* (Gould) Parodi, which occurs on the Edwards Plateau, and *B. hybrida* (Gould), which is known to occur near Del Rio in Val Verde County. Also, Kelly Allred (pers. comm.) has seen a specimen of *B. wrightii* (Hack.) Henr. from Jeff Davis County (Davis Mountains, 18 Apr 1930, *S. E. Wolff 1635*, US), but he noted that the current existence of this species in the Trans-Pecos requires verification. According to Allred, *B. wrightii* resembles *B. barbinodis* except that it has smooth, glaucous stems, a short panicle with few branches, and glumes with a glandular pit.

Key to the Species

1. Plants weakly tufted, stems erect or decumbent, perhaps rooting at the nodes where frequently mowed, growing at roadside or in other disturbed habitats; inflorescence at maturity turning purplish because of color in spikelets; pedicelled spikelets about as long as sessile spikelets but usually narrower   **1. *B. ischaemum.***

1. Plants strongly tufted, stems erect or perhaps weakly decumbent in age, never rooting at the nodes, growing in native habitats and disturbed sites; inflorescence at maturity collectively appearing as a whitish, cottony mass because of long, white hairs. Pedicelled spikelets perhaps shorter and usually much narrower than sessile spikelets.

    2. Culm nodes glabrous or short-pubescent with hairs usually less than 1 mm long; sessile spikelets less than 4.5 mm long; awns 1.8 cm long or less   **2. *B. laguroides.***

Fig. 279. *Bothriochloa ischaemum* var.
songarica. Plant; spikelet pair.

2. Culm nodes bearded with appressed to spreading hairs 1–7 mm long;
   sessile spikelets 4.5–7.4 mm long; awns 2.0–3.4 cm long.
   3. Panicle axis usually less than 5 cm long; panicle branches usually
      2–7; culms usually slender, with nodal hairs spreading, 3–7 mm long
                                                              3. *B. springfieldii.*
   3. Panicle axis usually 5–20 cm long, or more; panicle branches usually
      9–30; culms usually stout, with nodal hairs appressed or spreading,
      1–6 mm long.
      4. Plants to 1.2 m tall; culms not bluish-glaucous below the nodes;
         culm nodes with appressed hairs 1–3 mm long; panicles usually
         7–13 cm long   **4. *B. barbinodis.***
      4. Plants to 2.5 m tall; culms bluish-glaucous below the nodes;
         culm nodes with spreading hairs 3–6 mm long; panicles usually
         14–25 cm long   **5. *B. alta.***

1. Bothriochloa ischaemum (L.) Keng var. **songarica** (Fisch. & Mey.)
Celarier & Harlan   KING RANCH BLUESTEM.   Fig. 279.   [*Andropogon
ischaemum* L. var. *songaricus* Fisch. & Mey.]. An introduced species abundant
at roadside and in other disturbed habitats. Presidio Co., 25 mi S Marfa toward
Plata. Jeff Davis Co., Wild Rose Pass. Brewster Co., Alpine, lawn on Sul Ross

Fig. 280. *Bothriochloa laguroides* subsp. *torrey-*
ana. Plant; spikelet pair and rachis joint, and
spikelet parts.

campus; 16 mi W Alpine; 23 mi S Marathon; Black Gap Refuge, 4 mi below
headquarters. Val Verde Co. 2,000–4,600 ft. Flowering Aug–Nov. Throughout
much of S TX. S and central Europe, and elsewhere. Mex.

The taxon occurring in Texas and the Trans-Pecos is *Bothriochloa ischae-*
mum var. *songarica*. The species was introduced as a pasture grass and has
since escaped and spread along the roadsides in Texas, probably reaching the
Trans-Pecos in the early 1960's, according to one herbarium record, but evidently not becoming widespread in the Trans-Pecos until the late 1970's or
early 1980's. Gould (1975) did not list King Ranch bluestem for the Trans-
Pecos area. Evidently King Ranch bluestem is highly palatable, but it is not
likely to ever furnish good forage in the Trans-Pecos, because it does not appear capable of becoming established on rangelands away from the extra water
it gets at roadside.

2. Bothriochloa laguroides (DC.) Herter subsp. **torreyana** (Steud.) Allred
& Gould   SILVER BLUESTEM.   Fig. 280.   [*Andropogon saccharoides* Sw.
var. *torreyanus* (Steud.) Hack. in A. DC.; *Bothriochloa saccharoides* (Sw.) Rydb.
var. *torreyana* (Steud.) Gould]. Infrequent to frequent in various soil types,
perhaps best developed at mid elevations in deep soil, in every county of the

Fig. 281. *Bothriochloa barbinodis* var. *barbinodis*. Plant; spikelet pair. *Bothriochloa springfieldii* is similar in habit and spikelet structure.

Trans-Pecos. 1,200–6,000 ft. Flowering Apr–Nov. Throughout TX. E to GA,
N to MO, KS, CO, W to AZ. NE Mex.

Silver bluestem is regarded as a good to fair forage grass for livestock and
wildlife. It is a hardy perennial and is easily re-established after droughts
and overgrazing. *Bothriochloa laguroides* subsp. *torreyana* overlaps in distribution with the common *B. barbinodis*, and also with the less common species,
B. springfieldii and *B. alta*. All of these taxa are similar in appearance, but under
most circumstances *B. laguroides* can be distinguished by its smaller habit, often glaucous herbage, shorter inflorescences, and culm nodes that are glabrous
or with short hairs. *Bothriochloa springfieldii* also is smaller in habit with
shorter inflorescences, but has spreading long hairs at the nodes. Both *B. barbinodis* and *B. alta* have larger habits, with *B. alta* being the tallest and with the
longest panicles. For many years silver bluestem was known as *B. saccharoides*,
but a recent study by Allred and Gould (1983) has clarified the taxonomy of
this grass complex.

3. Bothriochloa springfieldii (Gould) L. R. Parodi   SPRINGFIELD BLUE-
STEM.   Fig. 281.   [*Andropogon springfieldii* Gould]. Infrequent on mountain slopes, in alluvial basins, and in canyons, various soil types. El Paso Co.,

Fig. 282. *Bothriochloa barbinodis* var. *perforata.*
Spikelet pair.

Franklin Mts.; Hueco Mts. Culberson Co., Guadalupe Mts., North McKittrick Canyon; base of Signal Peak. Presidio Co., Chinati Mts., Pinto Canyon. Jeff Davis Co., Davis Mts. State Park, N part of county. Brewster Co., Mt. Ord; S slopes Cathedral Peak. Winkler Co. Crane Co. 3,500–6,000 ft. Flowering Jun–Oct. Also High Plains, TX. W to NM and N AZ.

Bothriochloa springfieldii appears to be most closely related to *B. barbinodis*, but in size it most resembles *B. laguroides*. Springfield bluestem is much more scattered in distribution and is less common than *B. barbinodis* and *B. laguroides*. Springfield bluestem is highly palatable, particularly early in the season.

4. Bothriochloa barbinodis (Lag.) Heter   CANE BLUESTEM.   Two varieties of *B. barbinodis* are recognized by Gould (1975). *B. barbinodis* var. *barbinodis* is distinguished by the absence of a glandular pit on the first glume of the sessile spikelet. *B. barbinodis* var. *perforata* (Fourn.) Gould has a round glandular pit at or above the middle on the first glume of the sessile spikelet of all or most all spikelets.

A.   *Bothriochloa   barbinodis*   var.   **barbinodis**   CANE   BLUESTEM. Fig. 281.   [*Andropogon barbinodis* Lag.]. Infrequent to frequent and widely distributed in various soil types and habitats, in every county of the Trans-Pecos. 2,500–6,200 ft. Flowering Jun–Nov. Throughout most of TX except deep E portions. To CO, UT, CA. Mex. Also Argentina and Uruguay.

Fig. 283. *Bothriochloa alta*. Panicle; spikelet
pair and rachis internode.

Cane bluestem is regarded as a good forage grass, particularly early in the season before the culms become fully mature and fibrous. This is perhaps the most widely distributed bluestem in the Trans-Pecos.

B. *Bothriochloa barbinodis* var. **perforata** PINHOLE BLUESTEM. Fig. 282. [*Andropogon perforatus* Fourn.]. Probably rare in mountains of the Trans-Pecos. Brewster Co., top Nine Point Mesa; Mt. Ord. 4,500–5,000 ft. Flowering probably Jun–Oct. NM. Mex. Argentina and Uruguay.

According to Gould (1975) this taxon has essentially the same distribution and habitat as the typical variety, but it is certainly rare in the Trans-Pecos compared to var. *barbinodis*. The roundish glandular pit on the glume of the sessile spikelet, which distinguishes this taxon, is very evident under magnification.

5. Bothriochloa alta (Hitchc.) Henr. TALL BLUESTEM. Fig. 283. [*Andropogon altus* Hitchc.]. Infrequent, mountains and basins, various soil types. Hudspeth Co., 8 mi W Sierra Blanca, Quitman Mts. Jeff Davis Co., 5 mi S Kent; between Madera Canyon and Mt. Locke; W slopes Mt. Locke; 4 mi S Fort Davis toward Marfa. Brewster Co., E side Alpine. 4,500–6,200 ft. Flowering Jun–Oct. Also S NM. W-central Mex. Reported from Bolivia and Argentina (Gould, 1975).

Tall bluestem is probably somewhat more common in the Trans-Pecos than current collections would suggest. It is similar to *Bothriochloa barbinodis*, and collectors possibly have not always distinguished the two taxa. In addition to the taller plants with larger panicles, *B. alta* can be distinguished in the field by the bluish-glaucous ring below culm nodes. Tall bluestem surely is as palatable to livestock as is *B. barbinodis*.

77. SCHIZACHYRIUM   Nees   LITTLE BLUESTEM.

Perennials (in our species) or annuals, cespitose, with or without rhizomes. Culms erect, rarely decumbent, usually much-branched above. Leaves with rounded or keeled sheaths; ligules membranous; blades flat or folded, slender. Inflorescence with flowering culms much-branched above, each leafy branch ending in a single spicate raceme. Spikelets appressed to or divergent from rachis; rachis joints and pedicels somewhat flattened, the joints cup-shaped or irregularly lobed at the apex; disarticulation at the base of sessile spikelets, with the rachis joint and pedicel falling with the spikelet, sessile spikelets perfect; glumes hard; lemmas, of both lower and upper florets, thin and hyaline; lemma of upper floret awned or awnless.

A genus of about 60 species distributed in warm grasslands throughout both hemispheres. The genus name is from Greek *schiz*, to split or cleave, and *achyr*, chaff or husks, presumably alluding to the disarticulating rachis joints in the inflorescence. *Schizachyrium* is distinguished from *Andropogon* by its single racemes and fimbriate internode tips in the inflorescence. The little bluestem grasses are noted for their good forage value. The three species recognized for the Trans-Pecos are all similar in macroscopic appearance. With good eyesight one can distinguish *Schizachyrium cirratum* from the other two species by the paucity of villous hairs on the inflorescence. All three taxa seem to overlap in distribution and ecological habitats, and there would appear to be some question about their taxonomic status.

Key to the Species

1. First glume of sessile spikelet pubescent on the back; rachis internode and pedicels typically hispid on the back and margins; rachis internodes thick (a character useful only by comparison with thin internodes in *S. scoparium*)   **1. *S. sanguineum* var. *hirtiflorum*.**

1. First glume of sessile spikelet glabrous or at the most scabrous on the back; rachis internodes and pedicels pubescent or not; rachis internodes thick or thin and flexuous.

   2. Rachis of the raceme glabrous except for rather short, stiff hairs at the ends, near nodes and the points of disarticulation; rachis thick; glume of sessile spikelet glabrous on the back, but scabrous to short-ciliate on the margins above the middle only   **2. *S. cirratum*.**

Fig. 284. *Schizachyrium sanguineum* var. *hirti-florum*. Raceme; spikelet pair on rachis.

2. Rachis of the raceme densely villous (long, white hairs along internodes and pedicels); rachis thin and flexuous; glume of sessile spikelet glabrous on the back and margins   **3. *S. scoparium.***

1. Schizachyrium sanguineum (Retz.) Alston var. **hirtiflorum** (Nees) Hatch. Fig. 284. [*Andropogon hirtiflorus* (Nees) Kunth; *A. feensis* Fourn.; *Schizachyrium feense* (Fourn.) A. Camus; *S. hirtiflorum* Nees; *S. sanguineum* (Retz.) Alston var. *brevipedicellatum* (Beal) Hatch]. Infrequent to frequent, mountain slopes and canyons, medium elevations. Presidio Co., W side High Lonesome, Brite Ranch. Jeff Davis Co., Little Aguja Canyon; upper E slopes, Major Peak, Kokernot Ranch; Davis Mts. State Park, picnic rocks at E entrance; Musquiz Canyon, 13 mi N Alpine. Brewster Co., 4 mi W Alpine, Paradise Canyon; Iron Mt.; Glass Mts.; one questionable record for the Chisos Mts., in Big Bend Natl. Park. 4,000–5,500 ft. Flowering Jun–Oct. GA and FL. W to E AZ. Mex. highlands. Central America.

Gould (1975) discussed possible relationships of *Schizachyrium sanguineum* var. *hirtiflorum* to other Trans-Pecos species of *Schizachyrium*. In Texas, *S. san-guineum* var. *hirtiflorum* is restricted to the Trans-Pecos mountains, and it is of more limited occurrence than any other Trans-Pecos little bluestem. This is

Fig. 285. *Schizachyrium cirratum.* Plant;
spikelet pair on rachis.

the only Trans-Pecos *Schizachyrium* with pubescence on the flattened back of
the spikelet (on the first glume).

2. Schizachyrium cirratum (Hack.) Woot. & Standl.   TEXAS BLUE-
STEM.   Fig. 285.   [*Andropogon cirratus* Hack.]. Infrequent to frequent on
rocky mountain slopes and in canyons. Hudspeth Co., W slopes Eagle Mts.
Culberson Co., Guadalupe Mts. Presidio Co., Sierra Vieja, 2 mi S Vieja; Capote
Mt., S slopes; 101 Ranch. Jeff Davis Co., Davis Mts., high ridge SE of Mt. Liv-
ermore; Rockpile; 2 mi N Bloys Encampment; Davis Mts. State Park; Fern Can-
yon, Mitre Peak Girl Scout Camp. Brewster Co., between Alpine and Fort Da-
vis; Paradise Canyon, 4 mi W Alpine; 9 mi S Alpine; Mt. Ord; Cienega Mt.;
Cathedral Mt.; Goat Mt.; Chisos Mts., above Boot Springs; E slopes Casa
Grande. 4,500–7,500 ft. Flowering Jul–Nov. W to S CA; Sonora, Chihuahua,
Coahuila, Mex.

This is the only Trans-Pecos little bluestem whose racemes appear to the
naked eye to be essentially hairless, the short hairs of the rachis joints being
present only at their ends. Texas little bluestem should be good forage for livestock and wildlife.

Fig. 286. *Schizachyrium scoparium*. Plant;
spikelet pair and rachis internode.

3. Schizachyrium scoparium (Michx.) Nash. LITTLE BLUESTEM.
Fig. 286. [*Andropogon scoparius* Michx.]. Infrequent to frequent, mostly on
rocky mountain slopes and in canyons. By far the most widespread and common little bluestem in the Trans-Pecos, occurring in probably every mountain
system in every county, in canyons of the western Edwards Plateau, and in the
sand dune area. 1,500–8,000 ft. Flowering Jun–Nov. Throughout most of TX;
throughout the E and central United States, into Canada. Throughout much
of Mex.

Gould (1975) recognized five varieties of *Schizachyrium scoparium* in Texas,
with the common variety in the Trans-Pecos being *S. scoparium* var. **neo-
mexicanum** (Nash) Gould (New Mexico little bluestem). Some Trans-Pecos
specimens also key to *S. scoparium* var. *frequens* (C. E. Hubb.) Gould (little
bluestem). No varieties are recognized herein because they could not be distinguished, with certainty at least, among the Trans-Pecos specimens. The
racemes have long-villous hairs in most Trans-Pecos populations, allowing
tentative recognition of *S. scoparium* without magnification. *Schizachyrium scoparium* is regarded as a good forage grass especially in early season.

Fig. 287. *Trachypogon secundus*. Plant;
fertile spikelet.

78. TRACHYPOGON   Nees   CRINKLEAWN.

A genus of about three species distributed in the warmer regions of Africa and the Americas. One species occurs in Texas. The genus name is from Greek *trachus*, rough, and *pogon*, beard, in reference to the plumose awns in the inflorescence.

1. Trachypogon secundus (Presl) Scribn. CRINKLEAWN. Fig. 287. Perennial, cespitose; culms 60–120 cm long, the nodes densely appressed-pubescent, becoming glabrate. Leaves with sheaths rounded to slightly keeled; ligule of lower and middle leaves membranous, brownish, 1–10 mm long; ligule of upper leaves short and fringed; blades to 30 cm long, 1–8 mm wide, flat or involute. Inflorescence a spikelike raceme, usually 10–20 cm long. Spikelets in pairs on a continuous rachis, one subsessile, staminate, and awnless, another with slightly longer pedicel, perfect, and awned; disarticulation at base of spikelet; spikelets linear, 6–8 mm long; first glume, rounded on the back, sparsely hispid; lemma of perfect floret with a stout awn 4–6 cm long, the awn twisted and plumose, the hairs 2–5 mm long, diminishing in length distally.

Reported from the Trans-Pecos (Gould, 1975), to be expected in loose,

Fig. 288. *Elionurus barbiculmis*. Plant; spikelike
raceme; spikelet pair.

sandy soils. Also South Texas Plains and Gulf Coast Prairies in TX. W to AZ.
Throughout Mex. Argentina.

Crinkleawn is a coarse perennial that is rare in the Trans-Pecos. It is of
limited forage value.

79. ELIONURUS Willd. BALSAMSCALE.

A genus of about 15 species in warm regions of the Old and New World.
Two species occur in the United States and in Texas. The genus name is from
Greek *eluein*, to roll, and *oura*, tail, in reference to the cylindric inflorescence.
Clayton and Renvoize (1986) point out the correct spelling for the genus,
Elionurus instead of *Elyonurus*.

1. Elionurus barbiculmis Hack. WOOLSPIKE BALSAMSCALE.
Fig. 288. [*Elyonurus muticus* (Spreng.) O. Ktze. var. *barbiculmis* (Hack.)
Beetle]. Perennial, cespitose; roots reddish, without rhizomes. Culms erect
35–85 cm long, pubescent below the nodes, nodes glabrous. Leaves hispid
especially on the upper sheaths; ligule a short, fringed membrane; blades slender, involute, usually ca. 1–1.5 mm wide. Inflorescence a spikelike raceme,
usually 3.5–10 cm long, raceme and peduncle densely villous; disarticulation

in the rachis. Spikelets awnless, in pairs, similar in appearance, one subsessile and perfect, 4.5–7.5 mm long, the other pedicelled and staminate, slightly shorter than perfect one; first glume of subsessile (perfect) spikelet firm to leathery, second glume thinner, the glumes of both spikelets densely pilose on the back; lemmas of both florets thin and hyaline, paleas absent.

Infrequent on rocky mountain slopes and in canyons. Presidio Co., Capote Mt., S slopes; Chinati Mts., Tigna Canyon; Wildhorse Canyon above Shely Ranch house; lower slopes Chinati Peak; Frenchman Hills 25 mi S Marfa. Jeff Davis Co., between Madera Canyon and Mt. Locke; 1.5 mi N Bloys Encampment; Barrel Springs; Limpia Canyon; near Mt. Locke; Davis Mts. State Park; Wild Rose Pass; Fern Canyon, Mitre Peak Girl Scout Camp; Haystack Mt. Brewster Co., between Alpine and Fort Davis; Sul Ross Hill; Cathedral Mt.; Chisos Mts., Basin; trail to Laguna. 4,000–6,800 ft. Flowering Jun–Nov. W to AZ. N Mex.

Gould (1975) reported one doubtful collection of *Elionurus tripsacoides* Willd. (Pan American balsamscale) from Jeff Davis County. *Elionurus tripsacoides* in Texas occurs normally in deep southern regions and has not been observed among numerous recent collections from Jeff Davis County. *Elionurus tripsacoides* is distinguished by knotty, rhizomatous bases, culms glabrous below the nodes, first glume glabrous on the back except ciliate near the apex, while *E. barbiculmis* lacks rhizomes, has pubescent culms below the nodes, with the first glume densely pubescent. The *E. muticus* var. *barbiculmis* combination in synonymy is by Beetle (1977). Woolspike balsamscale is palatable but not often abundant enough to provide useful forage.

80. HETEROPOGON   Pers.   TANGLEHEAD.

A genus of about six species in warm regions of the world, probably native to the Old World and adventive in the Americas. Only two species are reported for the United States and perhaps for Texas. The genus name is from Greek *heteros*, different, and *pogon*, beard, in reference to inflorescences with awnless, staminate spikelets below and awned, pistillate spikelets above.

1. Heteropogon contortus (L.) Roem. & Schutt. TANGLEHEAD. Fig. 289.   Perennial, cespitose. Culms to 80 cm long, glabrous, freely branching below and above. Leaves glabrous except near the junction of sheath and blade; sheaths strongly compressed and keeled; ligule a short, fringed membrane; blades flat, to 20 cm long, usually 4–6 cm wide, rarely wider. Inflorescence a terminal raceme, 4–7 cm long excluding awns. Spikelets in pairs, one sessile, one pedicelled; lower spikelet pairs awnless, staminate or neuter, the sessile spikelets upwards on the raceme all perfect, with a pointed, bearded callus and dark colored awn, this twisted and geniculate; staminate

Fig. 289. *Heteropogon contortus*. Plant;
fruiting spikelet.

spikelets 7–10 mm long, their glumes glabrous or sparsely pubescent, broad, thin, green, many-nerved; perfect spikelets 5–8 mm long, their glumes hispid, dark brown, slender, rounded; awn of lemma of perfect floret, usually 5–12 cm long, hispid, geniculate, weakly twice-geniculate.

Infrequent to locally abundant, various soil types, lower to mid exposed mountain slopes, canyons, and on mesas, in probably every county of the Trans-Pecos. El Paso Co., Franklin Mts.; Hueco Mts. Hudspeth Co., Beach Mts.; Eagle Mts. Presidio Co., Sierra Vieja; Chinati Mts.; Elephant Mt. Jeff Davis Co., Davis Mts. and foothills. Brewster Co., Glass Mts.; Cathedral Mt.; Cienega Mt.; Elephant Mt.; Cottonwood Spring, 02 Ranch; Packsaddle Mt.; Nine Point Mesa; Terlingua area; Black Gap Refuge, Stairstep Mt.; Big Bend Natl. Park, Chisos Mts.; Burro Mesa; Paint Gap Hills; Smokey Creek; Dead Horse Mts.; Boquillas area; Hot Springs. Pecos Co., 6 mi N Fort Stockton. Terrell Co., along Rio Grande between Reagan Canyon and Sanderson Canyon; mouth of San Francisco Canyon. Val Verde Co., 5 mi W Langtry. 1,400– 5,200 ft. Flowering (Mar) Jun–Nov. Edwards Plateau, South Texas Plains, and Gulf Coast Prairies in TX. NM, AZ, and CA. Warm regions of the world.

During the fall of the year, in the Trans-Pecos, dense stands of tanglehead

Fig. 290. *Hemarthria altissima*. Plant; spikelike
raceme; spikelets and spikelet parts.

can be recognized on hillsides from far away because of the clumps of rusty
herbage. Thus fall coloration of mature plants is characteristic of tanglehead
and some bluestems. Tanglehead is considered fair to good forage for livestock
before the plants reach maturity, after which the plants reportedly are too
coarse for some animals, including sheep, and the mature awns with sharp-
hard points are also troublesome for sheep.

81. HEMARTHRIA R. Br. JOINTTAIL.

A genus of about 12 species native to warm regions of the Old World and
introduced into the Americas. Five species are reported for the United States
under the genus name *Manisuris* L., and only one species occurs in Texas
(Gould, 1975). The genus name possibly is derived from Greek *haem*, blood,
and *arth*, joint. The pertinence of blood red is obscure, but the suffix doubtless
is in reference to the jointed racemes.

1. Hemarthria altissima (Poir.) Stapf & Hubbard. JOINTTAIL.
Fig. 290. [*Manisuris altissima* (Poir.) Hitchc.; *Rottboellia altissima* Poir.]. Per-
ennial. Culms usually 0.4–1 m long, glabrous, nodes numerous and short.
Leaves with sheaths usually keeled, glabrous or pubescent on upper margins;

ligule membranous, short, ciliate or lacerate; blades thin, glabrous, flat or folded, 3–8 mm wide. Inflorescence a spikelike raceme 4–12 cm long, glabrous, the internodes dorsally compressed and club-shaped; racemes typically developed at all upper culm nodes, enclosed basally by sheaths; disarticulation at nodes of rachis. Spikelets in pairs, one sessile and perfect, the other pedicelled and staminate or neuter, both somewhat sunken in the corky rachis; sessile spikelets awnless, elliptic-oblong, the apex attenuate, with a somewhat triangular basal callus; lower glume 4–7 mm long, the back flattened; upper glume obtuse to acute; pedicelled spikelets about equal to sessile ones, attenuate or acute; pedicels flattened, broadly linear, usually fused to rachis internodes.

In the Trans-Pecos known only in moist habitats, at the edge of water, along the Rio Grande. Brewster Co., Big Bend Natl. Park, near Hot Springs; between Solis and Mariscal Canyon; Mariscal Canyon. Ca. 2,300 ft. Flowering Jun–Oct. South Texas Plains and Gulf Prairies. Adventive in the United States. Warm regions of the world.

Plants of the jointtail most likely are palatable, but the plants are not abundant or accessible enough to be of much forage value.

82. TRIPSACUM   L.   GAMAGRASS.

A genus of about 13 species native to the Americas, particularly in warmer regions. Three species occur in the United States, with one species in Texas. The origin of the genus name is not known, but according to Hitchcock (1951) it could have come from Greek *tribein*, to rub, a reference to the smooth inflorescence joints. All of the species of *Tripsacum* are regarded as palatable forage grasses, but they are not often abundant. *Tripsacum* is related to *Zea mays* L. (corn or maize).

1. Tripsacum dactyloides (L.) L.   EASTERN GAMAGRASS.   Fig. 291. Perennial, cespitose, large, with knotty rhizomes. Culms 1.5–3 m or more long, glabrous. Leaves glabrous, sheaths rounded, smooth; ligule membranous, short, ciliate or lacerate; blades thin, flat, usually 30–75 cm or more long, 1.0–2.5 cm wide. Inflorescence a single spikelike raceme or of 2–3 spikelike racemes, these 12–25 cm long; raceme or racemose branches with awnless pistillate spikelets below and staminate spikelets above. Pistillate spikelets subsessile, usually single, hard and bony, usually 6–8 mm long, the glumes indurate, fused with rachis and enclosing other spikelet parts; staminate spikelets 2-flowered, usually 6–10 mm long, in pairs on one side of a continuous rachis; lemmas of perfect and sterile florets thin and hyaline, often reduced; pedicels and pedicelled spikelets usually absent, or a rudiment present; the pistillate part of inflorescence disarticulating at the nodes into hard, shiny, beadlike units, the staminate part deciduous as a whole.

Infrequent and scattered, moist canyons, watercourses, boulder fields, and other protected areas. Presidio Co., Capote Falls, Capote Mt.; along Capote

Fig. 291. *Tripsacum dactyloides*. Plant; pistillate spikelets with rachis joint and a pair of staminate spikelets with rachis joint.

Creek; Elephant Mt., N slope. Jeff Davis Co., Davis Mts., Rockpile; Limpia Creek 10 mi below Fort Davis; Little Aguja Canyon; Musquiz Canyon; Fern Canyon, Mitre Peak Girl Scout Camp; Pollard Ranch. Brewster Co., Chisos Mts., Cattail Falls; Oak Creek, Basin; Oak Creek Canyon, below the Window; Ranger Canyon, 5 mi W Alpine; Calamity Creek; Cienega Mt., E side; Whirlwind Spring, 02 Ranch. 3,500–6,200 ft. Flowering Apr–Oct. Throughout most of TX. E United States, N to NE. Also N Mex. West Indies.

Other than the river cane grasses and pampasgrass, eastern gamagrass is the largest grass in the Trans-Pecos, and it is the largest native species in the area. Eastern gamagrass is regarded as excellent forage, but it is not often abundant enough in the Trans-Pecos to be of much value.

83. ZEA   L.   CORN, MAIZE.

A genus of four species native to the New World, probably Mexico. *Zea mays* has been cultivated in the New World since before recorded history, and is known only from cultivated plants. The genus name is from Greek, *zea*, or *zeia*, a type of grain.

Fig. 292. *Zea mays*. Two branches of staminate inflorescence (tassel) and pistillate inflorescence (ear); pair of spikelets attached to rachis (cob) with mature grains, the second glume showing (lower right); single pistillate spikelet soon after flowering (lower left); staminate spikelet (upper right).

1. Zea mays L.   CORN, MAIZE.   Fig. 292.   Annual. Culms thick, 1.5 – 3 m long. Leaves with short membranous ligules; blades flat, broad. Plants monoecious. Inflorescence a terminal panicle of staminate spikelets and modified axillary arrangements of pistillate inflorescences. Spikelets unisexual; staminate spikelets 2-flowered, in pairs on unequal pedicels, on spikelike branches of the terminal inflorescence; glumes of staminate spikelets broad and thin with several nerves; lemma and palea of staminate spikelets thin, hyaline; pistillate inflorescences axillary, enclosed in leaflike sheaths, the spikelets paired, in rows on a thickened, corky axis (the "cob"); pistillate spikelets of one upper (perfect) floret and one lower (reduced) floret, the lower perhaps developed as a second perfect floret; glumes of pistillate spikelets broad, thin, shorter than mature grains; lemma of lower floret and lemma and palea of upper floret thin, hyaline. Caryopses large, thick, the "grain" of corn.

Cultivated in farming areas of the Trans-Pecos and in home gardens. Flowering late spring and summer. Cultivated throughout TX, and throughout all continents, perhaps the most widespread crop plant in the world.

The taxonomy of the economically important genus *Zea* has long been studied. Biologists in many fields of specialty have been involved in attempting to resolve two outstanding questions about the genus. From what taxon did cultivated corn (*Zea mays*) evolve, and what was the origin of the unique structure we know as the ear of corn? Recently these questions have been addressed again, so that there is much improved understanding regarding the taxonomy of *Zea* (Iltis and Doebley, 1980; Doebley and Iltis, 1980). And there has been a remarkable concept offered to explain development of the ear of corn (Iltis, 1983). The four species of corn recognized by Doebley and Iltis (1980) are: *Z. diploperennis* Iltis, Doebley, and Guzman, diploid perennial teosinte; *Z. perennis* (Hitchc.) Reeves & Mangelsdorf, tetraploid perennial teosinte; *Z. luxurians* (Durieu & Ascherson) Bird, annual teosinte from Guatemala; and *Z. mays* L. Four subspecies (teosintes) of *Z. mays* are recognized: *Z. mays* subsp. *mays*, the cultivated maize or corn; *Z. mays* subsp. *mexicana* (Schrader) Iltis of central Mexico; *Z. mays* subsp. *parviglumis* Iltis & Doebley of southern and western Mexico; and *Z. mays* subsp. *huehuetenangensis* (Iltis and Doebley) Doebley of the western highlands of Guatemala (Doebley, 1990). The new theory regarding the origin of the ear of corn was referred to as the catastrophic sexual transmutation theory by Iltis (1983), a highly complex and controversial concept that is now undergoing scrutiny as the most plausible origin of the corn ear.

Glossary

Abaxial. Located on the side away from the axis.

Achene. A small, dry, indehiscent one-seeded fruit in which the ovary wall is free from the seed.

Acicular. Needlelike.

Acuminate. Gradually tapering to a point.

Acute. Sharp-pointed, making less than a right angle.

Adaxial. Located on the side toward the axis.

Adherent. Sticking or clinging; adhering.

Adnate. Grown together with an unlike part.

Adventive. Introduced by chance or accident, not definitely established or naturalized.

Alluvium. Soils deposited by flowing water.

Annual. Of one-season or one-year duration from seed to maturity and death.

Anther. The pollen-bearing part of the stamen.

Anthesis. The period during which the flower is open and functional.

Antrorse. Directed forward or toward the apex; the opposite of retrorse.

Apex. The tip of an organ (pl., apexes or apices).

Apical. Situated at or forming the apex.

Apiculate. Terminating abruptly in a small, short point.

Apomixis. A general term for asexual reproduction, i.e., seed production without fertilization where meiosis and gamete fusion are completely or partially suppressed.

Appressed. Closely pressed against another organ; usually angled toward apex.

Arcuate. Bent or curved like a bow.

Aristate. Awned.

Articulation. A joint or node.

Ascending. Rising or curving upward.

Asymmetrical. Without symmetry.

Attenuate.   Tapering gradually to a slender tip.

Auricle.   An ear-shaped appendage; name applied to pointed appendages that occur laterally at the base of the leaf blade in some grasses and laterally at the sheath apex in others.

Awn.   A bristle or stiff, hairlike projection; in the grass spikelet, usually the prolongation of the midnerve or lateral nerves of the glumes, lemmas, or palea.

Axil.   The upper angle formed between two structures such as the culm axis and a branch or a spikelet pedicel.

Axillary.   In an axil.

Axis (of culm, inflorescence, etc.).   The central stem or branch upon which the parts or organs are arranged.

Barbellate.   Having short, stiff hairs.

Beaked.   Ending in a firm, prolonged tip.

Bearded.   Bearing long, stiff hairs.

Bifid.   Deeply cleft or two-toothed.

Bilateral.   Two-sided, arranged on opposite sides.

Blade.   The expanded portion of a flattened structure such as a leaf; the blade of the grass leaf is the usually flattened, expanded portion above the sheath.

Bloom.   In reference to grass herbage or spikelets, a waxy or powdery covering.

Bract.   A modified leaf subtending a flower or belonging to an inflorescence; the glumes, lemma, and palea of the grass spikelet are bracts.

Bracteate.   Having bracts.

Bristle.   Reduced branch of *Setaria* inflorescence.

Bur.   A rough or prickly covering around seeds, fruits, or spikelets, as the bur of the grassbur or sandbur, *Cenchrus.*

Callus.   The hard, usually pointed base of the spikelet (as in *Heteropogon, Andropogon,* and related genera) or of the floret (as in *Aristida* and *Stipa*) just above the point of disarticulation; in the spikelet, the callus is a portion of the rachis; in the floret, it is a portion of the rachilla.

Capitate.   Head-shaped; collected into a head or dense cluster.

Cartilaginous.   Firm and tough but flexible; like cartilage.

Caryopsis.   A dry, hard, indehiscent, one-seeded fruit with the thin pericarp adnate to the seed coat; the characteristic grass fruit; differs from the achene only in the fusion of the pericarp and seed coat.

Cauline.   Belonging to the stem, or the culm.

Cespitose (Caespitose).   In tufts or dense clumps.

Chartaceous.   With the texture of stiff writing paper.

Cilia.   Marginal hairs.

Ciliate. Fringed with hairs.

Ciliolate. Furnished with minute cilia.

Clavate. Club-shaped, thickened or enlarged at the apex from a slender base.

Cleft. Cut or divided into lobes.

Cleistogamous Spikelet. Spikelet in which fertilization takes place within the spikelet.

Collar. The outer side of a grass leaf at the junction of the blade and sheath.

Concave. Hollowed out; opposite of convex.

Connate. Union of like parts; fused together.

Contracted. Narrowed; in an inflorescence the opposite of open or spreading.

Cordate. Heart-shaped; with a broad, notched base and a pointed tip.

Coriaceous. Leathery in texture.

Corm. The enlarged, fleshy base of a stem.

Culm. The stem of a grass.

Cuneate. Wedge-shaped; narrowly triangular and broadest at the tip.

Cuspidate. Tipped with a short, sharp, rigid point.

Deciduous. Falling, as the leaves from a tree.

Dentate. Having a toothed margin, the teeth directed perpendicular to the margin.

Depauperate. Stunted, starved.

Dichotomous. Dichotomous branching is repeatedly forking into pairs.

Diffuse. Scattered; dispersed; spreading.

Digitate. Arising from a common point or base, as the fingers (digits) of the hand; bermudagrass, *Cynodon dactylon*, has an inflorescence of digitately arranged branches.

Dioecious. Unisexual, with staminate and pistillate flowers on separate plants.

Diploid. Having two chromosome sets; twice the haploid number.

Disarticulate. To separate at the joints or nodes at maturity.

Distal. Opposite the point of attachment.

Distichous. Distinctly two-ranked, in two rows.

Divaricate. Widely spreading or divergent.

Dorsal. The back side or surface; the surface turned away from the central stalk or axis; abaxial surface.

Ecotone. A transition zone between adjacent communities.

Ellipsoidal. An elliptic solid, twice as long as broad and pointed at the ends.

Elliptic. In the form of a flattened circle, more than twice as long as broad, and with pointed ends.

Endemic. Indigenous or native in a given region.

Endosperm. Nutritive tissue arising in the embryo sac of most angiosperms, adjacent to or surrounding the embryo.

Entire. Undivided; in reference to leaves or bracts, the margin continuous, without teeth or lobes.

Ephemeral. Lasting for a day or less.

Erose. Irregular and uneven, as if gnawed or worn away.

Escape. A cultivated plant seemingly growing wild.

Excurrent. Extending out; in grasses the nerves of the lemma may be extended out (excurrent) as awns.

Exserted. Projecting beyond the surrounding parts, as a stamen or stigma.

Fascicle. A cluster or close bunch, often used in reference to branches of the inflorescence.

Filiform. Threadlike; filamentous (filament, the stalk of a stamen).

Fimbriate. Fringed with coarse hairs or narrow segments of tissue.

First Glume. Lowermost of the two glumes.

Flabellate. Fan-shaped, broadly wedge-shaped.

Floret. In grasses, the lemma and palea with the enclosed flower; the floret may be perfect, pistillate, staminate, or neuter.

Floriferous. Bearing flowers.

Flower. Usually two lodicules (vestigial perianth segments), three stamens, and a pistil.

Fusiform. Spindle-shaped; rounded and tapering from the middle toward each end.

Geniculate. Bent abruptly, as at the elbow or knee joint.

Gibbous. Swollen on one side; with a pouchlike swelling.

Glabrate. Becoming glabrous; essentially glabrous.

Glabrous. Without hairs.

Glaucous. Covered or whitened with a waxy bloom, as a cabbage leaf or a plum.

Globose. Spherical or rounded; globelike.

Glumes. The pair of bracts (usually) at the base of the spikelet, below the floret or florets.

Grain. In grasses, the unhusked or threshed fruit; used in reference to the mature ovary alone or the ovary enclosed in persistent bracts (palea, lemma, glumes).

Habit. General appearance of a plant.

Habitat. The normal environment of the plant.

Herbage. The stems and leaves of an herbaceous plant.

Hirsute. With rather coarse and stiff hairs, these long, straight, and erect or ascending.

Hispid.   With erect, stiff, bristly hairs.

Hispidulous.   Minutely hispid.

Hyaline.   Translucent or colorless, rarely transparent.

Hybrid.   A cross between two species (or between other taxonomic entities).

Imbricate.   Overlapping, as the shingles of a roof.

Imperfect.   Unisexual flowers or florets; with either male or female parts but not both.

Indument.   A hairy covering.

Indurate.   Hard.

Inflorescence.   The flowering portion of a shoot; in grasses, the spikelets and the axis or branch system that supports them, the inflorescence being delimited at the base by the uppermost leafy node of the shoot.

Innovations.   The basal shoots of a perennial grass plant.

Internode.   The portion of the stem or other structure between two nodes.

Involucre.   A whorl of bracts or reduced branchlets that surround a flower or floret or a group of flowers or florets.

Involute.   Rolled inward from the edges.

Joint.   A culm, rachilla, or rachis internode together with a portion of the node at either end; term generally used in reference to the units of a disarticulating culm, rachis, or rachilla axis.

Keel.   A prominent dorsal ridge, like the keel of a boat; glumes and lemmas of laterally compressed spikelets are often sharply keeled; the paleas of most florets are two-keeled.

Lacerate.   Irregularly cleft or torn.

Lanate.   Woolly; covered with hairs resembling wool.

Lanceolate.   Lance-shaped; relatively narrow, tapering from below the middle to the apex.

Lateral.   On the side.

Lemma.   The lowermost of the two bracts enclosing the flower in the grass floret.

Ligule.   A membranous or hairy appendage on the adaxial surface of the grass leaf at the junction of sheath and blade.

Linear.   Long and narrow and with parallel margins.

Lobe.   A segment of an organ.

Lodicule.   Scalelike processes, usually two or three, at the base of the stamens in grass flowers; generally regarded as rudimentary perianth segments.

Membranous.   Thin, soft, and pliable, with the character of a membrane.

Midrib.   The central rib of a leaf or bract.

Monoecious.   Flowers unisexual, with male and female flowers borne on the same plant.

Monotypic.   Having a single type or representative, as a genus with only one species.

Mucro.   A short, small, abrupt tip of an organ, as the projection of a nerve on a leaf or bract.

Mucronate.   With a mucro.

Muticous.   Blunt; without a point.

Naturalized.   Of foreign origin, but established and reproducing as though native.

Nerve.   A simple vein or slender rib of a leaf or bract.

Neuter.   Without functional stamens or pistils.

Node.   Region of the culm, branch, or spikelet axis at which leaves, bracts, or branches are produced.

Nodulose.   Roughened with rounded protuberance or knobs.

Oblanceolate.   Inversely lanceolate, attached at the narrow end.

Oblong.   Much longer than broad and with nearly parallel sides.

Obovate.   Inversely egg-shaped, with the broader end near the apex.

Obtuse.   Blunt but pointed, making more than a right angle.

Opposite.   Set against, on opposing sides of an axis.

Oval.   Broadly elliptic.

Ovary.   The enlarged lower part of the pistil in angiospermous plants, enclosing the ovules or young seeds.

Ovate.   Egg-shaped, with the broadest end toward the base.

Palea.   The uppermost of the two bracts enclosing the grass flower in the floret; the palea usually is two-nerved and two-keeled.

Panicle.   In grasses, any inflorescence in which the spikelets are not sessile or individually pedicelled on the main axis.

Papilla.   A minute, nipple-shaped projection (pl., papillae).

Papilla-Based Hairs.   Hairs arising from papillae.

Papillose.   Bearing minute nipple-shaped projections.

Pectinate.   With narrow, closely set, and divergent units like the teeth of a comb.

Pedicel.   In grasses, the stalk of a single spikelet; the stalk of a cluster of flowers in other angiosperms.

Pedunculate.   With a peduncle.

Pendent, Pendulous.   Suspended or hanging.

Perennial.   Living for more than two years.

Perfect.   A flower or floret with both male and female functional reproductive structures.

Perianth.   A collective term used for the calyx and corolla together.

Pericarp.   The fruit wall developed from the ovary wall.

Persistent.   In reference to rachis or rachilla, one that does not disarticulate.

Petiole.   A leaf stalk.

Pilose.   With soft, straight hairs.

Pistil.   The female organ of the flower, ordinarily consisting of the ovary and one or more styles and stigmas, and bearing ovules.

Pistillate.   Having a pistil but not stamens.

Plumose.   Feathery; having fine, elongate hairs on either side.

Polyploid.   With three or more basic sets of chromosomes; of any ploidy level above the diploid.

Primary Inflorescence Branch.   Branch arising directly from the main inflorescence axis.

Prophyll.   The first leaf of a lateral shoot or vegetative culm branch; the prophyll is a sheath, usually with two strong lateral nerves and numerous fine intermediate nerves; a blade is never developed (=Prophyllum).

Puberulent.   Minutely pubescent.

Pubescent.   With short, soft hairs; downy.

Pulvinus.   A swelling at the base of a leaf or of a branch of the inflorescence (pl., pulvini).

Pungent.   Terminating in a rigid, sharp point.

Raceme.   In grasses, an inflorescence in which all the spikelets are borne on pedicels directly attached to the main inflorescence axis, or in which some spikelets are sessile and some pedicelled on the main axis.

Rachilla.   The axis of a grass spikelet.

Rachilla Joint.   See Joint.

Rachis.   In grasses the axis of a spike, raceme, or spicate raceme.

Reduced Floret.   A staminate or neuter floret; if highly reduced, then termed a rudimentary floret.

Reflexed.   Bent downward.

Reticulate.   Having the veins or nerves disposed like a network.

Retrorse.   Pointed downward or toward the base; the opposite of antrorse.

Rhizome.   An underground stem, usually with scale leaves and adventitious roots borne at regularly spaced nodes.

Rib.   The primary vein of a leaf or bract.

Rosette.   A whorl or cluster of basal leaves.

Rudiment.   In the grass spikelet, one or more partially developed florets.

Rugose.   Wrinkled.

Scaberulous.   Minutely scabrous.

Scabrous.   Rough to the touch, usually because of the presence of minute, angled, prickle-hairs (spicules) in the epidermis.

Scarious.   Thin, dry, and membranous, not green.

Second Glume.   The uppermost of the two glumes of a spikelet.

Secund.   Arranged on one side only, unilateral.

Semicircular.   Partially circular.

Serrate.   Saw-toothed, with sharp teeth pointing forward.

Sessile.   Attached directly, without a stalk.

Seta.   A bristle or a rigid, sharp-pointed, bristlelike organ (pl., setae).

Setaceous.   Bristly or bristlelike.

Sheath (of leaf).   In grasses and sedges, the basal portion of the leaf, the part that encloses the stem.

Spicate.   Spikelike.

Spicule.   Short, stout, pointed projection of the leaf epidermis; spicules often grade into prickle-hairs.

Spike.   In grasses an inflorescence with spikelets sessile on an elongated, unbranched rachis.

Spikelet.   The basic unit of the grass inflorescence, usually consisting of a short axis, the rachilla, bearing two "empty" bracts, the glumes, at the basal nodes, and one or more florets above.

Spine.   A stiff, sharp-pointed projection or tip.

Spinescent.   Becoming spinelike; ending in a spine; bearing spines.

Stamen.   The male organ of the flower, consisting of a pollen-bearing anther on a filiform filament; collectively, the stamens of a flower are referred to as the androecium.

Staminate.   Having stamens but not a pistil.

Stigma.   The part of the ovary or style that receives the pollen for subsequent effective fertilization.

Stipe.   A stalk.

Stipitate.   Having a stalk or stipe, as a fruit or an elevated gland.

Stolon.   A modified horizontal stem that loops or runs along the surface of the ground and serves to spread the plant by rooting at the nodes.

Stoloniferous.   With stolons.

Stramineous.   Straw colored; yellowish.

Striated, Striate.   Furrowed; striped; streaked.

Strigose.   With still bristles or hairs; these appressed.

Style.   The contracted portion of the pistil between the ovary and the stigma.

Sub.   Latin prefix meaning "somewhat," "almost," "of inferior rank," "beneath."

Subtend.   To be below and close to.

Subterranean.   Below ground.

Subulate.   Awl-shaped.

Succulent.   Fleshy or juicy.

Tawny.   Dull brownish-yellow.

Taxon.   Any taxonomic unit, e.g., variety, species, genus, or tribe.

Terete.   Cylindrical, round in cross section.

Terminal.   Growing at the end of a branch or stem.

Tertiary Branches.   With branches in third order of branching.

Tetraploid.   Having four sets of chromosomes.

Throat.   The adaxial portion of the grass leaf at the junction of sheath and blade.

Tomentose.   Covered with short, soft, densely matted, woolly hairs.

Translucent.   Allowing the passage of light rays, but not transparent.

Transverse.   Lying or being across, or in a cross direction.

Trigonous.   Three-angled.

Truncate.   Terminating abruptly as if cut off squarely at the end.

Tuberculate.   Covered with tubercles or warty protuberances.

Turgid.   Swollen from fullness.

Unilateral.   One-sided; developed or hanging on one side.

Unisexual.   Flowers with either male or female sex structures but not both.

Vernal.   Growing in the spring.

Verrucose.   Covered with warty protuberances.

Verticil.   A whorl.

Verticillate.   Having three or more members or parts attached at the same node of the supporting axis. Having inflorescence branches, for example, arranged in verticils.

Vestigial.   Rudimentary and almost completely reduced, with only a vestige remaining.

Villous.   Bearing long, soft, unmatted hairs.

Viscid.   Sticky; glutinous.

Whorl.   A ring of similar organs radiating from a node.

Woolly.   Having long, soft, entangled hairs; lanate.

Xeric.   Pertaining to condition of low moisture (a xerophyte is a desert plant).

Literature Cited

Allred, K. W. 1982. *Paspalum distichum* L. var. *indutum* Shinners (Poaceae). Great Basin Nat. 42:101–104.

Allred, K. W. 1984. Morphologic variation and classification of the North American *Aristida purpurea* complex (Gramineae). Brittonia 36:382–395.

Allred, K. W. 1989. Observations on seed dispersal and implantation in burrograss (*Scleropogon brevifolius*—Gramineae). Sida 13:493–496.

Allred, K. W., and F. W. Gould. 1983. Systematics of the *Bothriochloa saccharoides* complex (Poaceae: Andropogoneae). System. Bot. 8:168–184.

Anderson, D. E. 1974. Taxonomy of the genus *Chloris* (Gramineae). Brigham Young Univ. Science Bulletin, Biol. Series 19:1–133.

Anderson, R. C. 1982. An evolutionary model summarizing the roles of fire, climate, and grazing animals in the origin and maintenance of grass lands: An end paper. Pp. 297–308, *in* Grasses and Grasslands, Systematics and Ecology (J. R. Estes, R. J. Tyrl, and J. N. Brunken, eds.). Univ. of Oklahoma Press, Norman.

Arnow, L. A. 1994. *Koeleria macrantha* and *K. pyramidata* (Poaceae): Nomenclatural problems and biological distinctions. System. Bot. 19:6–20.

Bahre, C. J. 1991. A legacy of change. Univ. of Arizona Press, Tucson.

Barbour, M. G., J. H. Burk, and W. D. Pitts. 1987. Terrestrial plant ecology, 2d ed. Benjamin/Cummings Publishing Company, Inc., Menlo Park, Calif.

Barkworth, M. E. 1990. *Nassella* (Gramineae, Stipeae): Revised interpretation and nomenclatural changes. Taxon 39:597–614.

Barkworth, M. E. 1993. North American Stipeae (Gramineae): Taxonomic changes and other comments. Phytologia 74:1–25.

Barkworth, M. E., and R. J. Atkins. 1984. *Leymus* Hochst. (Gramineae: Triticeae) in North America: Taxonomy and distribution. Amer. J. Bot. 71:609–625.

Barkworth, M. E., and D. R. Dewey. 1985. Genomically based genera in the perennial Triticeae of North America: identification and membership. Amer. J. Bot. 72:767–776.

Barkworth, M. E., and J. Everett. 1987. Evolution in the Stipeae: Identification and relationships of its monophyletic taxa. Pp. 251–264, *in* Grass Systematics and Evolution (T. R. Soderstrom, K. W. Hilu, C. S. Campbell, and M. E. Barkworth, eds.). Smithsonian Institution Press, Washington, D.C.

Barkworth, M. E., and J. Maze. 1979. Proposal to reject *Stipa columbiana* (Poaceae) and nomenclatural changes affecting three western North American species of *Stipa* (Poaceae). Taxon 28:621–625.

Baum, B. R., J. R. Estes, and P. K. Gupta. 1987. Assessment of the genomic system of classification in the Triticeae. Amer. J. Bot. 74:1388–1395.

Beetle, A. A. 1977. Noteworthy grasses from Mexico. Phytologia 35:221–223.

Beetle, A. A. 1981. Noteworthy grasses from Mexico. IX. Phytologia 49: 36–37.

Bock, J. H., and C. E. Bock. 1992. Short-term reductions in plant densities following prescribed fire in an ungrazed semidesert shrub-grassland. Southwest. Nat. 37:49–53.

Box, T. W., and F. W. Gould. 1959. An analysis of the grass vegetation of Texas. Southwest. Nat. 3:124–129.

Branscomb, B. L. 1958. Shrub invasion in southern New Mexico. J. Range Management 11:129–132.

Bray, W. L. 1901. The ecological relations of the vegetation of western Texas. Bot. Gaz. 32:99–123, 195–217, 262–291.

Brown, A. L. 1950. Shrub invasion of southern Arizona desert grassland. J. Range Management 3:172–177.

Brown, D. E. [ed.]. 1982. Biotic communities of the American Southwest— United States and Mexico. Desert Plants 4:1–342.

Buffington, L. C., and C. H. Herbel. 1965. Vegetation changes on a semidesert grassland range from 1858 to 1963. Ecological Monographs 35:139–164.

Burgess, T. L., and D. K. Northington. 1981. Plants of the Guadalupe Mountains and Carlsbad Caverns National Parks. Chihuahuan Desert Research Institute, Contrib. No. 107.

Campbell, C. S. 1983. Systematics of the *Andropogon virginicus* complex (Gramineae). J. Arnold Arb. 64:171–254.

Casey, C. B. 1972. Mirages, mysteries, and reality, Brewster County Texas, the Big Bend of the Rio Grande. Pioneer, Hereford, Tex.

Clayton, W. D., and S. A. Renvoize. 1986. Genera Graminum, grasses of the world. Kew Bulletin Additional Series, Royal Botanic Gardens, Kew, London.

Corning, L., Jr. 1967. Baronial forts of the Big Bend. Trinity Univ. Press, San Antonio, Tex.

Correll, D. S., and M. C. Johnston. 1970. Manual of the vascular plants of Texas. Texas Research Foundation, Renner, Tex.

Cottle, H. J. 1931. Studies in the vegetation of southwestern Texas. Ecology 12: 105–155.

Crepet, W. L., and G. D. Feldman. 1991. The earliest remains of grasses in the fossil record. Amer. J. Bot. 78:1010–1014.

Crins, W. J. 1991. The genera of the Paniceae (Gramineae: Panicoideae) in the southeastern United States. J. Arn. Arb., Suppl. Series 1:171–312.

Cronquist, A. 1988. The evolution and classification of flowering plants, 2d ed. New York Botanical Garden, Bronx, N.Y.

Cronquist, A., A. Holmgren, N. H. Holmgren, J. L. Reveal, and P. K. Holmgren. 1977. Intermountain Flora. Vol. 6. Columbia Univ. Press, New York.

Davidse, G. 1987. Fruit dispersal in the Poaceae. Pp. 143–155, *in* Grass Systematics and Evolution (T. R. Soderstrom, K. W. Hilu, C. S. Campbell, and M. E. Barkworth, eds.). Smithsonian Institution Press, Washington, D.C.

Davila, P., and L. G. Clark. 1990. Scanning electron microscopy survey of leaf epidermis of *Sorghastrum* (Poaceae: Andropogoneae). Amer. J. Bot. 77: 499–511.

deWet, J. M. J. 1981. Grasses and the culture [sic] history of man. Ann. Missouri Bot. Gard. 68:87–104.

Dewey, D. R. 1982. Genomic and phylogenetic relationships among North American perennial Triticeae. Pp. 51–88, *in* Grasses and Grasslands, Systematics and Ecology (J. R. Estes, R. J. Tyrl, and J. N. Brunken, eds.). Univ. of Oklahoma Press, Norman.

Dewey, D. R. 1983a. New nomenclatural combinations in the North American perennial Triticeae (Gramineae). Brittonia 35:30–33.

Dewey, D. R. 1983b. Historical and current taxonomic perspectives of *Agropyron, Elymus,* and related genera. Crop Sci. 23:637–642.

Doebley, J. 1990. Molecular evidence for gene flow among *Zea* species. Bioscience 40:443–448.

Doebley, J. F., and H. H. Iltis. 1980. Taxonomy of *Zea* (Gramineae). I. A subgeneric classification with key to taxa. Amer. J. Bot. 67:982–993.

Dorr, L. J., and P. M. Peterson. 1993. Typification of two Buckley grass names revisited: *Muhlenbergia texana* and *M. monticola* (Poaceae). Sida 15:589–591.

Echols, W. H. 1860. Camel expedition through the Big Bend Country. U.S. 36th Congress, 2d Session, Senate Ex. Doc., doc. 1, pt. 2, U.S. Serial Set No. 1079, pp. 36–50.

Esen, A., and K. W. Hilu. 1991. Electrophoretic and immunological studies of prolamins in the Poaceae: II. Phylogenetic affinities of the Aristideae. Taxon 40:5–17.

Estes, J. R., and R. J. Tyrl. 1982. The generic concept and generic circumscription in the Triticeae: An End Paper. Pp. 145–164, *in* Grasses and Grasslands, Systematics and Ecology (J. R. Estes, R. J. Tyrl, and J. R. Brunken, eds.). Univ. of Oklahoma Press, Norman.

Fernald, M. L. 1950. Gray's Manual of Botany, 8th ed. American Book Company, New York.

Gardner, J. L. 1950. Effects of thirty years of protection from grazing in desert grassland. Ecology 31:44–50.

Gehlbach, F. R. 1981. Mountain Islands and Desert Seas. Texas A & M Univ. Press, College Station.

Gillis, A. M. 1991. Should cows chew cheatgrass on commonlands? Bioscience 41:668–675.

Gould, F. W. 1951. Grasses of the Southwestern United States. Univ. of Arizona Press, Tucson.

Gould, F. W. 1962. Texas plants—A checklist and ecological summary. Tex. Agr. Exp. Sta. MP-585.

Gould, F. W. 1968. Grass systematics. McGraw-Hill Book Company, New York.

Gould, F. W. 1969. Texas plants—A checklist and ecological summary. Tex. Agr. Exp. Sta. MP-585/Revised.

Gould, F. W. 1975. The grasses of Texas. Texas A & M Univ. Press, College Station.

Gould, F. W. 1978. Common Texas grasses: An Illustrated Guide. Texas A & M Univ. Press, College Station.

Gould, F. W. 1979. The genus *Bouteloua* (Poaceae). Ann. Missouri Bot. Gard. 66:348–416.

Gould, F. W., and T. W. Box. 1965. Grasses of the Texas Coastal Bend (Calhoun, Refugio, Aransas, San Patricio, and northern Kleberg counties). Texas A & M Univ. Press, College Station.

Gould, F. W., and C. A. Clark. 1978. *Dichanthelium* (Poaceae) in the United States and Canada. Ann. Missouri Bot. Gard. 65:1088–1132.

Gould, F. W., G. O. Hoffman, and C. A. Rechenthin. 1960. Vegetational areas of Texas. Tex. Agr. Exp. Sta. L-492.

Gould, F. W., and R. B. Shaw. 1983. Grass systematics, 2d ed. Texas A & M Univ. Press, College Station.

Gregg, J. E. 1933. The history of Presidio County. Master's thesis, Sul Ross State University, Alpine, Tex.

Grover, H. D., and H. B. Musick. 1990. Shrubland encroachment in southern New Mexico, U.S.A.: An analysis of desertification processes in the American Southwest. Climatic Change 17:305–330.

Hall, S. A. 1990. Pollen evidence for historic vegetational change, Hueco Bolson, Texas. Tex. J. Sci. 43:399–403.

Hanselka, C. W. 1989. Forage quality of common buffelgrass as influenced by prescribed fire. Tex. J. Agr. and Natural Res. 3:15–18.

Hastings, J. R., and R. M. Turner. 1965. The changing mile. Univ. of Arizona Press, Tucson.

Hatch, S. L., and D. A. Bearden. 1983. *Stipa curvifolia* (Poaceae)—Studies on a rare taxon. Sida 10:184–187.

Hatch, S. L., K. N. Gandhi, and L. E. Brown. 1990. Checklist of the vascular plants of Texas. MP-1655. Tex. Agr. Exp. Sta., Texas A & M Univ. System, College Station.

Henrard, J. E. 1950. Monograph of the genus *Digitaria*. Univ. Pers., Leiden, 1–999.

Henrickson, J., and M. C. Johnston. 1986. Vegetation and community types of the Chihuahuan Desert. Pp. 20–39, *in* Second Symposium on Resources of the Chihuahuan Desert Region, United States and Mexico (J. C. Barlow, A. M. Powell, and B. N. Timmermann, eds.). Chihuahuan Desert Research Institute, Alpine, Tex.

Herbel, C. H., F. N. Ares, and R. A. Wright. 1972. Drought effects on a semi-desert grassland range. Ecology 53:1084–1093.

Herrera A., Y., and J. F. Bain. 1991. Flavonoids of the *Muhlenbergia montana* complex. Biochem. Syst. Ecol. 19:665–672.

Hill, A. 1991. Grazing as a management tool. Wildflower, J. National Wild-flower Research Center 4:13–18.

Hill, S. R. 1982. Vegetative apomixis ("vivipary") in *Bouteloua hirsuta* Lag. (Poaceae). Sida 9:355–357.

Hitchcock, A. S. 1935. Manual of the grasses of the United States. U.S. Dept. Agr. Misc. Publ. 200.

Hitchcock, A. S. 1951. Manual of the grasses of the United States, 2d ed. (revised by A. Chase). U.S. Dept. Agr. Misc. Publ. 200.

Holechek, J. L. 1991. Chihuahuan Desert rangeland, livestock grazing, and sustainability. Rangelands 13:115–120.

Humphrey, R. R. 1953. The desert grassland, past and present. J. Range Management 6:159–164.

Humphrey, R. R. 1958. The desert grassland. A history of vegetational change and an analysis of causes. Bot. Review 24:193–252.

Iltis, H. H. 1983. From teosinte to maize: The catastrophic sexual transmutation. Science 222:886–894.

Iltis, H. H., and J. F. Doebley. 1980. Taxonomy of *Zea* (Gramineae). II. Sub-specific categories in the *Zea* complex and a generic synopsis. Amer. J. Bot. 67:994–1004.

Johnston, M. C. 1963. Past and present grassland of southern Texas and north-eastern Mexico. Ecology 44:456–466.

Johnston, M. C. 1981. *Andropogon spadiceus* (Poaceae), a Coahuilan species now known from Texas. Southwest. Nat. 25:557.

Johnston, M. C. 1988. The vascular plants of Texas, a list up-dating The Manual of the Vascular Plants of Texas. Self-published, 3905 Ave G, Austin, Tex.

Johnston, M. C. 1990. The vascular plants of Texas, a list up-dating The Manual of the Vascular Plants of Texas. Self-published, 3905 Ave G, Austin, Tex.

Kellogg, E. A. 1989. Comments on genomic genera in the Triticeae (Poaceae). Amer. J. Bot. 76:796–805.

Kellogg, E. A. 1992. Tools for studying the chloroplast genome in the Triticeae (Gramineae): An EcoRI map, a diagnostic deletion, and support for *Bromus* as an outgroup. Amer. J. Bot. 79:186–197.

Kerr, R. A. 1990. New greenhouse report puts down dissenters. Science 249: 481–482.

Koch, S. D. 1974. The *Eragrostis pectinacea-pilosa* complex in North and Central America (Gramineae: Eragrostoideae). Illinois Biol. Monographs 48: 1–75.

Koch, S. D., and I. Sanchez Vega. 1985. *Eragrostis mexicana, E. neomexicana, E. orcuttiana,* and *E. virescens*: The resolution of a taxonomic problem. Phytologia 58:377–381.

Langford, J. O., and F. Gipson. 1952. Big Bend, a homesteader's story. Univ. of Texas Press, Austin.

Lonard, R. I., and F. W. Gould. 1974. The North American species of *Vulpia* (Gramineae). Madroño 22:217–230.

Löve, A. 1982. Generic evolution of the wheatgrasses. Biol. Zentralbl. 101: 199–212.

Löve, A. 1984. Conspectus of the Triticeae. Feddes Repert. 95:425–521.

McBryde, W. D. 1958. A study of vegetational changes that have occurred on Bar-SR-Bar Hill from 1929–1957. Master's thesis, Sul Ross State University, Alpine, Tex.

Macfarlane, T. D. 1987. Poaceae subfamily Pooideae. Pp. 265–276, *in* Grass Systematics and Evolution (T. R. Soderstrom, K. W. Hilu, C. S. Campbell, and M. E. Barkworth, eds.). Smithsonian Institution Press, Washington, D.C.

McNeill, J. 1979. *Diplachne* and *Leptochloa* (Poaceae) in North America. Brittonia 31:399–404.

McPherson, G. R., and H. A. Wright. 1990. Effects of cattle grazing and *Juniperus pinchotii* canopy cover or herb cover and production in western Texas. Amer. Midl. Nat. 123:144–151.

Martin, W. C., and C. R. Hutchins. 1980. A flora of New Mexico, vol. 1. J. Cramer, Publ., D-3300, Braunschweig, West Germany.

Morden, C. W., and S. L. Hatch. 1981. *Polypogon elongatus* H.B.K. (Poaceae) new in Texas. Sida 9:187–188.

Morden, C. W., and S. L. Hatch. 1986. Vegetative apomixis in *Muhlenbergia repens* (Poaceae: Eragrostideae). Sida 11:282–285.

Morden, C. W., and S. L. Hatch. 1987. Anatomical study of the *Muhlenbergia repens* complex (Poaceae: Chloridoideae: Eragrostideae). Sida 12:347–359.

Morrone, O., and F. Zuloaga. 1991. Estudios morfologicos en el subgenero *Dichanthelium* de *Panicum* (Poaceae: Panicoidae: Paniceae), con especial referencia a *Panicum sabulorum*. Ann. Missouri Bot. Gard. 78:915–927.

Muller, C. H. 1947. Vegetation and climate in Coahuila, Mexico. Madroño 9: 33–57.

Nelson, J. T. 1981. The historic vegetative aspect of Fort Davis, Texas. Fort Davis National Historic Site, National Park Service, Fort Davis, Tex.

Nelson, J. T. 1987. Was it grassland? A look at vegetation in Brewster County, Texas through the eyes of a photographer in 1899. Tex. J. Agr. and Natural Res. 1:34–37.

Parker, K. W., and S. C. Martin. 1952. The mesquite problem on southern Arizona ranges. Circular No. 908. U.S. Department of Agriculture, Washington, D.C.

Parry, C. C. 1857. *In* Emory, W. H. 1985. United States and Mexican Boundary Survey. U.S. 34th Congress, 1st and 2d Session, Senate Ex. Doc., doc. 108, vol. 2, pt. 1, U.S. Serial Set. No. 833, pp. 9–26.

Parsons, J. A. 1990. W. B. Mitchell and the early days of the Trans-Pecos cattle industry. J. Big Bend Studies 2:59–71.

Perry, G., and J. McNeill. 1986. The nomenclature of *Eragrostis cilianensis* (Poaceae) and the contribution of Bellardi to Allioni's Flora Pedemontana. Taxon 35:696–701.

Peterson, P. M. 1988. Chromosome numbers in the annual *Muhlenbergia* (Poaceae). Madroño 35:320–324.

Peterson, P. M. 1989. Lemma micromorphology in the annual *Muhlenbergia* (Poaceae). Southwest. Nat. 34:61–71.

Peterson, P. M., and C. R. Annable. 1990. A revision of *Blepharoneuron* (Poaceae: Eragrostideae). Syst. Bot. 15:515–525.

Peterson, P. M., and C. R. Annable. 1991. Systematics of the annual species of *Muhlenbergia* (Poaceae-Eragrostideae). Syst. Bot. Monographs 31:1–109.

Peterson, P. M., and L. H. Rieseberg. 1987. Flavonoids of the annual *Muhlenbergia*. Biochem. Syst. and Ecol. 15:647–652.

Pohl, R. W. 1983. *In* Reviews, The Grasses of Baja California, F. W. Gould and R. Moran. Madroño 30:197.

Powell, A. M. 1988. Trees and shrubs of Trans-Pecos Texas. Big Bend Natural History Assoc., Big Bend National Park.

Quinn, J. A. 1991. Evolution of dioecy in *Buchlöe dactyloides* (Gramineae): Tests for sex-specific vegetative characters, ecological differences, and sexual niche-partitioning. Amer. J. Bot. 78:481–488.

Raven, P. H. 1960. The correct name for rescue grass. Brittonia 12:219–221.

Read, J. C., and B. J. Simpson. 1992. Documented chromosome numbers 1992:3. Documentation and notes on the distribution of *Melica montezumae*. Sida 15:151–152.

Reeder, C. 1985. The genus *Lycurus* (Gramineae) in North America. Phytologia 57:283–291.

Reeder, J. R. 1986a. Another look at *Eragrostis tephrosanthos* (Gramineae). Phytologia 60:153–154.

Reeder, J. R. 1986b. Type specimen of *Bouteloua ramosa* Scribn. *ex* Vasey (Gramineae). Taxon 35:149–153.

Reeder, J. R., and C. Reeder. 1978. *Tragus racemosus* in Arizona. Madroño 25: 107–108.

Reeder, J. R., and C. G. Reeder. 1980. Systematics of *Bouteloua breviseta* and *B. ramosa* (Gramineae). Syst. Bot. 5:312–321.

Reeder, J. R., and L. J. Toolin. 1987. *Scleropogon* (Gramineae), a monotypic genus with disjunct distribution. Phytologia 62:267–275.

Reeder, J. R., and L. J. Toolin. 1989. Notes on *Pappophorum* (Gramineae: Pappophoreae). Syst. Bot. 14:349–358.

Rominger, J. M. 1962. Taxonomy of *Setaria* (Gramineae) in North America. Illinois Biological Monographs, no. 29, pp. 1–132.

Sauer, J. D. 1972. Revision of *Stenotaphrum* (Gramineae: Paniceae) with attention to its historical geography. Brittonia 24:202–222.

Schlesinger, W. H., J. F. Reynolds, G. L. Cunningham, L. F. Huenneke, W. M. Jarrell, R. A. Virginia, W. G. Whitford. 1990. Biological feedbacks in global desertification. Science 247:1043–1048.

Schmidly, D. J. 1977. The mammals of Trans-Pecos Texas. Texas A & M Univ. Press, College Station.

Shaw, R. B., and R. D. Webster. 1987. The genus *Eriochloa* (Poaceae: Paniceae) in North and Central America. Sida 12:165–207.

Shreve, F. 1939. Observations on the vegetation of Chihuahua. Madroño 5:1–13.

Shreve, F. 1942. Grassland and related vegetation in northern Mexico. Madroño 6:190–198.

Simpson, B. B., and M. Conner-Ogorzaly. 1986. Economic botany: Plants in our world. McGraw-Hill Book Company, New York.

Smithers, W. D. 1976. Chronicles of the Big Bend. A photographic memoir of life on the border. Madrona Press, Inc., Austin.

Snow, N., and G. Davidse. 1993. *Leptochloa mucronata* (Michx.) Kunth is the correct name for *Leptochloa filiformis* (Poaceae). Taxon 42:413–417.

Soderstrom, T. R., and J. H. Beaman. 1968. The genus *Bromus* (Gramineae) in Mexico and Central America. Pub. Mus. Michigan State Univ. 3:469–519.

Soderstrom, T. R., and H. F. Decker. 1965. *Allolepis*: A new segregate of *Distichlis* (Gramineae). Madroño 18:33–64.

Soderstrom, T. R., K. W. Hilu, C. S. Campbell, and M. E. Barkworth (eds.). 1987. Grass systematics and evolution. Smithsonian Institution Press, Washington, D.C.

Soreng, R. J. 1991. Systematics of the "Epiles" group of *Poa* (Poaceae). Syst. Bot. 16:507–528.

Soreng, R. J., and S. L. Hatch. 1983. A comparison of *Poa tracyi* and *Poa occidentalis* (Poaceae: Poeae). Sida 10:123–141.

Stebbins, G. L. 1981. Coevolution of grasses and herbivores. Ann. Missouri Bot. Gard. 68:75–86.

Stein, R., and J. A. Ludwig. 1979. Vegetation and soil patterns on a Chihuahuan Desert bajada. Amer. Midl. Nat. 101:28–37.

Stoddard, L. A., and A. D. Smith. 1955. Range management. McGraw-Hill Book Company, New York.

Stubbendieck, J., S. L. Hatch, and C. H. Butterfield. 1992. North American range plants, 4th ed. Univ. of Nebraska Press, Lincoln.

Trent, J. S. 1985. A study of morphological variability in divaricate aristidas of the Southwestern United States. Master's thesis, New Mexico State University, Las Cruces.

Trent, J. S., and K. W. Allred. 1990. A taxonomic comparison of *Aristida ternipes* and *Aristida hamulosa* (Gramineae). Sida 14:251–261.

Turner, R. M. 1990. Long-term vegetation change at a fully protected Sonoran Desert site. Ecology 7:464–477.

Valdés-R., J. 1985. A biosystematic study of the genus *Erioneuron* Nash (Poaceae: Eragrostideae). Ph.D. dissertation, Texas A & M University, College Station.

Valdés-R., J., and S. L. Hatch. 1991. Lemma micromorphology in the Eragrostideae (Poaceae). Sida 14:531–549.

Van Devender, T. R. 1986. Pleistocene climates and endemism in the Chihuahuan Desert flora. Pp. 1–19, *in* Second Symposium on Resources of the Chihuahuan Desert Region, United States and Mexico (J. C. Barlow, A. M. Powell, and B. N. Timmermann, eds.). Chihuahuan Desert Research Institute, Alpine, Tex.

Van Devender, T. R., and W. G. Spaulding. 1979. Development of vegetation and climate in the southwestern United States. Science 204:701–710.

Veldkamp, J. F. 1984. The identity of *Andropogon nutans* Linnaeus (Gramineae). Taxon 33:95–97.

Warnock, B. H. 1970. Wildflowers of the Big Bend country, Texas. Sul Ross State University, Alpine, Tex.

Warnock, B. H. 1974. Wildflowers of the Guadalupe Mountains and the sand dune country, Texas. Sul Ross State University, Alpine, Tex.

Warnock, B. H. 1977. Wildflowers of the Davis Mountains and Marathon Basin, Texas. Sul Ross State University, Alpine, Tex.

Warnock, B. H. 1982. A new three-awn grass from Trans-Pecos, Texas. Sida 9:358–359.

Watson, L., H. T. Clifford, and M. J. Dallwitz. 1985. The classification of Poaceae: Subfamilies and supertribes. Aust. J. Bot. 33:433–484.

Wauer, R. H. 1973. Naturalist's Big Bend. Texas A & M Univ. Press, College Station.

Webster, R. D. 1987. Taxonomy of *Digitaria* section *Digitaria* in North America (Poaceae: Paniceae). Sida 12:209–222.

Webster, R. D. 1988. Genera of the North American Paniceae (Poaceae: Panicoideae). Syst. Bot. 13:576–609.

Webster, R. D. 1993. Nomenclature of *Setaria* (Poaceae: Paniceae). Sida 15: 447–489.

Weddle, R. S. 1990. Madera Canyon: Historic corner of the Davis Mountains. J. Big Bend Studies 2:43–58.

White, J. F., Jr., P. M. Halisky, S. Sun, G. Morgan-Jones, and C. R. Funk, Jr. 1992. Endophyte-host associations in grasses. XVI. Patterns of endophyte distribution in species of the tribe Agrostideae. Amer. J. Bot. 79:472–477.

Wipff, J. K. 1992. *Tragus roxburghii* (Poaceae: Zoysieae) new to the New World. Sida 15:111–114.

Wondzell, S. M. 1984. Recovery of desert grasslands in Big Bend National Park following 36 years of protection from grazing by domestic livestock. Master's thesis, New Mexico State University, Las Cruces.

Worthington, R. D. 1989. An annotated checklist of the native and naturalized flora of El Paso County, Texas. El Paso Southwest Botanical Miscellany No. 1., El Paso, Tex.

Wuerthner, G. 1989. Texas' Big Bend Country. American Geographic Publishing, Helena, Mont.

York, J. C., and W. A. Dick-Peddie. 1969. Vegetation changes in southern New Mexico during the past hundred years. Pp. 157–166, *in* Arid Lands in Perspective (W. G. McGinnies and B. J. Goldman, eds.). AAAS, Univ. of Arizona Press, Tucson.

Index

Boldface indicates Latin names and page numbers of principal reference. Latin names considered as synonyms or those not of principal reference are in *italics*.